peter david

BUT I DIGRESS

Edited by Myra & Peter David

Published by

krause
publications

700 E. State Street • Iola, WI 54990-0001
Telephone: 715/445-2214

Library of Congress Catalog Number: 93-80099
ISBN: 0-87341-286-9
Printed in the United States of America

About the Author

Peter David is a pseudonym for David Peters, who gave up the world heavyweight title to play center field for the Mets. After suffering a crippling injury at a World Series game (the manufacturer of the candy wrapper settled out of court), David turned to the wacky world of comics. Since then he has run Marvel and DC into the ground and formed his own company, Reflection Comics.

He lives in Los Angeles with his manager and six cats, one of whom wrote this bio.

Contents

Harlan Ellison

Introduction

An associate of Sartre — one of the first to perceive racism as a result of socioeconomic factors and political oppression rather than as (in the mid-50s, a view much in vogue) a psychological aberration — the late Martiniquan psychiatrist and philosopher Frantz Fanon completed, just months before his death from leukemia in 1961, a classic volume on oppression and violence titled **The Wretched of the Earth**.

Nowhere in this introduction — search mightily if you feel so inclined — will I again mention the author of these columns, Peter David.

Essayists are the *literary* Wretched of the Earth. Those who write essays of "confessional literature" — defined as a "type of autobiography involving the revelation by an author of events or feelings which normally are discreetly concealed" — find themselves in short order the target of calumny, social ostracism, print retaliation, personal umbrage, death threats, challenges to come onto the schoolyard to duke it out with loudmouth bullies long on meanspiritedness but short on intellectual skills . . . and life long enemies whom they have never met, nor who have ever met them.

Rousseau's **Confessions**, Ralph Waldo Emerson's **Essays**, Michel de Montaigne's **Essays**; the writings of Mencken, Karl Kraus, Ring Lardner, E.B. White, Mary McCarthy, FPA, Dorothy Parker; the essays on journalism by A.J. Liebling and the exquisitely phrased literary comments of Cyril Connolly; Joan Didion and Virginia Woolf and Rebecca West and Pauline Kael; Bernard Shaw's *Introductions* (frequently more inspired than the plays they introduced), Graham Greene's ruminations on lost childhood (far more passion-evoking than even the best of his "entertainments"), Stephen Jay Gould's science columns (a rock in the surging river of scientific illiteracy and religion-based obscurantism that threatens to swamp us).

The essay, the column of personal opinion, the closely-reasoned argument of special pleading. The form that more often sways the minds and hearts of masses than a hundred thousand more-praised novels or short stories.

Yet the essayist is despised.

Enemies beset the commentator from the moment the first line of opinion is written. Not only from the Right, and its boneheaded belief that "conservatism" means "concretization," but from the Left, as well, where equally boneheaded parvenus and adherents of paralogia insist that political correctness is more important than a good heart and a sane mind.

No writing is more evanescent than what the essayist brings forth. It is valuable — usually — only for the moment in human history where the terminology is *au courant*. Use the word "keen" or "nifty" and the piece is automatically fodder for the dustbin of arrogant youth a mere twelve months later. What is "bad to the bone" today is "bitchin'" tomorrow and "narrow" the day after. Word!

The essay is not a piece of journalism. The essay is not journal. The essay is not panegyric or screed. Nor is it a piece of thinly-disguised fiction, a representation of history, or item on a secret agenda intended to masquerade special pleading as common sense. Yet, because we are the most duplicitous species ever mutated, it can be *all* of the above. And there be classic examples of the essay one could easily identify as subscribing to the above-noted conceits. Yet the essay, in its most translucent form, is reason and rationality and high honor set to the music of flowing language. Words are the river, and the accomplished essayist knows how to ford every sand bar, shoot every rapid, backwater around every hidden snag so that the journey down that river is a song sans cacophony.

But even given the skill and the tempered self-confidence of a hotshot essayist, more is required. *Because* essayists are the wretched of the literary world, they must be gunslingers. Never sit with your back to the door, never play into a straight line, never respond to a phone call in which the mysterious communicant says, "I can't talk to you on the phone . . . meet me at the corner of Hudson and Christopher, and I'll bring the black bird with me." Never draw to an inside straight. Never pause long enough in a supermarket check-out line to let an *Enquirer* headline register on your consciousness. Never mistake vanity for heroism.

Essays tell the truth. As the essayist perceives it.

That doesn't mean they're always accurate, or realistic, or proper, or courteous, or even — simply — right. What is means is: the essayist is out there, his or her visceral material exposed, vouchsafing this or that belief, and willing to take the lumps for having said so. Anyone who is afraid of being reviled should seek a job in Kansas City writing for Hallmark, and never *ever* undertake an essay. As Lawrence Durrell wrote, "Trivial or impure dreaming literally rots the fabric of the future." The sullied truth stinks from the head, like a week-old grouper.

The essayist is, in some ways, though I just said s/he is not . . . a journalist. And (he dropped quote again) as Joseph Pulitzer assured us decades ago, "The purpose of journalists should be to afflict the comfortable."

What joy! What bad cess to those who hog the mike and own the marketplace and whine when anyone dares to point out their lack of savory or flavorful existence. The essayist goes after them. And, if done properly, there is the rending of flesh, the ripping of garments, the woebegone tugging of forelocks as the once-mighty crawl around on hands and knees bleating how unfairly they've been treated. Case in point (though even this example will out the slavering beast):

Couple of California brothers, both Atheists, family is of the Atheist persuasion, refused to swear allegiance to god, or to be precise in the terms of the Boy Scouts oath, to God...no wait, make that GOD...um...G★O★D!! So the BSA gave them the boot. For having a belief different from that of the owners of the mike, the hoggers of the dais, the mouth that speaks for All of Society. So the father of these kids, who just happens to be a lawyer, takes the Boy Scouts of America chapter in Garden Grove, or Anaheim, or La Puente, or wherever the hell it was, takes them to court. And here it is, going up the ladder from court to appellate court to maybe even the Supreme Court. And at every step, the BSA, espousing the name of G!O!D! by God, is heaving its bosom and carping that it's not getting equal time to present its side of the question.

As if there hasn't been something like two thousand years of proselytizing, inveighing, Inquisitioning, missionarying, and just all-around free-floating espousal of God As The Answer. (You'll notice that on Sunday morning, amid all the 700 Clubs and Crystal Cathedral importunations, there ain't *The Hour of Atheism* on any cable or network channel.)

Well, the essayist would write about that sort of thing. The essayist would step up to the plate, all innocence and dimples, and suggest, well, maybe there *ought* to be a little Equal Time for the right of whoever desires it so, to be free *from* religion for a while, as opposed to the standard freedom *of* religion, which is nice, too, I suppose. The essayist would suggest coyly that such a consistent presentation of the bent of the majority is as religiously fanatic as the most demented Fundamentalist bomb-thrower. Because neither cares to permit anyone else to have a differing point of view by which they can exercise their right to free choice.

The essayist is the one who talks about such matters.

The essayist takes chances.

The essayist hammers the blinders from your eyes.

The essayist speaks to you in languages you've never heard.

The essayist goes logically from presumption to inescapable truth you refuse to accept.

The essayist won't take anything on faith.

The essayist is a practitioner of guerrilla warfare.

And for this, the essayist, the columnist, the setter-down of personal — *informed* — opinion is treated like a mangy dog.

But as Super Chicken said to his crony, Fred, "You knew the job was dangerous when you took it."

Any writer worth his or her salt and/or cayenne, who seeks succor and approbation and nights of sweet sleep, should book passage on the Trans-Continental Dirigible for Kansas City, where greeting card doggerel awaits him or her who cannot stare down the barrel of the assassin's rifle and delude him- or herself into believing s/he can catch that damned bullet between Adamantium teeth.

This has been an introduction to the writings of one Peter David. Believe it or not.

A Depreciation

Three years ago, when this foray into insanity began, it seemed harmless enough. I figured it would last a few months; I would get some notoriety; the Comic Book Legal Defense Fund would make a few bucks; and that would be that.

I never foresaw 36 months of this or a "Best of —" volume. Or the notion that the simple act of turning out a weekly column would somehow, through sheer week-in, week-out diligence, result in my having some sort of impact on the business of comics and even on the lives of some of the individuals in it. That *Comics Buyer's Guide* readers would actually look forward to my column or even turn to it first.

When the column began, I had no clue as to what I'd discuss or how I would possibly maintain it. Don and Maggie Thompson, my esteemed editors, wouldn't even promise that it would be weekly. The most that they would assure me is that they would "try."

Here, then, is my first column. Notes to follow:

Installment 1

BECAUSE HUE DEMANDED IT (July 27, 1990)

The first query came from Bob Greenberger during the course of my daily crabbing-about-certain-licensors phone call. Bob, my editor on *Trek*, said, "So — you gonna do the column?"

What column?

"The column for *CBG*," he prompted.

Seems somebody had suggested to Don and Maggie Thompson that I write a column. Suggested it in print. And they said it sounded good to them and tossed the ball over to me.

I didn't want the ball, so I tossed it back.

But it kept being thrown at me. People asked me at Marvel. People came up to me at the Heroes convention in North Carolina and asked me. I couldn't believe it. This was a three-line squib in the back pages. Does everyone read *every* line of the paper?

Guess so.

"Write a 'How-To-Write' column," Don and Maggie suggested.

No way. Writing a how-to-write column, to me, implies that you've reached a pinnacle and are now ready to dispense wisdom from on high. Let's face it. What such a column really means is, "I will teach you how to write like I do." Believe me, you don't want to write like I do because then you'd have to think like I do. That's too hideous a fate. The only person who's figured out how I think is my wife, Myra. And she won't tell me.

To think like I do means that you could be watching Showtime one evening and see the words "This program is close-captioned for the hearing impaired" appear on the screen. And then a voice solemnly intones, "This program is close-captioned for the hearing impaired." And you suddenly wonder, "Wait a minute. Who are they saying it for? What is the purpose of *saying* 'This program is close-captioned for the hearing impaired'? Because if you are deaf you won't know they said it, and if you aren't deaf you won't care.

But I digress...

"Talk about how to break into Marvel," Don and Maggie suggested.

I don't know. Lock picks, I suppose. If that means how to get started in comics, you can't use me as an example. I wasn't trying to break in as a writer. Instead, I was cheerfully toiling away as direct sales manager at Marvel when "it" happened.

No reader understands, or cares about, what a sales manager does. This puts them on par with most editors.

Once I was at a convention sales repping Marvel comics, and a fan came up to me and said, "What do you do at Marvel Comics?" And I said, "I'm the sales manager." And he thought it over for a moment, then shrugged, and said, "Oh — well — I guess I'll get your autograph anyway." He felt he'd do me a favor.

Certainly, I'd made a vague attempt or two at selling a story along the way. I had not been awesomely successful. I tried submitting a couple of *Moon Knight* plots to Denny O'Neil. I still haven't heard back from Denny on them and, frankly, I'm starting to think I never will.

Then Jim Owsley became the editor of the Spider-Man comics and he was more than happy to make time for me when I kind of drifted by and said, "I've got an idea for a Spider-Man comic." And that story became *Spec Spidey* #103, which, if you hunt around, you can probably find in a three-for-a-dollar box somewhere.

Besides, when people ask, "How did you get into comics?" they don't really want to know, anyway. They want to think there's some secret word that professionals know, and all you have to do is whisper the word and you're in. They don't want to hear about 95 percent luck. Can't blame them. When I was on the other side of the autograph table, I sure didn't want to hear that, either.

So a "how-to" column was out.

I knew I didn't want to write a gossipy "Behind-the-Scenes" type column, because I'd lose every friend I have in comics. No one would ever talk to me about anything, because they'd be wondering whether they were providing grist for a column or not. So that didn't sound like fun.

People kept asking, and here I had no idea why I should, because I had no idea what I would write about.

What finally made me decide to write this column was my appearance at the aforementioned Heroes convention (a fun series of conventions run by Shelton "Well Hush My Puppies" Drumm, proprietor of "Heroes Aren't Hard to Find," a nice guy and new husband of Cynthia Drumm. They got married at the most recent con. The guy'll do anything to boost attendance. But I digress).

I was scheduled to speak at noon on Sunday. Then I noticed that nothing was scheduled after me until 2:30. And I said, "No way am I going to stand there and fill two-and-a-half hours. I'll talk and field questions until I run out of things to say and/or the audience gets bored with me and leaves," which was fine with Shelton. No one really expected me to fill that huge block of time.

I never ran out of things to say. They dragged me offstage at 1:45, and the room was still full. Everyone seemed to be enjoying themselves — either that or, being southern, they were just too polite to leave.

The thing is, my talking style is much like my writing style. When someone asks a question, I will talk and, as things occur to me, I'll go off on a tangent and just keep going and then vaguely come to a stop and say, "Did I answer your question somewhere in there?" This rambling style of mine is currently accepted as my rather offbeat style. When I'm old, it will be cited as evidence of senility and be more than enough reason for my children to have me put in a home.

The point of all this is that, if I can fill up time at conventions with such ease, then I can probably fill up a column.

And if I find the fan who got me into this, I'll throttle him.

*(Peter David writes **Hulk**, **Dreadstar**, **Star Trek**, **Atlantis Chronicles**, and other projects he'll shamelessly plug. And when he writes short bios about himself at the ends of articles, he uses "he" to make it sound as if someone else wrote them. If you have questions or issues you'd like him to address, send them to him c/o **CBG**, and maybe they'll be addressed there. Or maybe not.)*

What amazes me the most, in retrospect, is how off base I was. I said I would not write a "how-to-write" column. Yet in this collection are half a dozen columns on the art of writing. "How to Break In?" That's covered, as well.

The thing I did manage to avoid was turning *But I Digress* into a gossip column. Miraculously, I have managed to keep my column separate from my daily interactions with my peers — although occasionally, when a confidence is being shared, some will still hesitate momentarily and say, "This is off the record, you know." I must continually reassure my friends and associates that casual chats do not end up grist for my column — unless, of course, they're feeding me grist for my columns.

I have tried to cull the most genuinely memorable — not to mention some of my personal favorites — from the column's three years of life. Some readers, upon learning of the preparation of this volume, suggested just printing them all. This is not possible. Aside from the format constraints, some columns simply do not age well. They were pertinent at the time but now simply seem irrelevant. The ideal notion was that this volume would stand on its own. Besides, who knows? If this thing takes off, we could always do a "Second Best."

A number of people must be thanked. First and foremost is my wife, Myra. Not only has she been a source of inspiration for a number of column ideas (not to mention my first-line editor), but it was also her suggestion that the money I get paid for the column be donated to the Comic Book Legal Defense Fund. It was an idea I embraced wholeheartedly, since it meant I could natter on for whatever length I wished and not second-guess myself that I was padding a column out for the purpose of making a few extra bucks. It's about time, though, that she was given the credit she deserves. I know any number of professionals whose spouses exhibit tolerance at best — and outright disinterest at worst — in the comics field. Myra has made the effort to embrace it, understand it, and better it.

Second are Don and Maggie Thompson, the intrepid *Comics Buyer's Guide* editors, who have gone from cautious "no promises" about my column being weekly, to nowadays when, if I'm running late, Maggie's calling me up and saying, "Where is it?" Aside from a few *contretemps* here and there, as is inevitable during a lengthy creative association, the column's production has been remarkably trouble-free.

Third is Greg Loescher, *CBG's* publisher who listened to the demands of the fans and spearheaded this compilation.

Fourth is everyone in the professional community who ever wrote to *CBG* and attacked me, sometimes blithely distorting and misquoting the column in order to do so. Praise is wonderful, but the assaults have not only provided me with additional material, they've also made for some of the most entertaining reading.

Such missives have also served as a reminder of the power of the written word. When people see things in print, there is a far greater need to respond than if the same things are said in casual conversation. As Neil Simon's Eugene observes in *Biloxi Blues,* people figure that if it's written down, it must be true — otherwise the author would not have taken the time to write it down.

Fifth, I would like to thank Harlan Ellison, whose own forays into column writing served as a personal inspiration and challenge.

Sixth, all those friends in the industry — particularly Pat O'Neill, Jo Duffy, Bill Mumy, Carol Kalish (bless her), Bob Greenberger, Carrie and Mart Nodell, Julie Schwartz, Stan Lee, Terry Stewart, and many others — who have been so supportive of these efforts.

And lastly, to the thousands of letters I've gotten from people who were touched, in a variety of ways, by these columns. I've added **Historical Notes** after those columns which resulted in particularly memorable responses.

And for those of you who are reading these columns for the first time — boy, are you in for some weirdness.

Peter David
Writer of Stuff
New York
August 1993

SECTION 1

Comic Books — Variations on a Theme

or
Up, up, and Oy Vay

The production of comics — ranging from the editorial content to the publishing and distributing of them — is an endlessly fascinating and varied topic.

I've been working in this industry for more than a decade now, and in many ways feel that I'm still scratching the surface.

We read comics for so many reasons. Some say that they want pure escapism, embracing those stories that focus primarily on big guys hitting each other. Other folks want more substance in their comics: more fiber in their diets. Some want only super-heros in four colors; others go for elves and aardvarks in black and white.

Comics, in all their permutations —

DEAD AND RECOVERING NICELY... (Aug. 3, 1990)

Who killed death in comics?

This calls for a baseball metaphor (as do most things in life). Asking who killed death in comics is like asking who a runner steals a base on: the pitcher or the catcher? The former says the latter; the latter accuses the former. So it is with comics death. The fans will blame the writers, and the writers will pin it on the fans.

Follow:

Comic books are second only to soap operas in terms of being a fan-responsive medium. When Stan Lee would smilingly proclaim that readers are "the real editors," he wasn't kidding. Fan letters (and fans' ultimate vote, their dollars) can determine a great deal about how things proceed.

Not that any writer worth his salt does everything readers say. It's gutless, and, besides, fans can be remarkably shortsighted. Remember the "kill that obnoxious Wolverine" pleas from *X-Men* letters pages, circa issues 97-107? Still, fan reaction was, is, and will be a powerful influence.

And fans hate to see characters die.

Except characters they hate or characters that are felt to have "no potential." (And after what's been done with Swamp Thing, Animal Man, and others, can anyone comfortably say that about *any* character?)

But if the fans have any sort of emotional attachment to a character, they don't want to see that character go. Worse than that — they don't believe the character is really dead. Why should they? They've seen resurrections far too many times to take any of it seriously.

And that's where we, the writers, have shot ourselves in the foot. By trying to placate the fans by reviving popular characters (I stress *popular*. You don't see anyone plotting to bring back The Ringer) we have robbed ourselves of the ability to tell stories with any meaning (myself not excluded, in case you think I'm getting holier-than-thou).

In any action film you see, tension is generated because somebody you like might die. In *Die Hard*, might be Bruce Willis or his wife. In a Bond film, might be his latest lady love. And so forth.

But comics have a built in fail-safe mechanism — someone dies, we can bring 'em back — and so we are unable to get anyone to take death as a serious threat.

Case in point from personal experience: The Death of Jean DeWolff.

Here was a relatively minor supporting Spider-Man character who was blown away to kick off a four-parter. (Short digression: An editor at a comic-book company [no longer in the field] took me aside and informed me quite seriously that this story violated the "rules" of comics. That when a character died, it had to be at the climax of the story, preferably with the character giving his or her life heroically to save the hero. That was a rule. Killing Jean on page 4 of an 88-page story was "ridiculous." Old, dopey me.)

So Jean dies in *Spec Spidey* #107, and we get deluged with letters. The majority of them contained recurring themes: First, that Jean was the letter writer's "favorite character." This was odd considering Jean had hardly appeared at all for many issues previous, and letters demanding more of her were nil. The second theme was the more disturbing — people didn't believe she was dead.

I was unnerved by this. If readers didn't accept her death, they wouldn't accept everything that flowed from it. *Spidey* Editor Jim Owsley was even told by confident fans at an Atlanta Con, "Nah, she's not really dead."

I couldn't understand it. I had called the damned thing "The Death of Jean DeWolff." I'd had her entire upper torso blown away at close range by a shotgun. I had her funeral and planted her in the next issue. What did I have to do? Decapitate her on panel? She was dead, cold, wormfood.

And people refused to believe. They were willing to accept the most outrageous contrivance (clones, replicants, LMDs, secret S.H.I.E.L.D. plots — all these and more were suggested) rather than handle the simple truth that Jean had joined the bleeding choir invisible.

The fans have made it too easy on us writers. They'll swallow it all rather than live with death. Perfect example: Elektra. Elektra's death was devastating. Frank Miller pulled it off perfectly. No one was deader than Elektra.

And Frank brought her back, and everyone was happy. Everyone. And it was accepted without question. And Elektra is walking around somewhere in the Marvel universe, waiting for her graphic novel. No one thinks this odd.

The following is not meant as criticism — I think Frank is a freaking comics genius. But consider:

Elektra was stabbed to death. Not turned to stone like Thanos or fried in mystical energies like the Lord Papal. Not molecularly disassembled, not scattered on the four winds of the cosmos, or any of the countless pseudo-scientific/fantastical means by which you can at least justify, to some degree, that someone might come back.

She wasn't immortal, alien, interdimensional, or extragalactic — she was just a human.

After she expired in the most mortal of ways, she was then autopsied. Now, when they perform an autopsy, they cut you open to discover what made you die. They remove and examine your organs.

They then put the organs back but, since your future need for them would seem limited, they don't put them back in place. They just dump them all in your chest cavity — liver, spleen, kidneys, everything — stitch it up and ship you off.

For most people, this is where it ends. But Elektra, as they say, "got better."

When I was sales manager at Marvel, after Elektra returned, fans would ask me at conventions, "What's Elektra going to do now that she's returned?" And my reply was always, "Slosh." But people just stared at me.

Elektra's return was always accepted as "ninja magic." Why not? It's no sillier than, say, shrinking to microscopic size to avoid a gamma bomb blast.

They die, and the fans protest, and they return. Robin, Marvel Girl, Gwen, Ma and Pa Kent (well, OK, no one protested, but the Kents came back, anyway), the list goes on and on. Writers try to please the fans by giving them what they want.

So-and-So is dead? No! Shock follows shock, as So-and-So returns (usually accompanied by a cover illo of the hero saying, "It can't be! You're — *dead*!", thereby proving that super-heroes never read comic books or they wouldn't be surprised by this sort of thing).

And what happens? The fans complain. What, someone has died, say the fans? Ah, the jaundiced, jaded fans, who cock a knowing glance and nod their heads and say, "Suuuuuuure, they're dead. You expect us to believe that? Come on. No one ever dies in comics. Because writers are too gutless to really kill someone and have them stay dead."

Which brings us back to the original question: Whose fault is that?

What do I think?

I think the runner definitely steals on the pitcher.

*(Peter David is the writer of **The Hulk**, among other things, and wishes to address something that seems to confuse people but is completely off topic — namely, if the gray Hulk gets mad, does he turn into the green Hulk?*

The answer is: of course not.

The two Hulks are aspects of Bruce Banner. An angry Bruce Banner gets you an enraged green Hulk. An angry gray Hulk gets you a quick trip to the nearest Emergency Room. The gray Hulk has never had any trouble dealing with anger and so would have no need to vent his rage in another persona. It's that simple. I think.)

THE GREEN AND THE RED (Sept. 21, 1990)

In order to be extremely accommodating, as this column is wont to do, this ninth installment of *But I Digres*s — will feature two subjects: one that is fairly serious and I've been giving some thought to; and one that is utterly pointless and even vaguely humorous, which occurred to me in a comic store.

Therefore, depending upon your mood, you can read the first entry (the pointless, vaguely humorous one) or the second entry, which is serious and disturbing and may even be regarded as insulting to a long-standing comics character (although it's not intended as such).

If you're of a broad mind this day, you can even read both and dwell on how the world can be both thoughtful and pointless all at the same time.

First, the pointless, vaguely humorous bit.

I was visiting Amazing Comics in Sayville, Long Island, wherein there was a display of the new line of action figures being released with Marvel and DC characters.

Now, I love action figures. They are the toys I wish I had had when I was a kid but am glad they're here now, since it means I don't have to beg my parents to buy them for me.

(Actually, have you ever done that as an adult? Like, when you see those 900 numbers that say, "Get your parents' permission to call." And you're 33 years old and you call your folks and ask if you can call this 900 number. And your parents say no. Then you call it anyway and revel in the idea that you can still be defiant, just like when you were a teenager. Makes you feel young. Try it sometime. But I digress...)

Anyway, I'm looking at this line of action figures, and I'm very impressed. Unlike the earlier, awful line of Marvel action figures (the ones that were really stiff and didn't bend at the knees or elbows, and the black ink from Daredevil's DD insignia smeared off on your hands. The only one that looked cool was the Spidey in the black costume, and it was tough to find. And they came with these stupid secret *shields*, for pity's sake, that had nothing to do with anything), these action figures are really cool.

They bend just as well as the original DC action figures (some of whom make their reappearance, such as Hawkman) and they come with great accessories.

The only problem was — The Hulk.

Not a problem, really. The Hulk looked cool, and he was green, but since the green guy came back I can live with that (although a gray one would look even cooler). It was the accessories he came with: an iron bar and a boulder. A big, plastic boulder.

Now in truth, I don't know what I would have had him come with myself. The problem was that it made me start thinking of action figures and raving about them, and The Hulk expressing his annoyance over the boulder. And it sounded just like what was to me: one of the most heart-tugging moments in the old Charlie Brown special, *It's the Great Pumpkin, Charlie Brown*.

Really! It would go like this:

Cap: Look! I got this great shield launcher that throws my shield when you squeeze the trigger!

Surfer: I've got a gleaming, shining surfboard!

Hulk: I got a rock.

Punisher: I got all these fantastic machine guns to blow bad guys away!

Daredevil: I got a billy club launcher that really launches my club!

Hulk: I got a rock.

Spider-Man: I got suction cups on my hands so I can actually stick to walls!

Doc Ock: I got suction cups on my mechanical arms so I can chase after you!

Hulk: I got a rock.

Get a bunch of friends together and read this out loud.

Really. You'll feel so sad for The Hulk.

Go out and buy lots of Hulk action figures. Make him feel better. Help him get his rocks off.

See? Told you it was pointless. By the way, has anyone seen the supposed action figure of The Blank from Dick Tracy? I've seen everyone but.

More serious things now.

I was travelling and I turned on the hotel TV and, so help me, *Red Sonja* was on. So I'm watching Red Sonja and Arnold going through their paces and I start thinking about Sonja — really *thinking* about her — for the first time in years.

And I start to get this sick feeling in the pit of my stomach, the kind I always get when I realize that something's going to occur to me that should have occurred to me years ago, except I didn't realize it.

Sonja's one sick puppy.

What prompted me to realize this was, of all things, *Atlantis Chronicles*.

In *Atlantis Chronicles* #3, a character named Cora is brutally raped (said rape resulting in the birth of the hellish Kordax). Writing that sequence and the subsequent storyline, was easily the most difficult story I've ever written. I felt so deeply for Cora and for what she went through. My sister, Ronni, asked me why I had written it, if it was so upsetting to me. And I told her, "Because that's what happened." Which is really the only answer I could come up with.

So I was watching *Red Sonja* for the first time since I'd written *AC* #3. And I started thinking about Sonja. And I started getting chills.

Sonja, as most every comics fan knows, was raped as a teenager. With the help of a passing goddess, some magic, and a convenient sword, Sonja embarked on a career as a swordswoman with a personal viewpoint on chastity that most fanboys know by heart. It rolls as trippingly off the tongue as does Green Lantern's oath or the line about what burns at the Man-Thing's touch.

Red Sonja vows that she will never give herself to (i.e., have sex with) any man except one who could defeat her in combat.

I've known this for years. I never thought anything about it, except sometimes I occasionally wished that Conan would clobber her once and for all and get it over with. But now I thought about it, and it really started to upset me (as did my attitude).

Follow:

Sonja was raped. She was brutalized. Control over her body was taken by a man, who overpowered her and had forced intercourse with her.

And she swore that no man would ever touch her except — who? A man who could beat her. Overpower her. Defeat her. That's creepy.

A gentle man does not have a chance with Red Sonja. A poet couldn't woo her. A singer could not sway her. A man of grace or charm, a man of breeding and education who would never think of striking a woman, much less raping one, won't get to first base with her. In short, the sort of man who, with patience and understanding, could put the pieces of this woman's sex life back together again is automatically out of the running.

Instead, the only man that she will have sex with is a man who can re-enact the single most traumatic and devastating event of the woman's life. Someone who is capable of overpowering Red Sonja, as her rapist did, is the one she will give herself to. She has doomed herself to disdain all normal sex, searching instead for someone who can remove control of her body from her once more and force her to relive her rape.

Red Sonja is a sick, sick woman. She is a living incarnation of the oldest and most insidious beliefs that men can have — namely, that women want to be raped. "But your honor, she was asking for it. Begging for it. Really. It wasn't my fault. She wanted it."

Red Sonja stalks the world of Conan with a philosophy that says, "Come on, take your shot. Think you're man enough? Come on. Come on."

I guess the thing that disturbs me more than the nature of the vow itself is that it took me this long to glom to it. I viewed this philosophy of hers, not as the viewpoint of a sick woman, but as a challenge. This was the gauntlet she threw down to the world, rather than a cry for help.

She's a sick character? Well, so is Bruce Banner. So is Bruce Wayne. (Must go with the name.) But to the best of my knowledge (I don't pretend to have read every story Sonja's been in) she hasn't been treated that way. The high tragedy of who she is and of the trauma of her brutalization have not really been explored.

And I'm annoyed with myself that I ever wanted Conan to beat her so he could give it to her, already. What in hell was I thinking? Some of the scariest things in the Hyborian world aren't conjured up by evil wizards.

(Peter David welcomes any comments c/o **Comics Buyer's Guide**. *He writes* **Hulk, Atlantis Chronicles,** *and other sick titles.)*

Historical Notes:

*1) David Schwartz, who runs a store called "Comic Collection," maintains that he was the first one who suggested to me the notion of the Hulk saying, "I got a rock," **a la** Charlie Brown. I have no reason to doubt him, and it even seemed vaguely familiar, when he brought it up at the Diamond Trade Show in 1993, so I'm making note of it here. I went on to use the same gag in a Hulk annual.*

*2) The observations on Sonja resulted in the full gamut of letters. One, from John Byrne in **Oh So,** took me to task for saying that I was upset over the rape in **Atlantis Chronicles,** stating that it only happened because I wanted it to happen and that the writer is in full control at all times. That's a world view with which I soundly disagree.*

Another letter, which came to the column, was one of the most affecting I'd ever received. It was from a woman who had been raped and felt extremely moved by my self-realization over Sonja's plight. I printed the letter, which I described as being from a rape victim, and stated how moved I was that she had written this poignant confession of her personal difficulties to me, a relative stranger.

This response, to my astonishment, landed me in deep water, as I was furiously informed by another correspondent that the term was rape "survivors," not "victims." It was my first experience with being Politically Incorrect.

I was also taken to task by that same correspondent over my use of the word "confession," which implied to some that I was granting the letter writer absolution. Being Jewish, that literally had never occurred to me. So it was also my first experience with having my meaning totally misconstrued.

Fortunately the "Sonja" letter writer understood my intentions and never took umbrage — and, eventually, I even made peace with the other correspondent who was so angry with me. Nevertheless, I was quite startled when it happened.

THE GIFT THAT KEEPS ON GIVING (Dec. 14, 1990)

With the holiday season upon us, it occurs to me that there might be some who are still stuck for presents to give their loved ones, or even their hated ones.

Now, of course, *CBG* has its annual holiday supplement with suggestions from various folks for ideal gifts. If you're still stuck for possibilities, *But I Digress* cordially offers you these options by other respected individuals within the comics industry, who were unable to contribute in time:

James W. Fry, penciller of *Star Trek, Blasters,* and others:

1) Ideal for any *Twin Peaks* fans — remove the clothes from any blonde fashion doll, paint her lips blue, wrap her in plastic, and you've got the Laura Palmer Inaction Figure. Small letters to stick under her fingernails are optional.

2) The Battery-Operated Battery Recharger — Insert batteries, insert batteries, and presto.

Bruce Banner, noted physicist:

I believe strongly that books make an ideal gift. I would recommend some of my personal favorites:

1) *A Simple Introduction to Particle Physics*

2) *The Yo Yo Syndrome: How to Deal With Abrupt Weight Loss and Weight Gain*

3) *Sybil*

4) *Dr. Jekyll and Mr. Hyde*

5) *Bix: The Unauthorized Biography of Bill Bixby*

Thanos, noted demigod:
1) A soul gem
2) A soul gem
3) A soul gem
4) A soul gem
5) Gameboy from Nintendo

The Joker, Clown Prince of Crime:
1) *Stacked Deck*, the new collection of Joker stories
2) Fake dog crap in a bag. Or at least, say it's fake.
3) Video assortment of *One Flew over the Cuckoo's Nest*, *Chinatown*, and *The Shining*
4) Electric cattle prod — great at parties
5) Plenty of lip gloss

Lex Luthor, businessman and philanthropist:
In this time when war seems to hang over us once again, casting a pall upon our fair world, I strongly feel it's time to set aside differences. There may be people whom you consider to be enemies. Colleagues with whom you've had disagreements. Business rivals who have attempted to screw you over on past occasions.

It's time to put those hostilities behind you. I would strongly suggest giving gifts to those who were once your enemies. Mend fences. And the ideal way to do it is with jewelry.

Not diamonds, though, or rubies. Instead, I would suggest jewelry of the type I make sure these days to give to all my former enemies: Kryptonite.

I realized the wonders of this magnificent little gem when I started wearing a kryptonite ring. What it did for my hand, I can't begin to tell you. So I would recommend for your enemies:
1) a kryptonite choker
2) a kryptonite wrist bracelet (engraving optional)
3) a kryptonite ankle bracelet
But wait! Why stop at jewelry? For a woman who used to drive you insane and now you wish to give an intimate gift to, may I suggest:
4) a kryptonite underwire bra
And for the man in your life who fancies himself the athlete, he cannot do without:
5) the kryptonite protective crotch cup
Believe me — they'll never forget it. I certainly didn't.

Puma, businessman and hero/villain:
1) Nikes
2) Reeboks
3) Keds
4) Air Jordans
5) Pumas

Victor Von Doom, monarch:
1) A country, the ideal gift for the man who has everything
2) Diplomatic Immunity. It comes with owning a country, and I certainly don't leave home without it.
3) WD-40, a handy aerosol oil that can be used for hundreds of everyday applications, including rusty locks, squeaky door hinges, and stubborn armor joints
4) Show her you love her: Send her to another dimension for a vacation.
5) One hundred pairs of stretch socks

Bart Simpson, student:
1) Edible shorts
2) New skateboard
3) Simpsons T-Shirts, dolls, figures, lunch box, etc.

4) The "Trump" board game, so you can change the rules and make him come out a real loser

5) The answers to your next major test

Captain America, patriot:

1) U.S. Savings Bonds

2) An Amtrak "See America" rail pass

3) The deluxe edition of *Profiles in Courage*

4) A chain-mail flag: bulletproof and it won't burn

5) A Flexible Flier with red and white concentric circles

Barry Allen, police scientist

1) A microwave oven

2) A crate of Jolt

3) A Federal Express account

4) Coupons for Domino's Pizza and their guaranteed 30-minute delivery

5) A ring to keep your clothes in (I used to have an outfit I kept in a ring. Now I have a new version of the outfit, and I'd need a ring about five feet wide to accommodate this sculpted monster).

Darkseid, Lord of Apokolips:

1) Power

2) Fear

3) Terror

4) Total Domination

5) Superstar Barbie

(Peter David, writer of stuff, wishes he could have a big, huge, impressive, incredibly long deadline.)

Historical Notes:

1) Beverly Martin, in Corpus Christi, Texas, was so taken by James Fry's suggestion that she actually made a limited run of Laura Palmer dolls. I have one, James has one, and Miguel Ferrer has one. And you don't. So there. Nyah.

GIRL TALK (Jan. 4, 1991)

It's been a truism in the comics that a female lead cannot sell a comic book.

Now, of course, *X-Men*, in its free-flowing membership, has boasted line-ups that were sometimes more than 50 percent female, but the title has *Men* right there, so it was OK to buy it. For that matter, although there was demand for years for Marvel to publish an ongoing comic book featuring Wolverine, when fans discuss series for the female characters it's always, "When will Rogue (or whoever) get her own *limited* series?" Is there any demand for an *ongoing* series with an X-Woman? Probably not, because, if there were, Marvel would publish it.

What other females are currently carrying their own titles? *She-Hulk*, but that boasted John Byrne, who was doing some really good work. If it had been launched with less popular creators, it probably would have fared as well as the original *Savage She-Hulk*. No others at Marvel, methinks. Over at DC, we've got the perennial *Wonder Woman*. Any female leads in their own title? Uh — have they canceled *Huntress* yet?

Ah, but the independents! The new wave of comics! Certainly they boast lots of — Uh — hmm. Nope. And no, *Ms. Mystic*, the world's only biannual monthly, doesn't count. And, I'm sorry, but *Flare* shouldn't count.

Now, oddly, this column is not actually about the dearth of women leads. It's about why the audience doesn't support titles that do feature women.

You could argue that, most times, the titles have sucked. Well, that's true to a degree. But there have been many titles that have been slow starters or even gotten off to downright poor starts. Sometimes the comics get themselves together, sometimes they don't. But if it's a female lead, chances are the comic book won't make it past six issues unless it hits the ground running and never stops.

Now, years ago, when the vast majority of comics readers were under 10, the answer was very simple. The readership thought, "Girls are dumb," and that was that. But nowadays the readership tilts heavily towards the high-school and college crowd who, I hope, don't feel that way.

But it doesn't matter. There is a perception throughout society at this point that women cannot carry a lead. That their contributions to a title, be it comic book, movie, or TV show, are minimal at best.

On the flip side, male contributions to the same properties are disproportionately rated. Patrick Swayze was offered millions if he would do a sequel to *Dirty Dancing*. But what about the star of *Dirty Dancing*, Jennifer Grey? A couple hundred thousand. Granted, a couple hundred thousand is nothing to sneeze at, but we're talking equity here.

Or take the following item that appeared in the December 9th *Newsday:* "Ten-year-old Macaulay Culkin, while not breaking the bank, will take a large chunk of it with his next film. Culkin, the star of Fox's hit comedy *Home Alone*, will receive a reported $1 million for his next picture —

"The film will also star Dan Aykroyd and Jamie Lee Curtis. While Culkin's salary may be record-setting (for a child actor), the other salaries on the film are not. Word has it that Aykroyd will receive around $2 million for the film, while Curtis will receive only $800,000 —

"It's safe to say that his fee has increased tenfold," Feldsher (his agent) says. "These are not outrageous fees for an actor in a very successful film."

Yeah, Feldsher, but for his next film? Only if it's an actor and not an actress. Meryl Streep, Sigourney Weaver, Cher: None of them became overnight sensations, and most of them — especially Streep — have been very vocal about payment inequities in Hollywood.

What takes this particular item about outrageous salaries and puts it right over the top? Why, the name of the film young Culkin is starring in: *I Am Woman.*

Part of the problem is that the contents of successful comics can easily be paralleled in the contents of successful movies. The only actors who can get films "green-lighted" (i.e., their involvement in the film guarantees a studio will want to make it) are guys like Sly and Bruce and Arnold. Action film guys. No female stars have that kind of bankability.

That's because a film heavy with females is almost invariably a relationship film. Tempers explode. But in a film with Bruce Willis, airplanes explode. Studio executives don't like emotional damage: they like property damage. It looks flashier on *Entertainment Tonight*. Look at *Postcards from the Edge*. A female relationship picture, but what scene did you always see a clip from? The one really big fight between Meryl Streep and Shirley MacLaine, on the stairs. Unfortunately, no punches were thrown.

Therefore, if movies with females are to be made that execs will like, it means action pictures. But then you have a problem. Who are the females going to fight in the action films? Well, by and large, you're limited to two genders — male and female.

Now you're stuck.

If your heroine beats up on a bad man, the males in the audience feel threatened and are not going to like her. If your heroine beats up on a bad woman, then the perception is that the villain couldn't have been that much of a threat, because, after all, it was a girl, and any healthy guy can beat up any dumb girl, right?

It's significant that the only action/adventure film with a female lead that was successful, in my recent memory, was *Aliens*. Why significant? Because the female lead beat up on alien beings who were non-gender-threatening (merely life-threatening).

Same thing with comics. Comics are, by and large, locked into the action/adventure format. That's what sells. That's what's successful on a large scale. *Love & Rockets* does fine for Fantagraphics, but I can't see Marvel putting it out and expecting it to keep pace with, say, *Iron Man*.

Now, readers can deal with a female who beats up on villains, if the female has lots of help surrounding her. I mean, I personally would be willing to take on Juggernaut if I knew that I had Wolverine covering my back.

Men generally see disputes in matters of black and white, to be solved quickly with as much maintaining of *machismo* as possible. This attitude is reflected in the world of super-hero comics as well as in the Middle East, where America is currently trying to show that we are the real-life Justice League of the World.

Women, however — and I'm going to make sweeping generalizations about gender here, admittedly, but I have been until now, so why change? — women don't share this attitude. And yes, I know there are women armed forces in the Middle East, but I would tend to think that, if women were running the show, we wouldn't have armed forces in the first place. Women see things in shades of gray and will usually want to talk things out rather than punch things out. That's why women watch *Oprah* and men watch *Monday Night Football*.

But when you have women super-heroes, they acquire the mental attitudes of their male counterparts. They have male thinking layered on them, which is kind of like frosting a cake with cement. The result is that, while male super-heroes embody idealized machismo, female super-heroes also embody idealized machismo. As a result, they are subtly unrealistic, and the fans perceive them as such and don't accept them as genuine characters. They'll suspend disbelief for the purpose of costumes and powers, but not for the difference in man/woman emotional make-up.

What's the answer? A mainstream comic about a non-super-powered female? A single mother, perhaps? How would that sell to the mutant fans? Probably about as well as a mainstream comic book about a non-super-powered male. Fans have a tendency to vote with closed wallets in cases like this.

And yes, I know there are some females in comics who act like real females, aside from those in *Love & Rockets*. There are exceptions. There are *always* exceptions. It would just be nice if there were enough exceptions to prove the rule. But more realistic females in comics would doubtlessly lead to fewer fight scenes, which would mean lower sales, which would mean the end of the world as we know it.

Or, to quote Steven Wright: "Women. Can't live with 'em. Can't kill 'em."

(Peter David, writer of stuff, has a screenplay about a female baseball player he wrote several years ago that he's still trying to get made. Any takers?)

UNINVITED GUESTS (April 12, 1991)

To guest, or not to guest, that is the question,
Whether 'tis nobler in the mind to suffer the slings and arrows of outrageous fandom
Who will take arms against a sea of guest shots
And by opposing, end them.

The original speech, of course, is about whether to die or not. And some months ago, I did a column about the tendency to revivify dead characters, focusing mainly on both the fan demand and abhorrence for the practice.

So we turn to another fan-powered notion, that being the featuring of hot characters in various titles. Are they overexposed? Is it a *bad thing* when writers do that? And more to the point — can I guest-star The Punisher or Ghost Rider in *The Incredible Hulk* without being shot?

The concept of cross-pollinating characters is nothing new, of course. It goes back to the very essence of the team concept that prompted the creation of the Justice Society of America, namely: Spud-Man has "x" number of readers. Captain Coleslaw has "y" number of readers. Put them in the same comic book, and you have x + y = a lot of sales.

Of course, I'm not privy to the sales figures of five decades ago, but I can only assume it did well, because the tradition has continued. The Barry Allen Flash teamed with the Golden Age Flash; Superman teamed with Batman in the long-running *World's Finest*. (When it was canceled by DC in the 1980s, a DC spokesman declared, "Batman and Superman never really worked well as a team." I thought this was a panic, considering that Batman and Superman were a team at a time when all the spokesman was old enough to do with a comic book was wipe his/her nose with it.) Iron Man teamed up with The Angel (through a special arrangement, we were told, with the publishers of *X-Men* magazine; darn nice of those publishers, I think.) And one of my personal favorites, Daredevil teamed up with The Fantastic Four.

And who can forget the immortal first teaming of Spider-Man and Superman, a Pre-Crisis event that had fans debating whether it took place on Earth 1, Earth 2, Earth S — where, in what reality, did it occur? (The answer, of course, is that it occurred on Earth $, otherwise known as Earth Bucks, which is not to be confused with Earth Barks, which is populated, of course, by talking ducks.)

Team-ups, guest shots, special appearances, cameos, walk-ons abounded. And those were some of the most memorable issues. The payoff was twofold: 1) They were the types of comics that gave us our first real feeling that the heroes lived in one big universe; 2) They were the types of comic books (again, we presume) that translated into $ucce$$ in the only way that publisher$ under$tand.

But because the guest shots happened every so often — and because it *wasn't the same characters* — fans didn't consider the team-ups from the profit-center point of view.

The change in viewpoint started slowly. For example, Spider-Man seemed to appear with startling regularity in the third issue (or so) of every new series. In a way, it seemed as if it was a way of making a new character or series "official" — Spidey's showing up was one manner to make the newcomer "genuine." He or she (yeah, right) was clearly a part of the Marvel Universe, because here was the most recognizable character in the MU come out to greet him or her. Feel at home. Pull up some increased sales and kick back.

In point of fact, what this also did was serve as a buffer against dropping interest. The first issue of anything generally sells well (OK, aside from *Night Nurse*). The second issue feeds off of the first — especially if you've got a continued story. Once you get to the third issue, however, you're more or less flying solo — unless you bring in an established guest star to bring in the *Spider-Man* fans.

And it was so easy, because Spidey was such a likeable, easy-going character who fit so easily into so many situations.

And then, somewhere along the way, Spidey's status was not so much thrown off as — displaced a bit. Because a new guest star megastar came onto the scene.

Wolverine.

Considering the once-fierce "Dump Wolverine" campaign that raged through the pages of *X-Men*, it's impressive to see how far the character had come. He went from outsider to the bread-and-butter character of the series.

And writers found him an intriguing character to work with. There was a lot there to explore, and he was also the first of a new breed — the strong, silent type who took no crap from anybody. The same thing that made him appealing to the fans also made him appealing to writers.

(A small digression here — I'm speaking in generalities. It's not as if I've done tons of research here. This is a theory, to be taken as such. Other writers might say differently.)

Wolverine started popping up in other comics, as well, and, lo and behold, sales started popping up, as well.

I believe that Wolverine was the first character to really underscore just what sales impact a guest star can have, even more than the customary Spidey guest shot. Even more than the multiple-sales theory of team comics.

Why? Because of the reader base from which the characters fed.

You've got Spider-Man appearing in *Spud-Man*. That means you're going to get the interest of the Spider-Man readers. But when you've got Wolverine guest-shooting in *Spud-Man*, that's going to attract the *X-Men* readers. And *X-Men*, as anyone who looks at the circulation statements can discern, sells somewhere in the neighborhood of three to four times as many copies as Spidey's comic books do (putting aside the multi-million "McSpidey" comic book).

When we guest-starred Wolverine in *The Incredible Hulk*, I did so for both of the obvious reasons: I liked the character and I liked the prospect of drawing some attention to the comic book, since sales were pretty crummy. But when retailers ordered the book, they blew it big time, even though their orders were double what they usually ordered on *Hulk*.

Why did they blow it? Because doubling pretty crummy gives you moderately crummy. What they should have done is place an order that was equal to, say, two-thirds of their *X-Men* order. But they didn't, and now that issue goes for, what, $20 a pop? $30?

Give them credit, however. The retailers learned. Fans snapped up anything in which Wolverine showed his adamantium-reinforced face. They increased their orders over time, and fans continued to vote with their wallets, and the vote was a resounding "Yes!"

Then The Punisher began to increase in popularity after the Grant/Zeck/Duffy *et al.* mini-series breathed new life into him (mercifully, else he'd still be shooting jaywalkers). Also, the grittiness and the "Code against killing, yeah, sure" attitude mirrored the mutant flavor of the decade, Wolverine. And as his series took off, the Wolverine phenomenon worked its magic on Frank Castle, turning The Punisher into yet another guest-shooting star. When the inevitable Punisher/Wolverine meeting occurred, it was like printing money.

What happened next? Lobo, who was a cross between Punisher and Wolverine (with some Charles Manson thrown in). Personally, I find Lobo about as appealing as nose hair, but I'm hardly an arbiter of taste in the comics universe. I mean, I gave *New Warriors* six issues, maximum. Credit Fabian Nicieza for pulling that one off.

Then, of course, came *Ghost Rider*. A character whose first series run could generally be found in the four-for-a-dollar box (right next to *Atlantis Chronicles* and *Justice*), Ghost Rider makes his re-debut and he's — guess what? — a hit. He punishes guys like Punisher, he is torn by inner demons like Wolverine, and he rides a sharp vehicle like Lobo. So who does a guest shot? Punisher.

Ideally, you would think that the fans would be pleased. Once again, they are being given what they ask for.

Instead, as is not surprising, the fans complain. Worse, they're cynical. At least, with bringing back dead characters, it can be chalked up to creative bankruptcy. But with Ghost Rider appearing all over the damned (literally) place, it's ascribed completely to profit motivation.

Now, I think that's a tad unfair. Sure, profit motive has some place in it. But to put a less monetary gloss on it, I think the motivation for success should also be factored in.

When I had Wolverine appear in *Hulk* #340, my hope was that it would cause *Hulk* to be more of a success. Yes, that translates into more money for me down the line. But I was more interested in the idea of it translating into more *readers*. As a writer, I wanted to increase my audience base. My ego and desire to tell stories are only served if as many people as possible are listening to, or reading, my stories. A successful writer is one who manages to get people's attention and hold it.

Furthermore, as I mentioned before, characters such as Wolvie and Ghost Rider attract readership, because they're interesting guys. If the readers can find them intriguing, why can't writers? And why shouldn't writers avail themselves of the opportunity to make use of those characters? I mean, if you went to the average fan and said, "Hey, want to write a Hulk/Punisher team up?" he'd jump at the chance. And no one would think the less of him. So if I do it, why should it be written off as an act of greed?

When Chris Claremont guest-starred The Hulk in two issues of *Wolverine*, you think he did it because he thought it would boost sales of the latter? Wolverine outsold Hulk maybe three-to-one. If The Hulk's appearance caused an increase of one percent, I'd be astonished.

Despite what some fans seem to believe, there is no editorial edict that says, "Punisher must guest-star in 10 comic books before the end of the fiscal year," "Ghost Rider's quota for the first quarter has not been met." It doesn't work that way.

As long as the fans continue to buy them, the crossovers will continue to occur. It would be nice if the companies could, however, coordinate matters a tad so that the characters aren't everywhere at once. If nothing else, it strains the suspension of disbelief — although this contention is pretty much shot considering that Spidey's in four titles every month and no one questions how he pulls that off, time-wise.

There is always concern about a character being overexposed. One problem: It has yet to happen. Spidey sells better than ever. Wolverine blows out of the stores, as does every guest appearance. More Punisher titles and one-shots are in the offing, and DC is heavily promoting a match between Lobo and The Demon.

I personally am eagerly awaiting the Wolverine/Lobo crossover. I can't stand Lobo but, if they offered it to me, I'd do it just so I could have Wolverine kick his butt.

I bet it would sell, too.

*(Peter David, writer of stuff, just saw the Michael J. Fox/James Woods film **The Hard Way** and was thrilled to hear them say, several times, "That only happens in movies; this is real life," indicating they must read his column. What was interesting what that he could swear he saw the storyline — actor teams up with hard-bitten cop to bring reality to a screen portrayal — in several episodes of **Hill Street Blues**. Then he saw that one of the writers for the film used to be with **Hill Street**. If you're going to swipe, swipe from yourself. That way you steal from the best.)*

DEAD AGAIN (April 26, 1991)

Stephen Sondheim wrote, "Every day a little death, in the heart and in the head."

From having discussed death in comics, and last week (although somewhat tangentially) violence in comics, we now move on to violent death. Specifically, to *Hulk* #380, a story about which I've received a great deal of electronic mail on the various computer nets I'm on, not to mention the April 5 issue of *CBG*.

For those who weren't paying attention, *Hulk* #380 featured our resident shrink, Doc Samson, being called in to testify in regards to the sanity of an assassin named Crazy Eight. At issue: whether she was cognizant of her actions at the time of murders she committed. At stake: whether she receives life in prison or the electric chair.

Samson's testimony in court results in her being given the chair, and her electrocution is clearly depicted on-panel.

To quickly address two assertions by the *CBG* letter writer: First, "Crazy Eight" wasn't inspired by the Barbra Streisand film *Nuts* (although I have seen it). It was inspired by an article in the local newspaper about a psychologist being called to testify at the sentencing hearing of a murderer, combined with the fact that I'd come up with what I thought was a nifty character name — "Crazy Eight" — and I wanted to use it in a story.

(Although, for the record, *Hulk* #383-384 is definitely a *Phantom of the Opera* riff. Maybe next I'll do a piece about where you draw the line between "inspired by" and plagiarism.)

As for the ongoing (which is a polite way of saying, "Jeez, are we *still* talking about this?") question of ratings, it should be clear by now that the usual violence level and occasional nudity (particularly in mutant books) makes Marvel Comics a standard PG, perhaps even PG-13. Therefore, anything that doesn't cross that line should be acceptable.

Actually, *Hulk* #380 was an exercise in writing mechanics. I had a story I wanted to tell — and I wasn't sure I was going to be able to do it effectively. I was afraid that, due to the climate of comics, it wasn't going to work.

Here was a story that hinged on death being a reality. Death was going to come to this character, Crazy Eight. She was going to die. Dead dead dead. A character whom the reader had never seen before and wouldn't see again.

My problem was twofold: I was asking the reader to care about what happened to this character whom they were only going to know for 20 pages, and I was asking the reader to believe that this character was really, absolutely going to die.

In approaching the first half of the equation, it meant that I was going to have to do everything I could to draw Crazy Eight as vividly as possible. I was going to have to make her so much bigger than life, so memorable, that she would make an instant impression. Her behavior in her interview with Doc Samson — her mood swings, her attempts to seduce him, her recollections of an abusive father that never occurred, and her stubbing out of a cigarette in her palm, all helped to grab the readers by the throat and make them pay attention.

Bill Jaaska's art was so effective that, by the time we got to the electrocution sequence, I had become so fond of the character that I was sorry she was going to die. The problem was that die she had to, or the story lost all its bite. Besides, the plot had been written and was drawn already. It wasn't as if I could change my mind just because the dialoguing stage had drawn me closer to the character.

The problem was I wasn't that sure the readers would take the death sequence seriously. That was something over which I had very limited control.

Wolverine routinely hacks up hordes of goons. The Punisher perforates criminals all the time, by the carload. Those "young readers" about whom a number of correspondents — not just the *CBG* letter writer, or I'd never have brought this all up — express such deep concern, think Freddy Krueger and Jason are cool.

And not only is death routinely depicted in comics (and glorified in slash/hack films appealing to the same audience base), but death is also routinely undepicted. I was worried that readers would get to the end of the story and say, "Oh, but she's not *really* dead. She survived somehow." That's what quite a few said about Jean DeWolff, and she didn't even have paranormal strength.

Death, in comics, has no meaning. But the story was about death; therefore, the story would have no meaning.

So to drive the point home — to give it as much (you should pardon the expression) grounding in reality as I could — I depicted the electrocution on panel. You couldn't see her face — it was covered by leather strapping. You couldn't hear her scream; her mouth was covered (all you "heard" was a muffled "nnnnnnnn" which grew smaller and eventually blanked out). No huge, comic-book-style, jagged lines of electricity. Her back arched, her fingers outstretched, her feet left the ground, but that was all.

One panel.

In comparison to books featuring page upon page of routine slaughter, it was one panel.

One little death.

And people got upset.

Good.

Dammit, good.

I'm ecstatic that people got upset. I'm thrilled. I am dancing on the ceiling and bouncing off the walls that people got upset. I want people to get upset.

I wanted that scene to turn people's stomachs, to nauseate them, to make them want to look away. I wanted that scene either to make people stare at it in morbid, horrified fascination, or else look away because it was too upsetting for them to take.

You see, *Hulk* #380 had a theme. Killing is wrong. The cold-blooded, state-planned murder of another human being is wrong. When I stated that on a computer board, I was accused of using a comic for expounding my own beliefs, which was ostensibly a bad thing.

Horrors. Imagine that. A comic book with a point of view. A comic book with a theme. Actually, most comic books do have themes, and they're consistent ones: Might Makes Right and Winning Is Everything. In the old days, you occasionally had Love Conquers All, but you rarely see that now.

Might Makes Right. And Winning Is Everything. The theme of the country. If someone is your enemy, step on them. Kill them if you can.

One little thing, though. Unless I tell you that *Hulk* #380 is an anti-capital punishment story, you probably won't pick up on that. I never *say* in the story that capital punishment is wrong. That would be intrusive. That would be preachy (much like this column). Instead, I simply showed it. I showed the harsh reality — the shaving of the head, the pulling of the switch, the human being's muffled screams. I gave the reader the courtesy of drawing his or her own conclusion.

One little death.

One small death is what I wanted the readers to care about. To make them take death seriously, accept it as a reality in comics and in life.

Several people told me that they were annoyed because they read comics to escape. They want mindless entertainment. Sorry, guys — you might not realize it, but it's insulting to ask me to turn my mind off when I write. I would never insult *my* readers by expecting the same of them when they read. If someone came to me and said, "This issue of *Captain Cauliflower* you wrote is stupid, mindless pap" and I replied, "You mean you *think* when you read comics? Boy, is that a waste of brain power," I feel that would be pretty damned offensive, don't you?

Of course, do objecting readers say, "Whoa, this is upsetting, we should do something about the death penalty"? Nah. They say, "Whoa, this is upsetting, we should do something about the comic book." Now *there's* a case of having your priorities in order.

As for the charge that younger readers shouldn't be subjected to seeing this happen: Why not? After all, it's not as if I'm depicting prostitution or mainlining; the seamier, illegal sides of the dark adult world. No, no. This is state-approved. Their parents may even have voted for this. This is legal. This is OK.

Except it's not OK, is it? It's really hideous, isn't it? It really is gut-wrenching, stomach-turning.

One death. One little death.

Of course, people who complain about the younger readers being upset are generally upset themselves but don't want to admit it. Same as people who say "I'm not in favor of censorship" always follow up with the word "but," thereby undercutting the first half of the statement.

But let's focus on the youngsters for a moment. If we're not to show them the horrors of state-mandated death, what should we teach them? Indeed, what are we teaching them these days on the subject of killing?

Well, we teach them to celebrate the death of 100,000 Iraqis. The general expression I hear is, "We kicked butt." What makes it OK is that only a handful of Americans were killed and, besides, Iraq was the enemy.

One hundred thousand people.

Take a hundred thousand pennies and count them, one by one. Stack them in your living room. Watch the pile grow. Imagine each penny to be a body. A man, a woman, a child. One hundred thousand deaths.

Now try to make a life to replace one of those deaths. Takes nine months and a small miracle. Lot of work. Do it 100,000 times. You can't. No one can.

But it's OK. It's to be celebrated. We won.

And it's OK to kill criminals, because they're bad guys. We have the technology. We have the laws. We have the might on our side.

Winning is everything. Might makes right.

Who says comics don't mirror real life?

(On a lighter note, Peter David Isabella, writer of stuff, appreciates brother Tony's kind invitation — especially when he recalls that brother Tony once instructed readers of Justice Machine to ship pizza boxes to Peter at the Marvel offices, which did not endear Peter to the Marvel mailroom. Still, the surname addition is kind, although Tony's long-standing obsession with the fact that Peter has two first names is curious, considering that Tony Isabella also has two first names, just like Peter David. Of course, at least Peter and David are both men's names —)

NYA-HA-HA-HA-HA! (Jan. 3, 1992)

What is it that makes a really, really good villain?

There are tons of them: Some of them memorable, many of them not. They certainly outnumber the heroes — in fact, if the heroes did not have right on their side, they'd have been obliterated long ago. Also, villains are the ones with the game plan.

Heroes are reactive. They exist to stop the villains, period. By and large, they don't have any sort of grand scheme to better the world. They don't use their powers or minds for the general betterment of humanity (with the occasional exception of The Squadron Supreme or Miracleman). If villains did not exist, heroes would have nothing to do. They'd be bored.

Villains, by contrast, can have a variety of goals. If heroes did not exist, villains would not be bored. Villains would be in charge. So heroes need villains, but villains could get along just fine without heroes, thank you very much.

But what specifically elevates a bad guy from mere villain, above good villain, above really good villain, to really, really good arch-enemy? What kicks him upward into the stratosphere of super-popular nasty?

Is it a powerfully alliterative name, such as Doctor Doom? Is it a memorable visual, such as Darkseid? Sheer inventiveness of the schemes, such as The Joker?

Certainly those factor in. But I believe that there's another element to big-time supervillainy that really does not get focused on:

The really, really great villains get away with it.

They are above punishment. They are above the law. And even when they're supposedly subjected to the legal system and slapped in jail, it is painfully clear to all concerned that they are simply catching their breath. The only reason they're in jail is because they haven't bothered to plan their escape yet. But as soon as they've decided it's time to leave, they're gone. In the meantime, they're getting free room and board on the taxpayer's dime.

Think about it: Who is Marvel's top, most renowned villain? Gotta be Doc Doom. Here's a guy who defined being above the law — to quote *Not Brand Echh*, he's "the boss of a whole, complete country!" He's got diplomatic immunity. He can do anything, *anything* he wants to The Fantastic Four, and all they can do is act in self-defense. He cannot, however, be called to task for his actions.

(Actually, I've often wondered about something. Is it enough that Doom is the monarch of Latveria, or does the United States have to have diplomatic ties with Latveria in order for him to have immunity? If it's the latter case, then all that has to happen is that the United States severs ties with Latveria, recalls its own diplomats (have we ever seen any U.S. diplomats to Latveria?) and bam, the FF can nail Doom.)

Who else is big at Marvel? Really big? Well, there's Magneto. He's had setbacks (such as being turned into an infant) but, during the time that he was a villain, he was also waaay above the law. Proof? Because eventually he was brought to trial for his crimes in international court, and what happened shortly thereafter? He *stopped* being a villain. By being brought to justice, he lost that upper-class air that made him a true arch enemy. So it's not surprising that, in recent days, Magneto's return to villainy has been accompanied by the reinstatement of his "You Can't Touch This" attitude. The villain-turned-hero Magneto says, "Put me on trial, I'll have my say." The hero-turned-villain Magneto says, "I'm above your laws; I'm creating my own haven for mutants, so buzz off."

Meantime, in the DC Universe, arguably the top two bad guys are the aforementioned Joker and the ever-popular Lex Luthor. Now in the old days, as noted, even their occasional jailing seemed more along the lines of humoring the penal system. Luthor was so undisturbed by the notion of incarceration that he frequently wore his prison grays even after he'd busted out.

But these are the new days, the new DC — and, consciously or unconsciously, DC has made efforts to bring its top nasties in line with the notion that the best bad guy is one who can laugh off justice.

The Joker is literally doing so. Now you can't even *jail* him. He can never, ever be held responsible for his actions because he's a nutball and tucked away at Arkham Asylum. Arkham is more than a simple replacement for the prisons that were just way stations in The Joker's career.

At least when he was in prison, The Joker was ostensibly serving some sort of sentence. But in Arkham, there's no pretense that he's doing anything more than biding his time until the next go-around. Hell, if we can believe the distasteful ending of *Killing Joke*, even The Caped Crusader thinks the guy's a million chuckles. Batman himself joins The Joker in laughing at the system. Since he's bonkers, he is as invulnerable to prosecution as —

As Lex Luthor. No prison fatigues for the new Lex. No longer was he the guest of Metropolis prison facilities. Instead, through Lexcorp, he was practically running the city. Superman couldn't lay a finger on the guy. Either people thought Lex was a perfectly straight businessman, even philanthropic; or else they knew what kind of guy he really was, but were too scared of him (or too much a part of his dealings) to do anything about it.

Sure, sure, supposedly Lex Luthor died in an airplane crash.

How many people seriously believe that Luthor is really, truly dead? I say this not because I have any sort of inside information (I haven't consulted Mike Carlin on it); it's just healthy skepticism as a result of years of being involved in comics. I don't believe Lex is gone for good. Chances are, neither do you.

This is all, of course, just discussing mortal villains. There are also gods: for example, Darkseid, who is answerable only to other gods and some vague prediction that someday Orion's going to mess him up real bad; or the godlike Galactus, who is purportedly above good and above evil (and, with my luck, above my house right now).

Now — here's where we get to some real fun stuff.

You see, people are always saying that comics are far too removed from real life. And I will agree that we don't generally have guys running about in zippy costumes with dastardly names. But what started me thinking about the subject of this column was several recent examples in the news of how truly despicable individuals can profit from their misdeeds and even, on an international scale (just like Doc Doom), be totally invulnerable to retribution.

For example:

Starting on a national scale, the Supreme Court overruled unanimously New York State's Son-of-Sam Law (the name taken by David Berkowitz during his extended killing spree) — which stated that criminals cannot make money from books, movies, or what-have-you that are based on their activities. Instead, all such money is to be put in escrow and given to the victims of their crimes. Not any more, though: The Supreme Court decided that it was contrary to the rights guaranteed by the First Amendment.

Now I can grant the argument that New York's law is too broad. For example, it also covers people merely accused of crimes, and there is this bizarre notion about innocent until proven guilty. But The Shadow's often-repeated statement that "Crime does not pay," supported by the Son-of-Sam law, has now been undercut by the Supreme Court.

I'd like to put forward two arguments, neither of which would fly with the Supreme Court, but I don't care — I'm no lawyer, and this is no court of law.

First, yes, an argument might be made that First Amendment rights are being abrogated by the state of New York (and the other states which have similar laws on the books). However, the act of becoming a criminal means that you have acted in a manner that is harmful to society and, in that act, have forfeited rights to certain things. Like liberty. Like the pursuit of happiness. Like, in some instances, life. To commit a crime means that you have done something wrong and are to suffer for it.

I do not see why it should be out of the question to limit the First Amendment rights of a criminal, exactly in the same manner that other rights of his are limited because of his crime.

The second aspect is that First Amendment rights end where the public safety is threatened. Or, as the old saying goes, you cannot falsely shout "Fire" in a crowded theater, thereby prompting a panic, and then claim that you were simply exercising your right to free speech.

It seems to me that, if criminals know that they can profit from a flashy enough crime — get their picture in *People*, become celebrities — it takes some of the edge off taking the chance of committing that crime. Considering what publishers, movie studios, and television programs are paying nowadays for anyone connected to any sort of high-profile criminal proceeding, such payoffs might be considered incentive for someone who doesn't mind the prospect of spending time in jail.

Granted, civil suits can be brought by the victims of the various crimes against the perpetrators. The criminals might have to turn over some or all of their blood money to the people who suffered at their hands. Then again, they might not. Terrific. Just what the overburdened judicial system needs right now: more litigation to accomplish what the New York law was already doing.

Long-time readers of this column know that I have stridently spoken in favor of the most liberal interpretation of the First Amendment. "I disapprove of what you say, but I will defend to the death your right to say it," a quote attributed to Voltaire. I agree with the sentiments, but I'll add that I draw the line at defending it to the death when that death might be at the hands of the guy who's exercising his free speech in the first place.

Besides, no one's suggesting we stop criminals from publicizing their misdeeds — just from making money off it. Where in the Constitution does it guarantee the right to make money? It's called free speech, after all. Not Paid Speech.

But if you want to talk about having it all — money, publicity, invulnerability — then you have to think about the Real World equivalent of super-villains: namely, the Lebanese terrorists who, over the past several weeks, released a slew of hostages including six-year-veteran Terry Anderson.

I, of course, am pleased as Punch that these people are free and have returned to their families. I hope they have all the luck in the world. They're certainly entitled.

However —

It angers me that they were released one at a time, for the purpose of heightening media attention, dragging things out, and allowing the captors to get off on their feeling of power.

It angers me that, to the best of my knowledge, absolutely no effort is being made to hold the terrorists accountable for their actions. The odds are slim that they will ever be punished for their crimes.

It angers me that we apparently ransomed them from a foreign government. What my news accounts don't seem to mention at all, or bury towards the end of the story, is that the hostages were released, with startling timing, several weeks after the United States released Iranian assets: assets that Jimmy Carter — in one of his few aggressive steps dealing with the hostage issue that eventually overshadowed his presidency — froze back in 1979 as retaliation for the Americans that Iran decided to take prisoner.

In essence, $278 million was forked over to Iran — and lo and behold, out came the hostages. In other words, we paid a ransom and got the kidnap victims back. We sent a message loud and clear, and that message was: "Kidnapping works. Terrorism works. Do what you want, suffer no consequences, get plenty of attention." Do you believe that, after receiving that message, terrorists are going to hesitate for one minute to repeat their acts of terrorism? To try to find new captives? Make new demands? Why should they? Just as, with Doc Doom or Darkseid, it's a case of do whatever the hell you want.

Of course our government denies any cause-and-effect. Just coincidence. Uh-huh. As startling a coincidence as when the Iranian hostages were released a decade ago, within 24 hours after Ronald Reagan was sworn in. This coincidence has prompted speculation that a deal was cut between GOP hopeful Ronald Reagan and the Iranians — one which George Bush supposedly helped set up — the deal being that the hostages were to be kept under wraps, poisoning Carter's chances of re-election, until such time that Reagan was safely in office. A goodly number of people seem rather intrigued by the notion.

Comic Book World versus Real World. Similarities abound. Is Luthor dead? No way. Are a sitting President and an ex-President part of a scheme which bartered human lives for an election? Quite possibly. How interesting that we have far more confidence in our fictional villains than in our real-world leaders.

(Notice that Peter David, writer of stuff, did not bring up the notion of "Getting away with it" in connection with the recently concluded William Kennedy Smith rape trial. Why? Because CNN legal experts claimed that Smith's celebrity worked against him to some degree. The attention focused on the alleged crime made them more anxious to prosecute than they would have been if he'd just been Joe Shmoe from Tallahassee. Prosecutors don't like rape cases; they're tough to win. And if you disagree with that assessment, don't bust my chops about it — go yell at CNN or your local prosecutor's office.)

Historical Notes:

1) The foregoing resulted in several learned letters from a variety of learned attornies, all of whom informed me that I was dead wrong. And there was some sprightly conversation about it on computer nets as well.

I remain unconvinced.

The New York law was subsequently revised so that the effect was the same, but there was no Constitutional question.

EXTINCTION? (Aug. 28, 1992)

Do we need publishers?

Forget "Do artists need writers?" or "Do writers need artists?" The question on the floor is, "Do we need publishers?"

The answer to that is: Yes, of course — if you're a publisher.

When I first started entertaining the notion of becoming a professional writer — back when I was 12 — I subscribed to magazines about breaking in. I also saved my allowance for quite some time and eventually purchased my very own copy of *The Guide to the Writer's Market*, so I wouldn't have to keep running to the library every time I wanted to find a potential market for my latest bad short story.

And in reading about the ins and outs of becoming a professional, I came across — and even absorbed, to a degree — the utter disdain and contempt that "real" writers felt for that lowest form of publishing: The Vanity Press.

"Real" writers produced work that was publishable. "Real" writers brought their wares to publishers: great, God-like entities who were capable of ruling on the quality of the work and deciding whether or not it was, in fact, publishable. And if it was not publishable, then the publisher would not want it.

But there was still an outlet: The Vanity Press. The term dripped contempt. What would happen is that you would take your book to a Vanity Publisher and you would pay that publisher for the cost of printing the book (with, presumably, some degree of overhead built in, so the Vanity Publisher could turn a profit). And there you had your book. Good luck getting it distributed, of course, since bookstores regarded Vanity projects with the same contempt as everyone else in the industry.

Vanity publications were, by definition, not any good at all, because — it was reasoned — if they were any good, then the writer would have been able to find a publisher. Q.E.D.

It was not until I got older that I came to realize what "publishable" actually means.

Publishable doesn't necessarily equal "good." Publishable means that the publisher feels that he can make money off it. Period. It can be trashy as anything but still be publishable — hell, that probably makes it even *more* publishable.

Furthermore, the decision on what's publishable and what isn't is made by human beings, not omniscient demi-gods. And human beings can just flat-out screw up. There are countless stories of books that made the rounds of publishers, collecting rejection after rejection before finally stumbling across someone who recognized the work's merits — and, lo and behold, it leaped onto the best seller lists.

(Of course, best-seller lists are pretty much manufactured. Publishers decide ahead of time what's going to be a best seller and market it as such. A book that's slated as a "mid-list," with a modest print run and no promotion, has no chance whatsoever of becoming any sort of best seller, even if it's the greatest novel in the history of humanity. We're not talking literary merit; we're talking salesmanship.)

Despite all that, however, Vanity projects — self publishing — are still not regarded as "real" books in the book industry. Vanity projects are works that simply weren't good enough, or saleable enough, to cut it. They are the last, desperate attempt by a despairing author to get his work out to an audience, even though the authorities on the subject — the publishers — have already rendered their verdict, stating that either the work isn't any good or, to use the popular phrase, "does not suit (their) present needs."

Quick — name some popular book publishing Vanity projects. Chances are you can't.

Now name some popular comic-book publishing Vanity projects.

Elfquest. Cerebus.

Oops.

Elfquest, in particular, was rejected by publishers and should have — under "traditional" publishing rules — been lousy and hidden forever from public view.

But no one — including me — can possibly dispute the quality and cutting-edge nature of these and other self-published titles.

Or look at Image Comics, which fits even more the definition of Vanity Press because — unlike Warp Graphics, which was created for the purpose of publishing *Elfquest* — Image involves another, pre-existing publishing entity to do the "dirty work," as it were. The line is too young to determine whether it's ever going to advance the form in the way that a *Cerebus* or *Elfquest* has done. But no sane person can deny the sales success. And, since publishers value salability more than anything, by the standard that matters above all else to a publisher, Image is thus far an indisputable triumph.

There are major differences between the worlds of book and comics publishing — differences so vast, in fact, that it's hard to believe they're both theoretically part of the same discipline.

• Both have work-for-hire set-ups. They publish series of works featuring some lead character (cowboy, scourge of crime, what-have-you). But in book publishing, more often than not, the writer is forced to hide behind either the name of the original creator of the work (if that work is handled by an independent packager) or else behind an utterly fictitious "house name" invented by the publisher. This is done to suit the display needs of bookstores, since they rack the titles by the last name of the author.

But comic-book titles are racked alphabetically by the title of the comic book (when they're racked in any pattern at all). It doesn't matter *who's* writing it. It's still displayed in the same place. So comic book publishers not only have no need to stick fake names on their titles, but, in fact, actually benefit from followings that build up for specific creative talent.

• Both have editors. But in book publishing, you can go head-to-head with an editor and win.

• Both pay royalties (or "incentives," as Marvel calls them). In book publishing, however, the average author frequently receives royalty statements late, and then gets to thrill to the complicated book-keeping legerdemain that explains why, once again, there's no check. In comic-book publishing, the statements come in a timely fashion, have exactly one number on them (copies sold) and usually have money accompanying them.

(At least, with Marvel and DC, that's the case. In terms of the other publishers I've worked for, Disney doesn't pay royalties on any of its characters [I sure didn't write *The Little Mermaid* to get rich, I'll tell ya], and First Comics sent me one royalty statement during the three years I wrote *Dreadstar*. It covered "sales" on 10 issues of the title, and enclosed a check for the princely sum of $13.64. I tried not to spend it all in one place.)

• To me, the most marked difference is the perception — both among professionals and readers — towards "Vanity" projects. In book publishing, a Vanity project is the lowest form of life — an attitude, I tend to think, which was probably fostered and nurtured by publishers.

In comic-book publishing, however, Vanity projects — or, as it's termed, self-publishing — is regarded as something to aspire to. It's considered a major accomplishment to break away from the creative constraints imposed by publishers — comparable to slaves bolting the plantation — and produce titles that are straight and undiminished from the brow of the creator.

I find this an intriguing development. Of course, I have the leeway to find it intriguing because I'm not a publisher. I'd tend to think that publishers find it somewhat disconcerting. The status is no longer quo. I doubt that Marvel and DC, a year ago, would have seriously entertained any scenario that would result in their being bumped from their industry-dominating positions of #1 and #2. These are the publishing homes of Spider-Man and Superman, after all.

Yet now — at least for the month of August — DC is #3, behind Malibu, and I can't believe that Marvel could possibly be complacent enough not to realize that just because everything has been a certain way for as long as anyone can remember doesn't mean that things can't change. If DC can be jolted, so can Marvel.

Of course, Marvel finds itself in a dicey position. Does it throw lots of money and perks at the creators who are still with them, in hopes of fostering good will and stopping the erosion? But (it could be argued) the highest-paid freelancers in the history of Marvel are now in head-to-head competition with their former employers. So clearly money — which is the only thing the corporate publishing mindset understands — isn't everything.

Does Marvel instead concentrate on boosting the visibility and promotional value of their characters? But to do that fosters the "characters-value-more-than-creators" tag (whether it resulted from a misquote or not) that currently hangs around Marvel's neck like an albatross — a viewpoint that, from a business point of view, has been the smart way to go over the long term. After all, Spider-Man has had consistent popularity over three decades, whereas the popularity of creators rises and falls with changing tastes.

Still — business-wise or not, it's a mindset that leaves creators with bad tastes in their mouths, and, from the short-term point of view, it could be catastrophic. And you never know when the short term can become the long term.

Yes, it's a tough time to be a publisher. Publishers are starting to look pretty superfluous. Upstart freelancers have been showing that they can do it themselves and enjoy as much — and even more — success than the publishers have traditionally allowed. Even in the case of Image, where there's a publisher involved, Malibu is really nothing more than a hired hand. Malibu is collecting (by a number of accounts) somewhere between 10% and 15%. That's not what a publisher traditionally makes. That's what an *agent* makes.

This, then, would seem to be something that publishers should consider. If they're going to have difficulty *being* publishers in the traditional sense, then what they may have to think of are alternative services they could provide to the creative community. Such as:

Agents. Malibu would seem to have pointed the way with its princely 10- to-15% cut. Take it further. Publishers could exist exclusively to represent characters and projects to movies, TV, T-shirt manufacturers, etc., all the time collecting no more than a minimal commission.

Copy editing. This is vastly distinct from an editor who says, "Sorry, the character wouldn't do this" or, "Sorry, I want to take the book in a different direction, so you're fired." A copy editor — in book publishing — goes through and points out basic errors in grammar and spelling. And in book publishing, the author has the option of saying — particularly when it comes to grammatical aberrations — "No, I did it deliberately. I don't care if it's a split infinitive; I want it split." In those instances, the author has the final say. So it's no challenge to the creative last word.

Travel agents. Publishers could field and negotiate all convention appearances, hammering out details like first class or coach, appearance fees, and limo services.

Faxing and photocopying services. This can be an extremely tedious chore. Wouldn't it be nice to be able to just summon your publisher over and say, "Knock off two copies of this for me. Oh, and fax this over to Spielberg — I've kept him waiting for two days, that's long enough to watch him sweat."

Groundskeeping. The lawn and bushes can sometimes grow to unmanageable degrees if you're busy hammering out your latest project. Imagine the convenience of sitting in your studio, and then looking up and waving out the window to your publisher, as he goes by pushing the old Snapper lawn mower.

Custodial duties. Hey, it's hard to find good help these days.

Procuring sexual favors. Creators have often been made to feel like high-priced whores. But by that reasoning, it follows that publishers are pimps. So obtaining "companionship" for lonely freelancers shouldn't be all that much of a stretch from business as usual, right?

Convenient tax dodge. Look at it this way: If you can't think of any other possible use for a publisher, you can list him on your tax return as a dependent and get a few hundred bucks' credit for him.

It's the least we can do.

*(Peter David, writer of stuff, is most appreciative to Michael Heisler for backing up his **Sesame Street** theory — apparently shared by lots of academic types, according to articles I've since received — and by providing a final bit of proof that had slipped past. **The Electric Company** was a wonderful program that promoted thoughtful analysis of words, encouraged reading rather than parroting, and required a decent attention span. It did not survive. Case closed.)*

Historical Notes:

1) As mentioned above, for the month of August 1992, Image loudly proclaimed that it had vaulted ahead of DC and was breathing hard upon Marvel. And indeed, in terms of orders, it had. However, only a fraction of the comic books solicited actually shipped — consequently, although they had the numbers on paper, that didn't mean anything. Retailers can't sell comic books that never arrive. DC, on the other hand, did ship the solicited comic books, so the Image claims of being the new Number Two (to quote The Prisoner) were premature.

2) The advent of Image Comics and the relegation of Malibu Comics to hired hand — which prompted this column — is covered in the Image section of "Fun with Publishers" beginning on page 64. The "Sesame Street" article alluded to is in "Social Studies," titled "Sesame Street and the Youngblood Generation," which appears on page 208.)

CODE IN MY NOSE (Oct. 9, 1992)

Yes. I see a hand raised. You, over in *Oh, So?*

The Comics Code Authority? What do I think of the Comics Code Authority?

Heavens. It's embarrassing to realize that I've been slogging through all manner of subject matter over the past two years and have never touched on the CCA — a truly hideous oversight which will now be corrected.

For those who are unfamiliar with the origins of the CCA (and readers can sometimes have short memories and shaky knowledge of history, as evidenced by one fan who was under the impression that Jim Lee created The Juggernaut), the CCA has been around for some four decades. It was created by comics publishers in 1954 in response to the charges that comic books (horror and crime comic books, in particular) were destroying and corrupting the youth of America.

This assertion was put forward by *Seduction of the Innocent*, which (as everyone knows) is the rock group that didn't play at San Diego this year. (There. *That* should cause some confusion. I eagerly await fans walking up to Bill Mumy or Al Collins and saying, "So *you're* to blame for the Comics Code.")

The Code was created with the notion that the publishers would then be able to police themselves, rather than have the government do it.

In a nutshell, the Comics Code Authority consists of a lawyer (or lawyers) who look over the titles of those publishers (Marvel, DC, Archie, etc.) which subscribe to the Code. The Authority makes certain that the comic books follow the guidelines, most of which were developed to put a halt to the types of stories being published in '50s horror and crime titles.

A title carrying the Code seal cannot have excessive blood and gore. An example of being "Code Aware" occurred in *Hulk* #398, when a character who had just been stabbed was depicted lying in a pool of blood — and the blood was colored purple. When I saw this, I figured it indicated that either the character was of noble birth, or else she was bleeding ink (which made sense, since she was — y'know — drawn).

The Code watches out for a variety of other things, ranging from explicit sex to such philosophical niceties as that evil cannot be portrayed in a positive light (which put a quick end to plans for the *Billy the Happy Pusher* comic book). Some Code rulings have fallen by the wayside. For example, *Amazing Spider-Man* broke new ground back in the '60s when the storyline concerned drug abuse. The Code Authority refused to put its seal of approval on the issue, despite the fact that drugs were portrayed in a very negative light, because the Code said that you couldn't have drugs *at all*.

Marvel went ahead and published the two-part story anyway — and shortly thereafter, the Code was revised. As a result, a few months later DC published a far more intense drug story in *Green Lantern/Green Arrow*, and that one carried the seal.

Then there was the rule that "zombies" could not be depicted. This one held for a far longer time than the drug rule, presumably since zombies have been a less pressing social issue than drug abuse. Yes, before Marvel was able to benefit from Marvel Zombies, it had to create, instead, zuvembies — which were just like zombies except they were called something else.

(One cannot help but wonder, if a villain called The Zombie Master had been created, and his ability was to command armies of tall glasses, each filled with liqueurs, fruit juices, and a couple of jiggers of rum, whether the CCA would have let that go.)

Somewhere along the way — I'm not sure when, but somewhere — zombies by name started popping up in comics again, and the Code folks didn't do much of anything about it.

That's the CCA in a nutshell. The question is what I think of it.

What can any creative individual think of it? I think it stinks, is what I think.

Pure and simple, I consider it censorship.

I don't care that the publishers helped put it together. I don't care that it's voluntary.

I consider the very idea to be antithetical to the ability of not only writers and artists to produce the stories they want to tell, but to the ability of the publishers to publish what they want to publish.

Ah, but they can ignore the CCA, you point out. Stan Lee did it decades ago. True enough. But the problem is that the publisher has to make the conscious decision that it's going to drop the seal for that issue. The concern about making that decision creates a chilling effect. Does the publisher want the potential hassle? Generally, a publisher wants money from published comic books. Period. So the question becomes: Is the publisher willing to go through hassle to get that money? The answer is: Whatta *you* think?

Publishers should have the right to publish whatever they want, without having to second-guess themselves or try to please some lawyers. Lawyers are not writers or artists. Lawyers are not editors. Lawyers are people who are conditioned to play things safe — and, if you're trusting them to allow you to push the envelope, you can pretty much count on the envelope staying tightly sealed.

If the publishers hadn't created the CCA in the '50s, would they really have wound up with the government regulating them? Banning them? Clamping down of them? On the one hand, I find that difficult to believe. Certainly those actions would have been challenged in the Supreme Court, and one would like to think that the Court would have remembered about this thing called the First Amendment, which tends to frown on such activities.

On the other hand, one can't help but notice the local laws being made around the country lately, limiting or even banning the various gangster cards. Still, these are local governments — and one wonders whether such laws would stand up to Supreme Court scrutiny (although frankly, these days, that's something of a crap shoot).

It's easy, with four decades' worth of hindsight, to declare that the publishers should have stood firm, told the government to take its best shot, and published whatever the hell they felt like publishing. But this wouldn't have served their short-term business interest. Compromise did, and so was born the CCA — as I said, useful in the short term.

But now we're four decades older and we're still stuck with the damned thing.

What purpose does it serve? None that I can see. Keeping things suitable for younger readers? It's hard to believe that, if the CCA vanished tomorrow, the floodgates of profanity, gore, and sexuality would open in the average issue of *New Warriors* or *Superman*. I tend to think that publishers are very much aware of what their audience wants and expects from specific titles, and no one is going to go berserk if newfound freedom were bestowed.

A net for editorial blunders? Do the publishers really think that their own editors are incapable of producing comics adhering to specific guidelines? If not, then the Code is redundant. If so, then they need better editors.

Protection? An umbrella if trouble hits? You can't really be serious.

A hypothesis: The XYZ Club, dedicated to preserve morality and God-fearing thoughts in America, declares that *Dr. Strange* should be banned because its members feel that the comic book promotes — I dunno — Satanism.

"Ah, but, XYZ Club," protests Marvel, "look here. The comic book has the CCA seal of approval on it."

Would the XYZ Club zealots say, "Oh, dear. We didn't see the Comics Code label. We're sorry, Marvel. This comic book is OK by us"?

I'm sorry, but no. The CCA label would not deter the XYZ club in the slightest. It doesn't know the CCA. It knows Satanism.

Furthermore, if action were taken, it would not be taken against the CCA. No, the action would be taken against Marvel. It would be Marvel which would get the letters; it would be Marvel which would be picketed; it would be Marvel stock that would drop; it would be Marvel ads being yanked (due to pressure exerted on the advertisers); it would be Marvel getting the calls from Wal-Mart saying, "You better not be putting any *Dr. Strange* into 3-packs"; it would be Marvel that would be up a creek.

In the meantime, the CCA would be conducting business as usual, poring over the next flight of Marvel comic books, looking for violations of the Code. And you can bet it'll probably reject the next issue of *Dr. Strange* — which would help to cover its own posterior but wouldn't do a damned thing for Marvel.

(And, in case anyone thinks I'm just ragging on Marvel for some reason, substitute DC for Marvel, Batman and Robin for Dr. Strange, and child endangerment and lack of family values for Satanism. You've got the same scenario — and, even better, you'd have Warners looking to find whom to hold responsible. Would it go after its own people or the Code? You decide.)

The CCA is the publishing equivalent of using the rhythm method for birth control. It's approved by those in authority and people submit to it voluntarily. But (absolutely no offense intended) it's not tremendously reliable and it's not particularly safe — or, to put it succinctly, you can use it faithfully and still get consequences you won't like.

So why's it still around? Habit. Habit and inertia. Publishers may still be clinging to the quaint notion that having the CCA around makes them "honest," makes them "safe," makes them — in some way, shape, or form — better publishers.

But it doesn't. What it does do is give new publishers the opportunity to say, "Ah, we don't bother with the Comics Code. We publish whatever the hell we want." And even if the material they publish would result in a Code-approved comic book, it doesn't matter. It still has that edge of anarchy to it.

It is, to my mind, unconscionable that any publisher would voluntarily submit to any sort of outside censorship. If it was felt that it was necessary 40 years ago, well, I'm sorry, but I consider that to have been a mistake in the long run. And in the long run, everyone involved with any Comics Code publisher is still paying for that mistake.

Essentially, the publishers created a parent organization for themselves.

It's high time they stopped kidding themselves and grew up.

(Peter David, writer of stuff, thinks the term "Marvel Zuvembies" would have been a pretty darned silly one.)

Historical Notes:

1) This column prompted a letter from the head of the CCA describing how the Authority was, in fact, a wonderful organization, and how I was completely off base.

In the meantime, they continue to crack down on, say, the depiction of blood in comics (it must be black, not red), language, mature themes, and other matters not to be inflicted on America's youth.

They remain censors.

SECTION 2:

The Chalker Papers

His name was Vic Chalker, and he was intended to be the Fan Boy from Hell. A lampoon of every blustering, blowhard, arrogant fan who ever stalked the aisles of a comic book convention. His first appearance was easily the most vicious column I've ever written, and it was easy to do because, to all intents and purposes, it wasn't me.

Over time, however, Vic metamorphosed into a handy alternate voice. Whenever I wanted to do something that was off center — particularly make-believe "panels" that presented all sides of an issue in a way that I, as a single voice, never could — I'd bring all the "sides" together and let Vic, my alter ego, moderate it. He gradually become a relatively lucid, and even sane, individual. It's nice to know that fictional fanboys, at least, can grow up.

Like the "I got a rock" gag, Vic made his way into my comic book work, showing up as a demented scientist in *X-Factor*. He was honored to participate.

TRADER VIC (May 17, 1991)

Peter David, writer of stuff, unfortunately has absolutely no time to do this week's column, what with deadlines he's racing to meet before he heads out to Oakland's Wondercon. However, rather than run two "TOP 10" columns in a row, he is instead going to turn the column over this issue to one of the more outspoken and aggressive members of the IBIDS (Intrepid But I Digress Staff), Mr. Victor Chalker. Vic (no relation to Jack Chalker, it should be noted) is a long-time associate (friend might be too strong a word) with very distinctive views on comics and the industry. Peter hopes he's not making a serious mistake. So without further ado: Mr. Vic Chalker.

Ladies and gents, mud will be slung tonight.

Welcome to the first installment of

Chalk Board

My hope is that enough people will like what I have to say; appreciate my candor; my style; my straight from the hip honesty; that you'll want to see more of my opinions besides what Dave is willing to let me have for a one-shot appearance.

If it makes it sound like I'm ungrateful, I'm not. I've known Dave (Peter David to you) for years. The reason he likes me; not that he'll admit it; is that I keep him honest.

Because I remember him before he became the self-appointed conscience and hotshot that he's mutated into here in the pages of *Comics Buyer's Guide*. Now he goes around, spouting political philosophy and self-conscious claptrap as if anything about him [besides his legs] carried weight. I remember him when the only date he was able to get was off a calendar. I remember him when the only writing he did was on bathroom walls, scribbling down his own phone number with the message "FOR A GOOD TIME CALL —

And now this closet dweeb has the gall to set himself up as some sort of weekly columnist. It is to laugh.

The only reason he became a writer is because it means he doesn't have to interact with people in any way other than through a computer. It's perfect for someone who used to slink through high school corridors terrified that someone would notice him.

If I sound like I'm being harsh on Dave, I'm not. I really do like the guy because he does have a shred of talent. Nothing deep, mind you; a certain facility with the language, giving a nice surface gloss to his work; The strategically placed humor he's acclaimed for makes it all go down easy. Give it up,

Dave. Surface gloss and glitter. He's the writer equivalent of the writer/artist; able to cover his inadequacies with glitz. And of course, you guys never notice.

Why should you? Most comics fans haven't had their mental taste buds grown in; either that, or they've been scalded away through years of being pummeled, like water against the surf, into nothingness.

Not that I blame you. It's not your fault. Week after week, year after year, the claptrap that comes down the chute which passes for entertainment can only have a demeaning and destructive effect on you; I've been reading it for so long that I wasn't certain whether to call this column "Chalk Board" or "Chalk Bored."

I mean, Dave's no wiz, but compared to some of the doo daa that's out there, he's practically Tolstoy.

Look at the comic book out there that you guys have made number one: The Advantageous Spider-Man! Can you believe that thing? This comic comes out bagged, which is appropriate; if there's ever been anyone who should bag it as a creator, it's McFarlane!

This guy is the writing equivalent of Scuds; he launches his story with no clear direction, and it lands somewhere completely weird, causing random havoc and destruction.

A show of hands now. Who in the world buys this thing and doesn't feel like some sort of idiot? Of course, The McFar's visual storytelling deftness hasn't atrophied (unlike Marvel's artistic morals) and so it looks reeaaaal purdy, and you dweebs actually snap it up. There's nothing more pathetic than watching comics fans bravely going, "Well, gee, I think his writing's improving, don't you?" No, I don't! Give it up!

And Byrne! Now there's a winner. Finally, for the first time since *Fantastic Four*, he's found a book he'll stay on longer than twenty minutes. *Namor the Sub-Mariner*. Well, now gee — here's a comic book about a guy who is imperious, arrogant, snotty, conceited, pompous, superior, and usually all wet. Is there any wonder why this bozo would be someone Byrne-baby-Byrne could identify with? It can't be too hard for him to draw; all he has to do is look in the mirror! Give it up!

And good lord — has anyone read *X-Men* lately? *Can* anyone read *X-Men* lately? This reads like Chris Claremontezuma's Revenge! Claremontezuma's favorite movie has got to be *The Neverending Story*. You can sure tell from this book; Mutant Massacre? Mutant Messacre is more like it.

This thing just goes on and on and on and on and on and on and on — It's like the comic book equivalent of those old Timex commericals with John Cameron Swayze; you feel like you want to take Claremontezuma, tie him to an airplane wheel, send him through a blender, lash him to a propeller, drop him underwater, inflict all manner of physical punishment on him; and then you bring him up and the guy is still going, even though his works are waterlogged and going in circles.

And now there's going to be a new X-Men book! Cripes, we weren't expecting that now, were we? This one'll be bagged, I bet, which is good — because that way, at least unlike other mutant books, we won't be able to detect the stench! Give it up!

All of which is overseen by Tom Da Flako, nominal editor in chief. Da Flako obviously feels nothing decent has been done in comics since the 1960s, and clearly he's decided to maintain that tradition; this guy is the Piltdown Man of comics. Boy oh boy, I just can't wait to see what he does with *Fantastic Four*. I'm sure it'll be right up there with what he did with *Thor*, which in turn is right up there with dysentery and cholera. Give it up!

If I took over Marvel, the first thing I'd do is kill off all the mutants; all of them; especially Wolverine. I can't stand any of them. No one I know can stand any of them. People don't even read the books any more; they just buy them so they can continue their collection. What's the point of producing stories if no one reads them? None, except to make money. Marvel, the House of Recycled Ideas, should be above that.

I'd kill off all The Avengers, and I'd keep Spider-Man, but knock it down to one title. Marvel did just fine throughout the '60s with only one Spider-Man title; keep McFarlane as artist, and get someone who can write. Someone who'll put a new slant and fresh perspective. Like Gary Groth. I bet Groth would be spectacular at fiction; have you read his editorials?

I'd drop all the licensed titles. Those are insults. It's like the old days of DC Comics. Remember when their top book was *Jerry Lewis*?

Not that the new days of DC are much better; here's a whole company that will publish anything as long as it comes from abroad; why don't they just change DC to UK?

Ever read one of those science fiction, alternate world stories in which the British won the American Revolution, and they speculate what the world would be like?

Wonder no more; just read DC Comics, chockful of tons of stories which are written in a confusing and oblique style; and readers everywhere are afraid to admit that they're lousy stories, because they were produced by British guys, and everyone knows Brits are better than Americans.

The claptrap that comes rolling across the English Channel is turgid, confusing and dull, and yet fans still attach all sorts of artistic merit to it because they're impressed by the snooty accents of the nominal creators. Look at some of the "acclaimed" works:

Arkham Asylum? The ones who belong in an asylum are those who think there's any merit to this overpriced nightmare. Is the whining wimp hero of the story supposed to be Batman? He has to enter a building, filled with a whole bunch of *losers he already beat,* in order to rescue some people. Whoa, scary stuff. Does he just climb up the side of the building? Does he sneak in in disguise? No. He walks in and lets The Joker goose him. Yeah, sure.

The Killing Joke? Batman yokking it up with a guy who, a few hours earlier, tortured Commissioner Gordon and hospitalized his daughter; what's next? High tea with Charles Manson?

And what about Alan Less-is-Moore's acclaimed *Swamp Thing*? Remember "American Gothic"?; What a dog and pony show that turned out to be. A supernatural odyssey that climaxes in a cosmic handshake? What the hell was that supposed to be? Why not a cosmic high-five?!

Doesn't anyone notice that virtually every single Brit-produced comic; from *Animal Man* to *Marshal Law Takes Manhattan* to *Shade*; is filled with page upon page of anti-American and anti-super-hero invective? These people, as a country, clearly are envious and hating of Americans and do nothing but write comics that put us down.

And what do we do? Praise them for it, give them piles of American bucks [worth far more than their puny pounds] and invite them to insult us again. Give it up!

If I ran DC, I'd knock off all Batman titles except one, keep Superman except make him interesting, get rid of all the other "heroes" in the DC universe since they're ruined anyway. Green Lantern is a drunk driver? The Flash as the fastest whiner on Earth? Come on! And I'd stop producing high priced graphic novels and similar price-jacked material, because it's unfair to ask fans to keep buying them.

Not that my ideas for improvement are new; I've been writing to Marvel and DC for years with them. But they are so hidebound that they continue to ignore my suggestions; even though they would bring about a new age of quality and style to the comics industry.

Likewise, they ignore my story ideas. I presented my twelve-part epic, "The Final Crisis," the incredible Marvel/DC crossover that would, once and for all, knock off the vast majority of their characters so that it would leave the way clear to create new and exciting concepts. Also, I have submitted story and character ideas to various so-called editors on the average of two a week for the last three years.

I have yet to hear anything.

And that, people, is what infuriates me most of all. Because "The Big Two" are so married to people like David, McFarlane, Byrne, Claremont, Moore, Morrison; all of them; that they're afraid to let in someone who will really give the fans what they've been clamoring for.

I'm serious. There is more entertainment value in one page of "Nick Shan, the Esoteric Man" (one of the three titles of my proposed "Aesthetic World" cycle) than in any five entire issues of the average Marvel or DC Comic.

But no. They keep their blinders to the wind and continue to produce the sort of pablum that fans are forced to suck up. Pablum that will, sooner or later, completely erode their market base and send comics companies spiralling down into the financial toilet that they so richly and justly deserve.

And I, for one, will be standing over them laughing when it happens.

That's it for this installment of "Chalk Board." Now give it up!

So— how many of you, at some or all points in the preceding, found yourself nodding or agreeing or just saying, "Yeah!" On the other hand, how many of you also wondered whether the foregoing was legit or not?

No, it's not legit. Vic Chalker doesn't exist.

Except I see his soul mates: in letters to me, or letters in letters columns, or in computer postings. Many of the preceding statements, in some form or other, have appeared in those forums, filled with bile and vituperation — not to mention mixed metaphors and bad punctuation.

No. Vic doesn't exist.
I think.

Historical Notes:

1) The coda at the end was added at the insistence of the Thompsons, who were convinced that people wouldn't realize it was a gag. It would appear they had a point, because a number of fans told me that they, indeed, found themselves agreeing with much of what Vic said, and even saw a great deal of themselves in him — and then were appalled to realize it. Jo Duffy, however, saw through it immediately. Trust another writer to recognize a style, even disguised.

MACHO MEN (Sept. 13, 1991)

The following is a transcript of a panel entitled "Men In Comics," held behind closed doors at Non-con 13 in New York on August 10-11. Participants include Spike Jackson, artist on *Blood and Gore*; Bud Wolff; writer/artist of the forthcoming detective comic series, *Dying Is for Pansies*; Zack Dekker, writer/artist for the vigilante tales of *The Defenestrator*; and Mike "Mad Dog" Miller, editor of *Hi Test-Tosterone, the Killer Mutant Gas Jockey.* Moderator is convention organizer Vic Chalker.

Vic: The door's bolted? The "No Girls Allowed" sign up? OK, good. I'd like to welcome all the real men in the audience to the "Men In Comics" panel —

Zack: *Urrrp*

Spike: You're supposed to crush the beer can —

Zack: *Cruuunch* *Sploosh*

Spike: — after it's empty.

Vic: Every time you go to conventions, you always see these "Women in Comics" panel. And you get a bunch of pasty-faced broads up there moaning and whining about how comics are insensitive to women creators and crapola like that.

Mad Dog: Whining little wusses.

Bud: Look, let's get real up front about this, OK? The reason nobody cares about "women" in comics is because comics is a men's medium, OK? It's for guys. It's for people with a "y" chromosone, OK? It's the last bastion of male supremacy.

Zack: Absolutely.

Spike: Chicks are going to stand around and whine and crab because here's something else that they're just not good enough to compete with the big boys on. They just haven't got the, whaddaya call it — ?

Mad Dog: Equipment.

Spike: Right. Mental or physical. Just don't have the kahonies, y'know?

Vic: But there are women super-heroes, you know. Rogue, Storm, Wonder Woman —

Mad Dog: Pansies and wusses. Whiners. All of 'em.

Vic: You're saying Ms. Tree is a whiner?

Bud: If she were any good, she'd be monthly.

Zack: *Urrrppp*

Vic: Do you think that women super-heroes serve a purpose?

Zack: Someone's gotta get the coffee, y'know? *(Raucous laughter)*

Bud: Zack, pass a beer down.

Zack: Beer Hunter! Let's play Beer Hunter!

(One can is shaken and then they're all mixed around. Panelists open them one at a time as panel continues.)

Spike: Here's the purpose they serve: Sales consideration.

Vic: In what way?

Spike: The problem is that most comic books lose their readers once the readers discover girls. So in an effort to try and hold on to those readers, you've got some broads in the books so that, when their hormones kick in, you give the kids something to look at. Something soft to focus on.

Zack: It's not just sales. There's emotional involvement. Some of the love letters we get addressed to May Hem, the usually undressed love interest in *Defenestrator* — they'd tear your heart out. So when we have female characters, we try and be aware of the difficult emotional baggage that our readers carry, and act accordingly.

Vic: What do you look for in a female character?

Zack: Big hooters.

Mad Dog: Huge gazongas.

Bud: Absolutely. Knockers the size of Pawtucket.

Spike: Gotta have 'em. They gotta defy gravity.

Mad Dog: We're talking monster truckers here —

Bud: And skimpy costumes.

Zack: A must. An absolute must.

Spike: We try to work in at least one shower or bathing scene in every issue of *Blood and Gore*.

Vic: Isn't that gratuitous?

Spike: Oh, absolutely. Our readers constantly express their gratitude.

Bud: Frequently they express it on paper.

Mad Dog: Yeah. Gets pretty disgusting, too.

Zack: It works either way. Women undressed or women in tights. Our readers like women who are *real* women. Women in tight fitting costumes —

Vic: We got a question from the audience.

Fan: Yeah, I was wondering — you were talking about tights and stuff. Whenever I think of tights, I think of women and also ballet dancers —

Mad Dog: All male ballet dancers are pansies. It's a medical fact.

Fan: But most super-heros wear tights too. Doesn't that ever make you — y'know — wonder?

Mad Dog: Makes me wonder about you, you sissy boy.

Vic: Now wait, he's got a point there. I mean, you wouldn't catch me dead in tights. And how about you guys? Be honest now.

Bud: *Splooosh* *Arrrggghhhhh*

Spike: Hah! He got the shaken can!

Zack: That Bud's for you, Bud!

Spike: Y'know, that guy has a point. I sure wouldn't dress in tights. None of us would. That's because we're all real men. Kevin Costner, there's a real man — wouldn't wear tights in *Robin Hood*. Not like that Nazi pinko Errol Flynn.

Mad Dog: Yeah, I never thought about it — tough to be a real man when you're wearing tights. Some guys can do it, though. Most are wusses, though. That's why we publish the comics we do — to provide comics for real men with real men heroes. Not pansy heroes like —

Vic: Like who? Let's have the audience toss out suggestions, and you guys will decide whether the heroes mentioned are real men or wusses. Okay. Suggestions?

Fan #2: Wolverine.

Panel: Wuss!!

Vic: Wolverine is a wuss?!

Bud: Oh, he *used* to be a real man. Then he got involved in all that samurai crud, and now he hangs out with jailbait like Jubilee. And simpering about robot girls!

Zack: Wuss city. Next?

Fan #3: Lobo.

Bud: Real man.

Mad Dog: Absolutely. Guy takes no crap, and blew away his old teacher. She had it coming, too. Next?

Fan #4: Sandman.

Zack: Wuss.

Mad Dog: Dead on there. Major wuss.

Spike: Might as well just write off any books written by Limeys. Whole wuss country. Run by a queen. Whattaya expect?

Fan #4: Now hold it. What about Judge Dredd? That's done by British guys. Judge Dredd is a wuss? *(Dead silence.)*

Spike: OK, one non-wuss British thing slipped through.

Zack: Law of averages. Had to happen.

Vic: Anyone else?

Fan #5: Batman.

Vic: Which one?

Fan #5: 1950s.

Panel: Wuss!

Fan #5: 1960s "New Look" Batman.

Panel: Wuss!

Fan #5: O'Neil/Adams Batman.

Panel: Real man.

Spike: Though he got a little wussy whenever Talia was around. Never liked her.

Fan #5: Englehart/Rogers Batman.

Panel: Real man.

Spike: Same complaint about Silver St. Cloud. Although he walked in on her when she was standing there in the towel — that was a real man in action, lemme tell ya.

Fan #6: Spider-Man.

Panel: Major wuss.

Fan #7: Thor.

Mad Dog: A few of the Lee/Kirby issues were real man stuff. Otherwise, though, major wuss.

Zack: And that stuff when he turned into a frog? What the hell was that all about?

Bud: The hair should be enough of a tip, y'know?

Fan #8: The Hulk.

Bud: Gray Hulk was a real man. New guy's a wuss.

Fan #9: Superman.

Panel: Wuss.

Fan #10: Green Lantern.

Bud: Which one?

Fan #10: Hal Jordan.

Panel: Wuss.

Fan #10: Guy Gardner.

Panel: Real man.

Fan #11: The Punisher.

Mad Dog: A man's man. The ultimate man.

Zack: No two ways.

Spike: Especially when you've got a real man's man writing him. Like that Joe Duffy. He's got The Punisher down to a tee. That Joe, I'd like to go out and knock back a few beers with him and tell him he knows what makes a man a man.

Bud: You bet.

Zack: I couldn't agree more.

Mad Dog: I'd stake my rep on writers like that Joe Duffy guy —

Vic: Uh — guys? I think the panel's just ended.

Spike: Why? We still got — why's the audience laughing? Where're they going?

Mad Dog: What's with you pansies!! What —

Vic: This has been "Men In Comics." Thank you all for coming.

Zack: Why're they all walking out?! We mention a real man like Joe Duffy and they can't take it? It's not like we brought up that Chris Claremont broad!

Vic: Just shut up, OK? Just shut up.

*(Peter David, writer of stuff, cannot recommend highly enough the great new book, "**Where's Dan Quayle?**" A take-off on the "Waldo" books published by Collier Books, it's a dandy ice-breaker if you keep it around as a coffee-table book.)*

COLUMN WITHHELD (Oct. 18, 1991)

Historical Notes:

CBG had, shortly before this column, run one of its most notorious letters: Signed simply "Name Withheld" but purportedly from an artist in the industry, it claimed rather stridently that writers were neither needed nor wanted by the far more talented comics artists. The comics community was stung both by the vituperative and arrogant nature of the letter, combined with the base cowardice involved in not signing a name to it.

Since then, it should be noted, Image publishing has produced parody comics of its beginnings, and one of the creators — corresponding to Erik Larsen — is designated "Name Withheld." Draw from that what you will.

When this particular column ran, a tape that read "Name Withheld" was stripped in over my name in the column masthead.)

The following is a transcript of a panel focussing on the work of writer/artist Randy Kingman, at Wrathocon II in Passaic, New Jersey, Sept. 21-22. Present are Kingman and interviewer Vic Chalker.

Vic: Randy, it's good to see you. I'd like to welcome you here on behalf of the Wrathocon Audience.

Randy: Thank you, thank you.

Vic: Randy, of course, most people are familiar with your career. You started as artist on *Brickman*, working with noted writer Buck Grissom —

Randy: Actually, I dislike the term "working with," Vic. The relationship between writer and artist, in which the artist has to curb his own superb artistic impulses to suit the visually uninspired natterings of the "writer," well — "working with" makes it sound like it's something I readily agreed to, rather than a situation that I tolerated.

Vic: Well, how would you describe it?

Randy: I would say I was "creatively indentured."

Vic: That sounds brutal.

Randy: Oh it is, it is.

Vic: You must have felt it liberating when the writer was fired, or quit — reports still differ — and you took over the series yourself.

Randy: Well, it was a while in coming, but it was inevitable. I don't mean to badmouth Buck, but, for example, he'd write pages of people just standing there and talking, y'know? Just talking. Now that's not what the fans want to see. It's certainly not what I want to draw. So I'd try to give it visual kick by turning those boring, chatty scenes into interesting pin-up pages. Or I'd stick in a fight scene. And Buck would crab about the pacing being screwed up, saying it's not the story he wrote. And he'd complain to the editor, and the editor, he knows what side his bread is buttered on, y'know?

Vic: And now I understand you're starting up a brand new title with orders already over twelve million for the six different editions. Tell us about it.

Randy: You mean *The X-Cels*. Yes, that would be my series about a group of mutant cartoon characters who once were simple drawings on celluloid, but came to self-awareness and broke free of their restraints and now fight those who threaten freedom of imagination.

Vic: It sounds a bit autobiographical.

Randy: You're quick, Vic.

Vic: You're writing and pencilling it?

Randy: Writing, pencilling, inking, coloring, and lettering. Let's face it, the artist is what makes the book sing. Everyone else is just hired hands. That's "artist" as opposed to "inker," by the way. I've heard inkers refer to themselves as artists. They trace lines and they want to be called artists. Five-year-olds can trace lines.

Vic: Your chores on this title sound ambitious.

Randy: Hey, the art is the tough part. I do that already. The rest of the stuff is a cakewalk.

Vic: We have a question from a young lady in the audience?

Young Lady: Mr. Kingman, I just want to say that you're a strikingly handsome individual.

Randy: Why, thank you. You'll notice that most artists are lean and good-looking. This is as opposed to most "writers" who are shorter and usually overweight. I imagine this physical jealousy is part of what prompts so many writers to be envious of artists. The fact is that, in every way, artists are better than writers. They can't stand that. They're old news. Fading history.

Vic: How would you account for this physical difference?

Randy: Gravity. Writers sit there in front of their typewriters and sag while writing their recycled plots. Artists are taut and lean, stretched out over their drawing boards. Physical demands of the job. That's what does it.

Vic: Could you tell us who some of your artistic influences are?

Randy: Oh, lots of people have influenced me at various times. Russ Manning. Frank Frazetta. Steranko. Eisner. Burne Hogarth. Plus constant sketching from real life. Friends posing for me. That sort of thing.

Vic: And who are your writing influences?

Randy: I'm sorry, what?

Vic: What writers have influenced your work?

Randy: Well, writing is nothing special. Anyone can write. Why should some writer influence me? It's art that's important.

Vic: But —

Randy: After all, you know what one picture is worth a thousand of, don't you.

Vic: But you should have *some* knowledge and understanding of what other writers have done? I mean — what do you think of Hemingway's writing?

Randy: Which one wrote? Mariel or Margaux?

Vic: Let me put it another way: when you write a story —

Randy: I don't "write" a story. The story's just there. I start drawing it.

Vic: OK, how about, when you tell a story, what themes do you explore?

Randy: You mean like music? TV themes?

Vic: *Themes*! Topics! Subject matter! What comments on the human condition are you trying to make? You know, the things that writers should be doing!

Randy: But are writers doing that? Hell no. It's all recycled garbage: yesterday's stories in modern dress. Don't tell me that comics writers are exploring — what'd you call it? — themes. They can't even *hum* themes, much less explore them.

They're old, tired, and used up. But artists have new, fresh ideas. Look at this advance copy of *X-Cels*, each page brimming with vitality — each page new and different.

Vic: It's fight scenes.

Randy: Yeah?

Vic: It's twenty pages of fight scenes. And two pages of exposition, being told by women with their hips outthrust.

Randy: Isn't it great?

Vic: But comics writers are accused of rehashing. You said so yourself. What in the world is new and novel about fight scenes?

Randy: Because they're being drawn by people who have a grasp of how to tell things interestingly in a visual manner. Writers don't.

Vic: They all look like pin-up pages.

Randy: Right. Writers don't care about important stuff like that because they don't get art pages back. And they gripe about it and ignore the needs of the artists. It's deliberate.

Vic: I'm not following. What do pin-up pages have to do with getting art pages back?

Randy: It has everything to do with it. If I drew what those so-called "writers" wanted, with pages that had six, seven, even eight panels of people talking — or pages of fight scenes with smaller panels instead of big ones — those pages go for less than half of what pages with big images go for.

Vic: "Go for?"

Randy: On the art market.

Vic: Wait a minute. You're saying that when you create stories, one of your major concerns has to do with how much you can sell the pages of artwork for?

Randy: Of course. Pages that have two or three images on them — preferably two or three small panels, combined with an extremely large image (usually a dynamic pose or a fight pose) — those go for a couple of hundred bucks easy. Those look great up on walls. Those are genuine pin-up quality. But pages with small images of this character interaction garbage: Those go for peanuts. Those don't look good up on walls. That's one of the reasons Buck quit off *Brickman*. I'd take his boring, low-value character scenes and turn them into vibrant, valuable collectibles. He hated that. Jealousy.

Vic: But — but that's crazy!

Randy: No it's not. It's economics. It's dollars and cents. Publishers understand about economics. Artists understand about economics. Writers don't.

That's why publishers are selling millions of copies of titles, artists are pushing out writers and making big bucks on the art market, and writers are finding themselves out in the street and wailing about how they're being ignored and shafted. They just brought it on themselves with their unimaginative rehashing.

They don't have what it takes to be a writer/artist.

Actually, we're a new breed, and I prefer a different term to refer to us, namely "wartist." They're just not wartist material.

If they hate it so much, why don't they pick up pencils and learn to draw? They're just a bunch of lazy crybabies.

Vic: Can I quote you on that?

Randy: Sure, but don't use my name.

(Peter David [whoops, sorry, that should be "Name Withheld"] Writer of Stuff, had been thinking of doing this column for over a month, but was concerned it might come across as an unprovoked attack. He is most grateful for the provocation.)

SNOB APPEAL (Jan. 24, 1992)

(The following is a transcript of a panel from Non-Con III, held during Christmas in Verona, New Jersey. The topic of the symposium is "Comic Art Versus Real Art." The panelists are Louis Lance, noted comic-book critic and publisher of *Comic Intelligence — The Magazine of Acerbic Comic Absurdities*. and also publisher of the "Uno" comics line; and Matty Michaels, publisher of Spectacular Comics, the number-one comics line in the country. The moderator, as always, is professional fan Vic Chalker.)

Vic: First, I'd like to thank both you gentlemen for taking time out from your busy schedule to join us. The first thing I think we have to do is define our terms. Gentlemen, I put it to you: What is art?

Matty: Art is what tells a story.

Vic: Maybe I wasn't specific enough. I meant, "How would you define 'fine art'?"

Matty: Art that tells a story that sells over a million copies.

Louis: God, this is pathetic.

Vic: Look, Matty —

Matty: Oh! Oh, I see what you're getting at. *Fine* art.

Vic: Yes, precisely.

Matty: Well, I'll tell ya, Vic, I don't generally get involved in discussions of quality grading. Fine, near mint, mint — we leave that to collectors. We're just out there trying to publish the most masterful comics we can.

Louis: Let me shoot him. Please. Before he procreates and further sullies the gene pool.

Vic: Uh, Louis — maybe you'd care to field this one?

Louis: To be blunt, Vic — and you'll find that I'm not one to prevaricate or obfuscate — the concept of art is something that's dying in this country. Art is something that elevates the human spirit, comments on the human condition, and will invariably stand the test of time.

Vic: Can you give us any examples of comics that you think will fit that category?

Louis: Well, there's *Beanbag, Femmes and Fishnets, Window on a Warped World* —

Vic: Pardon me, Louis, but aren't all those published by your own Uno line?

Louis: That's right, Vic. Available at less-blathering comics stores everywhere.

Vic: Can you think of comics published by anyone besides yourself that would constitute "art"?

Louis: No.

Vic: No? Not a one?

Louis: No. Any comic book with true artistic merit is, by definition, being published by me.

Vic: Well that's very interesting. Matty, would you agree with Louis' definition? About art being something that lasts?

Matty: Sure. That sounds good.

Vic: Is Spectacular publishing anything that, in your opinion, will have lasting value?

Matty: Oh, absolutely. It's a need that we've definitely been dealing with.

Louis: I can't wait to hear this.

Matty: Yeah, gang, that's why we've been publishing special editions of our classics in air-tight bagged editions.

Louis: I knew it.

Matty: Those things will last for your great-great grandkids. That enough art for ya, Lou?

Louis: I cannot believe that this oaf's comic line outsells mine one thousand to one. Then again, maybe I shouldn't be surprised. Commercialization has been nothing but detrimental to our society. It's blanded out the audiences, stuffing garbage up their nostrils until they can no longer recognize the stench.

Matty: Now there I gotta disagree with ya, Lou. Our comics don't have commercials. That's television.

Louis: Oh for crying out —

Matty: Smart guy like you, don't know the diff between print and TV. Geez, I dunno. Sure, we got ads, but readers can skip right by th —

Louis: Commercialization, you Neanderthal yahoo! Pandering to the lowest common denominator for the sole purpose of turning a buck! Letting monetary concerns be the sole dictator of what the great unwashed of this country can hope to be exposed to in the name of art!

Vic: But Louis, is it unreasonable for a publisher to be concerned about the monetary bottom line? He is trying to stay in business, after all.

Louis: A publisher has a responsibility as a sentient human being — or whatever Mr. Michaels here is — to not toss shovelful upon shovelful of manure upon the public, even if they're clamoring for it.

Vic: Well now I'm a little confused here, Louis. You are also the publisher — under other publishing names — of such titles as *Super Terrific Hero* magazine, and then there's this one: *Wee Willie and his Wonderful Winkie*, which is little more than smut by any definition. Aren't you just turning a buck, same as any other publisher?

Louis: The difference is that those publications — the need for which I abhor — helps to support my more worthy ventures, publications that can benefit humanity as a whole. Mr. Michaels and his immoral ilk are simply out to make money for the sake of making money.

Matty: Yeah, but we aren't going around pointing fingers and calling names, saying that we hate our audience on moral grounds, but don't mind taking their money. Least we're honest.

Louis: How splendid. Honest, pandering hacks.

Matty: We're not hacks.

Louis: Of course you are. Oddly enough, it's not even a derogatory word, so I don't understand why you sound offended.

Vic: I always thought of a hack as someone who didn't care about what they were producing, that they were just going through the motions.

Matty: Me, too.

Louis: Hardly. A hack is simply someone who turns out material with his primary concern being that of making a buck at it. He's not someone with true vision; he's simply a working stiff with no real artistic invention, working his trade or craft. You would compare the hacks who turn out comics for Spectacular to genuine artists in the same way that you would compare a decent carpenter to a gifted architect. Hacks and carpenters can hammer nails straight, but don't expect them to design lasting works. You can be a good hack.

Matty: Bull. When we say a guy's hacking it, we mean he's not giving it his all. Ya can't sit there and say, "Oh, I say this guy's a hack, but it's not an insult." It's as if I talked about how wonderful and convenient urinals are, and then said that calling a magazine *The Comics Urinal* was intended as flattering.

Louis: You're mixing apples and oranges, although I suppose in your beer circles that might actually pass as humor.

Matty: I see what you're all talking about with this "fine art" stuff and what makes art and what's lasting and all that.

Louis: Finally.

Matty: You ask me, all this stuff about what's art and not, that's just snobbery. Guys like you, Lou — and you're a smart guy, I'll give ya that — but guys like you have lots of learning and education, and you read a lot of books by a lot of smart guys. And you decide that, based on all that, you know what's real art and what's not. And you also figure that, since you know so much more about stuff than the average joe, your opinion is not only worth a lot, but theirs is worth nothin'. Which means that anything the average guy likes has gotta be less important, less artistic and less good than what you like. All you critics set your critical standards, but what it really boils down to is that it's just your opinion, and one guy's opinion is just as good as the next guy's.

Louis: So if one "guy" is a Nobel scientist who says the Earth is round, and the other "guy" is a working stiff who says the Earth is flat, both are equally valid?

Matty: Now you're the one who's juggling fruit. Facts is one thing. You can back up the Earth's shape with pictures from space. But opinion is just opinion. The regular guy is just as entitled to his art as you are to yours.

Louis: The regular guy gets precisely what he deserves: Unremitting swill from people whose only concern is not elevation of the ideal man, but elevation of their stock values. At Uno Publishing our valued "commodities" are artists, not stocks.

Matty: So how come your artists are talking about coming on board with us?

Louis: Nonsense.

Matty: It's true. They're getting nervous because you keep badmouthing distributors and retailers in *Comics Intelligence*, badmouthing the guys who get your product out there. And the distributors are saying, "Hey, the only reason this guy's got an audience is because we give him one. Why are we doing this to ourselves?" You've made enough enemies — and your "art" books make so little money — that if the distributors felt there was no point in carrying your stuff any more, you'd be belly-up inside of a month.

Louis: My people are loyal to me. They respect that I won't toe the line of cronyism and will continue to speak my mind and criticize the offal state of our society regardless of whatever economic guerilla tactics my opponents may employ.

Vic: I think we're getting off the subject here. A question from the audience?

Audience Member: Could each of you cite an example of what you consider to be a great work of art?

Louis: Well, there's so many — none of them courtesy of Mr. Michaels and his work-for-hire drones, of course. I don't know. Michelangelo's rendering on the ceiling of the Sistine Chapel.

Matty: That was work-for-hire.

Louis: Oh for heaven's —

Matty: It's true! The Pope went to him and said, "Hey, Mike, decorate the ceiling for us!" You think Mike did it out of the goodness of his heart? He got paid for it! Heck, he didn't even get as good a deal as we give.

Vic: How so?

Matty: He didn't get his art back.

Louis: This is reaching new lows.

Matty: Why? Because I'm reminding you of the roots of your precious "fine art"? People we consider to be great artists fall into one of two categories: Either there were critics like you around to say what slobs they were so that they never got anywhere; or else they were popular and had wealthy patrons or commissions to keep 'em going. They didn't set themselves up, like you do, and say, "We're making art. Look how great we are." You go back and tell Bill Shakespeare that a couple hundred years later, people would still be doing his plays, and he'd've laughed in your face.

Louis: He would certainly have laughed in yours. But he would hardly have been alone.

Vic: Matty, name a great work of art.

Matty: *Action Comics* #1.

Louis: Oh, for the love of God! You're comparing the primitive scribblings of two teenagers to a breathtaking masterpiece like the Sistine Chapel?

Matty: It elevated the human spirit — kids thrilled to his adventures and dreamed about what it would be like if they had super-powers. It commented about the human condition — it said, "Wouldn't things be better if we had a guy with super powers to watch over us?" Heck, there are whole religions where the basic idea isn't much more than that. And ol' Superman has staying power — he continues to be one of the great American heroes. It fits all the definitions you came up with.

Louis: This entire discussion has been utter rubbish — which means it will probably end up being transcribed into some mindless column somewhere, to be read by the sort of brainless, gibbering boors to which Mr. Michaels caters. As for me, I've had more than my share. I ask you all to read Uno comics — the only true intelligent exchange of graphic art currently being published.

Vic: We have time for one more question.

Audience Member: Yes, I want to ask Mr. Lance something about Uno comics.

Louis: Thank heavens, *someone* with a modicum of taste.

Audience Member: Yeah, I want to know if you're going to be having a big crossover where all the characters in your comics meet each other and have a big fight. You know, you could release multiple editions and it'd be really really good —

47

(Peter David, writer of stuff, regrets that the transcript ends here rather abruptly. Anyone wishing to help post bail for Louis Lance while he awaits trial on his assault and battery charges can send money care of the Comic Book Legal Defense Fund.)

Historical Notes:

1) Matty Michaels is a thinly disguised take-off on Tom DeFalco, Marvel's editor-in-chief. Louis Lance is an even more thinly disguised riff on Gary Groth, editor of **Comics Journal**. *Groth had written a vicious piece about the late Carol Kalish (see "Character Sketches," "Carol," page 113), using her passing as simply another opportunity to rag on Marvel Comics. I was furious, wanting to rip into him on the one hand, but reluctant to give him any publicity on the other, or even possibly prompting people to run out and buy the latest "Journal" to see what he'd said. So I settled for parodying him.*

SECTION 3:

Fun with Publishers

or
Biting the Hand

When I first started the column, I didn't give any real thought to the notion that, sooner or later, I was going to have to start taking shots at some of the folks who enable me to sustain a living in the comic book industry — namely, the publishers. I suppose if I *had* given it any thought, I might have punted the whole idea of the column right then.

Nevertheless, it became clear to me that if I were going to be doing any sort of weekly essay that purported to be about the comics industry, then sooner or later I was going to have to talk about the publishers themselves. Like as not, the talk might not be particularly flattering. So I decided the best approach was to be as even handed as possible, and take no prisoners. If I fry Marvel one week, they can take consolation in the fact that next week I might be going after DC. Stick to giving analysis of what's on the public record, avoid character assassination, and try to maintain a sense of humor throughout.

Thus far I am still gainfully employed in the industry, and there have been any number of occasions where employees or executives of companies that I criticized have told me privately, "You were absolutely right," which is always gratifying. Not that I necessarily think that my little essays have necessarily gotten anyone to rethink their practices — but you never know.

I've divided this section into four parts and run them alphabetically: DC, Defiant, Image, and Marvel. Specific comments preceed each section.

Cry havoc, and let slip the teeth that bite the hand—

Part 1: DC, Where Legends Die

In compiling this book, I was astounded to find that of the four columns focussed on DC that I thought worthwhile for inclusion, three of them dealt with the "Death of Superman." Sad to say, DC didn't really *do* much else worth discussing in the previous years. Go figure.

Still, the gimmick-ridden temporary demise of its cornerstone character, and the remarkable brouhaha that ensued, remains formidable proof of what can happen when CNN has a slow news day.

The only other noteworthy mentions of DC Comics involve their continued disinterest, as of this writing, in collecting a series I wrote for them called *The Atlantis Chronicles* into a trade paperback, and "The Return of the Blasters" which can be found reprinted in "Useless Stories," page 223.

As for me, I still find the "Superman versus Doomsday" story something that works only if you are willing to accept that Superman had lost all his cleverness, and was reduced to a slugging machine.

IT'S A BIRD, IT'S A PLANE, IT'S DEAD (Oct. 2, 1992)

Front page news.

"The Death of Superman" has finally hit the media, landing with a very loud splash on the front page of *Newsday*. And since *Newsday* is a tabloid, front page means the whole page.

DC publicists were not ready to talk about it, which is nothing new. It's been ages since I've seen a general media event that was planned, orchestrated, and launched by any comic-book company publicity department. Instead the news events just sort of happen, with leaks coming from distributors or creators or retailers, and then the PR folks madly scrambling to say something intelligent in response (which can frequently be boiled down to "No comment" or "We'll get back to you on that").

So it would seem that those who were writing off DC's future and market power were premature. DC has not taken its being knocked down to the No. 3 company for August lying down.

(Although here's a homework assignment for anyone with access to the sales numbers: Remember that the August numbers that made Malibu/Image the No. 2 company were based on *orders*. It'd be interesting to see how many of those items actually *shipped* in August, versus how many DCs actually shipped. This would determine whether Malibu/Image was *de facto* No. 2, or whether it only held that status on paper. I have no idea one way or the other. I'm just interested. After all, orders don't pay bills. Sales do.)

No, DC has fought back. For some time now, DC has wrestled with a difficult (you should pardon the expression) image problem. On one hand, it has carved out a niche for itself as publisher of some high-quality, award-winning titles, mostly produced by British guys. And it's developed one Wolver-inesque success in Lobo.

But the three jewels in its British crown have been *Watchmen*, which was a limited series; *Swamp Thing*, which hasn't been written by a Brit in years (although Nancy Collins is doing some nice work); and the award-winning *Sleepwalker*-Done-Wrong, *Sandman*, which is scheduled to end when Neil Gaiman leaves. As for Lobo, the character has yet to prove that he can sustain anything beyond specials, one-shots, and limited series.

This puts DC's long-term hopes back where they've always been, namely with its established characters.

The problem is that Superman, *et al.*, have been around for so long that DC is constantly in the position of having to reinvent them, so that modern readers can embrace the characters without dust flying. Kind of a comic-book equivalent of the "This is not your father's Oldsmobile" commercials. Indeed, I keep waiting for an ad with Batman standing there, looking kick-butt and serious, declaring, "This is not your father's Batmobile."

DC perpetually embraces the latest trends in this reinvention of itself and characters. The announcement at San Diego of its intended crossovers with Image reminds one of the college professors in the 1960s who grew beards and wore Nehru jackets and love beads in an effort to show the younger generation that they could be groovy, too.

Furthermore, DC characters have been, for some time now, becoming grimmer and grittier. It's a trend that has become more and more pronounced throughout the line. Terrified of being viewed as old fogies, DC is doing whatever it can to "de-fogy" itself.

How else to explain, for instance, the abrupt cancellation of *Justice Society of America*? I don't know what sales were, but were they *that* bad that they warranted the decision to drop the axe *that* fast? Was it sales, or was it DC believing that it has already got enough "old" characters in its stables, and shouldn't be adding any more?

One of the greatest benefits of this is that, whenever DC makes any sort of major change, it gets the company headlines because its characters have such high recognition. Also, the stories have masterfully easy hooks for the media to latch on to.

"Batman Gets Old!" *Dark Knight* in three easy words that make great headlines. "Jimmy Olsen Gets Fired." "Superman Gets Engaged!" — and now "Superman Dies!" (Me, I'm waiting for "Wonder Woman Becomes Single Mother!" The GOP would just *love* that.)

There have been the occasional backfires, of course, because the simplicity that newsfolk crave makes it difficult to handle any development of complexity. Remember the "Superman Gets Married" story of some years ago — except it turned out (to bewildered reporters and newcomers) to be the Superman of Earth II.

For that matter, try to explain to your average feature writer (who hasn't read comics in years) the entire "Crisis on Infinite Earths" concept. Though the idea was developed to simplify the DC Universe, you had to describe to the writer all the circumstances that made the DC Universe so confusing in the first place — by which point the reporter was hopelessly lost. ("So *which* Earth is ours?")

Then, of course, there was the Dial-M-for-Murder-of-Robin fiasco. It started out as a nifty-enough novelty story, but backfired when Robin was actually killed, to the horror of America. The problem was that the average man-on-the-street (or reporter on the beat) couldn't mentally distinguish between Jason Todd's obnoxious Robin and the cheery, gosh-wow Dick Grayson-Robin of the 1960s *Batman* TV show. Go explain that Dick Grayson was safe and sound as Nightwing of the Titans ("Who of the what?")

Despite these snags, DC and Image have generally managed to stir up some genuinely great PR for themselves (as opposed to Marvel, which these days generally gets media attention along the lines of "Major Marvel Stockholder Arrested for Having Sex with Sheep").

And now, DC's latest — and possibly greatest — publicity coup: Killing the Man of Steel.

No comics fan is fooled by this for a microsecond, of course. In most fiction, "And then he dies" is usually followed by "The End." As opposed to comics, in which the same statement is usually followed by "Oh really? And *then* what?"

It is, as noted before, eerie timing coming hard on the heels of the death of Joe Shuster.

(Although, purely as a side note, I'm happy to report an amendment to my earlier statements over DC's placing Siegel and Shuster on a $20,000-a-year stipend. I commented that $200,000 seemed more appropriate. Well, a source at DC has informed me that the amount has escalated dramatically over the years — wildly beyond normal inflation adjustments — to the point at which Joe Shuster was getting around five times that amount every year when he passed away. Still less than I thought they should get, but certainly a lot closer to equity. Cheers for DC.)

Thus far, initial sales impact seems promising. Comics store owners are reporting a lot of interest from non-readers. Signs are already going up at stores offering a reserve system. Hell, I must admit that, if I weren't on the comp list, *I'd* buy a copy of the storyline, just to enjoy the mechanics of it.

What's interesting, although understandable, is that Superman's dying is, quite simply, not a story. Joe Shuster dying, that's a story. Fay Vincent resigning, that's a story. But Superman getting knocked off is, in and of itself, meaningless, because in comics death is, in and of itself, meaningless. *CBG's* own Don Thompson put that in perspective for *Newsday.*

No, Superman's death is not an event. It's plot mechanics. What makes this whole thing so intriguing is what DC intends to do *after* Superman dies. "What next," as mentioned above. Thus far, editor Mike Carlin has been quite correctly cagey on the entire topic.

What, then, *is* going to happen next?

Here's my guess —

And no, you're not going to see any sort of spoiler warnings or anything, because that would imply knowledge. I have deliberately refrained from asking anyone in authority — not that they necessarily would have told me, although I imagine I could have wormed it out of *someone*. But, since I haven't chanced finding out anything, my guess is no better or worse than yours. Besides, I've written about so many things in the past without knowing a damned thing about them, why ruin a perfectly good track record.

My guess is that, after Superman dies, he'll enter some sort of chrysalis or transformational state — caterpillar to butterfly type of thing. This could be based either on the nature of his death (whatever that is) or something having to do with his Kryptonian physiology. And once he does come back — what then?

Probably a two-pronged approach.

First, his powers.

I don't think they're going to change them radically in nature because, well, he's Superman. Sure, they've mucked around with him in the media. But I doubt we'll suddenly see him acquiring some of the abilities from the old TV series, such as splitting into two Supermen or phasing through walls. Nor will he suddenly display the talents that showed up from nowhere in the Superman films, such as turning back time, multiple-imaging, or even the dreaded Kryptonian "S" Frisbee. (Not to mention the dreaded anti-gravity vision displayed by the Kryptonian villains.)

No, when comics have toyed with his powers, it's generally been in the realm of power level. When a "major change" was made, as Denny O'Neil did in the 1970s and John Byrne did in the 1980s, the move was towards making him weaker. No drop kicking planets and such.

But since he's not all that powerful now, maybe the move will be to increase his powers. I've even heard a rumor or two on the fan circuit to that effect. Maybe DC is tired of Superman flying through space with an oxygen mask. Maybe it wants to make Superman more Super — which will make it that much more challenging for the writers to come up with someone who's going to be a serious threat to him.

I don't think, however, that the important change is going to be in the powers. I think it's going to be in the personality.

My guess — and I stress, it is a guess — is that the watchwords of Superman are going to be, basically, the kid gloves are off. I think we're standing on the eve of Grim and Gritty Superman.

I mean, let's face it: If somebody kills you, that's *got* to be more than a little annoying. So when (not if) Superman comes back, my guess is that he's going to react in one of two ways: Either he's going to become ultra-tentative, reluctant to risk dying again — which, somehow, I don't think is going to play all that well. ("Up, up and Far, Far Away.") Or else he's going to become ultra-aggressive, determined not to give anyone the chance to knock him off again.

The fact is that Superman's image hasn't been the same since *Dark Knight*. Frank Miller did wonders for Batman, but his portrayal of Superman as the ultimate representative of the *status quo* seriously damaged Superman's likableness. One of the attractions of super-heroes is that they're wish fulfillment. They do what we wish we could do, be what we wish we could be. But who really aspires to becoming a blue-and-red-costumed embodiment of the Reagan era?

Writer Kurt Busiek put his finger squarely on the problem when he made a rather canny observation about a Jim Croce lyric from the song, "You Don't Mess Around with Jim." You know, the line that goes: "You don't tug on Superman's cape."

Kurt's view on this was simply, "Why not? Why *wouldn't* you tug on Superman's cape? *What's he gonna do?* He's *Superman*, for crying out loud. What's the absolute worst that's gonna happen? If you tug on Superman's cape, he'll just look at you and say, 'Don't do that, son. It's not nice. And — isn't this a school night?' Nothing is going to happen to you if you tug on Superman's cape.

"Now — you don't tug on *Batman's* cape. Tug on Batman's cape, you're toast. Or you don't tug on *The Spectre's* cape. But Superman? Tug away."

In a comics universe that features psychotics, drunk drivers, crippling sociopaths, homicidal maniacs — and that's just the *good* guys — Superman would seem to be something of a relic. Whereas once he pointed the way for all super-heroes to follow, now he seems to be a giant anchor, dragging them back in a direction that they don't want to go. Which means that — in my opinion — he's either going to have to follow the migration or be left behind.

Superman B.C. — Before Corpse — is a square. My guess is that Superman A.D. — After Death — is no longer going to be a nice guy.

Because we all know where nice guys finish.

(*If Peter David, writer of stuff, turns up dead of strangulation, and Mike Carlin's fingerprints are found on his throat, that will be a good tip that his guesses were correct. Place your bets.*)

Historical Notes:

1) The reference to the Siegel and Shuster stipend appears in the "Character Sketches" section, in "Bigger Than Life" on page 119.

2) John Byrne wrote in to say that I didn't know what I was talking about (big shock there). However, as it turned out, I was twenty-five percent right, as you will see in the subsequent "Will the Real Superman — ?" article. As of this writing the return of the real Superman is imminent, and the long term effects of his temporary dissolution remain to be seen.

TRUTH, JUSTICE AND STICKER FUN (Dec. 18, 1992)

There's definitely something wrong with me.

I'm missing the boat. I'm out of the loop. I'm just not with it.

Why? Because I've gone beyond the saturation point with the marketing surrounding the death of Superman. I am now solidly repulsed by it.

I just received a kit from DC (which, after this column, will probably take me off its kit mailing list). There's a cover sheet describing the contents, complete with such goodies as:

1) A cardboard coffin. I believe it's just large enough to accommodate my old Captain Action-costumed-as-Superman figure;

2) A set of stickers, including one showing the grotesque image of a sobbing Lois Lane cradling the dead, blood-soaked body of Kal-El — certainly a portrait that every spiritual, life-celebrating American school kid would want plastered on his or her spiral binder;

3) A press release and ad slick, which are guaranteed to "generate excitement in your local market" ("Hey Timmy! Superman's dead! I'm so excited!").

Plus posters, rack header cards, etc.

I'm sorry. I guess I'm being squeamish. I guess I'm being old fashioned. But this whole thing is really starting to sicken me.

This is no criticism of the stories. I haven't read the stories yet. I don't begrudge DC the success; I don't begrudge the royalties for the creative teams, or the opportunity to be part of what the promotional kit refers to as a "landmark comics event" (and I guess they're right. I mean, hell, back in *Crisis on Infinite Earths*, Wonder Woman — who is only a few years younger than Superman — was turned into a lump of clay. That didn't rate so much as a six-graph obit — or even a promotional glazed ash tray which, DC might have claimed, was made from genuine Wonder Woman).

But what's starting to get to me is the chop-licking joy that, boiled down, is: "Wow! People are really upset and grieving! Let's wring every nickel we can out of it!"

I mean, I like angst as much as the next guy. But good lord, the "grieving Lois" sticker and the coffin (which can be used to display the lovely clip-on Superman R.I.P. pins) are the last straw.

I've written before about how we have a new breed of heros who revel in pain and suffering. And now we know what they do in their off hours. They work for the promotional and marketing departments of comic book companies. (And I'm not singling out DC here; I'm sure that if Marvel caught a PR tiger by the tail like this one, it would be riding it for all it's worth.)

I've also written before about a tendency in this country to enjoy tearing down icons. How people seem to enjoy dragging that which is great and wonderful and "better" down to a level that will make them feel comfortable about themselves. Some people wrote in and said I was being overly sour. But the Death of Superman is merely the latest incarnation of that trend.

And the biggest aspect of all this is that, although comics fans aren't really buying into the notion that Kal is gone for good, there are a lot of civilians who do believe it and are genuinely upset (as was pointed out in a *CBG* editorial cartoon).

I was at one public place where I heard some guy (who was not a comic-book reader, but instead, had gotten all his information from news reports) talking with utter conviction about how Superman was gone for good, and Doomsday was going to be the new mainstay at DC Comics— which the guy declared was "cool." And there have been people who have struck up conversations with me (not knowing of my connection with comics, but instead being prompted to do so because of my Spider-Man jacket) who are clearly quite distressed by what they perceive as the permanent demise of one of their childhood friends.

No doubt, in their mind's eyes, they're seeing George Reeves lying lifeless in his black-and-white Superman outfit, with Noel Neill sobbing over his prostrate form.

And DC is sending out toy coffins and stickers.

But I guess I shouldn't be surprised. Only the intensity and glee with which Superman's death is being pushed can be considered new. *CBG* pointed out at length the number of times that Superman has been killed. Knocking off dearly beloved popular idols, however, is hardly limited to Superman.

One need look no further than the end of the 19th century, when Arthur Conan Doyle decided to rid himself of a literary albatross named Sherlock Holmes. Convinced that the master detective was drawing attention away from work that Doyle considered less frivolous, ACD crafted "The Final Problem," in which Holmes went over the Reichenbach Falls, locked in mortal combat with his arch enemy and "Napoleon of Crime," Professor Moriarty.

Unlike (presumably) Superman's writers, Doyle didn't develop the story to answer the question of, "Well, what do we do that's new and exciting with Holmes this year?" He didn't intend to bring Holmes back — although, let's face it, he could have put a bullet through Holmes' brain "on camera," and shut the door completely. Obviously he left himself an out. But let's give him the benefit of the doubt and presume that he really did intend for Holmes to buy it.

I think, however, we can agree beyond doubt that Doyle did not manufacture arm bands with the letter "H" on them; or distribute magnifying glasses with "RIP" inscribed on the glass and that the *Strand* magazine did not develop a special Reichenbach Falls counter display with a Moriarty header card. Londoners were in genuine mourning for their fallen hero. What Doyle *did* was attempt to placate them by giving them the "untold tale" of *The Hound of the Baskervilles*. But that wasn't sufficient, and when (as I recall the story) Doyle's own mother started ragging on him, he finally resuscitated Holmes. Then again, Doyle always was obsessed by life after death. Maybe this was just a manifestation of that.

More dead icons (besides Elvis, I mean)? Let's jump forward three quarters of a century to 1976, and Robin Hood of Sherwood Forest.

Although Robin's accomplishments (robbing from the rich, splitting the arrow, defeating Sir Guy/ The Sheriff/Prince John/whoever) were widely known, less celebrated were the stories of his demise. So screenwriter James Goldman wrote the singularly downbeat *Robin and Marian*, a 1976 Columbia picture. Starring Audrey Hepburn, radiant as Marian, and Sean Connery as an aging Robin (presaging his cameo fifteen years later in *Robin Hood: Prince of Thieves*, in which he would be more effective in his 30 seconds of screen time as King Richard than Kevin Costner was as Locksley in the preceding two hours), this was a no-holds-barred tear-jerker.

Returning dispirited from the Crusades after the demise of an aging Richard Lionheart (Richard Harris), Robin and Little John (Nicol Williamson) link up with Friar Tuck and Will Scarlet, played by Ronnie Barker (of *The Two Ronnies*) and Denholm Elliot (which, with the third "Indiana Jones" film, means that there were two movies in 15 years that featured Sean Connery, Denholm Elliot, and a "last crusade"). They engage in one final campaign against the Sheriff of Nottingham, played with dignity and elan by Robert Shaw.

The climactic battle between Robin and the Sheriff was absolutely heart-stopping, and the final scenes of that film made one of the few times I've actually gotten misty-eyed in a theater. It was funny, sad, beautifully acted, well-directed —

Yet, as I recall, *Robin and Marian* did not do particularly well in the box office. Clearly it was a movie made before its time. Release it now, and we would see Columbia flood the market with black arrows, memorial swords, and the like. Action figures that can actually die a variety of ways would hit the toy stores.

Death, destruction, misery, and shattered dreams are big business, and *Robin and Marian* would be a smash. As it is, it's consigned, dusty and forgotten, to the video shelves and the occasional appearance on cable.

Obviously, milking death for all it's worth is tremendously effective. At comics stores, 90% (and, on some days, 100%) of the phone calls are inquiries about the Death of Superman. People were lining up for blocks when the comic book hit. *CBG* editors "Dan and Margie" were flooded with calls from newshounds.

Even *Saturday Night Live* took the opportunity to haul the super-hero costumes out of mothballs once more and stage a Superman funeral service. (Please, God, let Tony Isabella have been watching Sinbad as Black Lightning, the super-hero they wouldn't let in. Me, I was getting off on the dead-on accurate Hulk gag.)

I think, then, it's only a matter of time until other licenses and properties start tumbling to the marketing possibilities and develop death scenarios, along with attendant marketing strategies to pump up interest.

Perhaps, within the next couple of years, we'll thrill to:

"The Death of Spider-Man" — Harry Osborn, The Green Goblin, goes berserk one final time and teams with Venom to destroy Spider-Man. Aunt May is killed as an innocent bystander, and Spider-Man goes completely berserk. He kills Venom and is about to kill the Goblin as well, but restrains himself at the last moment — at which point Harry blows them both to Kingdom Come with a pumpkin bomb.

Harry's young son, Norman, is griefstricken over the misery that his father has caused. Then Norman is kidnapped by an enraged Doctor Octopus, who is infuriated that he didn't have the opportunity to kill Spider-Man. Doc Ock subjects Norman to a series of experiments which causes him to age 19 years and acquire the powers of a spider — at which point Norman beats the stuffing out of Ock and becomes the new Spider-Man.

Look for spray cans of specially made black webbing, black Spider-signal flashlights, special cardboard "Death of Spider-Man" dioramas, Spider-Man's widow's black veil (got to have something for the female readers), and ten different editions of the new *Spider-Man* #1 featuring the debut of Norman as Spider-Man.

"The Death of Tarzan" — Tarzan is updated, and the saga of La of Opar is turned into a redo of *Fatal Attraction*, including such gut-wrenching moments as Jane discovering Cheetah the monkey (or, for purists, Manu the Monkey) floating dead in a pot of bouillabaisse. La then kills Jane, and a final battle results in a climactic elephant stampede during which the enraged Tantor inadvertently steps on both Tarzan and La. Korak, the son of Tarzan, in whom no one is remotely interested, becomes the new Tarzan.

To be marketed with black loincloths; bagged stuffed monkeys, fake gold bars (straight from Opar) with "RIP" engraved in them, clip-on daggers, and elephant-foot umbrella stands complete with genuine Tarzan and La smear on the underside.

"The Death of Steve Urkel" — Please. Somebody. Anybody. Kill this character. Slowly. Make him suffer.

"The Death of Mickey Mouse" — Black Pete, enraged by his being completely diluted on *The Goof Troop*, cuts off his leg, replaces it with a peg leg, and then goes berserk attacking the other characters by beating them with his severed limb. In a devastating three-hour battle that levels Disneyland, Mickey valiantly fights to the death. Mickey's nephew, Morty, vows to change his name to Mickey and maintain the ideals that Mickey stood for.

To be accompanied by Mickey memorial cheese; little black buttons that say "RIP" on them; special displays shaped like mouse traps; souvenir peg legs; a special reunion/funeral TV special of the Mouseketeers; all theme parks throughout the world shut down for a 24-hour period of mourning, and the various Enchanted Castles festooned with black wreaths; the slogan of Disneyland officially changed from "The Happiest Place on Earth" to "Life Sucks"; the official theme song changed from "When You Wish upon a Star" to "Nowhere to Run to, Nowhere to Hide."

Also, announce preparation for next year's release of Death of Pinocchio with trailers featuring Pinocchio becoming infested by termites while Figaro eats Cleo in the background, all set to the tune of "Funeral March of a Marionette."

"The Death of Charlie Brown" — Lucy pulls the football away from him once too often. Charlie lands wrong and dies from a broken neck, shattered spine, and cerebral hemorrhage. Lucy is arrested, tried as a minor, and sent to reform school. Schroeder composes his first funeral dirge. Pigpen is contacted by the *National Enquirer* and dishes dirt. A devastated Linus hangs himself with his blanket. Snoopy starves to death waiting for Charlie Brown to feed him.

Look for the special black memorial football, the special black blanket, a special CD featuring every *Peanuts* related song including "Snoopy and the Red Baron" (original and Christmas-themed sequel); an updated version of the musical *You're a Good Man, Charlie Brown*, revised to *You're a Dead Man, Charlie Brown*; special line of Peanuts figures in black mourning clothes; dead Snoopy keychains; and, if it happens around Halloween, special trick or treat bags filled with rocks.

And then, in a shocking twist, a new strip is begun in which the ghost of Charlie Brown is denied entrance to the hereafter and condemned to walk the earth trying to find someone who will like him — and he changes his name to Casper — which would explain a lot.

(Peter David, writer of stuff, hopes he gets royalties if any of the above ideas are used.)

WILL THE REAL SUPERMAN... ? (Feb. 12, 1993)

Well, the word is out about the return of Superman. An assortment of press releases and coming-issue blurbs have crossed my desk, confirming the rumors that have been floating around for weeks.

"Four beings simultaneously appear," proclaims the general media announcement, "each claiming to be the Last Son of Krypton. Is one of these the real Man of Steel?" Is it:

"The cyborg from space — half-machine, half alien? He proclaims himself a Superman retooled from the future, and no one has the guts to contradict him.

"The cold super-being who sets up shop in the Fortress of Solitude and relentlessly takes the law into his own hands?

"The super-powered teen-ager who appears to be cloned from the first Superman? He must be a clone — why else would he have no memories of a previous life?

"The steelworker, John Henry Irons, buried alive during Superman's battle with Doomsday, who, like a man possessed, uses his talents to create a high-tech suit of armor and weaponry to literally become a Man of Steel?"

Split infinitives aside, it sounded like the next words should be, "Or is it — someone else? Match wits with Ellery Queen and see if you can figure out — who done it?" The fans can guess all they want, but if Jim Hutton were still around, he and David Wayne would have this thing sorted out in no time.

The other "Coming Comics" articles outline in more detail the information disseminated fairly succinctly in the first release.

What I found somewhat lacking was any detailed discussion of the creative teams. The biggest rap on Marvel is that publicity always seems to emphasize the characters over the creators (An article in *Entertainment Weekly* about Wolverine, for example, quoted Editor Bob Harras extensively, and even featured a photo of him — while Len Wein, who created the character, and Chris Claremont, who defined him, were never mentioned.)

DC, on the other hand, was ostensibly the place where creators are emphasized over characters, with such maneuvers as splashing the creator names all over the covers.

So one would think that the Superman spotlight would be the ideal time to get some serious ink for the creators. But the only person mentioned by name in the main press release is Editor Mike Carlin — indisputably *the* central figure in all this, but even so, he's not writing or drawing the comic books.

No, the folks who merely write the stories and draw the pictures are mentioned (out of five pages worth of material) precisely once. None of them are quoted. Even more, we're not told which writer is working with which artist, or which titles they're working on. Jerry Ordway's departure from the series is mentioned off-handedly, with no clue as to why.

Indeed, the only mention of the creative teams is in conjunction, not with their respective titles, but with their contributions to *Adventures of Superman* #500, in which they'll be "documenting four 'sightings' of Superman."

It's a sign of the times when you read five pages of material and learn more about the cover gimmicks than you do about who's producing the comics inside the cover. If DC is going to follow Marvel's lead on something, why did it have to be this?

At any rate —

Thus far, *BID* has made several speculations about Superman's return. The first, as John Byrne so kindly reminded us, was that we would see a grim and gritty Superman. If I were a less mature individual than I am, I might be inclined at this point to say:

"Nyaah nyaah. Told'ja, John. Told'ja John. Told'ja so, told'ja so, told'ja so. I was right, you were wrong, neener, neener, neeener."

However being the mature, sophisticated patron of the arts that I am, you'd never seen such a childish display in this column.

The second speculation, as outlined in "Ask the Self-Proclaimed Experts," was that DC was going to have to define just who Superman is before they could then determine where to go from there. Little did we suspect at the time that this statement would be so literally correct.

Now, putting aside all the carping about the ignoring of the creative teams, I happen to be jazzed about this entire development, for four reasons:

1) It perpetuates the mystery without committing DC to any particular direction. One of the greatest successes of the mutant titles has been their continued ability to pose question after question without offering any concrete answers. Any sane person would think that this would quickly lead to boredom, but the fans keep coming back for more, so there must be *some* merit to this approach. So it augers a continuation of the interest in the adventures of DC's oldest costumed super-hero.

2) It introduces some new characters to the DC Universe under very high-profile conditions — characters who, if they develop their own following, could stay around long after this whole business is finally resolved.

3) Pat O'Neill has pointed out that this would be the ideal manner in which to reintroduce a Superboy into continuity — simply by continuing the adventures of the young Super-whatever-he-is. This maneuver would eliminate the two long-standing raps against Superboy: a) You don't have a sense of everything being moot because everyone knows he grows up to become Superman; b) you don't make yourself crazy trying to figure out what time period to put him in. (Remember when Superboy was so far back in continuity that he met Bonnie and Clyde?)

Of course, again, the likelihood of this is contingent upon how they resolve the storyline.

(One would think, logically, that the resolution will come in one of two ways. I tend to think it's going to be an all-or-nothing proposition: Either none of these guys is Superman, or all of them are Superman — that is, different aspects of his "soul," as it were, splintered and inhabited these four beings. This would then suggest a climactic storyline in which they all unite in some manner and the "real" Superman, whole once more, returns. This resolution would, on the surface of it, call for the disappearance of all four characters, eliminating the possibility of any of them continuing. So perhaps the success of this multiple Superman plan (or lack thereof) will determine where they go from here.)

4) And most important — it's real.

What do I mean by "real?"

I mean that I like stories that have a real world feel to them.

All too often, super-hero comics exist in their own reality, divorced from considerations of how the real world would react to the goings-on.

Rarely does any one sue for property damage after a battle.

We rarely see heroes reading scandalous stories about themselves in supermarket rags ("Mr. Fantastic's Tortured Sex Life!" "The Thing and Alicia: Is Their Sex Life on the Rocks?").

Name all the stories in which some woman has come forward stating that she's carrying someone's super-lovechild.

Super-heroes are not, by and large, hounded by paparazzi (aside from one memorable sun-bathing experience for She-Hulk). They're not constantly tied up in court testifying against villains. In short, except for rare occasions, you don't get a sense that these people exist in the same world that we live in, a world that exploits and devours anyone of any notoriety.

And that is the kind of world we live in, make no mistake. If three network films in a week about Amy Fisher didn't convince you of that, then nothing will.

Considering the real-world reaction that the death of Superman incurred — a world in which, let's face it, Superman was and is a fictional character — I think it fairly safe to say that, in the DC Universe, Superman is unquestionably the most popular, the most idolized, the most famous man. I mean, that's the whole point of "World without a Superman," right?

And that's why these new developments ring so true.

Because we know that, in a world where there was a Superman, these new occurrences are the logical progression. Devastatingly logical — so much so that I'm, frankly, annoyed that I didn't see it coming.

Why so logical? Even — inevitable?

Because it's happened before, that's why.

It's happening right now.

I mean — c'mon. Superman was the king of super-heroes. The biggest. The best. We've seen him young, we've seen him older.

It's so obvious what DC is doing. It makes so much sense.

He's no longer merely Kal-El.

Now —

He's Kal-Elvis.

Yes, that's right. Intentionally or not, the Superman creative team has perfectly paralleled the life, and, more importantly, the afterlife, of Elvis Presley. The King.

It's all there, right in the press releases.

First it begins with the Superman sightings. Now how many times — *how many* — were we subjected to continued reports of Elvis being spotted here, there, and everywhere, long after he died.

Elvis at K-Mart. Elvis at Burger King. Elvis at Red Target stores. Elvis at the A&P. He wandered through *Bloom County*. We saw him picking up his newspaper in *Eerie, Indiana*. There was a song, for crying out loud, called "Elvis Is Everywhere" ("Why are ships vanishing in the Bermuda Triangle? Elvis needs boats") and for a while that seemed pretty true.

I, however, still cling to the belief that Elvis is dead, but Andy Kaufman, the world's greatest bender of reality, is in fact alive and going around doing his Elvis impression for gullible shoppers at King Kullen.

And that leads us into the next step of Elvis worship, which is being faithfully followed by DC — namely the Elvis/Superman imitators. Oh, sure, there were people who did Elvis impressions before he died, but that's nothing compared to what we've seen since.

Elvis impersonators by the truckload have paraded across the American consciousness. And now DC, in presenting the life of Kal-Elvis, is dutifully giving us four Superman impersonators.

Does it matter if any of them really looks like Superman? Of course not. Look at the real-life parallel.

We've seen young Elvis. Old Elvis. Fat Elvis. Thin Elvis. Black Elvis. White Elvis. Hawaiian Elvis. Japanese Elvis. Baby Elvis. Toddler Elvis. *Honeymoon in Vegas* gave us the Utah chapter of the Flying

Elvises. Some look and sound authentic; others aren't remotely so. It doesn't matter. They're still walking around, singing around, twisting around, and calling themselves Elvis.

Some people, of course, know that they're just dressing up. But I saw a guy interviewed who said, with all seriousness, that Elvis was channeling through him — that he *was*, in fact, Elvis.

And since comic books are a heightened, exaggerated reality, we're seeing an exaggerated version (but not too much, really) of the Elvis-imitator syndrome. An alien takes up residence in the Fortress. Some determined Elvis imitator could occupy Graceland and maybe even start convincing people that he's Elvis back from the dead. Hell, I'll bet anything that tons of folks would believe it.

I just hope that DC really takes the opportunity to carry this all the way. Enough of these tasteless cardboard coffins. Let's go for tasteless and tacky.

I want my velvet Superman painting.

I want my Superman wine decanter (head or full figure, preferably both).

I want my *Superman Live!* stage show.

I want my TV show about a young Superman. (Oops — already had that. Sorry.)

I want the Utah chapter of the Flying Supermen, and baby, you'll believe they can fly.

I want my musical Superman sweatshirt, sold exclusively through QVC (playing "Up, up, and Away," I suppose).

I want my commemorative Superman plates, which may or may not go up in value. I want my Superman medals from the Franklin Mint. I want my Superman books, CDs, tapes, keychains, T-shirts, poseable dolls, collectible dolls, and toilet paper.

Dammit. I want my Superman postage stamp, so I can stand in line for two days to get one.

And best of all — I want DC to introduce women with small children who they claim are Superman's out-of-wedlock offspring.

("See here — Little Kal has a spitcurl, just like his dad. And he's invulnerable, too. Watch — I'll bounce this rock off his head. *Klonnk* Oh, look, he's pretending he's unconscious. He's so clever, just like his superdaddy was. Wake up, honey. ")

Yes, I want all that — and more. Why?

Because Kal-Elvis would have wanted it that way.

(Peter David, writer of stuff, will be organizing a pilgrimage to the Fortress of Solitude, where a candle lighting ceremony will be held. Send applications, and $10,000 in small, nonsequential bills to cover airfare and sundries, to To Be Continued, PO Box 239, Bayport, New York 11705.)

THE CON GAME (July 23, 1993)

Historical Notes:

(This is the one major DC piece that's not about Superman. Although the full names of all the principal players appeared in the original column, I have opted to use just the first names of some of the key individuals for this reprinted version. I'm not sure why, but my gut instinct is that I should, and generally I try to pay attention to such warnings. The events themselves are entertaining enough as is.)

I am about to tell you the shocking secret of The Con Game. Please do not tell anyone else, since you wouldn't want to ruin it for them.

The Con Game occurred at the recent Great Eastern Convention in New York. Last time I wrote about Great Eastern, you will remember, it was the site of the Image incite-the-crowd-to-riot fiasco. I wasn't there this time around, having a previous commitment for the weekend.

A week or so later, however, I received a phone call from friend and occasional collaborator James Fry. James, speaking with great ire, alerted me to something that had happened to a friend of his at the convention. It seemed such a bizarre story that I promptly contacted all concerned to find out just what had gone down.

And now *BID* will tell you:

Conventions routinely use volunteer workers to flesh out their staff. It's a fairly harmless *quid pro quo*: Volunteer workers are given free admission (plus free food at the classier conventions), and hobnob with the celebrities, in exchange for which they work their little keisters off doing whatever is needed to be done.

Charles, it would appear, has a shapelier keister than most. Charles, you see, is a professional female impersonator and "real life transvestite." And Charles, who intended to volunteer at Great Eastern, decided that he was going to endeavor to get into the spirit of things by engaging in a time-honored convention practice. He was going to show up in costume.

"It was my idea," he said. "I told them before I came that I wanted to do it."

Whoever it was that Charles told, it wasn't convention organizer Fred Greenberg. Nevertheless, Fred subsequently stated that, in principle, he "had no problem with it."

The "it" being Charles' choice of costume.

He showed up as Catwoman.

Specifically, in an eerily accurate recreation of the leather number that Michelle Pfeiffer sported in *Batman Returns*.

Charles entered the convention floor in full costume, before the convention even started.

By early that afternoon, he was being escorted out, at the direct request of DC Comics personnel.

The stated reason? Fred Greenberg was told, "We don't want (him) here because he's getting pictures taken (of himself). This is not how we want Catwoman represented." Charles was presenting, they told Greenberg, "the wrong tone" for the character.

Keep in mind, of course, that Catwoman — in current DC continuity — has an origin based in sado-masochism, lesbianism, and prostitution. Even the movie version had massive sexual overtones. Catwoman has never exactly been The Flying Nun, and her sexuality has only become more explicit over the years.

With all that baggage that the "real" character is carrying, the concept of being portrayed by a male would seem relatively tame. Particularly when the portrayal was so perfect that no one was tumbling to it — no one, up to and including Jim Balent, the artist on the Catwoman series.

The moment Catwoman made her appearance (for clarity's sake, we'll simply call Charles "her" when referring to the costumed persona) on the convention floor, Jim Balent spotted her. "The costume was very good," said Jim. "I was impressed that a fan had dressed up in that costume."

So impressed, in fact, that Jim immediately went over to her and brought her to the DC booth, to pose next to a Catwoman illustration. Jim himself also posed with her, spoke with her, and even talked to her about future modeling work for a series of fantasy artworks — all completely unaware of the model's gender.

Jim's offer was subsequently withdrawn (with no resentment on either side) upon learning that Catwoman was being portrayed by a man. "When I told the editors (that it was a guy), they laughed," he said.

Not laughing, however, were DC representatives Rich and Vince.

Late that morning, according to Charles, "My supervisor for the day came over to me and said that they (DC) didn't want me 'hanging around' their area." The reason was not stated. Catwoman was surprised, considering her earlier warm reception, but obeyed their desire that she keep her distance.

So although Catwoman's appearance and deportment was good enough to fool a professional artist and dozens of fans who were asking to have their picture taken with her, it was apparently not good enough to stay within proximity of the company that published her.

And, eventually, not good enough even to stay at the convention.

Because a few hours later, at about 2:30, according to Fred Greenberg, Rich called him over and informed him, in no uncertain terms, that the masquerade was to be brought to an end: That either Catwoman was to leave the convention entirely or change out of the costume into street clothes. "He said that this is just the exact kind of thing they didn't want," said Greenberg. "I was unclear on what the reason was."

Was Catwoman off the mark somehow? That didn't seem likely. The portrayal was so good, according to Jim Balent, that "I thought she was working for DC or Fred Greenberg."

Perhaps that was the concern: That the costume was so good, it seemed "official." But was Catwoman, then, to be penalized because the job was too good?

Of course, technically, parading around in a company-owned-creation costume is a violation of trademark. And if Catwoman had put up a sign that said, "Have your picture taken with Catwoman, $5," that would have been dangerously into the territory of unauthorized appearance.

Catwoman, however, was doing no such thing. Merely obliging various fans by posing.

Furthermore, in Greenberg's 17 years of putting on conventions, plenty of folks had shown up in costume and no one from DC had ever requested that they be removed. In fact, at shows such as the San Diego Comic Convention, DC gives out cash prizes at the masquerade for best costume.

So the sudden cold feet about the notion of a fan-in-costume struck Greenberg, he said, as somewhat odd.

Nevertheless, Fred felt he had no option.

He took Charles aside and apprised him of the situation.

"I made it clear to him," Greenberg said, "that it was not my doing. I was very much on the guy's side. But he was getting me into hot water with DC. I told him, 'DC doesn't want you to wear it. Either take it off or leave.'"

But Charles had no clothes to change into. "Would it really be preferable," asked Charles, "if I were walking around in my underwear instead of the costume?"

Trying to come to some sort of accord, Charles asked that he be allowed to speak directly to the folks at the DC table who wanted him gone. Fred agreed.

As they approached the DC table, a man walked over with his two small daughters. He had a camera, and asked Fred, "Can they have their pictures taken with Catwoman?"

"Not right now," Fred said hurriedly, and hastened Catwoman on her way, leaving the puzzled father and children behind. It was that single moment, Charles said, that he found more upsetting than anything else about the entire incident.

There was a crowd around the DC table, and Fred instructed Catwoman to hang back while he approached Rich. He told Rich of Catwoman's desire to try and sort matters out.

According to Greenberg, Rich told him, "Listen, I said I want this person out. I've said everything I'm going to say."

And that was that. Minutes later, DC reps had managed to accomplish what Batman hasn't managed to do in half a century: Get rid of Catwoman.

It didn't occur to Charles to turn around and buy a ticket into the convention. It would have put Fred into an interesting position because, as the convention organizer, he felt he had to accede to DC's wishes when it came to a volunteer worker. But would he have then kept out a paying customer? "It would have raised some interesting legal questions," he said. In all likelihood, Charles would have been able to march back in in full costume.

But the fact that he was ordered gone by DC had taken a lot of the fun out of it for him. However the cat, as the song goes, came back — by writing to DC, complaining of his treatment.

And DC, to its credit, moved quickly. After looking into the incident, DC veep Paul Levitz wrote to Charles. The letter said, in part:

"Please accept our apologies for the incident at the Great Eastern comic convention.

"For the record, neither our policies nor, based on our investigation, the motivations of our staffer, were based on the gender of the person in the costume or your possible sexual orientation. Our policies are simply to try to ensure that when a promotional event is staged — only the authorized licensee of DC provides the talent — to ensure that our trademarks are protected in accordance with the legal requirements placed on us by the trademark law. However, what you did, showing up in a comic convention in costume, is a tradition going back over two decades, and is one we are entirely supportive of.

"We believe that this experience aside, you have no reason to brand DC as homophobic, and that we have exhibited a sincere (as opposed to simply 'politically correct') commitment to nondiscrimination based on sexual preference — I hope you will accept our apology for this incident, and continue to be a satisfied customer."

It's a remarkable bit of irony, really. When Marvel Comics had Northstar publicly state that he was gay, it caused a major media brouhaha. Marvel then promptly closed ranks, issued terse, "No comments" to all subsequent inquiries, and a wave of conservatism swept through the editorial ranks (the first victim being my own story about abortion in X-Factor which was gutted and rewritten into near-incomprehensibility.)

This is as opposed to DC which, in its mainline comics and Vertigo line, has had consistent portrayals of people with all manner of sexual orientation — and nary a word has been said about it. And then, bam, this happens.

And it had to be Catwoman. Catwoman, the single kinkiest character in mainline DC continuity. If anyone should have an aura of "anything goes" surrounding her, it's Catwoman.

Now if any Marvel sales or promotional folks are reading this and chuckling to themselves, and thinking, "Wow, we'd never have reacted like that — "

Charles' next costume is going to be either Storm or Psylocke.

Tread carefully in how you proceed, gentlemen, lest the cat be once again be let out of the bag.

(Peter David, writer of stuff will be appearing as Wonder Woman at the next Great Eastern Convention — or maybe not.)

Historical Notes:

1) I was later informed that Catwoman's origin did not feature lesbianism. Sorry. I thought it did. Wonder how they missed it?

Part 2: "Defiant, Dammit"

As of this writing, the first issue of Defiant's new line, *Warriors of Plasm*, has hit the stands. I haven't quite been able to slog through it yet; then again, with dialogue like "He must have sensed my nodes tweaking! Stand ready, Zom! I wish to be dripping with splatter gore for my lust-mate!" being delivered by a female with breasts alternating between cantaloupe and watermelon size, it could take a while.

Nevertheless, I did not enjoy writing the following column. Some of that should be self-evident. I'll explain the rest at the end.

SHOOTER IN THE FOOT (June 18, 1993)

This is, like, so embarrassing.

I missed it.

I flat out missed it.

I come back from Romania, crack open *CBG*, and find Jim Shooter being pilloried. And I missed the article that kicked it off.

You have to understand: When I get *CBG*, I first do a cursory skim: read all the short items; save the long stuff for later. Except, with everything that's been happening over the past month, I never got a chance to go back and read the lengthy Defiant coverage that uncorked a massive flow of corrections.

Consequently, Messrs. Miller, Byrne, Gerber, Mlle. Duffy, *et al.*, have all beaten me to the punch.

Which means I must take another angle, because this can't be ignored. I shall endeavor to do so, therefore, by commenting not on the *CBG* piece but other pieces of disinformation that are floating around.

The thing that really hurts is that I like Jim. I think he's got a very clear creative vision, and you've got to give him credit for the fact that, like the Energizer Bunny, he keeps going and going.

A lot of people are asking: Does Jim Shooter *really believe* everything he's saying? I tend to think so: I mean, he'd have to be out of his mind to lie blatantly in such a public forum, and I hardly think he's nuts.

The problem, it seems, is that Jim is padding his resumé. This is not a federal offense. Lots of people do it. And most people do so in relative privacy. Jim, however, unwisely chose to do so in a public forum, and it's being seen — not wrongly — as an attempt to rewrite history.

What's a pity is that this revisionism — indeed, this entire "I am the greatest" chest-thumping by Jim and his major crony (to whom I shall get in a short while) — is wildly unnecessary. A lot of people admired what he achieved with Valiant. A lot of people thought he got shafted. And a lot of people were rooting for him with the birth of Defiant. He had more good will going for him now than ever before.

And he's blown it.

If Jim has ever wondered, in the past, why things keep happening to him — why he seems to be in a position of power and suddenly comes tumbling down from it — then this, the greatest and most needless P.R. debacle since Zoe Baird, answers the question beyond any doubt: He's bringing it on himself.

If only it were limited to *CBG*. But it's not. It's spreading, like a fungus or a rash, poisoning Defiant's send-off.

I read in amazement, for example, Jim's four-page presentation of his life story (which I hear was blown up to billboard size at Wonder-Con.) Breathtaking in its pomposity, it intersperses over-blown copy with sub-par art.

We witness, for example, Stan Lee (or his hand, at least) passing the editorial reins of Marvel to Jim (wearing a pinstripe suit with clashing tie).

Evocative of the Sistine Chapel ceiling, Stan's outstretched hand tells Jim that "Marvel's in your hands — !" and Jim replies, "I won't let you — or Spider-Man — down, Stan!"

After a number of questionable claims, we learn that "Jim was fired by the 'bad guys' for standing up for creators' rights, which were routinely violated by Marvel at that time. They even attacked his reputation, in order to erode the credibility of his accusations."

Now, generally, why someone is fired is their own business. But when someone makes a public proclamation of the reasons, then historical footnotes are being invited.

I mean, here I thought that Jim was fired because he managed to hack off just about everyone at Marvel. At one point he wrote a state-of-the-Marvel-union memo (admittedly at the behest of then-owners New World, who wanted his opinions) which thoroughly vilified everyone from Marvel President Jim Galton on down. That memo burned so many bridges for him that his power base was forever crippled.

Creator's rights? If that was the case, he might have done a better job letting creators know he was on their side and perhaps even gotten them onto his. As it was, one major creator had a party and burned Jim in effigy. Another major name sent a formal note to Mike Hobson, threatening to resign if Jim were not fired. Perhaps Jim considered himself a defender of creators, but there were far too many who were anxious to see him go. At the very least, Jim suffered from terminal communications problems.

He cites the same reason for his departure from Valiant: creator's rights. Now I've heard a lot of reasons, from all sides, as to why Valiant kicked Jim loose. And as close as I've been able to determine, the only creator whose rights were being screwed with was Jim.

After this we're treated to more sub-par art, featuring Jim raising his fist in defiance (naturally), protesting his fate and/or promising that he shall ultimately triumph. Well, not with too many more overblown "resumés" like this, he won't.

The most curious claims are that Jim was "a major contributor to the development of the Comics Direct Market." This immediately caught my attention. I was there during that time, and the main things I remember were that (a) Jim was constantly at loggerheads with direct sales department head Carol Kalish, (b) Jim frequently said that the sales department served no purpose and that the comics would sell themselves without the efforts of the sales department (a sentiment echoed twice in his resumé when he says that "All we had to do was tell great stories"), and (c) Jim pointed out a number of times that comics had been around long before the direct market — i.e., comics did fine before direct sales and would presumably do fine if direct sales went away.

What caught my attention even more was an interview in Capital City's May 1993 *Internal Correspondence*, in which Jim explains his recollections of the origins of the direct market. He describes how instrumental he was in developing and catering to the direct market, to the point where he even includes himself into the development of Marvel's cash register program, in which Marvel sold cash registers to direct retailers.

This I found particularly bizarre. Carol was the one who developed the idea of the register program, after her many trips to retailers discerned the repeated absence of this fundamental piece of in-store equipment. And I was the one who contacted register companies, came up with which models to sell, and learned how to operate them. Now if by "We did all that," Jim means Marvel Comics, then fine. But that's not remotely the way it comes across — and since Jim is a journeyman wordsmith, he should be aware of what he's saying.

In the same interview, he credits Marvel's expansion into the direct market to himself and Chuck Rozanski. The *Internal Correspondence* editors, in a lengthy footnote, immediately point out the inaccuracy of Jim's recollections. But the connection between Jim and Chuck is a bond that remains to this day — and one that served to send me absolutely ballistic not that long ago.

Chuck Rozanski of Mile High Comics and I go back quite a few years. I remember vividly when Chuck, through his distribution outlet "Alternate Realities," was returning box upon box of Marvel comics claiming that they were damaged and unsalable. Not only was his damage return rate many times higher than any other distributor, but the comic books he returned were of such pristine mint quality that other distributors who happened by the office when Chuck's "returns" showed up would snap up entire boxes.

When Carol and I (as her assistant) cracked down on him, Chuck retaliated. He told all his subscribers to write letters of protest to me (since I was the one checking over the comic books), falsely claiming that Marvel had revised its damage return policies. And his "Mile High" subscribers sent me a bunch of letters, variously questioning my sanity, my parentage, and my suitability to do my job. It was the first fan mail I ever got.

Even with Carol long gone, Chuck has apparently managed to nurse a grudge against her, and it came bubbling forth last month in his newsletter, "N.I.C.E. News Monthly."

In his opinion column, he put forward a theory as to how, in his judgment, Marvel had become a second rate market force. And in the course of this dissertation, he managed to pin all the blame on Carol, stating that she had single-handedly caused the downfall of Jim Shooter, the editorial emasculation of Tom DeFalco, and — apparently — precipitated the ruin of Marvel Comics and perhaps even the Western World.

If you thought that Jim was busy absolving himself of any blame for his misfortune, you ain't seen nothing until you've perused the gospel according to Jim's leading acolyte, Chuck Rozanski.

As far as Chuck is concerned, Jim Shooter was a helpless victim at the hands of the demonic Carol. Carol allegedly "used her guile to exploit the weaknesses in Shooter's interpersonal skills," driving wedges between him and creators and ultimately causing his downfall. Supposedly this lesson was not lost on Tom DeFalco, who (in Chuck's view) tremblingly toed the line, afraid of incurring the Wrath of Kalish. Carol ostensibly wanted nothing but to be president of Marvel Comics, steamrolled over everyone who stood in her way, and — when she died short of her goal — left Marvel rudderless.

At first I was willing to attribute all of this to Chuck's fevered imaginings. I was certain that Jim had too much class to try to pass the buck that way. Certainly, I reasoned, there would be no way that Jim would hold himself *completely blameless* in not one, but two major career mishaps.

Now, though, I'm not so sure.

Either way, Chuck has put forward a conspiracy theory that would give Oliver Stone the giggles.

So now one of the "bad guys" in Jim's resume is named. Carol Kalish got Jim Shooter fired from Marvel with her "guile." Curiously, Chuck doesn't bother to explain to his readers how Carol managed to reach not only across companies, but from beyond the grave, to get Jim ousted from Valiant.

No, he's too busy displaying his staggering ignorance of Carol's career goals. Carol, who was so determined to be president of Marvel that, during the height of Jim's reign at Marvel, she was ready to accept an offer at DC. She had one foot out the door and her hat on, but Marvel coaxed her back because it valued her contributions.

His scenario for her actions at Marvel once Tom took over are even more ludicrous. During the last year or so of her life, she wasn't even involved with marketing main-line Marvel editorial product. She was busy developing a line of religious books, Civil War comics, and "greeting card" comics to expand Marvel's market. I'm sure Tom would hardly share Chuck's characterization of his quaking in terror at Carol's presence — especially considering that, during the time that Carol and Tom's paths did overlap, Tom did not hesitate to shoot down any series concepts put forward by direct sales if he didn't want to do them editorially.

Furthermore, if Carol had been around another six months, she most likely would have been gone from Marvel entirely. She was all set to start her own publishing firm. So much for her plans to rule Marvel Comics.

Certainly this is not historical revisionism on par with, say, those who claim the Holocaust never happened (annoy a Jew, get a Nazi metaphor; happens every time). But Jim Shooter and Chuck Rozanski are trying to remake the world into a place where dark and sinister beings indulge in evil doings, and the proud warriors are being overwhelmed. Jim Shooter, Chuck Rozanski — two voices of reason and truth in a universe of malevolence. In short, a comic book continuum.

I am very, very afraid that Jim is going to be hurt by this column. I think he has viewed me as a friend, and I have been. Certainly I've lent a sympathetic ear on several occasions.

It is in that spirit, Jim, that I say this: You had it made. You had managed to portray yourself as an underdog, gaining support and sympathy even from those who couldn't stand you previously.

And now you're botching it.

All you had to do, in your own words, was "tell great stories." But in the comic books, for crying out loud. Not in your press release. Not in your resumé.

The American public has little patience for those who blow their own horn too loudly. It is far better to err on the side of being self-effacing than on the side of "I'm the greatest thing since the creation of fire" — particularly when you're trying to start up a company.

As it is, I find myself looking at the Defiant symbol with a new view. The solitary illuminated window, indicating — it now appears — that the lights are on, but nobody is home.

Furthermore, the castle tower itself makes me think of the matching chess piece. The one that's sometimes called the castle, but is also commonly referred to as the rook.

Someone is being rooked here, Jim. You, the readers, all those whose participation in Marvel Comics and the direct market growth is being usurped by you.

Pick up your rook, move it back a square or two, and take stock of the board — before it's too late. Before you've maneuvered yourself right out of the game.

(Peter David, writer of stuff, invites anyone who cares to tell Chuck Rozanski just what they think of his opinion of Carol to write to him at Mile High Comics, 2151 W. 56th Avenue, Denver, CO, 80221. And tell him I was happy to return the favor.)

Historical Notes:

1) When Chuck wrote his original revisionist look at Marvel history, I was so incensed that I wrote him a letter so filled with fury that I never sent it. If not for Chuck's original piece, I might never have written this one.

In response to the above, Cat Yronwode wrote a guest editorial in **CBG** *that made my column look like a love letter. In that same issue a response ran from Chuck, which basically claimed that he was actually trying to compliment Carol because he had hated her so much. Yes, you read that right.*

2) John Byrne wrote in and said "Score one for Peter." It was one of only two instances where he openly agreed with me.

Part 3: Multiple Image

On Feb. 21, 1992, the Image creators sent their publicity wagon rolling.

On that same date, I knocked the wheels off.

Image has never forgiven me.

In various interviews and public forums, Image representatives and their supporters have endeavored to ignore the substance of what I said and concentrated, instead, on all the varied nefarious reasons I *must* have had for saying them.

For Image, you see, was composed of freelancers. And in the freelance community, there are the freelancers (who are good) and the publishers (who are bad). So for me to criticize freelancers would mean that I was in opposition to good, which means that I was bad. Therefore I was jealous, or flacking for Marvel, or whatever else.

The truth was that Image wanted to be considered in the same ballpark as Marvel and DC. But while Marvel and DC took the considerable lumps that BID dished out with relative stoicism and even occasional good humor, Image proved remarkably thin skinned.

Did it ever.

IMAGE: THE LOONY BEGINNING (Feb. 21, 1992)

I must admit, I'm a bit spoiled.

To backtrack: People within the industry had been hearing the "buzz" (just as the press release says) about Image Comics for some weeks now. A group of friends band together to form their own business (friends and business; now there's a volatile mix; I hope everyone's got good lawyers going over the contracts) and produce their own comics.

And it wasn't just that they were creating their own titles. It's that, to varying degrees, they were walking away from Marvel, citing an assortment of reasons, none of which was particularly flattering to that publisher.

This is nothing new, of course. Any number of creators have become disenchanted with one or both of "The Big Two" and moved either to already-existing independents or self-publishing.

That's where the part about my being spoiled comes in. Creators such as Wendy and Richard Pini, Frank Miller, Alan Moore, Dave Sim: These are people with talent and vision whose muses have produced titles whose subject matter doesn't fit in with the Marvel and DC universes. Alan Moore did not cite disgust with DC's business practices and go off to develop a new character named "Muck Monster." He did *Big Numbers*. The Pinis had so much confidence in their elves that they were driven to produce *Elfquest* themselves, which thrives to this day, while Marvel's own "take" on elves, *Weirdworld*, vanished without a trace a decade ago. (Ironically, Marvel's Epic imprint later reprinted *Elfquest*.)

So when a creator boldly announces that he's off to start his or her own line, my presumption and hope is that it's going to be something new and visionary. It doesn't have to be highly marketable. Indeed, Marvel's and DC's main flaw is that titles are expected to draw significantly higher sales than an independent would reasonably expect for his piece of the market pie. So *Hard Boiled* doesn't have to sell like *X-Men*. No one expects it to.

If Todd said, "I've been dying to do a good romance comic book," I'd be thrilled. If Erik said, "My life's goal is to produce a solid Western," I'd be impressed.

So what's Image publishing?

Super-heroes.

Young super-heroes. SWAT-Team super-heroes. Young free-lance super-heroes. A group of super-heroes.

I mean — haven't we got Marvel and DC for that? Why have *X-Force* clones, when we've got *X-Force*?

I haven't seen them yet, of course. Perhaps there will be some startling vision that makes us see super-heroes in ways we've never seen them before. It's possible. After all, not all super-heroes are alike. *New Warriors* and *Watchmen* are nominally both about super teams, but are just a *tad* different in tone and style.

Can we get any idea in advance of publication as to whether the creators involved can pull it off, based on their previous work? Judging from their own press release, no, we can't get an idea. Why? Because of the alarming sentiments voiced by both Rob Liefeld and Erik Larsen. (And let me make it clear that I like both the guys personally; it's what's said in the press release that I'm reacting to.)

"I think that in many ways we've been holding back," says Erik. "Most of our best creations have yet to be seen and will be seen under the Image imprint for the first time."

Excuse me? *Holding back?*

Am I the only one stunned by this comment?

If you're unimpressed by Erik's recent work, don't worry. If you can barely remember such characters of his as Shrapnel, take heart. It has nothing to do with lack of ability or talent. By his own admission, Erik's just been dogging it — "holding back," as he says, withholding his full imagination until a better opportunity came along.

Unless I'm inferring incorrectly here, the concept that fans are plunking down good money while figuring that a creator is giving it his all, every time out, doesn't factor in. "Oh, this villain I just thought up is too good for Marvel readers! I'll hold back!"

Rob echoes the sentiments. The release states that Rob "confirmed that his enthusiasm for the new line of comics has him bursting at the seams." (What a concept. "Rob, are you bursting at the seams?" "Why, yes I am. Thanks for asking. These 501s are *tight*.") And Rob goes on to add, "Not only do we get to share with fandom our finest creations, but we get to own them as well. What better incentive to do your best work?"

Well, gee. Lemme think. Pride in workmanship? Commitment to a creative ideal? Are the retailers and fans who bought millions of copies of *X-Force* being told that their support was insufficient incentive?

It gives me the same queasy feeling that I get when I see one of those detergent commercials, wherein Woman X says to Woman Y. "What? How can you still be using Dayglo on your clothes? Don't you know about Dayglo *Plus*?" And she proceeds to tell us how wonderful the new product is in comparison to the old and clearly inferior product. Which makes you wonder why, if the original product wasn't all that hot, you were ever buying it in the first place. You feel like a fool because you supported the initial detergent. And you start to wonder if you're simply being taken to the cleaners.

I keep trying to determine what the guys might actually *mean* rather than what they're *saying*. Perhaps they mean that pride of ownership is what they take the greatest joy in. But again, here's where my selfish viewpoint kicks in. I happen to think that some of my finest creations, purely in terms of merit and the effect they had on the audience, are works involving characters I did not own. So it saddens me a bit that the guys seem to feel that lack of ownership is a stumbling block to full pride in their work.

Or perhaps it's just all hype, the same way as when Stan Lee would say, "Marvel Comics, the greatest works since Bill Shakespeare discovered the pen!" Now does Stan really, truly believe that Lee/Kirby *Thor* or *Fantastic Four*, as good as they were, are on par with, say, *Hamlet*? I tend to doubt it. I doubt anyone really thinks Stan believes it. But quality hype is stuff that's so over-the-top that you know to take it with a grain of salt.

Furthermore, quality hype should not denigrate the previous work of those people whose work you're now trying to sell. Those "fans and retailers" being offered a chance to "get in on the ground floor of an exciting new comics universe" thought they were doing that when they bought into the newly revitalized Marvel mutant universe, or the new *Spider-Man* title — and are now being told that the creators themselves don't consider that to be work reflective of their best efforts.

Speaking of Stan and Jack, I can't pass up Erik's claim that Image is "The most exciting thing to happen to comics since the creation of the Marvel Universe." Oh, honestly, Erik. Has it occurred to you that if Stan, Jack, and Steve had likewise been "holding back," there wouldn't have been a Marvel universe to bring you the measure of fame you now enjoy?

But you can point out that people like Jack Kirby and Steve Ditko did their best work for Marvel (and Siegel and Shuster for DC) and have not shared proportionately in the money generated by their creations.

You would be correct.

The troubles of the various creators in those instances, and many others, have been well-documented. No one covered themselves with glory. On the one hand, creators complained about perfectly legitimate deals that, with 20-20 hindsight, they wish they hadn't made. They wanted a bigger share to which they weren't legally entitled. On the other hand, corporations came across as heartless, inconsiderate, boorish and ungrateful to the people whose imaginations created the six-figure incomes some executives enjoy, the millions of dollars in licensing fees filling the company coffers.

It used to be that the only business considerations of comics were held by publishers. No more. We have a readership base that is made up, in large measure, of people who see comics, not as entertainment but as investments. And it would seem that we are also developing a creative base that is wising up, as it were. Who owns the story is becoming as great, if not greater, a consideration than what the story is actually about.

If Rob said, "I'm planning to do a series about a team of hermaphrodite bisexuals, and in the first issue they go back in time and discover Jesus was a vampire," my feeling would be, "Yup. That sure wouldn't have flown at the Big Two." But there's no discussion of subject matter that would have run afoul of corporate standards. Instead the release talks of crossover storylines, team-ups and a shared universe — all stuff that not only is S.O.P. at Marvel and DC, but occasionally gets flak as being a mere marketing ploy.

Instead, the main reason that the guys seem excited, according to the release, is that they own the characters themselves and, if there's money to be made with those same filthy business considerations that people use to castigate Marvel and DC, then, by gosh, the guys are going to make that money.

This is a significant consideration. Some headway has been made in the Big Two for creator remuneration, but not enough. For example, all those Spider-Man T-shirts: Todd didn't get a dime off those. That, to my mind, has been and continues to be unfair. But if a "Spawn" T-shirt comes out, the money goes to Todd — I presume.

Malibu Publisher Dave Olbrich discusses the business end in the press release, stating that the deal, in addition to creative freedom, provides "better earning potential for artists and writers than ever before. Malibu is proud and privileged to help pioneer this new relationship from which the creators will clearly profit as much as the publishing company."

Profit, indeed. Sources said that Malibu was offering Image anywhere from 70% to 95% of the line's net profits. In a separate conversation, Dave confirmed that the numbers were, indeed, "in that neck of the woods."

Eddie Murphy has commented (not to me, mind you) that an offer of sharing in net profits is "a monkey deal" — meaning you'd have to be as dumb as a monkey to make it. (Putting aside that an infinite number of monkeys working for an infinite period could produce the works of Shakespeare — although probably not an issue of *Thor*. Hey, maybe Stan was right after all.)

The point Murphy was making is that net means nothing. Gross is where the action is, and numbers can be crunched very easily, so that when it comes time for the net profits, you wind up with *nada*. Hollywood bookkeeping is legendary for this (Remember that *Coming to America*, one of Paramount's big summer hits, was still in the red when Art Buchwald won his lawsuit).

Dave Olbrich, however, promises better things for Image. "I'm thinking in the long term," he told me. Although obviously a few months of non-existent net profits would benefit Malibu, it would most probably alienate Image and, Olbrich pointed out, "When you do things in the long-term perspective, you have to keep that in mind. There's no long-term profit in violating trust."

Furthermore, Malibu and Image are agreeing ahead of time as to what type of expenses qualify as documentable costs, to reduce or eliminate the chances of unpleasant surprises. This is, of course, only a partial solution, since actual dollar amounts can't be predetermined. On the other hand, it eliminates the possibility of the sort of trickery in which movie studios engage. To make an outrageous example, Image isn't going to have to worry about going to Malibu and saying, "What's this part of the gross, where you took out $20,000 for limos," to which Malibu replies, "Oh, that's a legitimate expense. We hate to walk to work."

The bottom line for Olbrich is, he told me, that he's making every effort to deal in good faith since he's "not interested in winding up in a worse position than when I started."

I'm left, then, with only a couple of final thoughts. First, I can't wait to see what happens, if one of the creators has a falling out with the other guys and wants to take his character over to, say, Dark Horse. Can he guest-star characters he helped co-create for Image? What happens to licensing, particularly if the split is acrimonious?

Second, Image is going to boil down to the question of: What's really selling? Is it the specific creators? Or is it actually the comic books that the creators are on? It seems the guys are attentive to the monetary bottom line. If that's a major consideration, then what's going to generate more money in the long run for Rob Liefeld — *X-Force*, which he doesn't own, or *Youngblood* which he does. Which will bring in more for Erik — royalties on *Spider-Man* or *The Dragon*?

With the Marvel titles, they're backed up by thirty years of Marvel's aggressively cultivated audience base, distribution, promotion, marketing, and editorial power, all of which helped to push the masterminds of Image to the forefront of fan attention. But fan attention is notoriously fickle. They'll be counting on that selfsame audience base to support their solo efforts, without the benefit of one of The Big Two pushing them. The fact that *Youngblood* sold 300,000 copies is meaningless. Sold to distributors does not equal sold to customers. Just ask the retailers at the recent Great Eastern convention who had *X-Men* #1 in their three-for-$1 boxes.

To a degree, I see Image right now as a skier just hitting the upward ramp of a jump. Hurled upward into the air by forces of which he is only a part, he glories in the freedom that is his.

Then he looks down.

The question is whether Image is going to wind up looking like Jean-Claude Killy, or the guy who tumbles tail-over-teakettle at the beginning of *Wide World of Sports*.

As always, the fans will be the ultimate arbiters of that. Will the fans follow their faves? Or will it be like the movie actor who leaves Hollywood, goes to Broadway for a year and wins a Tony Award, only to return to Hollywood and discover that, as far as everyone there is concerned, he's dropped off the face of the Earth for 12 months? Thus far, it's seemed as if Marvel and DC are Hollywood, and if you're not working there, then to many fans, you're out of work.

I, for one, am certainly hoping they succeed. Any guys who are nervy enough to go head-to-head against The Big Two in precisely the same genre that Marvel and DC have had a hammerlock for three decades certainly deserve the best wishes of anyone in a creative endeavor. It's been a long time since Marvel and DC have had any serious competition from anyone besides each other.

I will be very interested to see whether Image develops into a portrait — or a silhouette.

(Peter David, writer of stuff, also hears there will be a title called "Wildcats." How nice. I love Goldie Hawn movies.)

Historical Notes:

1) And this was the other time John Byrne openly agreed with me. The exact words in his letter were, "When (Peter) is right, he's right, and this time he is very right." 2) Right after my column appeared, Jim Valentino called a press conference. I have no proof that cause and effect is involved, but the timing seems rather conclusive. In the course of the conference, Ken Krueger — one of the grand old men of comics distribution — asked him a playful question about whether I was welcome in the halls of Image. Valentino — good naturedly, according to Krueger — said that I wasn't. Unfortunately neither Jim or Ken gave thought to what this would play like in cold, hard type. Jim also said that I had gone on record as saying that I would "categorically" never work for them. All this factored into the next column, which apparently cemented my reputation as an Image-hater in a way that my potshots at Marvel and DC had never managed to give me a similar rep in regard to those companies.

AND NEVER DARKEN OUR DOOR AGAIN! (April 17, 1992)

Well, I'm taking a one-week break from my travelogue of my Scotland trip in order to deal (in as expedient a manner as I can) with a question I'm getting repeatedly: When in hell did I say that I "will categorically never do a book for Image"?

I must admit, I'm a bit surprised. My original article about Image contained meticulous references to the official Image press release (plus a phone interview with Dave Olbrich.) And Jim Valentino's response was to offer an unreferenced statement by me, which is causing a good bit of confusion.

The answer to when did I say it is: Beats me.

I know I didn't say it in *CBG*, and, since this all stems from material that appeared in this publication, it's a little confusing to readers.

Did I ever say I'd *never* work for Image? I don't recall. I say a lot of stuff. Did I say it at a convention? On a computer net? Maybe. I don't know. It would have been nice if Jim had placed the alleged quotes in context, just as I've endeavored to do every time I discuss Image. Since Jim didn't, then I'll take a stab at it — at the very least, put them into an historical framework so that, if I did make such a statement, it's clear why.

Jim says that the Image crew is pretty much agreed I won't be working for them. He says they can't concur on an editor, but they can agree that I'm *persona non grata*. Thank God everyone's priorities are in place. I'm glad they've decided I'm not welcome now — especially since I turned *them* down months ago.

In all deference to Jim's contention that Image was the best-kept secret in the comics industry, I'll presume he's referring to having it kept from the fans. People *in* the industry knew about it for quite some time. I found out about it a good month or so before the official announcement, when Sam Kieth called me up.

Image (although I don't think it was called Image yet) had contacted Sam and endeavored to sign him up, telling him he could write and draw whatever he wanted. Sam, a phenomenally talented artist, said that he felt he'd need to work with a writer, to help with dialogue and such. They told him to go out and recruit one, and I was Sam's first choice.

I told Sam I wasn't interested. Mainly, I don't generally like simply dialoguing a story. I rarely do it. To me, dialogue arises from character and situation, and if it's not *my* characters and situations, then I have little emotional investment.

I believe I said at that point that I couldn't see a circumstance in which I'd work for Image. It seemed a reasonable prognostication. Everything I'd heard (and have continued to hear) seemed to indicate that writer-artists were the creator of choice at Image. I didn't fit the writer-artist category. So I doubted I'd have a place at Image. End of potential participation.

(Sure, *now* Chris Claremont's aboard, but he's top-selling, 15-year mutant king *Chris Claremont*.)

But, although I wasn't interested on my own behalf, my feelings toward the enterprise itself remained pretty much *neutral*. And I was flattered that Sam had thought of me. I very much look forward to whatever projects he might turn out.

The other time I know for sure I expressed noninterest in working for Image was after I spoke with Dale Keown, the awesomely talented artist on *The Incredible Hulk*.

Dale apprised me of a phone call he'd had with one of the Image guys (who shall remain nameless), who had tried to convince Dale to ditch working on *Hulk*. The caller told Dale that he would never get anywhere working on that title; that it would always be a low seller, that it would never receive any promotion, Dale would never be famous while on it, and the title would never pick up in sales — a dead end, career-wise.

That sounds pretty darned "anti-Marvel," and I, as a creator (and Image is ostensibly "pro-creator"), felt kind of hurt. This line of argument, by the way, was derailed after Dale sanguinely pointed out to the caller that *Hulk* sales had doubled over the past couple of years.

(I should note, by the way, that I cleared discussing the above phone calls with both Sam and Dale — just in case anyone thinks that casual conversations with me can wind up as grist for this column. Fortunately, I only heard about the Dale conversation *after* I'd written the first column, or else, instead of simply analyzing the press release, I might actually have been annoyed.)

I'm sorry if it seems as if I have it in for Image. I don't especially. It's just that they keep *saying* things that I find irresistible to comment on.

Not all of them do. Jim Lee's presentations have been uniformly well thought out, classy, and impeccably presented. His piece in *CBG* was utterly unassailable, and if everything from Image had read like that, I doubt the imprint would have attracted much comment from me beyond, "That sounds neat; I look forward to it."

But Jim Valentino — I mean, jeez, Jim, I didn't even mention you. Why did you rush into the breach?

You seem to say that the only thing on which we agree is that I wouldn't be working for Image. Not true — we agree on a number of other points.

We agree that Erik Larsen's "holding back" comment is tough to defend. My approach was merely to criticize it. Jim's was to defend it by listing everyone involved who *didn't* say it and supporting *them*.

(I hope I don't sound naive when I say that I have no clue as to why people attacked my first piece using strange methods — either by rewording what I said to suit their requirements [as Don and Maggie pointed out in one instance] or, even better, fabricating arguments and motives for me and tearing them down to show what a clod I am. Was Jack Kirby "holding back" on *New Gods*? Was John Byrne "holding back" on *Next Men*? Uh, no. I don't *think* so. I never said or implied that they were. Or better yet — I'm *jealous* because next to the Image guys, I'm so gosh-darned uncreative. Oh. OK.)

Jim and I also agree that I wasn't there when they discussed what happens if creators want to take their characters elsewhere — the answer being that they can take them and go or return as they please. OK, fine. This, of course, doesn't answer the far more difficult question I posed of co-created characters, nor does it address the notion of creators walking off in a huff and not wanting farewell parties, but litigation. As I said to begin with, friends and business can be a very volatile mix.

Again, I emphasize that I'm asking these things not because I *want* such things to happen, but instead simply because — since we're dealing with, to a certain degree, controlled chaos (there's no final arbiter, by Jim's own declarations) — I find the entire thing so intriguing. Nothing like this has ever been set up. So why is it so cretinous to be curious about it?

We agree about the notion of doing away with gimmicks such as multiple covers. Good. I've been razzing Marvel about that for ages now.

I'm fascinated by the distribution of Image comics to chains such as Wal-Mart, Toys 'R' Us, etc. On the one hand, it's good to see that Image isn't just depending upon the direct market. On the other hand, they should be wary — it's outfits such as these that raise major protests when anything truly controversial is done. Which retailers do you think created the biggest stink when Northstar came out of the closet? Yup — major distribution chains such as those who will be carrying Image. Be sure, gentlemen, not to let their considerations shape your editorial content, as Marvel is in danger of doing.

We also agree that it's a serious injustice when DC (or whoever) makes a billion dollars off a character and the creators don't share in that proportionately. I think that's fairly incontrovertible, and indeed I have said as much before.

But the statement of Jim's that I find the most intriguing is, "We are all working for a common purpose and a common goal." Since Jim doesn't specify what that might be, I'm going to speculate that it's to create a line of titles that puts the creator, and creator rights, first.

Does that seem a fair guess? Terrific.

In which case, someone should alert one of Image's founding members, Todd McFarlane.

In an interview just released by Diamond Comic Distributors, Todd is asked, "Are all these creators going to be working exclusively on Image Universe titles?" To which Todd replies, "If I was the boss, I'd say yes. But some guys are not quite in the [popularity] position we are. I'd like to see that everybody is exclusive. I think you'll find that once we pour all our energy into it, and we're flying, guys will willingly become exclusive."

Wow. That's pretty amazing. The concept of mandatory exclusivity hasn't been a factor in comics since the 1960s. What a bizarre philosophy for an Image spearhead to espouse in the 1990s: Being in favor of a *more restrictive* policy than the much, maligned Marvel or DC currently have in force.

(I can't wait for the letters that say, "Where does Peter David get off saying that Todd McFarlane would like to see exclusivity as the norm for Image? What a slob! Would David want to see John Byrne forced to be exclusive with Dark Horse?" And so on.)

Todd goes on to say that, if Image can get "every single top creative person to work for our company, and Marvel and DC have to change a rule or two, then, on a personal level, I've won my battle."

I'm sorry, Todd, but no. Anyone who wishes he could make exclusivity mandatory doesn't get to take the moral high ground.

Jim states that they could never agree on who would be a managing editor. The lack of single vision doesn't bother Todd either as, in that same interview, he says, "There isn't really going to be all that many rules. Will the continuity be perfect? No. But the continuity isn't perfect at Marvel after all these years either. Continuity doesn't mean a whole heck of a lot to me. It's the story and art that matter, not the little details." Now there's a stainless piece of logic: Marvel's been inattentive to continuity for all this time — but now it's Image's turn!

Todd also says in an *Amazing Heroes* interview that anyone who is anyone is going to work for Image. I guess I'm not going to be anyone. And I'll have to live with that knowledge for the rest of my life.

Gentlemen, please — if I may inject a suggestion into the cheerful anarchy that would seem to be S.O.P. at Image: Install Jim Lee, if not as editor, at least as the official public face for Image. Step back, let him make the public policy statements, and you guys answer questions only about your individual titles. Get coordinated, find a company line, and stick to it.

The big news about Image is not the characters, but the creators involved. You guys have made yourselves the focus. That makes you news and worthy of analysis. Since I, and other people, are giving thought to the things you're saying, *you* might want to do so as well. It might not be as much fun, but it'll keep smart-mouth commentators like me off your backs.

I beg of you — don't make me have to do this again.

(Peter David, writer of stuff, must also point out to Todd that the big double-page ad of Spawn with the collar blowing one way and the cape blowing the other is really distracting. Speaking as an accomplished blowhard, I generally like to see wind coming from only one direction. Please fix that. Thanks.)

Historical Notes:

1) The artist alluded to in the above, who tried to talk Dale Keown into leaving **Incredible Hulk***, was Todd McFarlane, former collaborator whose own career didn't seem particularly tainted by his association with the title. Todd eventually did manage to talk Dale into leaving (boasting about it in interviews); and then, after Dale resigned off the book, Todd told people Dale had, in fact, been fired. Not true. Dale didn't have the opportunity to draw #400, yes — but that was because editor Bobbie Chase was convinced that Dale would never get the book out on time, especially since he'd already quit. Her suspicions were apparently well-founded: In the year's time since Dale left Hulk to produce an Image title, only two issues of that title have come out — both of them months late.*

2) Aside from Byrne's letter in support of my first column, other letters from creators took me to task for criticizing Image and claimed ulterior motives. Curiously, those creators wound up doing comics for Image — yet no one ever accused **them** *of having ulterior motives. Go figure.*

3) The Chris Claremont title remains unpublished by Image.

SELLING OUT (Nov. 20, 1992)

Talk about your non-issues (which of course, never has stopped me before about talking about your non-issues).

When it was first announced that Alan Moore, Neil Gaiman, and Dave Sim would be writing for *Spawn*, a number of people on various computer boards and at conventions came to me with attitudes ranging from simple curiosity to almost burning indignation and asked what I thought of this development.

And I kind of shrugged and said, "Well, I think it means that fans of *Spawn* will get to read some really well-written issues." That was pretty much it.

Then we had Gary Groth in *Comics Journal* express dismay and shock at Moore's participation in this endeavor, using a tone one would associate with, say, the Pope's discovering Mother Teresa turning tricks on Broadway and 42nd. That's to be expected of Groth.

But what surprised me was that no less than Dave Sim himself so felt the need to address the "situation" immediately that he actually wrote a guest editorial for *CBG*. He, too, had been deluged by people accusing him of selling out (no, I was *not* one of them, thank you very much) and was compelled to explain his motivations as if they needed explaining. Not only that, but he described at length how he was, in fact, not taking any money for it. So there, nyah nyah, you naysayers. Take *that*.

Now maybe I'm reading something into it that Dave didn't intend, in which case, if I am, I apologize in advance. But what surprised me, you see, was that Dave seemed so *defensive* about the whole thing, when in fact he had no need to be.

The concept of donating the money to the Legal Defense Fund is, naturally, noble. But it also was presented as final proof that Dave Sim had not "sold out" when, in fact, the notion that Sim, Moore, Gaiman, or *anyone*, for that matter writing an issue of *Spawn* represents some sort of "selling out" is seriously ridiculous.

Even if Dave had kept the money — even if he'd bought a Rolls-Royce with it — it would not have mattered one bit. It's still not selling out, because making money is not inherently evil, is not against the law, and does not automatically mean that you've packed up your morals and sent them to the Cote d'Azur for the winter.

It's the whole "selling out" thing that I find so entertaining because it seems to go back to the notion some people have that the only way one can remain artistically pure is if one is either (a) not widely popular or (b) poor. Preferably both.

I suppose we have some of the truly great artists in the past to blame for this. Ignoring the fact that most notable artists were scrambling for money (or wealthy patrons), just like the rest of us, some people in today's audience feel that a true creator's place is to be starving in a garret. And if the creator suddenly finds himself able to build a wing on the garret or install a sauna, it automatically cheapens him. Success equals diminished quality.

Let me make clear that I'm hardly talking about the entire audience for art, writing, and so on. But there is a definite sector of the population out there that proceeds along the following arc, every single time:

A) They discover a director or musician or writer who is generally unknown to the public and is probably living in a sublet loft in Soho.

B) They embrace said individual, raving about his work to people within their own sphere.

C) That individual grows in popularity. The small audience is pleased, because it shows how clever and tasteful they are.

D) The individual signs a three-picture deal with Paramount Pictures or gets a record deal with Warners or lands on the *Times* best-seller list for 37 weeks.

E) The individual buys a townhouse in Manhattan and a beach home in Malibu.

F) Suddenly the individual has "sold out." His latest work is automatically inferior to his earlier work, as far as his original audience is concerned. Invariably, the diminishing occurred because the individual is now popular with the general public.

This attitude — the same attitude that is responsible for stating that writing for *Spawn* equals selling out — shows a total lack of understanding of what selling out means. Or, at least, what it means to me — and, since this is my column, that's what counts as far as *I'm* concerned.

Let's stick with writing for the moment. When one writes something, the primary reason that one should be doing it is because it's going to be either enjoyable or challenging. Money is nice (even preferable, for crying out loud) but not always necessary; however, the presence of money does not obviate the presence of the challenge or enjoyment.

Dave stated that the main reason for writing *Spawn* is that he likes and respects Todd McFarlane. That should have been all he needed to say; whether he's getting paid or not and what he's doing with the money is frankly no one's damned business.

But we live in a society that is so geared to thinking that being well paid is some bizarre artistic sin, that even someone as morally centered as Dave Sim comes across as needing to explain how he had not lined his own pocket. How annoying for Dave that he felt he had to justify it — and expeditiously, through *CBG*, as if his rep was on the line. And perhaps he felt it was.

I must admit to some surprise when he characterizes some Image creators as being in favor of being an "Engulf and Devour" style corporation (a gag corporation from Mel Brooks' *Silent Movie* that was based on Gulf & Western), while others wanted it to remain a loose coalition of comic-book creators.

When Dave first described the schism in the letters page of *Cerebus*, he didn't say who was on which side. When he now ascribed Todd to the latter, I was astonished.

Considering that Todd has stated publicly and repeatedly: that Image intends to drain Marvel Comics dry of its creative talent; that Marvel now existed merely to serve as Image's "farm team"; and that he boasted in an interview that his seducing Dale Keown off *Incredible Hulk* meant that, in regard to me, he had "had the last laugh" — all that would have led me to believe that, if any one person at Image clearly had an agenda beyond just producing good comics, it was Todd McFarlane.

If personal conversations that Dave has had with Todd lead him to conclude otherwise, then that's fine. In which case Todd might want to consider having his public persona match his private one. Continuity and all that, don'tcha know.

Back to selling out.

Does Alan Moore working for *Spawn* mean that, as Gary Groth would have it, Moore is selling out, considering his past stated disdain for super-heroes? Not automatically, no. It can just as easily be argued that Moore finds super-heroes boring because of what's currently being done with them — and looks upon the opportunity of writing *Spawn* as a challenge and opportunity to "do it right," or even show the potential of the genre as he did with *Watchmen* (although I reread it the other day, and *still* think it falls apart at the end. But that's just me).

But if I'm so quick to say what selling out *isn't*, then I should give examples of what selling out *would be*.

OK. Since we began this with Dave, let's continue it.

Dave has stated that (a) he has disdain for the major publishers, (b) *Cerebus* is his own personal vision, and (c) it will run for 300 issues and then end. People like myself who have been there since the very beginning have an understanding with Dave — a contract, if you will — that he's guiding us through all the adventures of *Cerebus* with some grand destination in mind that he will see us through to, all things being equal.

Now —

Dave gets a call from Marvel or DC. "Dave!" they say. "We love the aardvark guy. We want to buy the rights for $5 million."

"Don't be ridiculous," says Dave. "Not a penny less than $10 million."

"Sold," they say.

"Done deal," replies Dave.

Cerebus disappears from the stands, only to show up six months later, full-color, bagged with a hologram card and embossed cover, pencilled by Joe Blow, inked by Jack Spratt. Dave is off to Tahiti and has nothing to do with *Cerebus* ever again.

That would be selling out.

Selling out means being willing to abrogate your principles and moral beliefs for the purpose of making money.

Let's take Todd, since we were discussing him. He has stated, loud and at length, that he feels Marvel treats creators with no respect and that he wants to have no part of it.

Now let's say Image goes belly-up and Todd blows all his money in a lousy real estate deal.

Would going back to Marvel and drawing *Spider-Man* as work-for-hire constitute selling out?

I'd tend to think so, yeah. Certainly the most charitable thing you could call it is knuckling under for economic survival. But it's still not something they pin a medal on you for. At the very least, it falls into the "You made your bed; now lie in it" category.

Another example, and this time I'll stick my *own* neck out:

I state, here and now and for the record, that I would not be interested in writing the adventures of the dumb, monosyllabic, "Hulk Smash" Hulk.

Now let's say the title suddenly switches editors. And the editor says, "I want to go back to the dumb green Hulk. Start turning in stories that ditch everything you've done up until now and write 'Hulk Smash' stories, instead."

And I say, "Forget it. I've already stated publicly that I'm not interested in writing the character that way. You'll have to get someone else."

And the editor says, "We'll up your page rate by $20 a page."

And I respond, "So when's my first deadline?"

That would be selling out.

In terms of Image, I feel mildly responsible for the notion that making money off Image is automatically dirty somehow. It seems to me that subsequent discussions of my first column about Image led people to think that I was implying that Todd and company were forming Image "only" for money, and that they were slime for doing so.

I never said any such thing, of course. What I *did* say was that ownership and making more money was a "significant consideration" in the formation of Image — which, of course, it was and is. And I said elsewhere in the same column that the notion of the guys breaking away from the super-hero-obsessed Marvel in order to produce — well — super-heroes, didn't send me through the stratosphere, because my personal bias is towards people who aren't working for Marvel and DC because they want to do stuff they *couldn't* do on a creative basis — the way Dave Sim does, for example.

So, creatively, Image didn't send me dancing in the streets.

I never said they *shouldn't* do super-heroes, and I never said they *shouldn't* be making a pile of money off it, if they can.

And we shouldn't have come to a situation where Dave Sim has to explain his actions just because he's doing something he's going to enjoy and get paid for it.

*(Peter David, writer of stuff, wants to make one thing clear, just in case some people start reading "between the lines" — he has not been asked to write **Spawn**, he doesn't anticipate being asked to write **Spawn**, and if asked, under no circumstances would he write **Spawn**, because then Todd McFarlane really **would** have the last laugh. He doesn't care if Sean Connery said "Never say never." Everyone who quotes that ignores the fact that **Never Say Never Again** was a lousy film. Connery should have stuck to his guns.)*

Historical Notes:

1) The foregoing, which could be loosely construed as being supportive of Image, prompted a letter claiming that I was backpedaling, no doubt because I was alarmed over how well Image was doing and was trying to retrench my position. Criticize them and you're out to get them; support them and you're panicking. Image continues to polarize opinions.

2) Frank Miller joined the group of writers who wrote issues of Spawn. The final results of the efforts were — mixed. It wasn't the writers' best work, and it sure wasn't McFarlane's. Sometimes the parts exceed the whole.

Part 4: Marvel, #1 With a Bullet Hole

Marvel continues to be my major source of income.

Marvel continues to be the major butt of my publisher-aimed potshots.

Again, go figure.

OUT OF THE PHONE BOOTH AND INTO THE CLOSET (Feb. 14, 1992)

About six years ago, when the Canadian team called *Alpha Flight* first appeared in its own title (and quite a hot property it was at the time), there was a character named Northstar. And there were little, between-the-lines hints dropped by writer-artist John Byrne that Northstar was gay.

But in those days, overt portrayals of sexuality were considered a no-no. It wasn't just limited to homosexuality, either. Over at DC, *Teen Titans* unwed lovers Dick Grayson and Koriand'r were shown in bed together, but at Marvel a similar scene between the married Bruce and Betty Banner was nixed.

As for homosexuality — forget it. The only overt portrayal of gay men in Marvel's history had been the homosexual near-rape of Bruce Banner in a shower at a YMCA, lovingly depicted in the pages of *The Hulk* magazine. Since Marvel's first portrayal of gay men came across as homophobic in nature, it was not a sequence that did much for Marvel, gays, Bruce Banner, or, for that matter, your local "Y."

As for Northstar, well, for a while there, he was actually dying of AIDS, and the fact that he was gay was going to be dealt with. It was dealt with, all right: The storyline was altered midway by a decree from upstairs. The declaration was subsequently made that Northstar was, in fact, a magical being and was dying because he was away from his magical homeland for too long. Yes, that's right: He wasn't gay; he was just a fairy. That's *muuuuch* better. And the protectors of super-heroic masculinity breathed a sigh of relief. That was a close one.

But times, as they say, have changed.

The news wires have been burning up the past week as, in the pages of *Alpha Flight* #106, writer Scott Lobdell (with the full support of editor Bobbie Chase and Editor-in-Chief Tom DeFalco) did away with the sly winks and nudges and had Northstar hold a press conference in which he came out as being gay. (Or, as one news reporter rather cattily put it, and here you thought comic books were something that were kept exclusively in closets.)

It was, of course, a terrific news story. Over at DC, where sexuality had been an open topic for quite some time, they must have been gnashing their teeth. The Pied Piper casually informed Wally West that he, the Piper, was gay, and then there's the supporting cast over at *Sandman*. But none of this had caused the sort of stir that Northstar's revelation did.

Why? Because Northstar's a hero, of course. Not only that, but an eminently macho super-hero, although I must admit I have trouble relating the beefed-up steroid case rendered by artists Mark Pacella and Dan Panosian to the sleek, limber character first drawn by John Byrne. The Piper doesn't seem remotely macho. Hell, you could even make jokes about how he goes around blowing on long, narrow instruments, and that should've been the tip off right there.

It's the same sort of reaction generated when Rock Hudson or Magic Johnson went public about AIDS. When AIDs was just a dark, loathsome disease that only "homos" got, society felt it easier to deal with. It barely warranted funds to try and cure it. But when the "good guys" got it, well, that was something else altogether.

(Although, on a side-note, I've wondered what the reaction would have been if, in fact, it had been Magic Johnson's *wife* who had turned up HIV positive, from sleeping around while her husband was out on the road. Would she have had books written about her called *The Heroism of Mrs. Magic*? Or would she have been pilloried as being a slut? But that's a whole 'nother discussion in itself.)

So there was Northstar, making startling personal revelations in the middle of a slugfest (which is the customary way that heroes make such disclosures.) For those of you who haven't read it, the story actually doesn't center on Northstar's sexuality, but rather on an abandoned newborn whom Northstar finds in a garbage can. He brings the scrawny infant to a hospital, drawn at times to look like a gymnasium, or perhaps a vacant parking garage — anything *but* a hospital. (The single stick of furniture in the place is the incubator that the baby's kept in, standing alone, like the cheese, in an otherwise empty room large enough to field a basketball game.)

Tests reveal the child has AIDS, and the terminal infant's plight becomes a *cause celebre* — except to one retired Canadian hero who's in-jokingly named Major Mapleleaf (after the sarcastic nickname Banshee gave Vindicator upon his first appearance). Apparently, the Major's son died of AIDS, but "because he was gay, he didn't *rate*." Society's cavalier attitude that gays brought AIDs upon themselves and, therefore, did not deserve sympathy, has stuck in the Major's craw for years.

Rather than seek therapy, the Major misplaces his aggression on Northstar, the fight ranging through a supermarket and winding up smashing into a moving van apparently owned by Editor Chase. In the course of the battle, Northstar reveals that he himself is gay, gets lectured about being a hypocrite (while being strangled: a sure way to drive home a point), and, once the dust clears, Northstar goes public.

Oh, and as if to assure us that all is "right," the final image in the comic is a pin-up featuring Logan, Puck, and Northstar (I *think* it's Northstar; the way he's drawn, it might also be Dick Tracy) cutting up and being macho guys in a bar, each of them chugalugging what appears to be entire pitchers of beer.) To be fair: It could be a gay bar. Who knows?

It was, as noted earlier, the ideal news story, in our world as much as the Marvel universe. Reporters love stories which can be boiled down to 10 words or less. "A super-hero announces he's gay! Film at 11!" For some reason I imagine people turning to each other and saying, "I knew it! I knew there was some reason Batman kept hanging out with that kid!" How disappointed the vast majority of Americans must have been to learn it was a super-hero they'd never even heard of.

Not only that, but since *Alpha Flight* is direct-only (a fact that none of the news stories I happened upon ever pointed out) the chances are that Joe Average wouldn't be able to find it. Anyone whose interest is piqued enough to try and seek out a copy would go down to his local 7-11, be told by the guy behind the counter that they'd never heard of *Alpha Flight*, and perhaps presume the whole thing was a hoax.

But the question now becomes: What happens next?

Frankly, what's happened until now hasn't been tremendously heartening.

Initial news reports stated that Marvel was offering "No Comment" on its groundbreaking publication. One reporter described Marvel reps as "skittish." No one could, or would, talk for attribution.

The message being delivered to the American public was clear. Someone high up, probably *very* high up (certainly higher than DeFalco), was extremely embarrassed by the story. Here various news agencies were ready to heap praise upon Marvel for daring storytelling, and the silence of Marvel's response was positively ringing. Not only did Marvel Corporate *not* seem proud of their achievement, but instead they came across as hoping that it would all die down very quickly.

Eventually a wire service story ran which quoted Marvel reps, but by then it was too late. Rather than seize the bull by the horns, Marvel had instead let itself get a bit gored by puzzled reporters who couldn't get a quote.

Ah, but what of Scott Lobdell, the gutsy storyteller?

Oh him. He's off the title.

I would love to be able to break the story here of how, in retaliation for writing an embarrassing story, Scott was fired. That, however, is not the case. (Indeed, if it *were* the case, I'd have put it a lot further up in this column — like, in the lead sentence. "Marvel writer fired for having Northstar come out of closet. Film at 11.")

No, Scott's departure occurred a week or so *before* the brouhaha hit. With Bobbie Chase taking on new editorial assignments (but still holding onto *The Incredible Hulk*, God bless her), *Alpha Flight* was switched to another editor, and that editor took Scott off the title and reassigned it for reasons (according to Scott) having nothing to do with the Northstar story. It is certainly not the first time that a new editor has come on and put new creative personnel on a title. However, this particular instance has got to go down in the record books as being one of the most ill-timed such maneuvers in the history of comics.

(For what it's worth, I think a truly professional comics editor is one who is assigned a title and has no other agenda than to make sure good stories are told. Sitting down with a writer and saying, "This story doesn't work for this and this reason, relating to dramatic structure " is absolutely proper. To sit down with a writer and say, "You're doing Story Type X, but I don't want to see that, I want to see Story Type Y, so *adios*," shows a lack of being able to delegate creative authority. It boils down to, "I want to see this book done the way *I* would do it if *I* were writing it." That does no service to anyone except an editor who wants to feel totally in charge.)

The question of Northstar's coming out ultimately, then, boils down to this: What next?

It could easily be argued that this was a simple step in Northstar's development and that the enlightened approach would be not to dwell on it, any more than finding out that a casual acquaintance is gay.

However, we do not live in an enlightened society when it comes to homosexuality (witness Marvel's own reaction). Besides, casual acquaintances don't call press conferences announcing their sexuality, offering it up as a way of countering homophobia. No, now that Northstar's made the declaration with a stated agenda, it would be unrealistic not to examine the fallout. (And no, I'm not pitching to write *Alpha Flight*. I'm more than busy enough, thank you very much.)

Northstar is a media figure and sure to become even more so. Will lovers of his who may *not* want to risk being high profile now shun him? For that matter, let's say you're a friend of his who's straight. How will you feel if your picture is snapped with him in a restaurant and run in a newspaper with the caption, "Northstar and his latest paramour?" Will you take it in stride, laugh it off? Or will you resent the intrusion — perhaps even resent Northstar?

For that matter, can you imagine Northstar fighting a villain who tauntingly shouts, "Look out! Here comes Canada's fighting fag!" Or even better, a villain who automatically assumes that, since Northstar is gay, he probably has AIDs — and surrenders on the spot rather than risk getting into a fistfight? How would such a "victory" make Northstar feel?

Then there's the guy who gets the snot kicked out of him by a group of gay bashers — and goes to Northstar, asking him to go out and beat up the gay bashers because homosexuals shouldn't have to suffer like this. Would Northstar consider it inappropriate to use his powers against mere mortals for the purpose of vengeance? Or would he consider it only fair since the gay bashers have no qualms about ganging up on one gay man?

Possibilities, all sorts of possibilities, which it would be almost criminal to ignore. A far cry from the generic "Villain shows up, fights hero, hero ultimately wins, the end." But will Marvel and the new writer and editor pursue those directions? Will there be pressure never to mention Northstar's sexual identity again?

Alpha Flight could be pretty darn interesting, depending how things go, and if the seeds that Scott Lobdell has sown are brought to — you should pardon the expression — fruit. A pity that the vagaries of editorial life have dictated he won't be there to do the gardening. Shed no tears for him; he's got other assignments coming up that should also be high-profile. Although I doubt that CNN will be calling him to find out about them.

If nothing else, he'll have some impressive clippings for his scrapbook. And Northstar will have — well — who knows?

(By way of promised update, Peter David, writer of stuff, can now play all the way through "Dragons Lair II: Time Warp," making this the third Don Bluth animated game he's gotten the hang of. The ending sequences are really touching, by the way.)

Historical Notes:

1) When I did a story about AIDS in Hulk, I depicted some gay lovers and never used the word "gay." I was worried it might cause a ruckus and prompt a backlash against other, mature stories. The story appeared and was highly praised. Then the Alpha Flight story appeared, with Northstar proclaiming that he was gay, and it prompted a backlash against other, mature stories. The first casualty? An abortion story in X-Factor written by me. Originally it was to go through unscathed. But then the word came down from on high to avoid anything remotely controversial, and the story was re-edited and rewritten into incomprehensibility.

BARREN REPORTING (March 20, 1992)

Well, a few weeks back, I slammed Marvel thoroughly for what I perceived as its rather craven and weak-kneed handling of *Alpha Flight* #106. So now, to confuse everyone completely, I'm going to turn around and defend Marvel on another matter entirely.

The topic of today's symposium is an article that ran in the Feb. 17 issue of *Barron's*, a weekly financial newspaper that has a great deal of influence in the world of investments — particularly for the small investor. In that issue, writer Douglas A. Kass elected to do what amounted to a hatchet job on Marvel, stringing together a series of "ifs," "ands, " and "maybes" and concluding that Marvel is "over-inflated and due for a fall."

The article had an immediate impact on the financial community, sending Marvel's stock into a tailspin and sending Marvel representatives scurrying into the position of damage control. Follow-up pieces in the *LA Times* and the *Chicago Tribune* detailed the panic seizing investors.

Unfortunately, none of the newspapers, nor any of the investors, were really aware that Kass's article was rife with half-truths, omissions, and shoddy journalistic techniques. It was also chock-full of sound effects, such as "Pow" and "Smash," which I must admit immediately put me off. I had thought that the *Batman* film had left those damned relics from the campy 1960s TV show far behind. But here's *Barron's* to bring it back for us again. (Apparently following *Barron's* lead, the *Times* and *Trib* likewise peppered their articles with "k-pows" and "biffs.")

Perhaps I'm a bit thin-skinned about this derisive attitude towards comics, but if they're running articles that are going to panic investors and cost companies thousands, if not millions of dollars, it seems the *least* they could do is treat the subject seriously.

Kass begins his article with a detailed analysis of just where the money from stockholders is going. Putting aside the annoying sound effects (and Kass's impression that Marvel publishes the "Shazam" Captain Marvel), I found this section of the piece informative and interesting. The majority of the money, it seems, is going to financier Ron Perelman. I must admit this comes as no shock, but the amount of money passing into his pocket is amazing.

Once Kass finishes his analysis, he concludes that Marvel's current stock value "might be tolerable if Marvel had strong growth prospects. Instead, Marvel already has wrung just about as much out of the market as possible and could run into unfavorable earning comparisons in the second half of this year."

Now, did Kass conclude this from talking to Marvel and learning what its publishing plans were?

No.

Did he contact distributors to get their opinions? Get a feeling for how they were planning to order Marvels, and how they viewed Marvel's growth prospects?

No.

He spoke to retailers. A dozen, to be specific. And, surprise-surprise, the retailers gave a very negative assessment of Marvel's future. They didn't like the price of Marvel comics. They had over-ordered and had too much backstock. Marvel was, creatively, nowhere near as interesting as independent comics.

From these sentiments, Kass concluded that Marvel's future was bleak.

I have no doubt that retailers told Kass these things. There's just one problem: When I was Marvel's direct sales manager, I talked to a lot of retailers, too. Far more than Kass did. I was on the road an average of one week a month talking to retailers all over the country. And many of them said the exact same thing that retailers told Kass, and predicted that Marvel was going to collapse.

But they were saying that to me five years ago. And seven years ago, and 10 years ago.

Marvel, in the meantime, has continued to grow and prosper. Sure, it's had its bumps along the way, but it is still the dominant force in the comic-book publishing industry.

What it boils down to is that many retailers simply *don't like* Marvel Comics. They don't like the titles they're publishing or the company's policies. Retailers would tell me that they hated ordering crossover titles or "yet another" mutant title — even if the comic books were selling for them. Retailers would also tell me that they would always recommend titles by independents to their customers, because they were the retailer's personal favorites and, as far as the retailers were concerned, those were the comic books that should be pushed.

All of which is fine. But, to Kass, the long-standing disillusionment that some retailers feel towards Marvel and indicates the beginning of the end, rather than a decade-long pattern.

He shores up his findings with "facts" that are misleading and contradictory. For example, he states that Marvel is in for trouble because "Consumers are no longer willing to keep shelling out anywhere from $1.50 to $2.95 for a comic book." He does not point out (or maybe he's simply unaware) that the majority of Marvel titles are, in fact $1.25 — including such top seeds as *X-Men* and *X-Force*. It is, in fact the independents which generally start at $1.75 and up, prices dictated by their lower print runs.

Yet Kass later claims that one of the things hurting Marvel is that "consumers... increasingly are turning to upstart competitors" and proceeds to list various independents which publish titles at higher cover prices. But I thought consumers were unwilling to pay $1.50 to $2.95 for a comic book.

This little gap in logic apparently does not deter Kass's evisceration of Marvel comics. But why use logic when you can fall back on groundless supposition? He characterizes *Alpha Flight* #106 as Northstar's "widely publicized gay 'outing,'" and implies that Northstar's revelation was "fortuitously timed to coincide with the January price increase."

He doesn't bother to point out that the publicizing didn't come from Marvel, but from news services who picked up on the story. His contention that Marvel saw *Alpha Flight* #106 as a means of making price increases go down easier, when in fact Marvel would have been much happier if the story had never seen print, is typical of his absurd logic. Marvel's handling of *Alpha Flight* #106 was not one of its more shining moments — but it was hardly a cold-blooded marketing maneuver.

Even on those occasions where Marvel looks bad, Kass manages to make Marvel look even worse. Kass describes Marvel's botched edition of *Cage*, where the promised fancy cover for the first issue failed to materialize. Retailers who thought they were getting an acetate-overlay, 3-D-effect cover, "accordingly stocked up on non-returnable orders" and, without that cover to give it the additional push, are "stuck with cases of surplus comics."

What Kass doesn't bother to mention is that, because the title was incorrectly solicited, all of those surplus comics are *fully returnable*. The retailers aren't "stuck" with them, at all. Certainly no one is happy that Marvel didn't deliver with the promised goods — least of all Marvel — but the company has a decade-old policy that if a book is mis-solicited, it's fully returnable. Distributors and retailers know this, but Kass doesn't. Nor did he check.

Kass (unsurprisingly) predicts bleak futures for Marvel's licensing side. Marvel has recently made tremendous strides in licensing, finally getting out action figures and playsets (whereas DC had such toys available years ago). Yet, incredibly, Kass actually manages to see this as a negative, claiming over-saturation. Has he bothered to call toy stores or manufacturers and ask if they're pleased with the sales or what their forecasts are? Need you ask?

He manages to downplay the announced *Spider-Man* movie by stating that the buyer, Carolco, has financial problems of its own. He states that if the *Spider-Man* movie doesn't materialize, it loses Marvel potential licensing fees.

Fair enough. However, Kass makes no mention of the *X-Men* animated series scheduled to run on the Fox network. Now, maybe that series will be lousy and it will have no impact on Marvel. On the other hand, an animated series generated millions upon millions for the heroes in a half-shell, so the cartoon *X-Men* could represent a major windfall for Marvel. More action figures, more playsets, more exposure for the comics. But, hell, why should Kass present a potential upside at any point in his article, when he's this far along?

Kass states that Marvel is vulnerable because three privately held distributors account for more than 50% of publishing revenues — and that if any of them hit financial problems, Marvel could have difficulties. OK, that's true. Did he contact Capital City to find out if they're having difficulties with receivables? Is there an indication that Diamond is flawed? Nope. Just more "what if's." And if Toys 'R' Us went belly-up, then Hasbro and Kenner would be in trouble.

Even the direct market itself is a negative to Kass. Nearly 80% of publishing revenues, he claims, are derived from the direct market.

Now — this is *good*. Sales to the direct market are inherently more economical and more profitable for publishers, because it means they can print exactly what they can sell. Minimum effort for maximum profits (as opposed to the "print three, sell one" situation existent in the returnable market.)

But no, Kass claims this is bad because — in essence — there's a recession on, and retailers are vulnerable. Of course they are. Everyone is. No one ever claimed that Marvel is recession-proof. *Nothing* is recession-proof. So why single out Marvel?

He claims that collector interest is waning in comics. His proof? He claims the Sotheby's auction was a "disappointment." By whose estimation? Sotheby's, which states that the money brought in didn't meet its estimates. But, in order to convincingly prove that collector interest is waning, Sotheby's should be able to compare the results this time with its previous auction, so it can say, "Look, a year ago we made X dollars, but now we made X minus $100,000."

Unfortunately, Sotheby's can't do that. Why? Because Sotheby's never had a comic-book auction before. So a quarter of the items failed to sell altogether. So what? Collectors gasped at a number of items which *did* sell, for many times what they were priced at in *The Official Robert M. Overstreet Comic Book Price Guide*. And who published a number of those high-selling comics? Why — Marvel.

More proof of Marvel's certain doom? Kass cites the "imminent exodus" of Rob Liefeld, Erik Larsen, George Pérez, Jim Valentino, and Todd McFarlane. Hot news flash, Kass: Todd hasn't done work for Marvel for close to a year; George Pérez is currently busy pencilling a two-issue "Hulk" bookshelf format comic book (I know, because I'm writing it; the first issue is already pencilled); and Jim and Erik, for all their talents, are not (no disrespect, guys) what I would term, in baseball parlance, as "franchise players." The only one who possibly fits that category right now is Rob, who has yet to prove his long-term selling power.

Who is an example of a franchise player in Marvel's history? The kind of people who, when they leave, makes you go, "Oh, my God."

Jack Kirby. John Byrne. Chris Claremont. The Simonsons. People whose work has been an underpinning for the success of Marvel Comics. And they've left. And Marvel has continued. And they came back, and Marvel has continued. And they left again and came back again — well, you get the idea. And Marvel has continued to grow. Not without its hiccups. But it's grown.

I'm sorry, but there is simply no historical precedent upon which to base Kass' contention that the defections of Liefeld *et al* "will create a serious threat to Marvel's creative franchise." Inconvenience and embarrass, yes. But *history* does not support the conclusion that Marvel is seriously threatened.

This is not to say that Kass might not be right. Perhaps Marvel will, indeed, run into major problems. But it's just as likely — indeed, based on historical precedent, *more* likely — that it will not. Kass, however, doesn't bother to point that out to investors. Why ruin a perfectly good butchering job by pointing out that the slaughtered cow has its own point of view?

There's only one point that Kass makes solidly enough to stick: that Marvel might become editorially timid, unwilling "to take artistic and literary risks."

One can already see that happening. Marvel's horrified reaction to the splash that *Alpha Flight* #106 made can only lead any thinking individual to conclude that Marvel will probably take steps to prevent it from happening again. That means editorial clampdowns and an inclination to play it safe whenever possible. Because Marvel is now answerable to licensees and investors, all of whom now have a stake in the company and want to make sure that nothing is going to come along and ruin their *status quo*.

This would be, of course, the single worst thing Marvel can do. Because, sooner or later, Ron Perelman is going to go away. He will have made his money and will sell the company. It's inevitable. But the characters and (with any luck) the readers will still be there. And if they become editorially stagnant in order to satisfy the desires of a transitory boss, that — and that alone — will the most damaging thing that could happen.

Marvel has already seen the results of trying to play it safe. It tried to ignore *Alpha Flight* so as not to upset all the investors, and *Barron's* came along and upset the investors, anyway.

The question becomes: What will Marvel learn from this *Barron's* piece? It could decide that playing it safe is no guarantee of anything and that you might as well go out there and publish the best damned comic books you can. Let the chips fall where they may.

Or they may decide that, since it can't control ill-informed gentlemen like Kass from stirring things up, it should do everything to control that which it *can* control, namely the contents of the comics. The reasoning will be, "We have to do what we can so that things won't get worse." This little piece of logic, of course, will not only *not* protect it, but *will* make things worse.

And Kass' little hatchet job will become a self-fulfilling prophecy.

(Peter David, writer of stuff, was not only amazed to discover that John Byrne shared his sentiments about the Feb. 21 BID column, but was further astounded to learn that that they both have a fondness for Edmund ("I have a plan so cunning you could brush your teeth with it") Blackadder. Good lord! Could the "great feud" be ending as common interests are discovered? Stay tuned —

Historical Note:

1) Douglas Kass wrote a follow-up article. He still said Marvel was a lousy investment. In the meantime, Marvel continues to make tons of money, and now the X-Men animated series is a smash success.

BEHIND CLOSED DOORS... (June 5, 1992)

Historical Notes:

Todd (There's That Name Again) McFarlane had a piece appear in an issue of CBG that explained his reasons for departing Marvel. He claimed that it was because the company gave him no respect. That prompted the following essay, featuring a cameo appearance by an old friend of BID...

(The following is a transcript of a super-secret Marvel comics spin-control meeting. Since it was difficult to determine which executives were speaking, they were simply identified by letters.)

Executive A: OK, gentlemen. I want answers. I want to know what it was that we did that turned Todd McFarlane into Toddney Dangerfield: this "I don't get no respect" stuff. It's embarrassing. We have to take affirmative action to prove that Marvel is, in fact, a loyal, loving company.

Executive B: I think the first thing we should do is fire somebody.

Executive A: Excellent idea. I think it should be McFarlane's editor. Who edited him on "Advantageous Spider-Man?"

Executive C: That would be Jim Salicrup.

Executive A: OK. I want Salicrup out of here before end of business today.

Executive C: Well, uh, actually, Salicrup's already gone. He left to ed —

Executive A: Already gone, you say? Good work! Good thinking. That's taking control of the situation.

Executive C: Uh, gee. Thanks.

Executive X: Don't you think that trying to assign blame doesn't really address the fundamental problem that McFarlane was bringing up?

Executive B: Which is what?

Executive X: That Marvel cares more about the characters than the creators.

Executive D: Of *course* we care more about the characters than the creators. The characters can't up and leave. They're the constant. Fans want to know what's going to happen next month to Spider-Man, and they're going to keep wanting to know that long after anyone remembers Todd McFarlane.

Executive X: But it's not like the characters think and feel for themselves. They don't materialize on the printed page from thin air.

Executive B: *Street Poet Ray* did. I can't believe someone actually wrote and drew that thing.

Executive X: OK, aside from that. It's the creators who developed them, who made the readers care about them. Don't they deserve respect for that?

Executive B: Of course they do! And we give them respect. We give them a lot of money.

Executive X: There's more to respect than money. There's recognition of loyalty, acknowledgement of a job well done —

Executive D: Look, fella, Todd may think he's Aretha Franklin, but the bottom line is, the way things are now is the best way that it could be for him.

Executive X: How so?

Executive D: If we measured respect by loyalty and jobs well done, Todd would never have gotten that Spidey title. He's only been with Marvel a few years. By rights, we should be giving John Buscema, Sal Buscema, Steve Ditko — all those guys — we should be giving them #1's with all the hype and jazz. Would Todd really like it better if he were still doing back-up stories in Epic Comics? Would that be more respectful of his talent?

Executive C: Yeah, I'll tell ya, I read that article of his — and I didn't follow it. I mean, a couple years ago, Todd was saying how he was asking Marvel for a chance to write. And how he would have been happy to get a writing assignment on some lower-rung book to start out. Instead we had enough respect for his abilities as a creator to give him a new title. He did it for 16 issues, quit, took a year's vacation, then came back and said we had no respect for him. I don't get it.

Executive X: But you only developed that title because you wanted to make money from it and him. You saw it as a potential hot property.

Executive B: So what? We're a publisher! We're supposed to try to make money! Money for ourselves, for the retailers and distributors, and for the creators! What's Image trying to earn with its publishing — Green Stamps? McFarlane made enough in royalties off *Spider-Man* to be set for life! Where's the lack of respect in that? What'd he want in addition? A Porsche? Candy? A tape recording of the bullpen singing "I Just Called to Say I Love You"?

Executive X: Maybe he didn't want things. Maybe he wanted those things — like the song says — that money just can't buy.

Executive A: Oh, for crying out loud. We're a business, not his mother.

Executive X: He said it would have been nice if his opinion had been asked on what sells.

Executive A: Why? No one asks the marketing director how to draw. So why should we ask creators how to sell? Besides, I'll bet you this: Every time you ask an artist what makes his book hot, he'll say the same thing: "I do."

Executive B: McFarlane himself said he had no great personal vision. What a great conversation that would've been. "Todd, how do we improve sales?" "I dunno." Gee, I'm sorry I missed that one. I might have learned so much.

Executive D: Y'know, talk about respect: We promoted that Spidey book up the wazoo. If left to its own devices, the first issue would've sold well, sure. But we developed the whole marketing and selling plan: the multiple covers, the bagged editions, the promotional campaigns, the reorder faxes. The promotion and marketing department worked their butts off. And Todd wound up making a ton of extra money off their labors. Did Todd ever thank them? Give them a pat on the back? An "atta boy"? Send them a gift or even a lousy telegram? Nope. Nothing. They were doing their job and taking pride in the fact that they were doing it well. They weren't there going, "Yeah, but what about me? Where's my piece? Where's my share? Why doesn't anyone notice me?"

Executive X: But Todd didn't ask for any of that stuff. The main beneficiary of all that was Marvel.

Executive C: I didn't see him turning up his nose at the incentive checks.

Executive X: Maybe he donated large portions of the money to charity. Or sent a nice gift to Steve Ditko.

Executive C: Might've been better if he used it to take writing lessons. Y'know, I was trying to figure out if he felt he wasn't respected because maybe he didn't like the editing. Well, I re-read those books and I'll tell ya — however much he was edited, it wasn't near enough.

Executive A: Right. I want that editor out of here.

Executive C: Salicrup. He's gone, remember?

Executive A: Oh, right. Right.

Executive B: You ask me, all these "creators" are ungrateful snots. As far as they're concerned, their contributions are the be-all and end-all of a company's success, and the publisher efforts count for absolutely nothing. So who's the more arrogant, them or us?

Executive X: Perhaps a sign of respect would be to cut creators in on subsidiary rights. Merchandising, dramatic rights and such.

Executive B: What's the point? What that translates into, bottom line, is giving them more money. We're giving them unprecedented amounts of money now, and they're *still* not happy. Besides, I thought this wasn't *about* money.

Executive D: If it's about equality, then the way Marvel is doing things right now is the most equal way imaginable. Yeah, maybe we do focus on the characters instead of the creators. We promote X-Men, we promote Spider-Man, we promote Hulk and Doc Strange and on and on. If we pushed Hot Creator #1 or Hot Creator #2, we'd be creating a tier system. We'd be saying to the public, "These are our first string creators, the ones worthy of promotion. These are our second strings, who are less so. And so on." Sure, the first stringers can go around and crow. But how's that supposed to make the second stringers feel? It doesn't matter if we promote one character over another because it's nothing personal. What's gonna happen? Wolverine is gonna thumb his nose at Iron Man and say "Ha ha, I got more readers than you?" This way, all the *people*, the *creators*, are equal. It means that a Scott Lobdell can step directly from a second string title like *Alpha Flight* right into *X-Men*. It means that we have more flexibility. It means no one *person* is "better" than any other person. Now *that's* fair.

Executive X: So you're saying that it's OK to treat everyone shabbily, as long as it's across the board.

Executive D: That's exactly what I'm — well, no. That's not what I —

Executive X: Like it or not, things are different. It used to be that, if a comic book was changing editors, editors were chosen with an eye towards their meshing smoothly with the creative team. But it's not that way any more. Now it's the editor's vision that's given the emphasis, and if he or she doesn't like the way things are being done on a title, then the creative team is gone. Doesn't matter how long the creative team has been in place — if a new editor comes on, his or her vision is given priority. How is that supposed to foster any sort of feeling of consistency or creative growth or good will?

Executive B: You know, he's got a point. Maybe we should change that.

Executive C: But we're more successful now than ever.

Executive B: Oh, OK. Keep it that way, then.

Executive X: Don't you see? You can't just brush off that concern. Face it: Marvel isn't the company that it was in the 1960s.

Executive C: No, it's not. In the 1960s we didn't return artwork, pay incentive bonuses, pay high reprint rates, pay creator royalties. Now we do.

Executive X: But —

Executive C: Marvel is a publishing concern and always has been. Some guys got a viewpoint of the business shaped by reading Bullpen Bulletins pages when they were kids — PR pieces that they took as gospel, and then they get steamed when the reality doesn't match the pleasant utopian view they have of Marvel from when they were growing up. If everything were always so wonderful, Kirby would never have left.

Executive B: I think we're getting off track here. This was supposed to be a spin-control meeting.

Executive A: You know, I've been thinking about it, and listening to everything being said here. Maybe we're looking at this from the wrong angle. Maybe this is the perfect excuse to save some major money.

Executive X: What are you talking about?

Executive A: Well, look. In the old days, we didn't return artwork, we didn't pay royalties, and what happened? Creators left. So now we do return artwork, we do pay royalties, and what happens? Creators not only leave but they crab about what a lousy company we are and start their own outfits — secured, no doubt, by the money we gave them as incentive bonuses. So here's what we do: We cut back or eliminate royalties altogether —

Executive X: *What*?!

Executive A: — and put the money back into the company. It'll help bolster Marvel's bottom line. Make up for any lost sales or revenues. The stockholders will be ecstatic — they won't care where the money's coming from.

Executive X: But that would be business suicide! It would put DC in the catbird seat!

Executive A: First, once they see the money we're saving, Warners would probably follow suit. Besides, we can head it off. If DC agrees to do the same thing ahead of time, then we're set. What, you think all the writers and artists are going to walk? You think they're *all* going to work for Dark Horse or Image? Get real. This'll work. Trust me. (*Buzzes intercom*) Get me Jenette on the phone.

Executive X: You can't do this! It's collusion! It's immoral!

Executive C: Wait a minute — what kind of talk is that? Who *are* you, anyway? And what's with the stupid nose glasses? (*Rips away Executive X's disguise*).

All: Gasp!

Executive B: Oh, my God! It's Vic Chalker! The Fanboy from Hell!

(*Vic turns and smashes through a window, his webbed parachute dropping him safely to the ground with only 19 broken bones.*)

Executive A: I don't understand. Who was — ?

Executive C: Don't you get it? That was Vic Chalker.

Executive D: Then that means this whole meeting was —

Executive C: Yes, I'm afraid so. It was entirely fictional. We're not really anyone in particular, but instead a pastiche of assorted opinions and possibilities for that stupid *CBG* column — a way of presenting a variety of points of view in an entertaining fashion without necessarily subscribing to any of them.

Executive B: So this whole meeting was a waste of time? Bummer.

Secretary: Sir? I've got Jenette Khan on the line.

Executive A: Hmm. Maybe it wasn't a waste at that. Hello, Jenette? How's it going? Listen, I got a proposal for you —

(*Peter David, writer of stuff, publicly announces herein that, at the San Diego Comic-Con, he's going to use some of the royalties money from the latest **Hulk** to take the sales department out to dinner, in appreciation for the heavy promotion they've been giving that title. Now, **that's** respect.*)

Historical Notes:

1) The full story on Vic Chalker appears in Section 2: The Chalker Papers, starting on page 37.

2) After this column appeared, I received an alarmed call from freelancers who swore that they had heard Marvel was, in fact, intending to do away with the royalties program as per my column, and did I have any inside information. It was, and is, a fabrication on my part. We can only hope that Marvel wouldn't be quite that suicidal.

X'D OUT (March 5,1993)

Talk about being stuck.

Over the past couple of years I have crafted for myself a reputation of being fairly straightforward with what I'm thinking, with what's going on in my life, and with my views (for what they're worth) on what's happening in the world.

For example: Gays in the military.

This has got to be one of the dumbest arguments I've heard in a while. Discussing whether gays should be allowed in the military is like discussing whether oxygen should be allowed in the atmosphere. It's kind of moot. It's already there, whether you want it there or not. The main question, to me, is what people feel more comfortable with: homophobia or the notion that the army is spending millions of dollars drumming gays out of the military.

Or another example: off-book domestic help, as popularized by Zoe Baird.

While everyone was busy pillorying her and other "cheating" employers, there was one thing that was never brought up. More than a year ago, we were considering hiring domestic help at *Casa* David, primarily in the form of child care, so that Myra could return to teaching while I continued my writing.

My accountant advised me that the best, the safest, way to handle things was to be completely above board. Hire someone, pay them through my corporation (a perfectly legit expense; without childcare, I couldn't write), do Social Security, withholding — the whole nine yards. The accountant was going to handle the reams of paperwork.

We contacted an agency, which sent over, or referred us to, nine different people. We told each of them that they were going to be paid above board, by check, on the books.

They all said forget it. If they weren't being paid in cash, off book, they weren't interested. And I have no reason to believe that our situation was unique.

I'm sure there are plenty of honest domestic-help type people out there. Nevertheless, shouldn't there be *some* discussion given to culpability on both ends? Huh?

As I said, I generally talk about what's on my mind.

Occasionally, however, I also put what's prompting me to write about a subject further down than it should be. In journalistic terms, it's called "burying the lead."

I have buried the lead in this column, which is that I'm leaving *X-Factor*.

My dilemma is that, as noted above, I tend to be square with readers. But on the other hand, I've always despised the notion of various creators airing lengthy grievances about ill-treatment at the hands of their employers — airing dirty linen, as it were. It's not, I figured, the kind of things that fans necessarily want to read about.

Besides, it's done with a certain degree of safety: Everyone in the industry knows that Marvel company policy is not to reply to attacks, so potshots can be taken in public forums with impunity. Sure, it's David taking on Goliath — but that wouldn't have been much of a challenge if Goliath had been buried up to his neck in sand.

At first, I simply wasn't going to say anything. But I knew it was going to be fairly obvious I had left under less-than-ideal circumstances; #89 is my last issue, and it's smack in the middle of a plotline. The usual Marvel line of "decided to move on to other projects" was not going to sound remotely convincing. And my going from outspoken to a terse "no comment" if others found out about it, would make me come across as two-faced: I don't mind talking at length about problems, as long as they're not my own.

On the computer service GEnie, therefore, I posted an explanation as to why I was leaving the series — which was then cross-posted for wider distribution (with my permission). I tried to keep all the aggravation and frustration I was feeling at the time in check. In re-reading it now, I don't know if I entirely succeeded. Also, my subsequent positive comments about Marvel's handling of the situation weren't part of the original post either — and I always think it's important to discuss all sides of something.

So — in an endeavor to be as "flame" free and as neutral about matters as I can possibly be — and, as I said, in an effort to have the laundry be as dirt-free as I can make it — here are my feelings and reasons about the *X-Factor* imbroglio:

I knew the job was dangerous when I took it so, ultimately, I blame no one but myself. This is as opposed to, say, Chris Claremont — the job when *he* took it was to stir interest in a newly revived series that was bi-monthly. I walked wide-eyed into the jungle; for him, it grew around him while he watched.

The circumstances surrounding the production of issues #80-#86 of *X-Factor* entailed a succession of artists and storylines that had to be either truncated or backburnered in order to accommodate crossovers.

What kept me going during this time was the notion that things were going to change.

Various circumstances, however, finally made me realize that I had been kidding myself: that it was not going to change but, instead, be more of the same. I could not stand to go through it all again — especially after having gotten off to such a strong re-start with #87.

If I had stayed on the title, I would merely have been going through the motions. And I've always felt that, if you're being paid to do a job, you have to give 100%. You can't (all together now) hold back. If you're giving less than 100%, then you're doing someone a disservice. It would not have been fair to the editors, to the other creators on the team, and, most important, to the readers.

Although I'm upset about the circumstances that have brought this about, I will also say — out of fairness — that the mutant editorial office has been nothing but considerate of my wishes. The editors are as trapped in this "Crossover *Uber Alles*" mentality as anyone else. The stockholders expect massive profits from the X-books, and crossovers remain the only way to give them what they want. (Proof? *X-Factor* sales doubled during "X-Cutioner's Song." The actual team members of X-Factor played a purely supportive role; in fact, in #85 and #86, none of the X-Factor characters were on the cover and they barely appeared in the issues. To me, these were less-than-successful stories. To stockholders, they were the best issues of the year.)

The editorial team had no desire to try to talk me into staying on the series if I was truly unhappy. We discussed my continuing to work with the mutant office without the strictures of writing storylines that often seemed mere filler material between crossovers: limited series, one-shots, and such, wherein I could still work with the *X-Factor* characters and be free of scheduling conflicts that constrict creative flow.

Furthermore, I had created what I had hoped to be a major opponent for X-Factor, who was to debut at the end of #89. I'd developed a name, backstory, powers, etc. A mutual decision was reached by the editors and incoming writer Scott Lobdell that it would be grossly unfair to me to have created this character, use him for exactly one panel (the last page of #89), and then lose control over him. So they kicked him back to me (making Scott's job none the easier), and I'll probably be using him in *Incredible Hulk*.

Furthermore, Scott called me to make sure it was cool with me that he was coming onto the title (at this point, only for a few issues until they know for sure what they're doing). I've known Scott for several years, and he's never been anything less than respectful of me as a person and creator. I have little doubt if I'd said, "No, Scott, I'm royally angry with everyone concerned, and if you get on the title I'll be angry with you, too," he would not have taken the assignment. But I didn't say that, because I didn't feel that way and still don't.

I've already seen a groundswell of "boycott *X-Factor*" on various computer nets. Folks — do not do such a thing on my account. I'm not a big fan of the mob mentality of boycotts to begin with, and I certainly don't want such a thing done in my name.

The fact is I had a lot of fun working on *X-Factor*. I worked with some good creators; I made a more-than-decent amount of money off it (and, with the Marvel royalty program, will continue to do so for the next nine months); and I enjoyed working with the characters and, with any luck, will still be able to visit with them from time to time in limited series and such.

The most important part of a writer's job is to try to imbue characters with the illusion of life: to get readers involved with people who, in their hearts, they know don't really exist. That, at its most basic, is suspension of disbelief. That's what I tried to do with *X-Factor*.

If you, as a reader, were involved with the characters, then for heaven's sake, *please* do not stop reading the series purely because I've left. I didn't want readers to care about *me*. I wanted them to care about the *characters*. If people stop buying the book solely because I've left, then I failed in the one aspect of writing that's most important to me. Readers would be doing me a *disservice* by deciding, before giving any subsequent writers a chance, that they no longer had any interest in the characters.

If you decide that you don't like where the series is heading that the characters no longer seem "right" to you, then you make a personal decision to drop it. But these organized boycotts and letter-writing campaigns people are talking about — Forget it. Please. Not on my account.

When people say, "Marvel is doing this," and "Marvel is doing that," they're missing the fact that *Marvel* isn't really doing anything. Marvel is, pure and simple, a corporate entity designed to make money publishing comics.

I don't deal with corporations, except to cash their checks. I deal with people. And right now, there are quite a few people in very difficult situations. Some of those situations are of their own making. Others are imposed from other directions. There's a great deal of stress going on there with a lot of folks caught in a lot of vises. It may be that, sooner or later, it all blows apart. Or the vises may hold everything together.

I dunno.

Meantime, it's not like I don't have anything else to do. So all those fans who are discussing what series I should take over:

Don't worry. I think maybe with the stress of producing *X-Factor* gone, I might try to take some time to do something else — like, maybe, breathe.

(Peter David, writer of stuff, can be written to at To Be Continued Inc., P.O. Box 239, Bayport, N.Y. 11705. Job offers need not apply. Gee, with me no longer on **X-Factor***, does this mean I'm off-book? Which means that Bob Harras couldn't be nominated for Attorney General, I guess —)*

Historical Notes:

1) **X-Factor** *#92, the issue that I resigned off the title rather than write, was Marvel's top-selling comic book for that month. Yeah, sure, I know I told people to give the series a chance — but I didn't think they'd give it that big a chance. If nothing else, it was just another reminder of how dispensable writers are, particularly on the Marvel mutant titles.*

SECTION 4:

The Write Stuff

The 1970s and early '80s were the time of the writer in comic books. Stories would boast copious captions by Don MacGregor, or wildly skewed visions by Steve Gerber, and the fans would eat it up.

That is far less the case nowadays. Creative matters always move in cycles, and tastes change. The artists who were the top creative names when I started reading comics could not get arrested in today's marketplace.

A few writers are still lauded nowadays. But comics have always been a visual medium, and modern readers raised in an increasingly visually-oriented society, have elevated the status of artists into the stratosphere. Magazines such as *Wizard* routinely list comics credits with the artist's name first, in defiance of the actual order in which the comic book was produced. And back-issue price lists oftentimes attribute an artist's commencement on a title, but rarely — if ever — the writer.

To some degree, comics writers have only themselves to blame. Many have settled for simply writing stories about huge guys hitting each other, submitting plots to artists that say, "Pages 5-22 — big fight. Knock yourself out." As if that actually constitutes a plot. Little surprise, then, that mindsets such as those belonging to the notorious Mr. Name Withheld — and the disenfranchisement of the writer in comics — have been the result.

Writing, however, is an art unto itself. And despite the intentions put forward in my first column, I have, from time to time, been presumptuous enough to discuss the art of writing in general and comics in particular.

Because, after all, I are a writer of stuff.

WHY WRITERS ARE SCUM (Aug. 17, 1990)

Crack out the violins. Proffer those hankies. I am now going to discuss why, by and large, writers are treated like scum. (Of course, you could argue that it's because writers *are* scum, but you have to get your own column to do that.)

This may actually seem like a controversial topic, but it's not. The low regard for writers is so legendary that it's the topic of the oldest joke in Hollywood, to wit: "Did you hear about the would-be starlet who was so dumb that, to land a part, she slept with the writer?"

Movies are, of course, made completely by directors. Directors regularly get the credit for clever characters, dazzling turns of story, and so on. Writers, on the other hand, are disposable, interchangeable. Don't like the way this script is shaping up? Roll in another writer.

The only place where writers are accorded any real sort of respect is the theater, but that's because they're "playwrights," a word inherently demanding respect because it's spelled weird.

The topic of writers in show business is fodder for a whole 'nother column at some future date. Let's focus on writers in comics. Just for kicks.

I was at a convention, sitting at a guest table and signing autographs and such, and a mother came by with her son. And the son was explaining the world of comics to his mom, who was nodding and beaming in approval at her child's mastery of his chosen hobby.

"That's Peter David. He's an artist."

Now I've stopped correcting people when they say this because, broadly speaking, writing is an art form. I especially didn't want to correct the kid in front of his mom. So I smiled and hoped that they would go away.

"You draw the pictures?" the mother asked, impressed.

Now I was stuck. "Actually, I'm a writer," I said.

Her face fell, her enthusiasm considerably diminished. "Oh. Well, then — what do you do in the comics?" She could not conceive that there was any function to a comic beyond the pictures on the page.

The son jumped in to explain matters. "The artist does the story, and then the writer fills in the words."

My smile pasted on my face, I bobbed my head slightly, pulled out my revolver and shot them both. You would have, too.

For the record, I write the plot and script. My plots run anywhere from 10 to 16 pages, containing the entire story — everything from probable dialogue to the way characters are standing during a scene to choreography of fight scenes.

I always try to involve the artist in terms of what he or she wants to draw or enjoys drawing. Also, I'm always flexible towards additions or substitutions the artist wants to make, as long as he or she calls me and discusses it first. They don't make story changes without asking; I don't redraw their pages. I think that's fair.

The plot is not dictated by the editors, as some believe. The editor has the final say, but generally I'm allowed pretty much free rein. I develop plot lines, short- and long-term, and carry them through. I also write the dialogue, captions, and sound effects once the art pages come back. I'll even proofread, if the editors get me photocopies in time.

So it's a little more involved than the off-hand explanation that the late kid offered to his late mom. But I suppose I shouldn't have been too upset. No less an authority than the *Village Voice* referred to a major comic-book writer as "a typist of word balloons." When at conventions, sure, I get my share of fans, but the lion's share of attention goes to artists. It always has and always will, because comic books are a visual medium. I know this, and I'm used to it.

But still —

It's not just comics. I also write novels, and if I tell a stranger this — on an airplane, for example — it almost always gets the same response. The person will say, "Oh, you know, I've always wanted to write a novel," or "I know someone who's working on one and is looking for a publisher." Impressed? Very rarely.

Tell people you're an artist, they'll want you to do them a sketch of Spider-Man. Tell them you're a writer, and they'll say, "That's nice." What are they supposed to say? "Ooooh, ooooh, write me a paragraph! Bang me out a word balloon!"

It's not just outside the industry. It's within as well, extending as far as corporate policy. When artwork is returned from a comic book, the penciller gets two thirds of the pages, the inker the remaining third. This can be a valuable money-generator because of the value on the art market.

The writer? The one who created the story that the penciller drew and the inker inked? We get to sit at conventions and watch stories taken from our heads sold piecemeal at $50 and up a page. One artist once said, "Hey, if writers are upset about it, I'll remove the word balloons and give them back."

In a marvelous musical currently on Broadway, *City of Angels*, a writer is infuriated over unasked-for and unauthorized rewrites on his screenplay by, of all people, a secretary who "just wanted to help." I paraphrase here, but the writer's response was something like this: "Everyone wants to help once it's done. But where are all the people who want to help when you're sitting there with a clean white piece of paper, blank — on both sides — and you have to take 26 letters of the alphabet and combine them and recombine them endlessly to create a story that will thrill and entertain. Where are all the helpers then?"

In other words, writers don't appreciate help. The problem is, in comics it's mandatory. Superb art can elevate a poor story, and shoddy art will kill Pulitzer material. A comic book stands or falls on the artwork, not the story, and that's an irritating admission for a writer to make.

If art is poor, people will stop buying the comic book, even if the writing is good. Not always, to be sure. But readers will abandon a favored writer far faster than they will a favored artist.

But whereas writers need help, the general perception is that artists don't. After all, comics are pictures. If you can draw the pictures, what more is there? Most readers believe this. Not a few artists do, too.

This viewpoint cuts to the core of why writers are treated like scum. Writers are viewed as nothing special, because, to most people, writers do nothing special.

Follow:

A civilian (defined as a non-writer and non-artist) meets an artist. Now, most civilians know whether they can or can't draw. The chances are they can't. Chances are they've tried to draw pictures for some reason — doodles and such — and they know their limitations. So when they meet an artist, they know they're meeting someone who can do something that *they themselves can't*. That engenders respect.

A civilian meets a writer. Now, let's assume that the civilian is literate. He can read a book and write a sentence, even paragraphs. He can write serviceable letters or memos. Maybe he even keeps a diary.

Well heck, he can write. Draw, no way. But write? Sure. It's easy to write. Anybody can write. If you know subject-verb-object, you can write a sentence. If you can write *a lot* of sentences, you can write a story. If you can write a *whole lot* of sentences, you can write a book. Heck, probably a better book than most of the trash that's out there on the best-seller lists now, right?

What's the reason that the civilian hasn't taken up a career in writing?

No time.

I hear this over and over again. "I have an idea I've been wanting to do." "I have a book I've always wanted to write." But they're too busy. Too busy earning a real living in a real world. "Something always comes up and I never have the time."

So a writer, by implication, is someone who has nothing better to do. Being a writer is something frivolous, something that the ordinary person could do in his or her spare time while making a genuine living. Try to explain to these people that writing is something you do because it's impossible *not to*, and you get blank stares.

Look at the legends built up around writers and artists. Artists starve in garrets, cut off their ears, and are rarely recognized in their own lifetimes. Romantic and tragic.

Writers get drunk. Wow.

Ironic that writers, masters of words, need better PR.

If all of the above sounds self-pitying, it's not meant to be. It's also not quite as sweeping as it sounds. Certainly there are comics writers who are respected by fans and industry, although by and large they have to fit one of two categories: either they're artists, as well, or they're from England (thereby proving that comics fans are no different than theater-goers or viewers of PBS in their adoration of all things British).

And there are artists who are superb writers, as well: writers with something different to say and a refreshing way of saying it.

And there are fans who do appreciate the contributions of writers and realize how important the story is. And, hey, sometimes artists even give me free pages: Esteban Maroto (a cover from *Atlantis Chronicles*), Richard Howell (from our work on *Action*), Todd McFarlane (the cover from *Hulk* #340, the Wolverine issue). None of these will ever be for sale, because I'm grateful for the thought behind the giving far more than I could ever be for the money I'd get from them.

The dichotomy really comes down to the purpose of the job. If the artist is doing his job, then he's seen. If the writer is doing his job, he's not. The writer should be the invisible man. The writer hides behind the characters, melting into the background. The writer's job is to make the characters take on lives of their own, to be real. (So yes, I disapprove of the writer putting himself into a comic book. It's self-indulgent and a disservice to the reader, in my opinion.)

I'll never forget the fan letter we got when I was writing *Spec Spidey*, from the kid who asked, "Dear Marvel: Does Peter David write Spider-Man's jokes, or are they ad libs?"

Writer-as-secretary. Spidey speaks, I jot down his *bon-mots*. Yeah, kid, they're ad libs. Writers may be second-class citizens, but still — listening to your heroes and taking down what they say and even telling them what to do — it's not a bad way to make a living. Sometimes you get cranky and, infantlike, kick and scream because you want more attention. But overall, it has its moments — like when you convince readers that Spidey talks with you.

And maybe I'll learn to draw.

In the meantime, anybody want to buy a plot?

(Peter David, writer of stuff, gets meaner the longer the Mets remain out of first place.)

Historical Notes:

*1) This, the fourth installment in my column, got me my first major fan letter — from Stan Lee, who wrote that it should have seen print in **The New Yorker**. I was tremendously flattered. I also, upon reflection, shouldn't have been surprised — it was, in fact, Stan himself that the **Voice** summarily dismissed as a mere "writer of word balloons," which I always thought did him a tremendous disservice. In the endeavor to give Jack Kirby his much-deserved due, it has apparently been decided that comic book history ain't big enough for both of them, and there have been concerted efforts to diminish Lee's contribution at every turn.*

Unfair, says I. If nothing else, Stan — not only through his creative efforts, but in his ceaseless PR drive promoting "The House of Ideas" — made comic books acceptable and even stylish for the college crowd — a change in demographics that the marketplace counts on to this day.

TRICKS OF THE TRADE (March 22, 1991)

Writers are manipulators. We create our own reality, stock it with whatever we need, and try to hornswoggle the audience into buying into these fantasies. There's a phrase for it: "Willing suspension of disbelief" (not "suspension of belief," as it's occasionally incorrectly called.)

If you blow the suspension of disbelief — if any of the seams of stitching together that fabric of unreality begin to show — then you lose your audience. There are, however, certain tried-and-true stunts you can pull, devices you can utilize, so that your audience will willingly go along for the ride.

1) **Audiences will forgive practically anything in order to have a happy ending**: So there we were at the end of *Back to the Future III* and it looked like Doc Brown was going to be stuck back in the Old West. Although Doc would have been happy, would the audience have felt good about it? Especially after having invested a collective six hours of movie-going time?

Heck no! So the movie makers pulled a rabbit out of their hat, produced an ending that was — to put it politely — unlikely, and got away with it. Why? Because the audience was with them. The audience *wanted* it that way and left the theater happy.

I pulled a similar stunt at the end of *Hulk* #372. At the climax of that issue, Bruce Banner is pursuing (on foot) a train which his wife, Betty, has just boarded. He's running down the track after it, trying to get its attention, but the train is picking up speed, turns a corner and is gone. Bruce sinks to his knees, sobbing and berating the fate that is his. The "camera" even starts to pull back on him.

The reader is now completely set up for a depressing Bruce-just-missed-her ending, extending a separation that's already gone on for two years.

And on the very next page, Bruce suddenly looks up in shock. Betty has come back around the track, *on foot*, carrying her luggage, shouts Bruce's name and leaps into his arms. Fade out.

I was asking a lot of the readers here. I was asking the reader to accept that Betty somehow *sensed* that something was wrong and, on the basis of a feeling, either leaped off a moving train (albeit still moving slowly) or forced it to come to a halt by pulling an emergency brake, then ran back to where her intuition was guiding her so that she could liplock the husband *she thought was dead*.

That's a stretch, even for me. Yet the response to that ending was uniformly positive. Every letter was pretty much the same — "I was so afraid that it was going to be another clichéd separation, and was *thrilled to find out I was wrong!*"

I had every confidence that the readers would be so pleased that I hadn't pulled a cop-out ending, that they would forgive the extremely suspicious means by which I did it. Which leads us to:

2) **Clichés can be your friend**: There are certain aspects of storytelling that are so standard, so overused, that audiences accept them. So when you make use of one of those clichés and abruptly stand it on its ear, you can catch the audience completely flatfooted.

The first two Indiana Jones films followed a basic formula — Boy Meets Girl, Boy Loses Girl, Boy Gets Girl. So audiences were properly shocked when *Last Crusade* turned into Boy Meets Girl, Boy Loses Girl, Boy Meets Grail, and on to An Unexpected Conclusion.

Use your audiences' expectations against them. In *Hulk* #345, The Leader announced that he was going to set off a gamma bomb in the center of an unknowing town precisely at 10 p.m. The Hulk got to the bomb an hour early, so The Leader obligingly set the bomb off prematurely, taking readers off-guard. Remember that villains do not have to play by the rules, and I don't understand why they so frequently do.

An immediate corollary to the above:

3) Make fun of clichés whenever possible: I had The Hulk, Sub-Mariner, and Doctor Strange running into each other, with dialogue to the effect of, "I thought you were dead." "*Me*? I was at *your* funeral," etc. Fans loved it.

Having a free-wheeling attitude towards clichés can also save your butt. Example: My running attitude with Rick Jones is that this guy has seen it all. He's encountered every single cliché from pseudo-deaths to space invaders. To a certain extent Rick is the jaded seen-it-all comics fan, except he's in the comic book. This saved me when I wrote myself into a corner in *Hulk* #375.

I had just had The Hulk and Betty leap clear of an exploding Skrull saucer and suddenly ground to a halt as I realized, to my horror, that I had forgotten to get Rick off the ship. I'd just blown Rick Jones to Kingdom Come.

What did I do? The next page, Rick floats safely to Earth, dangling from a parachute that he claims he always carries with him, just in the event that he has to jump from an exploding Skrull saucer. It's a gag I could only have pulled with Rick. And, when Bruce expresses total disbelief, Rick sanguinely replies, "Why? I had to, didn't I?", a defense to which Bruce can muster no response.

Which brings us to:

4) When in doubt, have the *character* be in doubt: One of the oldest writing tricks around.

What are the odds on a New York police officer visiting his estranged wife in L.A. on Christmas and arriving just in time to thwart a carefully conceived theft by a band of ruthless criminals? Slim — but acceptable. You have to have *something* on which to hinge a story. (Alfred Hitchcock called it "The MacGuffin.")

Now — what are the odds on that very same police officer, exactly one year later, crossing swords with *more* terrorists while his wife's life once again hangs in the balance? Ridiculous. Long beyond belief. Unacceptable.

Yet that is the premise upon which *Die Hard II* hangs. Joel Silver Productions knew it was absurd and knew that the audience would know.

So what did they do? They had Police Detective John McClane (Bruce Willis) comment on this extraordinary coincidence, expressing *his own disbelief*, at least four times throughout the film. And, for good measure, even wife Holly (Bonnie Bedelia) asks wearily, "Why does this keep happening to us?"

When a character states that he thinks something is absurd or unbelievable, it's the writer's way of signaling to the audience, "Hey, I know this is a weak point. I confess. And I respect you enough to know that *you* know, so now that we've all acknowledged it, let's move on."

Most times, the audience will subliminally think, "It's not just me. The character knows this is stupid, too," and will be satisfied with that.

That's what I had Bruce do when Rick Jones didn't die on the Skrull ship. I also feel — and this is purely my opinion, since I haven't spoken to him about it — that it's what Alan Moore pulled in the last two issues of *Watchmen*.

After 10 issues of a noteworthy series that was assiduously rooted in reality, Alan took flight with a plot twist that was a variation on a hoary science-fiction cliché — alien invader comes to Earth and all the countries automatically, within seconds, unite against it. It was a rather jolting, mad-scientist direction in which to go. But before I, as a reader, could express my disbelief, there was Nite Owl. Over and over and over again, he stated how outlandish the entire concept was, and how it would never work.

He was right, of course. The first thing that would happen, with the appearance of an "alien monster" landing in New York and killing millions, is that a dozen terrorist groups would all claim responsibility. Then the United States would accuse the Soviet Union of being behind it, accusations would fly, and so would missiles. The whole thing is absurd, but Nite Owl tells us over and over again that it's preposterous so that Ozymandias can make at least *some* attempt to convince us that it's not.

If you're eager enough to buy into it, then Nite Owl's protests and Veidt's rationalizations will be enough to ease you along. (Although, frankly, it kind of ruined it for me, and what happened to Rorschach really finished it. Why not let him go and try to convince people of Veidt's complicity? Who are people going to believe: the golden-haired, admired millionaire, or the escaped psycho with body odor? A case of tying off a loose end that didn't need to be tied.)

There are variations on the "expressing disbelief" stunt, by the way, such as:

5) Have a character acknowledge that he's acting out of character: In other words, when a character is doing something he should not, by rights, be doing, have the character say, "I can't believe I'm doing this." It's a tidy little dodge.

6) **Pretend you're not in the medium you're in**: The cop looks disdainfully at a plainclothes cop who is making a reputation for theatrical heroics and, in order to make clear that this is "real life," says sarcastically, "The guy thinks he's Rambo." The plainclothes cop makes a snide comment about Rambo in return.

The gag is that the plainclothesman is played by Sylvester Stallone, and the movie is *Tango & Cash*.

It's really one of the most common writing stunts when you're trying to simulate reality — You have a character say, "That stuff only happens in comic books or movies or on TV shows," etc; this is real life."

The one time I've ever heard the line used appropriately was in Woody Allen's *Crimes and Misdemeanors*, in which Woody Allen lays out for Martin Landau how, given a specific set of circumstances (which, unbeknownst to him, constitute the plot of the film), he would like to see things turn out. And Landau looks at him scornfully and says, "You've seen too many movies. This is real life." And, in fact, *none* of the things Allen anticipates happen. And you leave the theater thinking that you have indeed seen a slice of real life.

Now *that's* a genuine crime, if not a misdemeanor: Fabrication in the first degree. Guilty Guilty Guilty.

(Peter David, writer of stuff, still watches CNN and hopes that someday, at the beginning of a press conference, when General Schwarzkopf walks in, all the reporters shout, a la **Cheers***, "NOORRMM!")*

Historical Notes:

1) Several weeks after my column saw print, Garry Trudeau did that exact "Noooorrrrmm!" gag in Doonesbury, except he set it in Uncle Duke's Club Scud. Fans asked if I thought he ripped it off from me. I tend to doubt it — although I wouldn't mind trying to buy that particular strip if I ever have the opportunity.

THOSE CRAZY IDEAS (May 3, 1991)

"I hear that writers are always thinking even when they don't want to."
— *City of Angels*

Your name is Andy Kaufman. Although you charmed the country in **Taxi***, lately your career has taken something of a downswing. Your characterization of the woman-bullying wrestler, an insightful sendup of male machismo — is largely misunderstood by the American Public who have come to confuse the performer with the role. A telephone vote has banned you from* **Saturday Night Live***, one of your most visible arenas. Things are not going well. Sure, you still do a mean Elvis impression, but what makes you tick is messing with people's minds.*

And then a thought strikes you: the ultimate gag, a brilliant flimflam.

You fake your death, and start rebuilding. Slowly. Quietly. Doing routines under assumed names, getting back to your roots. Experiment with new comedy, with new ideas, out of the public eye and instead in the blissful quiet. Put the Elvis impression to use by showing up, as Elvis, in K-Marts and Shoprites, causing a wave of Elvis sightings. And someday, when you return — if you return — you will be applauded as the genius that you are. The scam of the century.

What an idea —

Where do writers get ideas?

They don't get ideas. Ideas come to them.

They come from the newspapers or books or TV shows. They come from movies, or friends. They come from happenstances that they witness or hear about second hand.

If I'm making it sound like ideas are a dime a dozen, well — they are. Probably less. It is so darned easy to get ideas, if you just set your mind properly.

The key to writing fiction is remembering just how closely linked fiction and reality are. Fiction is just like reality, except it's more elegant. It also makes more sense, unless it's written badly, in which case you've got bad fiction. I like stories that make sense; maybe I'm old-fashioned that way.

The only place where there is a clear-cut division between fiction and non-fiction is on best-seller lists where, if you come up with enough good ideas and execute them properly, you can wind up.

Execution. That's where it all is. You see, how you tell a story is more important than the idea. A hundred writers can have the same idea, and produce stories involving that idea that are wildly dissimilar. Look at the half-dozen movies that came out a couple years back involving a kid in the body of a man. The only one worth a damn was *Big*. Same concept. Better execution.

How you execute a story is the difference between a good story and a bad story (or one good story and a second good story.) It can also be the difference between being "inspired by" a source and plagiarizing a source.

Your name is Margaret Ray. It is the year 1998, and you are happily married to David Letterman, former talk-show host and now network executive. You met him in 1995 and married one year later. Your life has been generally pretty normal.

And then one morning you wake up and you're not in your Connecticut home. You're in New Jersey. You go back home only to find that no one knows who you are or believes your claims that you're Letterman's wife. Much to your shock, you discover that you've slipped backwards in time nearly a decade.

Everyone assumes you're insane and eventually you're sent to a mental hospital. The doctors don't believe you, of course — until you calmly detail the events of the Gulf War, months before they occur. Shortly after the end of the war — all as you predicted — the doctors turn their backs and let you "escape." They announce that they're not treating your escape as such. They're letting you go. Why shouldn't they? You're not crazy.

You return to your birthplace of Colorado, there to hope and pray that someday you're restored to your natural timeline. In the meantime, you rack your brains trying to remember who won the 1991 World Series.

What an idea —

When a writer sees a movie or reads a book, he invariably writes along with the writer of the work. It's automatic. You can't — as starlet Avril Raines, quoted above in the musical *City of Angels*, alludes to — shut it off. You analyze the themes being explored, the characterization, the style. And you usually wind up second-guessing, or trying to second-guess, the writer of the work.

Sometimes you anticipate where the writer's going, and sometimes you don't. But you may find that the storyline you've come up with is just as entertaining to you, or even more so, as what the writer came up with. And from that mental leapfrogging can develop a story.

This is called, "being inspired by." It's when somebody's work starts the wheels of your mind spinning. It's when you take a concept or an idea or a bit of business and twist it around and transpose it and make it into your own. This takes work.

It is also possible to take the aforementioned concept or idea or bit of business and put it in its entirety in your story. It's possible to do this unintentionally. This is called "happenstance."

And if you realize it while there's still time to do something about it, then either you excise it or else acknowledge the source. This is called "honesty."

However, if you do it deliberately, hoping to pull a fast one, that's called "plagiarism," from the Latin root meaning "kidnapper." To put it mildly, it's frowned upon. To put it unmildly, it's actionable in a court of law.

Have I ever plagiarized something deliberately, with intent to cover it up? Once. I was in sixth grade, stuck for a creative writing piece, and I cobbled a story from a comic book. I carry the guilt with me to this day and have lived in fear for the past two decades that they'll find out and make me repeat elementary school. I hope the principal doesn't read this column.

Your name is classified, but you work in a government lab experimenting with a virus that, when introduced into humans, will cause them to develop psionic powers. At this point, however, it's in the early stages. In fact, all it's doing is breaking down the immune systems of test subjects and killing them. You've still got a long way to go.

However, a screw-up on your part enables the virus to get out into the population, and you are horrified when people start dropping dead. You pray that no one traces the released virus, now called AIDS, to you. In the meantime, however, you are scientifically curious to watch and see if anyone of the affected subjects develops any paranormal abilities.

And then, somebody does.

What an idea —

I occasionally do riffs. Pastiches. This is sort of the opposite of plagiarism. This is a work that so screams of its origin that it's clear there's no intent to defraud. There is, to my mind, a fine line.

In an upcoming two-parter of *Hulk*, #383-384, I was so involved in a pastiche that I almost crossed that fine line before skittering back. As mentioned last week, those two issues are quite clearly a *Phantom of the Opera* riff, with a dollop of *Beauty and the Beast* thrown in (which, in and of itself, is a *Phantom* riff in many ways. Except *Phantom* is like the original *Beauty and the Beast* and — well, you get the idea).

Anyway, in the middle of the story, I had a plot element which was central to the second half. And after the story was already drawn, my wife read it and pointed out that it bore a strong — even uncomfortable — resemblance to a sequence in the film *Real Genius*. I hadn't been thinking about the movie when I wrote the story, but I realized that she was right. So I worked in an acknowledgement in the dialogue, and was quite satisfied with that. And acknowledging the source material, however unintended, is scooting safely back across the line.

In a *Star Trek Annual* a couple years back, I used the concept of telling a story chronologically backward, as Harold Pinter did in his play, *"Betrayal."* This was deliberate on my part — no accident here — and from the very beginning, it carried the credit line, "From a concept by Harold Pinter." This prompted a number of fans to think that Pinter was writing *Trek* comics for DC.

Even had I not acknowledged it, the treatments of the idea were so different that it might have slipped past a lot of readers. But when it comes to ideas and execution thereof, it's always better to be safe than sorry.

Besides, it's always embarrassing to have someone point it out before you do. It can have serious legal consequences (an episode of *Star Trek* comes to mind — and more, if Heinlein had chosen to make a fuss about Tribbles and Martian Flatcats; also there have been actions taken against comics stories from time to time.) It can tarnish your reputation (a reviewer on a computer net has pointed out that a currently running storyline in a major publication bears an almost scene-by-scene resemblance to the film *"Shane,"* again without acknowledging the source.)

Other works are just one of many sources of ideas. They're just the only source with potential legal ramifications and ethical considerations.

At their most basic, ideas come from the concept of "What if" (yeah, just like the comic book). You look at something that others take for granted, tilt it slightly, and see the possibilities.

One of the masters of this is Roger Stern, whose unused ideas are better than many ideas that see print. My favorite of his is the one in which Peter Parker learns that dear old Uncle Ben was actually a fence, and the burglar that shot him was angry over a transaction gone awry. Now wouldn't that mess with Peter Parker's head? Years of collaring criminals to make up for his uncle getting nailed, and then it turns out his uncle was a criminal, too.

Really, the trick to writing fiction is looking at reality, seeing what's behind it, and going from there.

Your name is Peter David. Your wife is four months pregnant, and you've just gotten back blood test results that tell you the child will not have Downs Syndrome or other ailments.

You joke to your wife, Myra, about how they seem to know so much about children in utero these days. You envision a doctor telling parents, "Congratulations. You're going to have a healthy, eight-pound, blue-eyed, black-haired, right-handed boy who shows talent for piano and the law. However, unfortunately, further tests indicate he will be a Red Sox fan, doomed to season after season of disappointment and heartbreak."

And as you're cracking wise, Myra looks at you and says, "You know — wouldn't it be interesting in the Marvel universe if they developed a test that indicated whether an unborn child was going to be a mutant or not? And women started considering abortions because there was, say, an 85% chance their child could be a mutant?"

And you realize she's right. You realize story possibilities. And, by a stroke of luck, you're going to be writing X-Factor. You run it past your editor. He likes it.

What an idea —

(Peter David, writer of stuff, hopes to see all and sundry at Long Island's ICON April 19-21, Oakland's Wondercon April 26-28, and Atlanta's DixieTrek May 10-12. Remember, you heard it here first.)

Historical Notes:

*1) The abortion story ran in **X-Factor** #77-78, but in greatly altered form. For details see "Out of the Phone Booth and into the Closet" in the "Marvel" section of "Fun with Publishers," on Page 73.*

*2) The reference to **Real Genius** prompted several fans on the GEnie computer network to request — no, demand — that the Hulk be seen sporting pink bunny slippers, as Val Kilmer's character did on occasion in that film. I complied and he wore them briefly in **Hulk** #390.*

THE TOOL BOX (Sept. 20, 1991)

(Historical Note: *The "lady in Philadelphia" referred to was letter-writer Mary McCool, who scolded me for not being, in her opinion, considerate enough of people's feelings in my column. She also gave me grief when I used the term "suffering from" in regards to an affliction, which is medically correct but not politically correct.)*

You are a carpenter, and you are banging away with your trusty hammer. The hammer is your friend, your ally. Without that hammer, you could not do your job. You could not be a carpenter. You would be helpless.

And then someone taps you on your shoulder and you turn around. And it's Mister Rogers.

"Hello, Mister Rogers!" you say. "What are you doing here?"

He points and says, in that polite way he has, "That hammer you have there — you know that can be used as a weapon, don't you?"

You look at the hammer. "This? This isn't a weapon. It's my primary tool."

"But it's a weapon just the same. You can hit someone by accident with it if you aren't paying attention. Or you can break someone's skull open with it deliberately."

You look at the hammer. "Yeah? So? What's your point?"

"You have to take responsibility for that, you know. You must only use that weapon for nice, polite, constructive purposes. You have to do only nice things with it." He smiles. "OK? So we can all be neighbors? Will you be careful with that hammer?"

"Yeah, sure. Fine. It can be used as a weapon, OK? I'll be careful."

"That's good," says a smiling Mister Rogers. "We all have to be polite to each other. No matter what we're actually thinking, we should be nice and say nice things and not offend anyone by hitting them with hammers. OK?"

And you realize the truth of Mister Rogers' words, because at the moment you're contemplating what it would be like to crush his skull with your hammer. But that wouldn't be nice. Not at all —

Bet you think I'm going to beat up on the lady in Philadelphia who wants everyone to be nice to each other, huh? Nah. After all, all she's doing is stating the obvious about how words can cut both ways, but adding to it a "Miss Manners" wounded air. Too easy.

No, no, I'm going after Don and Maggie.

In the pages of *Oh So*, Don and Maggie state that they're amazed at the "large number of professionals — who denigrate the power of words — while simultaneously boasting of their power and influence. You cannot have it both ways."

Silly Don! Silly Maggie! Of course you can. Short answer and long answer coming up:

Long answer first.

Let us contemplate the loaded revolver. A marvelous instrument of destruction. Something that, unlike a hammer — or words — has one use and one use only: to kill. Oh, you can say that it's also used to practice marksmanship. But what is marksmanship except honing your ability to hit your target and facilitate killing? (Great, now I just hacked off the NRA. The lady in Philly may not have to worry about me much longer at that.)

If Murray takes a loaded revolver, aims it at Solly's heart and squeezes the trigger, the bullet will strike Solly, penetrate Solly's heart, and kill him. It doesn't matter if Solly is in favor of gun control. It doesn't matter if Solly doesn't believe he will die. It doesn't matter if Solly thinks the gun is not loaded. In short, it doesn't matter how receptive Solly is to the entire concept of being shot and killed — if Murray shoots and kills him, Solly is shot and dead.

Loaded guns have that power. It is incontrovertible. It cannot be argued with or debated. They always, *always* have the power to kill or wound.

Words don't.

Because words are tools — friends, as I called them in one column, although, y'know, there's all *kinds* of friends — and what they are tools of is communication. Just as a hammer depends on the skill of the carpenter, so too do words depend upon the skill of the writer (or speaker) to use in conveying ideas. But just as important — even *more* important — is the willingness of the people who are receiving those ideas to believe, understand, and contemplate the ideas being conveyed.

That is where both the power and importance of words come into play and why saying that they can both accomplish great things and are lightweight is not at all contradictory. Because if the communicator and the audience do not connect, then the words have no power.

When you look at great moments in history that are connected with famous words or speeches, you cannot simply say, "Oh, these words and these words alone *caused* it to happen." You cannot separate the societal forces that caused those words to be spoken or written from the actual speaking or writing of them.

When words or speeches spurred on great achievements, it was to some degree because there was an audience who was ready and willing to listen to what the communicator had to say. Abraham Lincoln could credit Harriet Beecher Stowe all he wanted, but that ignores the fact that if the President of the United States had been vehemently pro-slavery, matters might not have proceeded as they did and

Stowe might have ended up strung up somewhere. (See, there's another one — a rope. It's your friend if you're hanging from a mountain, but it can also be used against you if you're hanging from your neck — ahhh, skip it.)

How many times have writers and philosophers and artists been considered "ahead of their time"? That's because the audience wasn't there for them, despite all the skill those communicators may have had. It's only "make-believe," if the audience will not take it as anything more than that.

For that matter, what about scientists or men of medicine who made great and wonderful discoveries — and all their words couldn't sway their contemporaries. Hell, some of them were burned as heretics. Talk about your tough audiences.

Words, in and of themselves, mean absolutely nothing. They have no power. Period. What matters is who says them, how they're said, and who they're said to. (Am I splitting hairs here? Of course I am.)

For example: "I hate you."

Very strong statement? Powerful statement? Nonsense. Means nothing. Three impotent words strung together. It's the context that's important.

Two people getting divorced, sitting across a table. One of the torn couple, with burning in his/her eyes, says "I hate you!" It speaks volumes. It speaks of a love gone sour, of two people who once shared their bodies unable now to even share a room. It has meaning, punch, pathos. Tragedy.

My daughter has just been told that she is to clean her room or there will be no television. She spins and, with her full fury, howls, "I hate you, Daddy!" I sigh. Yeah, right. Now go clean your room. There is no punch or pathos or tragedy, and the only meaning it has is that the kid is angry. And that, too, is evaporated a half-hour later when Dad comes up the stairs with freshly baked brownies.

The words mean everything. The words mean nothing.

Let's be more vicious with the following words: "Boy, you're a butt-ugly nigger."

I say it to a large black gentleman in the streets of Harlem. Chances are I'm going to be leaving with fewer teeth — if I'm ever seen again, that is.

Eddie Murphy says it to Richard Pryor, who responds, "You're not looking so hot yourself." No punches exchanged. No shots fired. Teeth all intact.

The words mean everything. The words mean nothing.

Words, words, words. You'll say things that are crystal clear to you and people just won't get it. When someone says, "It's not being politically correct to say that you don't want labels on anything or anyone," and you respond, "But that is the *essence* of politically correct — to have everything mean the same, to have nothing with any distinct meaning, to bland out society and stir it into one gelatinous mass of nothingness." And the guy will respond to you, "No it isn't," and you say, "Yes it is," and suddenly it's like having an argument with John Cleese.

Even intent doesn't matter, because people will make of words what they will. I'm reminded of when Mel Brooks caught flak from an organization on behalf of sufferers from Downs Syndrome, stating that the lummox character of "Mongo" in *Blazing Saddles* was clearly named that to make fun of so-called "Mongoloid idiots." An appalled Brooks explained that the character was named Mongo so that another character, upon hearing of the brute's arrival, could shout in alarm, "Mongo! Santa Maria!" thereby making a joking reference to the noted musician with that name. Brooks made clear that no such insult was intended — but I'll guarantee there are still people who take offense for that very reason.

Or there's the column I wrote some time back stating that I felt that the Vietnam War had had a developmental effect on *Star Trek*, discussing the humor content of original *Trek* versus *Next Generation*, and the impact humor had had on my own *Trek* work. So what did I hear from my sources at Paramount? That Gene Roddenberry was upset because "Peter David was saying he could write *Star Trek* better than Gene." I was stunned. I pulled out the column to double-check. No. Gene hadn't been mentioned anywhere. Nor had my relative writing prowess, for good or ill, been discussed. But someone, somewhere, had interpreted my piece to be some sort of self-aggrandizement at the expense of *Trek*'s creator, and relayed word back to Gene of that.

Be nice to each other, Mister Rogers? Don't wound people, Miss Manners? How about a couple of years back when that major earthquake hit San Francisco? I did a posting on a computer board asking whether regular board participants in the Bay area were all right. I was concerned. I was worried. And as a signoff, I quoted the William Thomas Cummings remark about "There are no atheists in the foxholes" — referring to the idea that, in times of stress, even skeptics — myself not excluded — might be inclined to offer up a prayer of hope on the chance that, if there is a higher power, then He might listen and help out.

That was polite, right? That was using words out of concern and consideration, correct? Who could fault me for that, right?

Well, there were a couple of people in San Francisco who replied to my message of concern by posting a series of vitriolic responses saying, in essence, how dare I challenge their right to be atheists and who did I think I was, and what a cretin I was, etc., etc. Like I cared that they were atheists.

See? Sure, I might offend someone when I do satire. On the other hand, people can get hacked off at me when I try to offer genuine words of concern. Hell, the very *existence* of this column offends some people.

So you see, how can anything as erratic and unreliable as words have any power? They can't. Unless, of course, you're lucky enough to hit the right audience in the right way, and get their minds thinking along the right track to lead to something, well, right. Then words can have power.

So you can have it both ways.

That's the long answer.

The short answer is from words — of course — written by Walt Whitman in *Song of Myself*:

"Do I contradict myself?

Very well then I contradict myself,

(I am large, I contain multitudes.)"

And you know what I bet? I bet that somewhere, some fat guy is going to read that and say, "Ah hah! He's saying that people who are large always contradict themselves! How insensitive to the difficulties of the fat — sorry, Sustenance Challenged — he is!"

Mister Rogers wouldn't approve.

*(Peter David, writer of stuff, has it on reliable authority that the eight people who voted in the **CBG** Poll stating that this column was their least favorite part of the paper, were the same eight hard-line Communists who endeavored to overthrow Gorbachev. Commie pinko creeps — got what they deserved, I say. Shows you what happens when you mess with me.)*

BLEEPIN' COMICS (May 22, 1992)

Words can be dangerous and tricky things, open to all sorts of reactions that one never anticipates.

No matter how long this column has been around, that's a fact of life that I'm reminded of with amazing frequency. Yet the most recent reminder of that truism came to me, not as a result of this column, but from Marvel Comics.

Of the two major comics publishers, Marvel — for more than a decade now — has been the more conservative when it comes to language. At DC you can pretty much get away with "hell" and "damn" with regularity. At Marvel, "hell" is occasionally tolerated if used tactfully, and "damn" never is.

And, of course, some words are *verboten* at both companies. Fortunately, in the liberal realm of Krause Publications, you can freely use such words as s*bleep* and f*bleep*, and even the dreaded m*bleeeeep*er.

But with all the unwanted PR Marvel's been getting lately — and with all the attention that's paid to non-editorial influences as the stock market or big shot chain stores — it appears that language restrictions are tightening up even further. With various creators boasting of how great it is that they can say or do anything in their own titles, now is the worst possible time for any major publisher to get more restrictive — yet that's precisely what's going on.

(And who knows? It was right at the release of the first *Batman* film that Warner went anal-retentive on DC, so maybe DC will get jumpy, too.)

In an idealized world, the only thing that should matter in editing a story is if it makes sense editorially. But we live in a world where Marvel actually got a letter several years ago (I saw it myself) in which a woman wrote in angrily about a villain saying, "I shall destroy you as easily as I would flick an insect off my shoulder" because she misread the "L" and "I" in "Flick" and thought it was a "U." Despite the fact that any reasonable in-context reading would have tipped her to what was being said, instead she wrote in and demanded to know how Marvel could be publishing such filth.

It's such an old gag that you shouldn't use "Flick" and, for that matter, not name a character "Clint" (and, consequently, the name "Clint Flicker" is definitely a no-no) that you don't expect it to crop up in real life.

But Marvel is now trying to anticipate all possibilities, and as a result, things can get a little, well, strange.

Now keep in mind that this isn't censorship. Marvel can publish, or not publish, whatever they want. Nor am I especially upset about it, because it's just words, and there's always plenty of words.

But even so —

In an upcoming issue of *The Incredible Hulk*, set in Las Vegas, I had a sequence where The Punisher was trailing someone, got spotted, and his van was rammed and knocked over. The Punisher burst out the back of his van, guns cradled in either arm, and announced loudly, "Somebody just crapped out."

Now my dictionary lists the term "crap out" as "to make a losing throw in the game of craps" and, in slang parlance, "to fail." The sequence took place in Vegas, remember — gambling capital of America (with all deference to Atlantic City). No reasonable person could possibly think, in context, that I was doing anything more than making a pun off of a popular Las Vegas dice game. Certainly I wasn't *intending* anything beyond that.

But the line of dialogue, after initially being accepted, was kicked back.

Why?

Because of alternate meanings of the word "crapped" — none of which had crossed my mind when I wrote it but might occur to that woman who complained about "flicked," or others like her. Then, of course, there's concern that some chain store manager might get a copy of *Hulk* shoved in his face by parents who decided to ignore the context so they can complain about the garbage in their kid's reading matter.

Well!

What a fix for a publisher to be in. What great sympathy this must elicit from the hearts of all writers, commiserating with Marvel's braintrust over the unenviable task of trying to anticipate every possible shade of meaning to every word in every Marvel comic book.

But take heart, Marvel, I'm here to help.

I'm always being asked by would-be writers what it takes to write for Marvel. Certainly if I, who have been at this full-time for over five years, can fail to perceive buzzwords or phrases, then newcomers would have even more problems. Think of the valuable editorial time wasted on reviewing key words and phrases that could possibly offend.

There are various words and situations that, on the face of them, would seem to be harmless. But they are in fact landmines of alternate meanings and should be avoided — not just by novices, but, by experienced professionals.

• "Crapped out" we already know about. Likewise, avoid referring to the edible North American freshwater fish called "crappies," do not refer to someone who has eaten himself sick as suffering from "crapulence," and do not use the term "crapshooter" since it might be interpreted as a slam at the editor of the Valiant line.

• Do not, under any circumstance, name anyone "Dick."

•Do not have anyone cock a fist. Do not have a sequence set in a barnyard wherein you refer to a crowing cock.

In sequences set in restaurants, do not have anyone toss around cock-and-bull stories while eating cockaleekie soup.

If their ship is sinking, do not have them leap into a cockboat. Even if they're certain they'll survive, do not have them be cocksure, and just to play it safe, don't have some guy who's the cock of the walk discussing the works of Jean Cocteau.

• Even if your character is ankle deep in a basement flooding with water, do not say that he's having problems with his plumbing. Do not refer to him having to deal with any sort of leak (*especially* don't use the word "taking" in conjunction).

• Do not, under any circumstance, have anyone eat shitake mushrooms.

• Despite the fact that the wood of this particular tree was used to make the Ark of the Tabernacle, make no reference whatsoever to the shittah tree.

• Don't bother coming up with a mutant team called "X-Crement." Better men than you have already tried it.

• Never describe two characters as walking abreast. Don't have them keep abreast of a situation. Don't have them, if ordering chicken in a restaurant, state a preference for breasts — or thighs, for that matter. Actually, legs aren't too good an idea, either. Have them order wings. That's safe. Set all chicken-eating sequences in Buffalo, N.Y.

• Don't have a character compliment a female grocer on her nice melons. If a female is selling a car, don't make reference to her showing a car with a nice set of headlights. In sequences set in stereo equipment stores, don't make reference to "woofers" or "tweeters" if females are present. In fact, just to be sure, if males are present, don't mention "equipment."

• Do not have a female character emphasize a point by ending with the phrase, "Period."

• If a man is wielding a very formidable gun, do *not* have another character comment that he's got his hands on a really nice piece.

• Do not call anyone an ass, even if he has fur and makes loud braying noises. For that matter, don't have anyone assimilate, never assume, and never assure.

• Don't have a character lay about, lay a foundation, lay a claim, or lay an egg.

• Don't have someone "queer a deal." Similarly, don't have a character who smokes a fag, and don't have them describe being exhausted as being "fagged out."

• Don't draw the faces of religious musicians onto comic-book covers, and don't write stories insulting Native Americans — neither of which has anything to do with the topic at hand, but it's generally good advice.

• Don't describe a character as frolicking in "gay abandon" unless you're prepared to appear on CNN.

• If someone's vacuuming, do not have another character admiring the vacuum cleaner by saying, "Boy, that really sucks."

• Do not depict a wine and cheese party wherein a character offers to cut the cheese.

• Do not have a deli owner bang his bologna or sling his salami.

• And whatever you do — under no circumstance — and this will get you fired, I guarantee — under no circumstance should you *bleeeeeeeeeeeeep*.

*(Peter David, writer of stuff, wished to announce that the new mascot of this column will be Fowlmouth, the little guy with all the profanity from **Tiny Toons**. Fowlmouth, when informed of the honor, was heard to say, "@*&#$!")*

Historical Notes:

*1) Suggestion #15 was a reference to the then-current stories of singer Amy Grant protesting that the cover artist for an issue of **Dr. Strange** had based a character on her likeness; and a comic called NFL Super Pro had featured Native American religious figures as villains, which resulted in yet more hot water for Marvel.*

BREAKING IN (July 31, 1992)

The most common question I get at conventions, the most frequent type of letter written to me at Marvel or c/o this column, features a variation on the following. (The exact wording is taken from the letter of one young man in Mansfield, Ohio. I'm not running his name because the letter wasn't in the column, and I don't want to violate confidentiality. But it was one of the better written letters I've received on the subject.) And it says:

"I want to be a comic book writer. At the moment, I'm a 16-year-old junior in high school, brimming with ideas. A question that seems to be asked a lot of me is, 'What are you going to do with your life?' and 'What are you going to be?' To most of them I say that I haven't decided yet. But, to those to whom I tell the truth, that I want to write comic books, they say, 'No, seriously.' That, along with a girl saying that she wants to just be friends, defines the low blow.

"The reason I'm writing is that I need a little help in knowing just how to get there."

Rather than answer the question over and over again, I figured I'd write it up for *BID*, make a bunch of copies of it, and send them out whenever I get asked.

This is not any sort of absolute "How To" essay. There is no absolute way. What there is is a very, very slim chance — and that's extra emphasis on "slim," particularly if you're trying to break into one of the Big Two. Unsurprisingly enough, though, I don't get a lot of people coming up to me and asking me how to break into Valiant or Dark Horse or Image. I'm usually asked about Marvel, and it's usually plot outlines for Marvel characters that I'm shown. So that's what I'll focus on, using my experience as a writer and also my time working for book publishers as well as my staff time at Marvel.

There are two things to be considered here: The nature of submissions, and to whom (and how) you should submit them.

Section 1: Nowhere near everything you need to know in order to be a good writer

I now give you some very brief, fairly practical advice in pursuing a writing career.

Rule 1: Don't listen to friends and family, no matter what they say. They will either tell you that your goals are stupid or unworkable, which won't help your ego. Or they'll tell you that you're a wonderful writer, which they're rarely in a position to do because their feelings for you cloud their judgment; you, however, will get delusions of grandeur. I'll never forget the first grade teacher who sent a manuscript for a children's book, claiming that it was a sure-fire bestseller because "I read it to my class and they loved it." Like the kids were going to shout out, "Boy, Mrs. X, your book really bites it."

Rule 2: Rule 1 is not absolute. If friends or family give you constructive criticism, take it.

Rule 3: Read.

Rule 4: Use a typewriter or computer with a letter-quality printer. 8 1/2 x 11 inches, double spaced, with at least one-inch margins all around (a pica inch is 10 spaces, an elite inch is 12. A vertical inch is six lines). Don't hand-write. Don't write on anything other than standard-weight white bond paper. I don't care what Abe Lincoln or Jack Kerouac wrote on; you're not Lincoln or Kerouac. And for crying out loud, don't use erasable bond. That wasn't a dodge the writer used in *Misery* to get Annie out of the house; no real writer types on erasable bond.

Rule 5: Use a dictionary. If you've got a computer, use Spellcheck.

Rule 6: Read.

Rule 7: Include your name and address on all correspondence.

Rule 8: Read.

Rule 9: Note the repeated emphasis on reading. Note that I don't keep saying "write." Many people will tell you that you have to write constantly. To me, telling a fledgling writer, "You should write" is like telling a fledgling auto mechanic, "You should fix cars." It's a given, it's obvious, it's self-evident.

If you want to write, though, you should be reading as wide a variety of things as you can. There's no better way to absorb the basics of writing than to see how others are doing it. And for heaven's sake, if you want to write comics, don't just read comics. What will make your stories fresh, vibrant, and, most important, noticeable, is bringing techniques and subject matter that you've learned from other writers along with you into the comics world.

The comics business needs new influences, not a recycling of the old ones. It's like all those artists who only learn art from comic books, rather than learning how to draw from life.

The more you distance yourself from outside influences, the more cloudy your vision becomes.

Rule 10: When you get rejected, keep in mind: It's nothing personal. Learn to mentally separate yourself from your work. If someone says, "Your writing is lousy," they're not saying that you are a lousy person.

Rule 11: Learn to type. Learn to type well and learn to type fast. If nothing else, you can pick up temp work to tide you over before those huge royalty checks come rolling in.

Section 2: How to give submissions in to comics

Rather than break this down into rules, I'll break it into questions. Keep in mind that there is nothing official in any of this. I'm not giving you word handed down to me from Marvel or DC management. In fact, future *Oh, So?* columns may have letters from comics companies stating that I'm completely off-beam. All I can provide is my opinion on how best to proceed.

Do I have to learn to draw? No. No more than you have to learn to letter or color. Learning to draw does make your work more accessible to the editor, in that it takes much less time to look at a few pages of art than it does to read over and critique a story. But does that make it easier to break in? No, not if the best you can be is a lousy artist.

Go with your strength. If you have a talent for writing and drawing, then by all means, develop both. Obviously, the more things you can do well, the more chances you have at success. If you have no talent for drawing, but know you can write, then focus on your strength. Why become a lousy penciller, if you have it within you to become a great writer?

Do I submit a whole story? You submit the gist of the story. Your initial submission should, ideally, be no longer than one page. It's not the easiest thing to do, and you'll find that it becomes almost an art form unto itself. What you should do is boil your story down to its essence. Ask yourself, "What is this story about? What are the themes? What does the character have to deal with that makes this story interesting, important, and, most of all, unique to this character?" Present the essence, the themes and conflict, and the resolution in the broadest of terms (you don't have to describe every moment in the story. Simply making it clear that you know how it begins and ends is fine).

If your story consists of "Wolverine runs around, fights guys, and comes up with a neat way to beat a villain," I can guarantee you it won't sell. You need to come up with some new slant, some new perspective, some new vision, that is both consistent with what's gone before and, at the same time, different enough to catch the attention of the person who reads it and make him or her say, "Hey, that's a neat idea. I like that."

I don't care if you've read stories that saw print and weren't about anything. Stories that had no subtext or depth. Stories that had no conflict other than people running around and hitting each other. How many times have you read a story and said, "Hell, I can write better than that?" Well, if you want to break in, you *do* have to write better than that. Sure it's not fair, but it's true. Besides, you don't want to aspire to mediocrity. Who wants to use the lowest common denominator to justify their work?

I have great ideas for all these new characters. Should I submit them to Marvel? No. Not if your goal is to break into Marvel. If you have a great idea for a three-part story, save it. If you dreamed up a 12-part star-spanning mega-series that incorporates every hero in the Marvel Universe, don't bother. You have to remember what it is you're trying to do.

So what am I trying to do? You're trying to make yourself useful to an editor.

An editor has one job and one job only: To get the titles he or she edits out the door to the printer. Everything they do — the phone calls, the meetings, the running around — everything funnels down into that one imperative. And if you come along and seem to be someone who can help them achieve that goal, then you've got a shot at getting on their good side. Not a *great* shot, mind you. The odds are still long, because editors don't always have time to nurse along would-be writers. But it's a shot nonetheless.

So do I submit stuff to the editor of a specific comic book? They may kill me for this, but my answer to that would be yes. Official policies may be otherwise but, as I said, I'm not official. And me, the smart-aleck freelancer, I figure, what've you got to lose? If the editor doesn't want to deal with it, he'll kick it over to someone else, anyway.

My reasoning is this: What an editor needs most is inventory material. Stories that do not have an immediate affect on the continuity. Stories that, after twenty-two pages, will leave the lead character the same as he was at the beginning in terms of his status and relations with the other characters. That way, if the regular team blows a deadline, the editor is prepared with a fill-in story.

The trick is that any good story is about — to some degree — change. Someone in the course of the story should, ideally, go through some sort of change. Something should happen to him wherein, at the end of the story, he views the world a little differently than when he began. So either the lead character (a super-hero, presumably) has to have an experience that makes him think differently about something when the adventure is over, or else you have to create some new character to interact with the super-hero so that, by the end of the story, the new character is different than when he began.

It's very difficult. It's not impossible. And when it's done well, it can be extremely memorable. Roger Stern's "The Kid Who Collected Spider-Man," for example, could easily have been a fill-in story, since it filled all those basic requirements, and I still get choked up when I think about it.

So what's the ideal scenario, if it all falls right? You submit a one-page story outline to the editor of the respective comic book. He loves it. He uses the self-addressed stamped envelope you included to write back to you and asks you to flesh it out into a full plot (presumably sending you a sample so that you have an idea of how to do it). You develop it as a full plot. The editor loves it, you get paid for it, and it gets sent off to an artist.

Do I get to script it myself? If you want to, sure.

Remember, you're trying to make it easier for the editor. If he or she has to find someone to script your work because you can't handle it, you have that much less value.

What if they steal my idea? The only thing slimmer than the odds of your breaking in is the odds of your ideas being swiped. There's simply no motivation for the editors to do so. Remember, ideally the editor wants writers to help him get the comic books out; not would-be writers who are angry because their ideas got filched. You must also keep in mind that you might submit something that someone else has come up with independently, and it's already in the works. Many a tyro has assumed that his idea was usurped, and went around badmouthing the writer and editor of the comic book. That's not a way to make friends and influence people, and it's also generally unfounded (unless you're Art Buchwald).

Is there any way to improve the odds a bit? Well, $10 clipped to your story submission might help.

Just kidding.

Yes, there are ways to improve the odds on becoming a writer for Marvel or DC. In fact, almost anything you do will improve the odds, because frankly, they can't get much worse than what they are when you submit a story cold.

Three commonplace ways to have a better shot at being a writer for Marvel:

1) Get writing credits somewhere else first. It doesn't necessarily have to be one of the independent comics publishers. As a pure digression, I must admit I'm a little fuzzy on the term "independents." Is Marvel still a British colony or something, that it's not independent? Is DC a British colony (well, maybe, yeah, now that I think about it). As for the so called "independents," sometimes they don't own the characters they publish. These alleged independents have less control over their fates, particularly if they are dependent on such things as the whims of licensors. Go figure semantics, huh?

If your cover letter can list professional experience in other forms of writing — news writing, copy writing, published short stories — anything that proves that you know how to put sentences together and meet a deadline will be of help. Not that you have to submit your résumé with every story. A couple of lines on your cover letter will suffice.

2) Go to conventions. Try to give an editor a face to put with a name. At smaller, less crowded conventions, it's possible for editors and writers to read your stuff and comment on your stuff. If you're going to a larger convention, such as San Diego, I suggest — as difficult as it may sound — that you boil your ideas down to verbal pitches of 25 words or less. If you grab an editor with a neat verbal hook ("Daredevil's hypersenses inform him that a politician's pacemaker is actually a bomb — but the politician hates super-heroes and won't trust him!") and get the editor going, "Yeah? Yeah? And then?" you can pull out your one-page outline with a flourish and hand it to him.

On a personal note: I will never read a plot outline, if it deals with characters I write. It's my way of avoiding possible hassles. But if time and circumstances at a convention permit, I will read outlines involving other characters. But please — if you see a writer or editor go into the bathroom, don't follow him in and slide your story under the door of the stall. I can't speak for others in the industry, but you won't like what I do with anything handed to me in that manner.

3) Get a job at Marvel or DC. To be honest, that's what happened with me. Except when I got a job at Marvel, it was in sales, and I didn't get the job because I hoped to angle into writing. My career was genuinely in sales. I tried the writing on the side, just for kicks. I had no idea that it would develop into what it has, or that eventually I would be writing columns in trade newspapers, trying to advise others on how to emulate what I laughingly refer to as my success.

If you're lucky enough to land an office job, it becomes that much easier because, of course, people will get to know you. Even if you don't get a job, the whole trick is to make a memorable and *positive* and memorable impression on the people to whom you hope to sell the story. Come up with clever, dynamic ways to get yourself — and your stories — noticed. What sort of ways? You're supposed to be a writer. Use your imagination.

(Peter David, writer of stuff, gives you the answer to last week's trivia question: The two films starring Michael Keaton and Danny DeVito are, obviously, **Batman Returns***, and not-so-obviously,* **Johnny Dangerously***. For you* **Johnny Dangerously** *fans (both of you), Weird Al Yankovic has a new videotape out called* **The Weird Al Yankovic Video Library: His Greatest Hits***, and it features the video of the theme song for that film, a zippy tune entitled "This Is the Life" that, for some reason, now makes me, think of certain guys at Image.)*

BREAKING IN, PART DEUX (March 19, 1993)

Delving into the *BID* mail bag, I found this letter on the top. It's a polite and respectful missive from Rick D. of Joplin, Missouri. Apparently endeavoring to maintain the skeptical nature of the "Show Me" state, Rick — after starting off with a terse "Mr. David" for a salutation, writes (and to be fair to Rick, who has his own writing ambitions, I'm leaving the missing words, misspellings, and improper grammar intact):

"Does your greed know no bounds? I read your article on breaking as a writer first in the *CBG*, and recently in the *Wizard Price Guide*. How can you be as arrogant as to give advice to a beginning writer? As an aspiring writer, I know that the only way to break in 'cold' into Marvel (or DC) is to know someone, which most of us don't. You however, worked for Marvel, and don't expect me to believe that you would have gotten published otherwise. The same goes for your *Star Trek* novels, which I don't doubt were helped by your involvement in the paperback industry.

"In addition to you being a poor example, you give poor advice as well. Since you've had it so easy I guess I could understand your not realizing the utter stupidity of submitting to the Big Two at all, much less to a specific title. No editor ever reads unsolicited plots. Instead of giving realistic, useful advice (such as start with independents, and find an artist collaborator), you're feeding these kids exactly what they want to hear, instead of what they need to hear. A lot of kids are being set up for a massive disappointment when those snotty form letters start rolling in.

"While much more advice for fledging writers should be offered, you are *not* the man to do it."

While this is not the most annoying letter I've ever gotten, I was impressed by your ability, Rick, to fit that much arrogance and that many incorrect assumptions into a relatively brief space. Since you yourself are an aspiring — or, to use your word, "fledging," as opposed to "fledgling" — writer, you would seem to have a bright future ahead of you — particularly if you wind up writing for certain acerbic comics publications.

There was much about the letter I found curious. Does my greed, in fact, know no bounds? I don't know. I believe my greed does, indeed, know bounds, although it remains shaky on state capitals.

If you're referring to my hunger to make money off this column, then apparently you're unaware that all the money for *BID* goes to the Comic Book Legal Defense Fund. If you're referring to the princely sum I got from *Wizard* for the reprint (*Wizard*'s people sought me out, by the way; I didn't go to them), I did indeed keep it, greedy devil that I am. It was enough, as I recall, to buy a week's groceries.

How can I give advice to beginning writers? I suppose if they stopped asking me, I could stop giving it.

Yes, absolutely, I worked for Marvel — in the sales department, as I've mentioned in the past. Curiously, this was both an advantage and a disadvantage. Sure, the editors all knew me — but they knew me as a sales employee. Back then there was a *tremendous* schism between editorial and sales. No one from the latter had ever, to my knowledge, done work for the former. There was a very simple logic involved, as far as the editors were concerned: If you were creative, you'd be working for editorial. If you were on the business side, you were not creative, because if you were creative, you'd be working for editorial. Q.E.D.

I was in sales for several years before I started showing story proposals around (using the format, by the way, that I advised in the column). I was not welcome. One editor (I was later informed) said, "Why should we hire *him* to write stories? Who do we hire next — people in subscriptions? Secretaries?"

Only one editor would touch my story ideas: Jim Owsley, who was always something of a maverick and didn't give a damn what people thought of him. When he bought some *Spectacular Spider-Man* plots from me, there were rumblings. When he assigned me to the book, there was full-fledged vituperation.

"It's a conflict of interest!" shouted some editors, claiming I would focus my sales attention on *Spec Spidey* to the exclusion of other Marvel titles. So I bent over backwards *not* to promote, or even push, any of my work —which is probably why sales on my issues weren't particularly good.

Eventually, when editorial saw that the sky didn't fall — and also, when Bob Harras (with the ice broken) offered me *Incredible Hulk*, a title that people weren't exactly falling all over each other to write — folks started to lighten up. Nowadays, crisscrossing between business and editorial is fairly common.

As for my *Star Trek* novels — sorry, Rick. Wrong again. No one at Pocket even *knew* I had worked in the paperback industry. They were interested in me because of my work on the *Star Trek* comic book for DC.

You seem to be under the impression that I had everything handed to me. I really hate to disillusion someone who is so completely sure of himself, but my first published fiction was in *Isaac Asimov's Science Fiction Magazine* — submitted cold, unsolicited. I sold an Op Ed piece to *The New York Times* — submitted cold, unsolicited. And I had 20 rejections to accompany every acceptance.

My novel, *Knight Life*, was agented — which hardly guaranteed it a free ride. It was first submitted to Judy-Lynn Del Rey of Del Rey paperbacks, who sent it back with a cover letter saying that the writing made her vomit. (And somewhere John Byrne is saying, "Ha! See! I'm *not* the only one who has that reaction!") It was subsequently rejected by half a dozen other publishers before finding a home at Ace.

Have I caught some breaks? Unquestionably. Then again, what is succeeding as a writer — or, for that matter, succeeding in *any* profession — if it doesn't involve catching breaks somewhere along the way? You can, however, increase the chances of catching those breaks, if you know some of the rules. That's all I was trying to do in the original column, as I said repeatedly: improve the odds a bit.

Another way of improving the odds is, unquestionably, getting some previous comic book experience. Hooking up with "fledging" artists, getting published by independents, or even yourself — these add valuable credits to your resumé and help prove that you can do the job. I kind of thought that was so self-evident that it didn't need to be mentioned. If I had thought it would have assuaged your wrath, Rick, I certainly would have brought it up. Besides, people weren't asking me how to break into the indies. They asked how to break into *Marvel*, and I gave them advice as to how to have, at the very least, a fighting chance.

But you claim that there's no point to that. "*No* editor even reads unsolicited plots," you declare. Well, you got me there, Rick. No editor does read unsolicited plots.

I never said they did.

As a matter of fact — *I said they didn't*. For those who may have missed the column, my contention was that submissions should be limited to plot springboards — preferably half a page, with a full page the maximum.

I started to wonder though, Rick: What if you're right? I mean, you were wrong about so many other things, I figured the law of averages had to catch up sooner or later. Was it true that no editor at Marvel was reading anything unsolicited?

Certainly a staggering percentage of Marvel's output comes from people who are now, or have been, on staff. Obviously, the absolute best way to break in is to get a job at Marvel; then again, that's not terribly useful advice to anyone not living in the New York/Tri-State area.

But is that tendency purely because of the convenience factor — or was there, as Rick implied, some sort of flat policy followed by Marvel's editors?

I decided to call up some editors and ask. I don't like to make flat assertions without having some sort of facts to back them up.

According to Mark Gruenwald, there is no official policy regarding unsolicited work other than "be nice" in dealing with those submitting the material. It's left up to the individual editors as to how to handle the actual process.

"Some editors send material directly to Glenn Greenberg, the submissions editor," said Gruenwald. "Some will write to the more promising ones, or call them since that's easier, if there's a phone number. There are some editors who won't deal with new writers because, due to their rather acerbic personality, they believe that silence is the best way to handle these things."

All the editors I spoke with stressed the long turnaround time, due to their own workloads. They handle it in different ways.

Bobbie Chase, for example, will allow material to pile up, sometimes as long as six months — at which point she'll then read through everything in one massive sitting. This, of course, means that it could take as long as half a year or as short as a week to hear back from her. But she will take the time to read the material herself.

Terry Kavanagh, on the other hand, strives for alacrity. Three to four weeks is as long as he'll let things sit, at which point he may then read them himself. Far more likely, though, is that he'll kick them down to Greenberg. It means that the material isn't read by him personally; on the other hand, it would theoretically be attended to more quickly.

"It used to be that I'd read 70-80% myself," said Kavanagh. "Now it's maybe around 35%."

"It takes forever to get to it," agreed Joey Cavalieri. He supported — as did all editors surveyed — the notion that would-be writers should stick to springboards. Some neos don't even settle for sending in plots. "People send me their novels," said Cavalieri in amazement. "They send me their screenplays."

Nel Yomtov left himself open to reading springboards "depending on my schedule. These days I have trouble finding the time."

"So much stuff comes in that I can't guarantee that I'll get to it," said Kelly Corvese. "I've learned the hard way that I can't promise to read everything." Corvese, however, does tend to read submissions, if he's discussed them over the phone first with the would-be writer — and the writer reminds him in a cover letter that they had already talked about the story idea. Again, though, time constraints weigh heavily.

Danny Fingeroth will automatically pass all submissions on to Greenberg. It's not just time limits that concern Fingeroth; it also relates to his "always being aware of being accused of using someone else's ideas."

Indeed, several editors noted that the most daunting concern about reading unsolicited manuscripts is that there may be ideas there that parallel material already in development. This can, in turn, lead to some more aggressive tyros accusing Marvel of plagiarism.

I can relate to this concern. I will never read any story proposals for characters on which I am currently working. For example, a letter was forwarded to me from DC which contained, I discovered, a plot outline for an *Aquaman* story. I took one look at the title: "Aquaman Battles the Deep Six," and tossed it across the room as if it had tried to bite me. Why? Because I was *already planning* to bring in those Kirby creations, and didn't need a fan accusing me of swiping the notion from him. I had Myra send it back to the writer with an explanatory note.

Similarly, I was extremely relieved that a *Hulk* bit featuring Betty Banner shunning a gamma-irradiated-chicken at the supermarket came out the same week as an identically themed *Bumpkin Buzz*. The timing precluded anyone saying I was swiping from Brian Ahern. (Although, c'mon — give me some credit. I wouldn't be *that* obvious.)

Tyro writers frequently refuse to believe that minds can work in similar directions, and that can make them very difficult to deal with.

Renee Witterstaetter reiterated the problem.

She pointed out a *Catch-22* situation in that if a tyro produces a story about a character who has his own title, the editor might not want to deal with possible plagiarism accusations. If the story features a character who's not in use, then who's going to want to publish it?

"Sending in a story for an existing book makes more sense," was what Gruenwald suggested. "You'd probably be better served trying to do a *Captain America* story or an *Incredible Hulk* story."

(Gee, thanks, Mark.)

Joey Cavalieri offers further advice. "Pick a title without a regular writer. Or one that seems to be having a lot of personnel changes, because (in those cases) clearly the editor is looking around."

Kavanagh — although he doesn't read the majority of material himself, as noted above — remains one of the only markets (with *Marvel Comics Presents*) for stories that don't feature mainline Marvel characters.

"I'm in a unique position," he says, "because I've got these eight-page stories. I can say to a writer, 'Work on this story, take your time, make it the best you possibly can.' And when it's printed, it's in a book with three other stories by writers with more experience. It's not on its own."

"The problem is," said Kavanagh, "I don't know if I would read a springboard and give someone an issue of *Namor*. It might be the greatest springboard in the world, but you don't know how long it took the guy to write it. You don't know whether he can actually produce the story."

Everyone agrees on one thing: It's difficult. As opposed to artwork which can be looked at in seconds, writing samples requires much more concentration — and willingness to develop stories — than some editors may have the time and inclination to provide. Some editors, though, have bought unsolicited manuscripts during their tenure at Marvel. (I won't say which ones, since I'm reluctant to "target" any of them as the most likely sources.)

Submissions Editor Greenberg has held the position for over seven months. In that time, he has not found one purchasable writing submission.

However, that may be attributable to the fact that the vast majority do not follow the suggestions outlined in my column.

"Most of the time I get these 300-page manuscripts or screenplays," said Greenberg, echoing Cavalieri's words. "People send these huge fantasy novels. And when they *do* send things in the right format, either it's only about characters they've created — or else it's just, 'Wolverine meets Sabretooth in the forest; they fight; Wolverine wins. The end.'"

So there you go, Rick. Now, of course, you might start claiming that all of the people I interviewed for this piece were lying to me — that *none* of them ever read anything that's submitted cold. I'm not all-knowing. Sometimes I'm even gullible.

Tell you what.

You contact all those editors and tell them they're full of it (although good luck if you had any subsequent plans of working for them). And then, you can write a piece for *CBG* and use your many years of experience to tell would-be writers what they *really* need to know, rather than the malarkey that various editors and I have been feeding them.

My, oh my. Where *were* you when I did "Ask the Self Proclaimed Experts?"

(Peter David, writer of stuff, is going to beg all you fledgling writers not to deluge with submissions the editors I interviewed for this piece — particularly the ones who said they read stuff themselves. Wait, oh, six months or so. But you can deluge Glenn right away. It's OK. He likes it. I also invite other companies' editors to write to tell us how they handle submissions, so that Rick won't have to have my opinions in this matter inflicted on him any more.)

Historical Notes:

1) Once again I have taken an editorial option, deleting Rick's last name from this reprint so that his fairly public drubbing won't be immortalized in a trade paperback. Besides, I figure he's got enough problems. No lie here: His brothers showed up at a convention. I thought they would be upset with me, but such was not the case. Not only did they back up the general impression one garnered about Rick from his letter, but they claimed that he had recently launched his college career with the unique feat of failing Freshman Orientation.

THE WACKO THEORY (June 4, 1993)

I haven't seriously annoyed bunches of people in a while, I think. Since I don't dare allow matters in *BID* to become too complacent, something must be done. Let us see now, what can I possibly talk about that will honk people off?

I know.

Something fun may be brewing in the letters pages of *Wizard* magazine. Let's see if we can cash in on it over here.

In issue #21 of that publication, a letter appeared from David Michelinie. David, being one of the more genuine gentlemen in the industry, very politely — polite to the point of bending over backwards, I would say — corrected what he felt to be a misstatement in the January issue. In that particular issue, David was referred to as the "co-creator" of Venom, the slobbering, hulking arch-enemy of Spider-Man and faint-hearted parents everywhere.

Not so, said David. Although his praise for Todd McFarlane was effusive, he stated that "there was only one person who actually created Venom, and that was me."

Indeed, although David doesn't mention it, I recall very distinctly when he was putting together the basics of the character — particularly because he discussed them with me. Not that I contributed anything to the character's development: I didn't. But there was a connection with the Sin-Eater/Jean DeWolff story I'd written, and David ran it past me in a "How does this sound to you as a tie-in" sort of manner. It seemed pretty keen to me. And Todd was nowhere in sight, or even connected with the title at that time.

But here's where things start to get fun. Because in issue #23 of *Wizard* (which, if I've timed this right, should be hitting the stands just about now) a letter runs that's signed by Erik Larsen.

Without going into detail on it, I will simply say that — using a somewhat more aggressive tone than Dave's letter — Erik proceeds to dismiss peremptorily all of Dave's contributions to Venom (origin, characterization, motivation — all that trivial stuff) as clichéd, unoriginal, and stupid. We're left to assume then, that all of Venom's success can be attributed to the teeth and tongue which Todd contributed.

What this calls into question is the whole notion of creating a character: Who created this character, who created that. It's probably an extension of the modern emphasis on character ownership. In the old days (note I do not say the good old days, 'cause they weren't good) the matter of who created what might have had less immediacy because the bottom line was that it didn't matter — not in the legal sense, at any rate. In terms of personal accomplishment, certainly. But, legally, it was all owned by the company.

Nowadays, though, the idea of who created what can translate into serious money for the individuals present in the creation. The stakes have gone way up. Not only are entire publishing entities springing into existence based on the notion of character ownership, but even avowed work-for-hire bastions such as Marvel have New Character forms which, when filled out by the creators of particular characters, guarantee the creators a piece of the action.

The valid point that Erik does raise is in pointing out all the pre-existing elements that went into Venom's creation.

Who *did* create Venom? Was it whoever came up with the idea of Spider-Man switching to a black-and-white costume? (Jim Shooter, who in turn may have been influenced by an intended costume switch for Spider-Woman, which became moot when her title was canceled.) Was it the person who decided that the costume was sentient? (Tom DeFalco and Ron Frenz.) Was it the designers of the black-and-white Spider-Man costume? (Mike Zeck and Rick Leonardi, among others.) Was it the creator of the Sin-Eater story with which it tied in? (Hell, no.) Was it the guy who struck in the tongue and teeth? (All Todd's.)

Considering the evolutionary nature of so many things in the comic-book process, is it possible for anyone *ever* to be termed the creator of anything?

Who created Venom? Dave and Jim and Tom and Ron and Mike and Rick and Todd? I wracked what I laughingly refer to as my brains for quite some time on this one before I came up with my answer. It's not a perfect answer. It's not an all-inclusive answer. But it's the only one I got.

Who created Venom?

Just Dave.

He's right. He's sole creator.

Because — and here's where it gets dicey — it is impossible, except in the most rare of circumstances, to have co-creators of any character. The vast majority of the time, a character has one creator. And of that majority, the vast majority of the time, the creator is the writer.

Now, c'mon. You knew I was going to say that. It's only fair. If artists get to sit there and proclaim that they're the be-all and end-all of comics, then writers are entitled to display some chauvinism every now and then.

First, we have to define our terms.

What is "creation?"

When we say that someone is creating something, what the hell are we talking about specifically?

Well, whenever I endeavor to define terms, I always crack open my *American Heritage Dictionary*. And in the reliable *AHD*, it states:

"Creation: (1) the act of creating."

As always, a big help. But if we jump to "create," we see:

"Create: (1) To cause to exist; bring into being; originate."

Now that's helpful. Before exploring it further, we can touch base with one of the better-known instances of creation, namely:

"In the beginning God created the Heaven and the Earth."

"And the Earth was without form, and void; and darkness was upon the face of the deep. And the Spirit of God moved upon the face of the waters."

"And God said, Let there be light: and there was light."

Two things can be discerned from the foregoing. First, it's interesting that, according to *Genesis*, God created the Heaven and the Earth before he created light. Some have held that this supports the Big Bang theory. Of course, if one wanted to be cynical, one could point out that apparently God created the Earth before He could see what the hell He was doing, which would certainly explain quite a lot.

The second is that, when one is talking about creation in its purest form, one is talking about bringing something from nothing. That's creation. To cause to exist. First there is nothing; then there is something. And the person who causes something to exist is the creator.

When one is creating life (aside from single-celled animals), that's a different story. Every single person reading this column is a genuine, indisputable co-creation. It took two to tango — and an X and a Y (or an X and an X) chromosome to get things rolling.

But the creation of a comic-book character is something else again. That's not creating life. That's creating a semblance of life. An illusion. And that sort of thing cannot be a co-creation, because, as described above, the creator is the one who sets it into motion. The one who makes it happen. And that is, also as noted, usually the writer.

The writer is the one who sits there with a blank sheet of paper or the blank computer screen. The writer is the one who has to reach into the ether of nothingness and pull forth from it, dripping and raw, something.

The writer is a character's creator. The sole creator.

I like to refer to this as the Writer As Creative King/Overlord theory or, more simply, the WACKO theory.

Now — although there are quite a few artists who would be quick to diminish a writer's participation in the creative process, no sane writer would return that favor (indeed, I understand that David Michelinie has declined to fire back at Erik's missive). Naturally the artist's visualization is vital to the development and, ultimately, success of a character. A crummy artist can drag down a creation into oblivion; a talented artist can cause the character to transcend what the WACKO has initiated.

But creating a look for the character is not the same thing as creating the character himself, and should not be lumped together. Did Spider-Man cease to be Spider-Man when he changed to the black-and-white costume?

Everything that comes afterward is other people — pencillers, inkers, whoever — building upon the concepts that the writer came up with. That makes the writer the creator and the penciller the — what?

"Developer," I suppose. Co-developer, because frequently the writer's input becomes instrumental for such trivial things as dialogue. That's if you want to be accurate. I'm reluctant to say that, though, because now we're beginning to understand why screen credits read the way they do. Because if Venom's pedigree were correctly (dare we say "politically correctly"? listed, it would be as follows):

Venom: A Marvel Comics Production. Created by David Michelinie. Developed by David Michelinie and Todd McFarlane. Based on ideas by Jim Shooter, Tom DeFalco, Ron Frenz, Rick Leonardi, Louise Simonson (since her handling of the costume in *Web of Spider-Man* established important foundations), and Mike Zeck.

You see how complicated it can get. That's why no one with any brains gets involved with this kind of argument. Of course, that does nothing to deter me.

Now of course, the WACKO theory only relates to writer/artist teams. If Erik Larsen the writer started arguing with Erik Larsen the artist about who created Savage Dragon, it would make a rather bizarre spectacle (albeit one that I'd certainly pay five bucks to see).

But when the artist and writer are two different people, you get into all sorts of problems. For example, according to the WACKO theory, Stan Lee is the creator of most of the key Marvel Comics. Why? Because he came up with the ideas.

Stan's creatorship of the characters, however, has been hotly disputed. I'm not going to get into that at any length because it's been done to death. But what I will point out is that, even as far as Stan's own recountings of Marvel's origins are concerned, there is one character who was indisputably created by the artist: Namely, The Silver Surfer.

Because, by Stan's own printed recollections, the art pages for *Fantastic Four* #48 came in and Jack had drawn a herald for Galactus that Stan had known nothing about. Jack's contention (according to Stan) was that someone as powerful as Galactus should have a herald. Therefore, the Surfer's pedigree would be: *The Silver Surfer*. A Marvel Production. Created by Jack Kirby. Developed by Stan Lee and Jack Kirby — according to the WACKO theory.

Ah, you say, but I stated that the character's visual was secondary to the character himself. So I did. But Kirby not only created the inspired and truly bizarre non-sequitur visual of an Oscar statue on a surfboard (a surfboard?! I mean, we take it for granted now, but — a *surfboard*? And the fans bought that? This silver guy shows up on Earth for the first time, riding a distinctly Earthian artifact complete with racing stripes, and no one commented on how completely insane this was?), he also developed the Surfer's reason for being and gave him the distinctly noble look that Stan keyed off on in dialoguing him.

The Surfer is a fascinating case study in how important a truly gifted team is. Without Jack, you wouldn't have had the Surfer to begin with because Stan didn't come up with him for the story. Jack is the all-important creator. However, without Stan — the as-important developer — you wind up with — well — you get The Black Racer.

Even worse — you wind up with Cable.

Cable might seem, on the surface, to defy the WACKO theory. Yet, in fact, he's practically the proof of it.

Who created Cable?

I've gathered the following from various interviews, and think I'm fairly accurate in describing the origins of the character as follows:

X-Editor Bob Harras decided one day that the New Mutants needed to have a new adult leader in charge.

Does that mean, according to the WACKO theory, that Bob created Cable? If it weren't for Bob's editorial directive, Cable would not have been created. But it's hard to designate Bob as Cable's creator because "They need a new leader" is a bit vague.

Then Rob Liefeld drew a cyborg character with a glowing eye and a big gun. When Louise Simonson suggested the name "Commander X," Rob declared that to be a stupid name and stated that he was called "Cable."

So did Rob create Cable? It would seem so, particularly if we look at the Surfer example. Except that (nothing personal, Rob) there's nothing particularly inspired or original about a cyborg character with one eye (see Deathlok or Cyborg of the Titans or even *The $Six Million Dollar Man*). Furthermore, whereas "Commander X" at least harkens to "Professor X," "Cable" conjures up associations with C-SPAN and Cinemax. He had a look and a name, but that was all. Like the Tin Woodsman, he had no heart.

So is Louise Simonson, the writer of *New Mutants*, Cable's creator? But she was third in the food chain by that point, behind Bob's editorial directive and Rob's visual. Furthermore, whatever plans and personality she had in mind for the character became moot when she left the series. Likewise with Rob when he left a year or so later.

As opposed to Venom (with David Michelinie exclusively handling the important Venom appearances — I'm not counting sales-jacking guest-shots) or The Silver Surfer (who was scripted by no one except Stan for years, at Stan's insistence), Cable was left with no writer or artist or even a wartist to guide him.

Who created Cable?

Ultimately — insanely — the only answer would seem to be: Marvel Comics.

There was no defining moment when Cable burst from the head of a writer as a character. He burst from the head of an artist as a visual. And when you look at a drawing for the first time, the natural inclination is to say — just as Stan did to Jack about the Surfer — "Who's that?"

With the Surfer, three issues later, we knew. His character, his essence, everything. Same with Venom.

With Cable, it's three years later, and we still haven't a clue.

Cable is the ultimate, perfect Marvel character. He has no personality. His background is nebulous and can be shifted to something else the moment readers start catching on. There's no writer attached to him who has invested a personal vision and will start fighting with the editor over what should be done. Readers will eternally be yanked around on the character's mystery, because he has nothing going for him *except* mystery. He makes the company piles of money without one of those gosh-darned irritating creators-with-a-vision to confuse things.

He's a zero, a cipher. He's the definitive company man, because he was not birthed by a WACKO. His was a bastard creation, and if the readers ever wake up to that, he's history. But don't bet on that happening any time soon.

So — the WACKO theory. There will always be those rare instances where a writer and an artist are sitting side-by-side and develop a character. But in the assembly-line atmosphere of Marvel, DC, and whoever else is developing a work-for-hire super-hero line this week, it's a different story. In those instances, the person who creates the character — the essence of the character's being and reason for existence — is the sole creator. Co-developers are incredibly vital, and their importance cannot be diminished. But if we're talking semantics, then there should only be one creator.

If nothing else, it'll avoid arguments of "I created this!" "No, I created it!" "Yeah, but I helped!"

When it comes to arguing over who created what, one is prompted to think of JFK's comment about the Bay of Pigs invasion — which he claimed was an old saying, but in fact wasn't all that old, having been coined by Count Galeazzo Ciano in 1942. And that observation was: "As always, victory finds a hundred fathers but defeat is an orphan."

Which is a highbrow way of saying, "Isn't it weird that we never see any arguments over who created Night Nurse?"

(Myra David, wife of Peter David, writer of stuff, says disputing creator credit is fairly silly and "a guy thing. Women don't get as worked up about it, because they've been spending years getting no credit for anything they accomplish. It's nothing new for them." She's probably right.)

Historical Notes:

1) Boy, did this start a hullabaloo, particularly on CompuServ. Two weeks of defending something that, to me, was largely tongue-in-cheek, but made more sense the more I had to explain it. Two further examples I used to illuminate it: (a) Who created Mr. Spock? Gene Roddenberry, of course. Even though Leonard Nimoy came up with the Nerve Pinch and Salute; even though others designed the costumes and prosthetics — Roddenberry is still "the creator" of Spock, and no one disputes that; (b) By the logic of those who say that an artist who first draws a character must be deemed co-creator, then whoever first drew the James Bond comic strip would be deemed the "co-creator" of James Bond. Which is, of course, ridiculous.

2) John Ostrander and Jim Valentino wrote in and disputed the theory — and Valentino stridently asserted that Rob Liefeld was Cable's creator, period. Walt Simonson wrote in in defense of wife Louise's participation, and said that I had made a dead-on analysis of Cable's place in the Marvel Universe. I think Walt was actually going to write in and challenge the WACKO theory as well, but got side-tracked by Valentino. John Byrne wrote in, criticizing Valentino's emphasis on character visualization to the point of excluding all else.

Valentino wrote back and apologized for possibly offending the Simonsons, and closed his letter with stating that John Byrne was irrationally jealous of Image, reaffirming that you can't disagree with Image, but only be jealous of them.

SECTION 5:

Character Sketches

Some of the best characters in comics are real.

The realm of comic books and science fiction is studded with some of the most memorable individuals one could ever hope to meet.

Several of the people who are profiled in the following essays — if you never met them before — you will never have the opportunity to do so.

Treasure those dear to you while you have them.

MAY THE SCHWARTZ BE WITH YOU (Dec. 7, 1990)

So I'm at the offices of DC Comics the other day, and coming toward me down the hallway, on their way to lunch, are Dick Giordano, Pat Bastienne, and Julie Schwartz. Collectively, they have about 3000 years of comic-book experience among them.

Dick tells me to stop writing fiction that I couldn't sell anywhere and write columns about real stuff. Pat — who is in charge of medical coverage — eyes me carefully to see if I'm coughing or anything, and Julie grips my shoulder firmly, stares me down and growls, "Do a column about me." OK.

Julie Schwartz
Where Legends Live

I will never forget the time I was in a comics store, talking with some older fans about comics history, and the name Julie Schwartz was raised. And a younger fan, standing nearby, glanced up from a rack of *Turtles* comics and said, "Julie Schwartz? Who's she?" Julius Schwartz, ya morons. Ya bozos. The man. The legend. The sexual dynamo. Describing Julie Schwartz brings to mind the (self-proclaimed) description of Captain Freedom from *Hill Street Blues*: Ten tons of dynamite in one hand and a neutron bomb in the other. When he walks, buildings tremble and bad guys wet their pants.

Julius Schwartz, whose very presence and air provides hope for future bald, old Jewish men everywhere (like myself, for example).

Julius Schwartz who — together with a host of others whose names would likewise be unfamiliar to fans who think that Gardner Fox was an old cartoon character — reshaped a comics universe.

They didn't need limited series, or fan favorites, or red skies, or mando paper, high-profile deaths, trade paperbacks, posters, fliers, store displays, inflatable figures, sponges, or bagged editions. All they needed was talent, imagination, and a sense of wonder, dammit.

Julius Schwartz, whose name is connected with one of the greatest disappointments I ever suffered at a convention.

It was at I-Con in Long Island last year, I believe, or perhaps the year before. There was a panel on the topic of redefining characters. Reshaping them, retooling them, and infusing them with renewed vitality for the modern readership (whatever might happen to be defined as "modern" at the time).

I was slated to be on the panel, presumably for my work with *The Incredible Hulk*. (For which, frankly, I still don't understand why I get all the credit. Bob Harras and Al Milgrom turned him gray and crafty, not me.).

I was asked to moderate the panel, but when I found out that Julie Schwartz was going to be on it as well, I refused. I felt it would be presumptuous and inappropriate. *Julie was there*, for crying out loud. So I helped retool one character. So what?

Julie helped reshape a comics *cosmos*. The stories he could tell about re-creating The Flash, Hawk-man, The Atom — an entire modern cast. And it had *never been done* before.

It doesn't matter how many new series they give Hawkman or how much they turn Catwoman into a slut, or how good any of the efforts are. Nothing will change the fact that when the Silver Age of comics was being hammered into shape on the anvil of creativity, it was the *first* time it was being done. We're talking uncharted water, unknown realms, where no fan has gone before.

I was really excited to be on this panel with Julie. I would have been happy to sit in the audience, or be a fly on the wall. I wanted Julie to moderate it. More than that, I wanted to just kick back on the panel and listen to Julie talk about what *it was like*. When I'm on a panel I can just talk and talk, but for this, I was ready to staple my mouth shut lest I detract.

So we show up for the panel at the appointed hour, Julie and myself and the other panelists (I don't remember who, I'm sorry, I apologize profusely) and I can't remember the last time I was so looking forward to a convention panel. Instead of a bunch of young hotshots discussing censorship or violence or whatever, we were going to hear about history in the making from someone whose hands got thick with the clay of the molding.

And no one showed up.

No one

Showed

Up.

I will grant you, it was the first panel of the morning.

Perhaps a number of attendees hadn't gotten there yet. But that's no excuse. We sat in that large lecture room, the bunch of us, for about 10 or 15 minutes, discussing this, that and the other thing — even about the start of the Silver Age — and listened to our voices echo in the empty room.

And no one

Showed

Up.

And after a while we all drifted apart to go look at the dealers' room, and the fans never bothered to come by and hear about the making of the character who was revived by Julie *et al.* so that he could eventually streak across your TV screen Thursday nights, accompanied by a Danny Elfman score.

(And hey, how come we don't see "Created by" credits on *The Flash*, the way Bob Kane receives credit in *Batman*? The official explanation — that they're combining several different elements of the Flash and that they can't, therefore, credit only one person — is a load of crap. What, are they paying for credits by the word or something, and they can't afford it? For that matter, I've seen script credits that read "Script by A, B, and C, from a story by C, X, and Z." Those fit on the TV screen just fine. Can't list one? List them all. They're entitled — their creation gave you guys a job.)

So I was bitterly disappointed with the fan apathy over that panel and if I'm ever on a similar panel, I'm going to do some audience recruitment with a 2 x 4.

I will note, though, that I was on a comics panel with Julie and some other guys that was designed as a "Comics Night" at C.W. Post, again on the Island, and we had a great turnout for that.

I will also note that Julie's ability to walk around conventions with various nubile young ladies at his beck and call, and his talent for charming the most formidable of women, is absolutely legendary. 'Tis a wonderment to behold. They just flock to him.

I have even seen him flirting, repeatedly, with Carol Kalish. And she loves it. *Loves it*. And she even *flirts back*.

To understand the magnitude of this, you have to understand Carol, I suppose. Carol is the head honcho of Marvel Comics Direct sales (that's the comic book specialty market).

She is tough, determined, aggressive, smart, a dozen other things — but not flirtatious. Carol is to the art of flirtation what Rembrandt is to skateboarding. She is my dear friend, but she's not someone you casually cuddle up to and rub faces with. She doesn't invite it and you don't ask.

Except with Julie.

The first time I saw it happen I was shocked. Julie was all over her. She was all over Julie. In *public*. Carol doesn't like having her picture taken, but the first time I saw her allow it, it was in Julie's embrace.

If Julie Schwartz can wrap Carol around his little finger, then the man is a master. An absolute master.

What's he got? I don't know. If I did, I'd seal it in Mylar and keep it in my basement, in a vault, so that I could access it when I'm his age (presuming I don't blow my brains out earlier on in envy) and make use of it.

Julie has appeared on the covers of comics more than any editor I can think of. In fact, when we had Bela Oxmyx an the cover of *Star Trek* #11, we had to change his likeness because we didn't have the right to use the actor's face. Bela wound up looking like Julie Schwartz, and we got quite a few queries about it. At a San Diego Con, Carol, Greg Theakston, Richard Howell and a host of cohorts sponsored a major birthday bash for Julie.

He deserves it, deserves it all. He certainly deserves that more than being wondered about as, "Julie Schwartz? Who's she?"

So now you know.

Okay, Julie — where's my ten bucks?

(Peter David, writer of stuff, is available for weddings, parties and Bar-Mitzvahs.)

Historical Notes:

1) At the very next I-Con, the identical panel was held. And this time there was a healthy crowd. A number of people told me specifically they had come because of my column. It was my first indicator that BID could really have an impact and get things done.

2) Julie gave me ten bucks. I kept it. I'm not stupid.

BAMF (July 12, 1991)

Something must said about this, the end of an era. About Chris Claremont making his surprising X-it from the X-books.

When I was about 19 or so, I had been cold turkey off comics.

For some years, I had quit them completely, as I noted in a previous column, when I was 13, because I was concerned that guys who read comics weren't cool-looking and were never going to get any girls. However, by age 19, I had a regular girlfriend and wasn't concerned about losing her (indeed, I didn't; in fact, a couple years later, I married her).

The other problem about buying comics years previously had been that the only comics outlet was a stationery/card store, where the owner looked at me like I was some kind of drooling idiot every time I purchased a "funny book." This, however, was in New Jersey, home of drooling idiots. (Hey! I lived there for 13 years. I paid my dues. I'm entitled to cut up New Jersey, if I feel like it. So there. Nyaah.) When I was 19, I was working part time for a newspaper in Pennsylvania, the humiliation of that Jersey card store long gone. And outside the newspaper office was a newsstand that carried comics. It was right on the way. I couldn't help but see them as I walked in.

And one day, I happened to notice that *X-Men* was on the stands.

X-Men, the only title in history to go into reruns during the numbering of its own title. X-Men, up until that time, probably held the record for as many stories reprinted as printed in the first place.

I had always enjoyed *X-Men*. There had been something about it that earned it its own special niche in my heart. Perhaps it was the fact that it was about an entire group of misfits. Kind of Spider-Man cubed. The Fantastic Four lived on their own little urban Mount Olympus and were revered. The Avengers were lionized. But everyone hated The X-Men's guts. For anyone who has ever thought, "Well, I'm just as good as this guy; so how come this guy has so many friends and I've got none?" this was definitely the group.

But this crew that graced the cover of *X-Men* #95 looked strange. In fact, I stared at them and thought, "How weird. Here's a title called *X-Men*, and it doesn't have any of the *X-Men* on it."

I looked left and right, to make sure that no one from the old neighborhood in New Jersey (roughly 100 miles away) happened to be wandering down the street. And then I bought it. I bought my first copy of a monthly comic book in more than five years.

I read it and immediately gravitated to these new characters.

At least Scott was still around, and Charles Xavier. I didn't know who the rest of the crew were, but they seemed likeable enough. Very colorful. The old *Trek* fan in me appreciated the ethnic combination, reminiscent of the bridge of the *Enterprise*. I thought Storm was a babe and wondered which of the other team members she was going to fall in love with. [*Answer: None.*] And I thought Wolverine was obnoxious, and so was Thunderbird, although that wasn't a problem for very long.

A few weeks after that, a comics convention was advertised. Fired up by this new group, I went to the convention and picked up a copy of *X-Men* #94, cover price. And I asked one retailer, "Have these guys made any other appearances?"

"Yeah," he said, and pulled out a copy of *Giant Size X-Men* #1. It was stickered at $1.50, but the convention was winding down, so he gave it to me for a buck.

After reading that, I discovered that Wolverine had first appeared in *Hulk* #180-181, so I sought out back issues of those and picked each of those up for about a buck or so.

Who knew?

Who knew that Chris Claremont would be picking up the reins of the team that Len Wein created and leading them on a mixed and merry chase for 15 years? I mean, it's crazy when you realize that there are now X-books coming out every single week, and when I started reading the comic book, it was coming out *bi-monthly*. Can you imagine Marvel's fiscal health, if the series had never gained the popularity it did and it was *still* coming out bi-monthly? Take away the mutant titles and what have you got? Well, *Ghost Rider. Punisher*. Ah, but it was the aggressive, kick-butt Wolverine who cleared the decks for hero/villains with weaponry and an attitude. Without them, that leaves —

Zip.

It has been stated that Alan Moore was the first writer to show that the writer and writer alone can make a difference in the sales of a comic book. I would disagree with that. Look at the history of The X-Men over the last decade and a half. Artists have come and gone, but the constant has been the writer. Has been Claremont.

There have been up periods and down, hot sequences and sequences that weren't so hot.

There's a reason for this. Claremont's human. Yes, true believers, despite what some may say, Chris Claremont has not been writing the comic books for so long that he's now a mutant.

Chris's strength has always been ideas and characterization (God knows it's not tying up loose ends), and the mutant comic books have always been replete with both. Sometimes to the point of obscuring the storyline. Sometimes to the point of making you scratch your head and wonder just what the hell the storyline was in the first place.

When I first picked up *X-Men*, it was eminently accessible. But there were only a few issues out. Now there've been a tad more, and it's extremely difficult to jump on board. The title's greatest strength — its complexity — can also be argued to be its greatest weakness. For some time now there have been promises that *X-Men* is going to be simpler, easier to follow. And it hasn't been. With Chris leaving, fans might now say, "Ah hah! Now things are going to get cleared up!"

Except —

Do you really want them to?

I mean, as much as fans crab and moan about the complexity, and the dangling storylines and the occasional total confusion, it also seems to be those same elements that keep people coming back month after month. I have generally found that fans want what they want until they get it, at which point they don't want it any more.

Lord knows, following the tangled skein of the mutant titles wasn't easy but, oddly enough, I don't recall reading a rule anywhere that said that just because a story was in a comic book, it necessarily had to be easy. *X-Men* broke a lot of the conventional wisdom of comics; it also sold the most for the longest period of time.

I wish John Byrne luck on following Claremont's act. I personally would not have wanted to attempt it. I personally would have felt too intimidated by the massiveness of the mutant universe that Chris has created. I don't need the aggravation or the fan microscope — I'm content with the relatively clean slate of *X-Factor*.

Although it was Dave Cockrum who helped breathe life into the characters at their inception (and reached new heights with the Starjammers storyline), it was Claremont and Byrne together who really put the series on the map.

Cockrum's favorite character was Nightcrawler, but Byrne's was Wolverine and, as the more picturesque berserker cut his way into the limelight (especially with his of-necessity slaying of a guard in the Savage Land), so, too, did the X-Men's star rise. But when Byrne left right after the Sigourney Pryde Meets the Alien issue, Chris was still there, plugging away.

It was his consistent hand, his understanding of the characters, and his unbounded imagination that kept the series ever on the rise, while other flashes in the pan have topped it, only to fall away or be canceled altogether.

Some fans grumble that Chris is only as good as his artist. Hot news flash, kids: Same goes for any writer, because the art is what people see, and the majority of readers will not cut through sub-par art, even for an above-average story. Not to mention the fact that artists, if their page layout or storytelling is poor, can hamper scripting abilities.

Did Chris repeat himself, repeat themes? Of course he did.

All writers do. Sometimes the overfamiliarity with Chris bred contempt among some readers who didn't realize the incredible difficulty and sheer feat of turning out a comic book month after month after month — or with even greater frequency, when you add in limited series, annuals, etc.

X-Men was (and, I hope, will continue to be) a series where anything could happen. Characters could die (and die and die and die and —), their personalities and interrelationships could change over time, their entire look could change (remember when punk Storm first walked on panel?), and, every so often, Chris could even poke fun at the characters (my favorite being when Wolverine was applying mousse to his hair, thereby answering the longstanding question of how he got it to stay that way; and in the course of doing so, moussed his hair and sideburns to give it the look it had during the Havok/ Wolverine limited series before he shook his head, said "Nah," and returned it to its usual state).

Chris has stated on various open forums that one of several points of contention that prompted him to leave was his intention to have, as an element of a storyline (and since it's not being used, I'm not giving anything away here), that Charles Xavier suffer the loss of his telepathic abilities as a consequence of battle. That he became the telepathic equivalent of a deafmute. That this loss of power would be a truly hideous thing for him to suffer through, far more devastating than any physical injury. And he was told that he couldn't do it, because it wasn't visual enough.

Two things occurred to me in this respect: first, that this is the second time Chris wanted to do a storyline like that. The first time was with Jean, when she went berserk as Phoenix. Chris wanted to have her psychically lobotomized. Living hell for a telepath.

And he was told then that he couldn't do it, because (according to all accounts on the subject) Jim Shooter said she had to die because she blew up the planet of broccoli heads. As a result, Jean died, causing a major loss of focus for the series from which, I feel, it never quite completely recovered.

So, if I can offer a piece of advice to future mutant writers, it would be to avoid storylines wherein characters lose telepathic abilities. It seems to be a really hexed plot. Either you lose major characters or else leave titles altogether.

The other thing I don't quite understand is the "not visual enough" objection. I mean, Peter Parker worrying about Aunt May wasn't visual. Reed and Sue's rocky romance wasn't visual (except when Namor kidnapped her and fought Reed for her, which was pretty neat — especially when an infuriated Reed turned his body into spikes). Cyclops and Jean thinking sad thought balloons about each other wasn't visual. Marvel built its entire foundation on inward angst. Why is it that such story elements now aren't acceptable? Is it going back to a response to the fan demand for simplicity? Is there concern that if it's not right there in the artwork, then fans won't "get it"? That it's not enough for emotional trauma to be a problem? I don't think so. I sure hope not.

Because if that's the case, then everyone could lose, and the Marvel Universe could just quite possibly wind up —

X-Tinct.

*(Peter David, writer of stuff is intending to stress character interaction and group dynamics in **X-Factor** and so far hasn't had a single problem with doing so.*

This is, of course, presuming he's still got a job after this column sees print.)

CAROL (Oct. 11, 1991)

There was Bill Mumy, writer-actor-musician, at the end of the San Diego Comic Con a few years back, along with comics mogul Steve Fischler, packing up Bill's car outside the Executive Hotel in preparation for the drive back to L.A. Heaving and ho-ing, they loaded box after box of comics and musical equipment into the car.

Partway through the loading process, an attractive, smiling young woman wearing a red vest appeared at their side and, with a polite nod of her head, started picking up boxes as if she'd been doing it her entire life. The job when that much faster and more efficiently, and when it was done, Bill turned to the young woman and handed her a nice, crisp, one-dollar bill.

She looked at it, and him, aghast. "Are you crazy?" she asked, in an educated voice that had a ring of East Coast to it — Boston, perhaps, or maybe Virginia.

Unsure of whether she felt it was just all part of her job, or perhaps she thought her work had been worth more than a buck tip, Bill smiled gamely, pressed the money firmly into her palm, and said, "No, really. I want you to have it."

She shrugged and walked away as Bill climbed into the driver's seat and drove off. Steve, in the passenger's seat, was staring at Mumy incredulously. "Do you know who that was?"

Bill shrugged. "Some hotel goon."

Steve shook his head. "That was Carol Kalish, the head of direct sales at Marvel Comics."

Thereafter followed some loud, inarticulate screams as the mortified Mumy saw his act of chivalry turn into an act of total embarrassment.

He got to know Carol Kalish in later years, and reports that in follow-up get-togethers they laughed about his well-meaning social gaffe.

No one who knew Carol was laughing on Thursday, September 5, 1991.

Ariel's birth had gone smoothly on Labor Day of 1991. Over the next several days I called a number of friends and joyfully informed them of the advent of my third daughter.

I didn't call Carol.

Damn me, I didn't call Carol.

I called Richard Howell and told him. I knew Richard, Carol's long-time companion (making him sound vaguely like Margo Lane, I suppose, but Carol as the mysterious unflappable Shadow isn't too off-base) would tell her. I didn't want to bother her because I knew how busy she was these days.

So I blew my opportunity to have a clear-cut, precise, "the last time I spoke to Carol was —" type of memory. I am such an idiot. Because now I can't say for 100% certainty when I last spoke to this woman who was one of the most important individuals in my life. Who got me into the comics industry, setting in motion a career in sales that eventually gravitated towards writing.

I didn't call her.

On September 5th we brought the baby home. I was seated in the living room, staring at the small bundle of new life that was on my wife's lap, and marveling at the wonder of her very existence.

And then the phone rang, forty-five minutes after Ariel came home, and it was Stevel Saffel at Marvel with the news that Carol was gone, just gone.

The phone slipped out of my fingers and, when I eventually found words, they were simply, "I'll call you back."

The next several days were an emotional rollercoaster. We had imagined that people would be calling to say congratulations about the baby. Instead every phone conversation was somber, tinged with mourning. Every word in the house became strained. All the happiness supposed to be associated with a child's homecoming was blackness and depressing, and worst of all I felt guilty and selfish over the shattered homecoming because how much worse was it for Richard, and Carol's sister Candace, and the rest of her friends? And for Carol —

Carol had loaned Fred Bauman, my sales assistant, $20 at a poker game at a convention the previous week. Now Fred was going to repay the loan, and Carol was in her office with a distributor. So Fred, without preamble, walked into her office, placed the $20 bill on her desk, said humbly, "Thank you for letting me work here another week, Miss Kalish," and exited without another word. The distributor went into hysterics and it's the only known time when Carol was at a loss for something to say.

I couldn't write. For the better part of a week, no words would come. My output consisted of a script page of *X-Factor*, a page here or there of something else.

It was announced that Terry Stewart of Marvel was putting together a memorial service for Carol and that people could get up and talk about her. I wanted to say something. I had even been asked to speak at the ceremony.

Still I was stuck. About her humor and good grace, her constantly sound advice, and the moral center she provided for so many things, I could not adequately express myself. I wasn't in shape to write a grocery list.

And I couldn't look at my new child without thinking about death. Or into the mirror without thinking, "It could have been me. Hell, Carol was in so much better shape than I was. On statistics alone, it *should* have been me."

Finally I sat down and had a talk with Ariel. Actually, I was lying down, and she was on my chest. I thought, Maybe she has answers somehow. Certainly none of the adults did. So I stared at her, propped her head up. She drooled on me a little.

And I thought about when she'd been first born. Lying there in the warming bed, and her grip on life had seemed so tenuous.

It was hard to believe that anything that small and helpless could possibly be alive. She seemed ethereal, as if, were we to turn away for just a moment, she'd vanish back into the ether.

And that's when I realized that it never really gets any more secure. When we lie there, naked and trembling and weighing under seven pounds, the thin thread that binds us to life is extremely visible. As we get older, can walk and talk and feed ourselves, we, in essence, polish up our act. We develop a certain degree of self-confidence about our invulnerability.

And we forget that the thread has gotten no thicker in the passing years. That our hold on life is just as flimsy and uncertain as in those first few seconds.

And I thought of what happened to Carol and realized that the question of "Why did that happen?" — to which there is no answer — can just as easily be asked when looking at this birth that had dropped into our lives. "Why did that happen?" Others struggle to conceive, others who are as much or more deserving. So why were we blessed? No one ever seems to question why the good things happen; they just rail at the bad, and the bad seems to drown out the good.

I wrote the first draft of my attempt to memorialize this splendid woman. I thought it was OK. I ran it past a writer whose advice when it comes to writing I respect above all others. He suggested changes which I implemented.

I dreaded going to the memorial, but it turned out to be a good thing, and I am indebted to Terry Stewart for organizing it. On September 5th, The Day the Comics Stopped, everyone who had known Carol was seized with an overwhelming sense of loss and a desire to do something — *anything* — because otherwise returning to normal function was going to be close to impossible. And the memorial service provided that, and people left feeling glad about having come together, not for Carol — because nothing we could do would help her — but for us.

And after I'd spoken, I felt ... better. Not great. But better.

And here is what I said:

As you flip through the pages of the book of your life, you find it studded with images. Existence caught in midmotion, like a camera in your head just snapped a photo of an instant.

Click.* JFK was shot. *Click* A woman you love just said she's pregnant, and you will always be able to envision everything from that moment with clarity you can taste, touch, see, and savor.

Because these are the moments something important has happened to us. We've gotten news, or learned something about ourselves, or someone else. In lives cluttered by trivia, crammed with nonsense and commercial breaks and garbage up to our nostrils, it is the important moments, the important people, that we keep with us.

Click It's 10 years ago, and Carol Kalish is in her office making a model kit of a pterodactyl. Carol's wearing a white blouse, blue jeans, and red-and-gold vest. She appears to be ignoring the résumé being pitched by her would-be assistant who had less weight and more hair than he does now. His voice trails off. Finally a burst of exasperation. "What are you doing?"

She answers. Her shoulders bubble up and down in sudden enthusiasm, her head bobbing like a miniature spring-head baseball player in the back window of a '63 Ford. "This is Rhodan, and when I'm finished, he's going to fly through the air and destroy Tokyo unless Godzilla stops him." As she speaks, she reaches across the desk for a stray pterodactyl leg and *shoof* her chair shoots out from under her and she vanishes underneath her desk. And then, from out of sight, she calls, "So why do you want to work at Marvel Comics?"

"She's crazy," I realize. "This is a crazy person. I mean, I'm nuts, but she's certifiable. God, I hope she hires me." She did. Time passed. Her hair got more silver. Her clothes got more uptown. She got no less crazy. She was boss, mentor, teacher, confidante, friend. She always had all the answers, even when she didn't have a clue. And she had the ability, as do all truly important people, to make you feel important as well.

And if she really liked you — she made you nuts. The more she liked you, the more nuts she made you. I think she must have liked me a lot. And this was perfectly fitting behavior for someone whose stated role models were Doctor Doom and Maleficent.

Click A report has been screwed up, and Carol shakes a wrathful finger at me and bellows, "You're a disgrace to the forces of evil!"

Click We are standing in front of the Marvel office, and I am screaming in her face, gesticulating like a madman. We had been heading out on a business trip, and we had to catch a cab to JFK. "Come on, let's catch a cab over on that corner," I said. And Carol replies, "No, that corner is better."

"Carol, that corner is one block further downtown. There's more empty cabs."

"But," she replies, "that corner is further uptown, we'll be one block closer to JFK."

"That's ridiculous! Let's go there!"

"No, let's go there!"

And back and forth, and suddenly I take a step toward her and say, "Black!" Without blinking an eye, she shoots back, "White!"

And I start jumping up and down and shouting, "I knew it! I knew it! All these months when you've been disagreeing with me about everything, making me always think I was wrong. But it wasn't me. It was you! You're trying to make me as crazy as you! But it won't work! See? Bwwaahhahah! *I'm still sane!*"

And there she stood, *click*, with this demented, satisfied gleam in her eye. I recounted this story to her friend, Paul Dini, and he said that Carol was Bugs Bunny and the rest of the world was Daffy Duck. He's right. That's what she could do to you. "Shoot me now! Shoot me now! I demand you shoot me now!"

She never, to my knowledge, lost a fight — except one. And even then, Death wouldn't take her in a fair fight because he was afraid he might lose. Why not? She was tougher, stronger, smarter than anyone else. So she got sucker-punched while her back was turned. Pitiful display. The Forces of Evil would have been proud.

Click The second we hear she's gone, and we'll all remember where we were, because that's how important she was. So important that we sit there, stunned, and go, "That can't be."

"How could this happen? We want answers! Who can we turn to for answers? I know. We'll ask — " And the silence of her passing becomes that much louder.

"It can't be," we say. "Not the superwoman of comics. It had to be ... a clone. Or a Skrull imposter. Or maybe she was spirited away by the CIA to testify against an international drug smuggler and then enter the Witness Relocation Program. *Anything* makes more sense than that she's just gone. Not Carol. Carol? That's ... crazy. That's just ... crazy."

Well — leave it to Carol that she did pull a victory from the craven attack. Because of how many people can it be said that, damn — right to the end, in death and life — they were consistent?

Carol comes into the office, and she's wearing a skirt. I mime fainting. I have worked for her for four and a half years and have never seen her legs because she never wears a skirt or dress. I had speculated aloud that she had wooden sticks or something rather than normal legs. She had said she'd wear a skirt on my 30th birthday. She did. I appreciated the gesture. And she had nice legs.

After the memorial I go out with about 30 or so people, in an expedition organized by retailer Lori Raub. We drink sodas to Carol's memory. And then I go home and hug my baby.

(Peter David, writer of stuff, misses his friend.)

Historical Notes:

*1) Carol's passing prompted an outpouring of grief in the letters page of **CBG** that is, quite simply, unparalleled in our industry.*

2) The week Carol died was one of only two times I didn't write a column (the other being when I was flat on my back with pneumonia and bronchitis). I simply requested that Don and Maggie slug an "In Memoriam" sentence into my customary space and box it. They did so.

3) This remains, to me, the single most upsetting column I've ever written.

THE GOOD DOCTOR (May 8, 1992)

There are going to be people far more knowledgeable than I who are going to write — or presumably have already written — essays on the loss of Isaac Asimov, one of the premiere and most visible modern writers of speculative fiction in the country, probably the world.

Since this column represents my very personal, and somewhat selfish, viewpoint of the world, I'm going to take this space to relate the first and last times that I had the opportunity to exchange words with this remarkable man — a man who, through his constant inventiveness, continued output, and sheer intellect, has always been one of my personal heroes.

My two major encounters with the good doctor were separated by a period of about fifteen years. The first was brief, the second much longer. But the first was funnier.

I was 19 years old. My then-girlfriend Myra (who later became my now-wife, Myra) and I were sitting in Penn Station, New York, waiting for a train down to Philadelphia. As was (and is) customary with Amtrak, things were running late. We were bored, and seated on the floor (since all the chairs were occupied).

It was April 1st.

In an effort to amuse herself, Myra suddenly looked up, pointed with great excitement, and said, "Look! Over there! It's Ben Bova!"

Thrilled at an opportunity for a break in the monotony — and perhaps a chance to chat with one of my favorite SF writers — my head snapped around and I said, "*Where?! Where?!*" She smiled smugly and said, "April Fool." Now, as April Fool jokes go, this wasn't particularly brilliant or even funny — especially if you're 19 and fell for it. If you're 19 and pulled it on someone, it's a laugh riot.

I made a face and a muttered "Ha, ha, very funny." We sat there a few more minutes, and then Myra went off to the ladies' room.

And Isaac Asimov walked by.

Of course, being a good SF fan and convention goer, I recognized him instantly. I waved and called out, "Hello, Doctor Asimov!"

He smiled, nodded, said, "Hello there," and walked on past. A minute or so later, Myra returned and sat on the floor, facing me.

"Guess what!" I said excitedly. "While you were in the women's room, Isaac Asimov walked past!"

She looked at me with a combination of pity and disdain. How pathetic I must have seemed. Apparently the best comeback I could develop was simply to try and get her back with a rehash of her own joke.

"Really!" I said. "He walked right past! And I said, "Hi, Doctor Asimov," and he said 'Hi' back!"

"Yeah, right," she said, not falling at all for this pathetic trick. "Sure. You bet."

And in one of those moments that would seem to provide evidence that there is, in fact, a God — Isaac Asimov walked past again.

Myra's back was to him, but I saw him clearly. So I waved and called out once more, "Hi, Doctor Asimov!"

Myra looked at me patronizingly. Unbeknownst to her, so did Asimov, who probably assumed that I was simply a moron. What was this odd compulsion I had to shout out his name every time I saw him? Nevertheless, he gamely waved back and said, "Hello, again."

Since Myra was looking right at me, I had full opportunity to see her stunned expression as she recognized his voice. She spun on the ground and stared at him in total shock.

He walked away. I never did find out where he was going or why he was there.

And for going on two decades now, Myra has never had the nerve to try another April fool's joke on me.

That was the first time.

The last time was under more professional and organized circumstances.

In connection with the yet-to-be-aired Sci-Fi Channel (yeah, I know, I know: everyone hates the term Sci-Fi. Don't bust *my* chops about it — I didn't name the damned channel), the folks who produce such licensed publications as the Official *Star Trek* Fan Club magazine had obtained the rights to produce a tie-in magazine for the Sci-Fi Channel. The cover feature was to be about Isaac Asimov, and they asked me if I would be interested in conducting the interview.

This was in November 1990. Because of the many subsequent delays with the start-up of the channel, the magazine has, likewise, experienced delays. No sense starting a tie-in magazine, if there's nothing to tie-in with. But at that time, no one knew that the Sci-Fi Channel was going to have trouble getting off the ground.

They gave me Asimov's phone number and told him that I'd be calling to set up a time.

I knew that Asimov's health had been flagging. I hadn't been at any conventions he had recently attended, but I'd heard that illness had caused him to lose an alarming amount of weight .and that he bore little resemblance to the gregarious, robust personality who had become such a staple of the world of SF. This seemed to be supported when the magazine guys told me that Asimov had wanted to make sure that I would not be bringing a photographer or camera of my own.

When I called Asimov to arrange a convenient time for him, he reiterated the condition. That he didn't want pictures taken, in and of itself, didn't bother me. Certainly if he was going to take the time to talk with me, he was well within his rights to make whatever stipulations he desired. But it did make me a bit apprehensive. Asimov was hardly camera shy; he'd been photographed hundreds of times and done commercials and television appearances. If he was suddenly reluctant to be photographed, what did that mean? When I saw him, I knew precisely what it meant. It meant that he was fully aware that his debilitated appearance did not remotely match the accepted image of Doctor Isaac Asimov. He made no bones about it; he knew how ill he was and he spoke more than once about dying. Certainly as great a visionary as he was capable of looking into his own future and not seeing all that much left to it.

As we spoke, with the tape recorder whirring, I proceeded very carefully. Despite the fact that it was 11 a.m., he was clearly tired. In a room filled with relics of his career, he almost seemed a relic himself. His famous mutton chops and hair were gray-white, and he wore lounging pajamas and a robe. He sat almost immobile throughout much of the conversation and at first when he spoke it was slow and obviously with great effort.

Fatigue hung over him like a cloud. I didn't want to overtax him. I felt like I was interviewing a china cup, and I decided that there was no way that I was going to go past half an hour in length. He was, quite obviously, no longer the man he had been.

Except he was.

As things progressed, more and more flashes of the old wit, and intelligence, and spirit surfaced — not because I'm a particularly great interviewer, but because he was the particularly great Isaac Asimov. We wound up going closer to an hour.

There were two points at which he became particularly animated — the first was when he was discussing the aborted attempts to produce a movie of I, Robot: Talking about Harlan Ellison — for whom it was clear he bore great affection — seemed to bring out the best in him. The second was when talk shifted to politics and the then-brewing situation with Operation Desert Shield. It was at that point that he became the most vehement, when all the fatigue and debilitation fell away. His voice rose and almost thundered in indignation, and he thudded on the chair for emphasis, as he ripped into the past and present administrations with an air of someone who didn't like the way things were going at present and was frustrated that he wasn't going to be around long enough to see them turn more to his liking.

I produce those two sequences for you here. I'm told that he didn't conduct all that many interviews in the last year or so of his life, so this unpublished excerpt should be something of a rarity. The interview will, naturally, be published in its entirety when the Sci-Fi Channel is eventually a go.

Asimov: (*continuing from a previous question*) — the only reason you'd have to go out to Hollywood would be to make a killing, and often they wind up killing you instead.

Me: One of the most vocal critics, and yet participants, in Hollywood has been Harlan Ellison. And he became involved in the attempted adaptation of I, Robot.

Asimov: I know that very well, and he put out a very good script. It was 90% Harlan Ellison and only 10% me, if that — but it was still a very good script. On the one hand it would have cost $30 million to put up on the screen, which at that time was a lot of money. (*Laughter*) And it was very doubtful that they would get their money back, because the script was not one of these easy Indiana Jones/Star Wars shoot-'em-ups.

I mean, it required thought. Horrors.

Then, too, Harlan is Harlan. He would fight with people. He has no sense of tact whatever.

I argued with him. I said "Harlan, they're going to want you to change things. The thing to do is say, 'Yes sir, I'll do it,' wait two to three months, and then bring back the same goddamn thing you had and say you made the changes. They'll never know the difference."

But nooooo. They ask for changes, he calls them names, y'know? One big-shot at the studio made it quite plain that he hadn't read the script. He was busy telling Harlan what was wrong with it, but it was obvious that he hadn't read it — that he had read some treatment that someone had given him. So Harlan told him he had the cranial capacity of an artichoke — which didn't go over very well —

* * *

Asimov: (*discussing the Strategic Defense Initiative* [SDI]) — I remember once science-fiction writer Jerry Pournelle approached me at a Nebula meeting and asked me, "Why are you against SDI?" And I said, "Because I don't think it's going to work." And he said, "Well so and so" — and he starts naming these scientists, and he says, — "Well so and so thinks it's going to work, and so and so thinks it's going to work." He sounded very belligerent.

He was larger than I was taller, wider, stronger, younger, drunker. And he said, "Do you question their expertise?" And I said, "No, I don't question their expertise; all I question is their sanity." He was shocked.

He went away and didn't kill me.

But it's true, it's true. Anyone can persuade Reagan to do anything, if only it's stupid enough. And he did that amongst a great many other stupid things. Unfortunately it's considered unpatriotic to blame him for our national debt; to blame him for our adverse trade balance; to blame him for the S&L fiasco, to blame him for the (*raising his voice*) *atmosphere of greed* that permeated the United States in the 1980s and resulted in having us now act as the world's policemen when we're only ticking on two cylinders. And it's all Reagan, all Reagan and the men who control him.

Me: Do you feel it's been perpetuated by Bush?

Asimov: Oh, yes. It's been completely perpetuated by Bush. Bush isn't as stupid as Reagan, because it's impossible to be as stupid as Reagan. But Bush isn't very much *smarter* than Reagan.

Unfortunately, we are living at a time when we imagine that we are still the United States of the 1950s. And we're not. The 1950s will never return. We are living in the world of the 1990s, which means that not only is the Federal Government short on money, but every single state, practically, has a shortfall.

And in every single state the populace knows only two things: one, they're not going to pay any more taxes, and two, they're not going to lift their noses out of the trough.

But you can't have it both ways.

God knows what's going to happen.

(*Peter David, writer of stuff, fully anticipates making a visit to a bookstore someday in the near year or so and finding a volume that has mysteriously appeared on the shelves. And the title would be* **Isaac Asimov's Guide to the Afterlife**. *If anyone could pull that off — he could.*)

BIGGER THAN LIFE (Sept. 4, 1992)

A curious and depressing sequence of events:

In *Oh, So?* there's a mini-debate over what constitutes something as being mythic.

Word starts circulating among fan magazines that Superman is going to die.

Joe Shuster dies.

Bill Mantlo is rollerblading and struck by a car. He remains in a coma for several weeks and the prognosis for a full recovery is not good.

All of which would seem to relate to the human spirit, the need for myths, and the need to be remembered. For myths are more than stories. Myths are stories that edge their way into the collective consciousness, stories that surpass their creators.

Stories that become fact.

When I was in Calgary some weeks back, I saw a commercial that featured a young Canadian boy boarding a train that was going to take him to America — Cleveland, presumably, since the boy was identified as Joe Shuster. The commercial has the excited young Shuster (already a teen) babbling to an older woman named Lois about this character he's created that can leap tall buildings, bend steel, etc., etc. Lois is patient but skeptical.

Just as the train pulls away, Joe tosses to Lois a quick drawing of the dynamic character who is bursting from his imagination — and who will shape an industry for the next half-century and more.

It's a fanciful little commercial. After all, although Canadian-born, Shuster in fact grew up in Cleveland. And he did have just a bit of help from childhood friend Jerry Siegel in creating the character that they would sell to National Periodicals for $130 as teens, which must have seemed like all the money in the world to them at the time. A deal that, with 20/20 hindsight, was the biggest rip-off since the legendary sale of Manhattan for a couple of bucks worth of chachkas.

In 1978, DC Comics was publicly humiliated into doing something approximating the right thing. With Siegel and the now-legally blind Shuster as walking Exhibits #1 and #2 against the comics industry business practices, DC restored their creator-credits and awarded them stipends of $20,000 a year for life, which allowed Shuster to move to a modest Los Angeles apartment.

To my mind, a stipend in the neighborhood of $200,000 a year would have been a bit more like it, so that he could move into a mansion. Even better: Imagine the publicity value of handing each of them a check for a million dollars in front of a cheering throng of press. The movie *Superman*, which came out that year, brought in $82.5 million from ticket sales and subsequent video rentals, so the words "drop in a bucket" come to mind.

But I digress.

I was talking about myths and legends.

It's a nice bit of irony that the Canadian commercial serves to start building a myth around the co-creator of what is arguably one of two America-generated 20th Century popular fictions that has crossed over into mythic status.

Yes, myths. I believe that Superman elevates Siegel and Shuster into the same pantheon as whoever first spun the stories of Zeus, et al.; or Chretien de Troyes, the French romance writer who decided in 1180 that what the tales of Camelot really needed was the great French literary tradition of the cuckolded husband.

And so de Troyes added Lancelot (a Frenchman, of course) to the Round Table for the purpose of bagging Arthur's queen.

T.H. Gastor states that a myth is a story or series of stories that serves as an underpinning for a society — a society being defined as two or more people.

And it's not only that. For something to become a myth, it has to worm its way into the collective consciousness of Joe Average as "fact." There's no absolute point of demarcation. It just sort of — happens.

(The second American myth, besides Superman, in case you're wondering, is *Star Trek*. With the entire fan-run "Starfleet" throughout the country, predicated on the structure and philosophies of the show, I think Gastor would unquestionably define *Star Trek* as a myth. In terms of how it "factually" fits in to the thesis, read on.)

For example: Ask your average guy, "Who is Fonzie?" The average response is, "He was this character played by Henry Winkler on a show called *Happy Days.* " Now: Ask your average guy, "Who is James T. Kirk?" The chances are, the response you'll get is, "He's the Captain of the original *Enterprise*." And you just know that when he says, "original *Enterprise*," he's not referring to the 70-ton British sloop that cruised Lake Champlain during the American Revolution, supplying British posts in Canada, was subsequently captured by Benedict Arnold, and then used in valorous combat against the British until it was beached and burned July 7, 1777.

No, he's talking about a starship — something that doesn't in fact exist, but is discussed as if it did.

Or ask your average guy, "Who is Superman?" And the response you will likely get is, "He's a strange visitor from another planet, with powers and abilities far beyond those of mortal men." Or, "Well, he's a super-hero, and in his secret identity he's Clark Kent, a mild-mannered reporter." There's no qualifier. Your average response will not be something to the effect of, "He's a comic-book character." Instead you'll get just as straightforward a response as if you asked Joe Average to tell you about his mother or a friend of his.

The starship *Enterprise*, registry number NCC-1701, is a "fact," as real to some people (even though "deep down" they know it's just a TV show) as the aircraft carrier *Enterprise*, registry number CVN-65. Superman's origin is a "fact." That he is Clark Kent is a "fact." And I would like to think that, to teen-aged Siegel and Shuster, he was also a fact. The best, the greatest creative minds are those who are able to transmit their own sense of belief in their fictions to their audience, so that the audience will believe, as well. The technical term for this is "suspension of disbelief." The romantic term for this is "myth making." Joe Shuster visualized a myth. He told an interviewer that "There aren't many people who can honestly say they'll be leaving behind something as important as Superman." This simple, irrefutable statement touches on the two most incredible aspects of Joe Shuster's life: first, that he was part of creating something that was far greater than himself, and, second, that he would be remembered for it.

Which brings me to Bill Mantlo.

The most recent time (I refuse to say "the last time") that I spoke to Bill was about two, maybe three months ago. He called me because in recently published interviews, when I'd been asked about origins for the Hulk's multiple-personality-disorder storyline, I had cited Bill's ingenious one-issue story that detailed Bruce Banner's history of being an abused child. I described how Bill had come up with something that was, to me, groundbreaking, and how the first 40 or so issues of my run had sprung directly from Bill's concept.

To me, this was simply answering the question — just the same as when people ask, "What made you turn The Hulk back to gray in the first place?" and I always respond, "Nothing. Al Milgrom did that. I just took it and ran with it." But Bill was extremely pleased and flattered that I had mentioned him in such glowing terms.

And he said, "It's nice that someone remembers."

It's nice that someone remembers.

It's better than nice. It's what many creators — writers, artists, what-have-you — are trying to do during their relatively brief time in this sphere. They're trying to create something of permanence. Trying to produce something that will be part of someone's consciousness long after they themselves are dust.

To be part of something that's bigger than themselves.

People are not remembered. People are never remembered.

It's the *accomplishments* of people that are remembered.

One of my favorite moments in all of movies is in a marvelous little film called *The Seven Faces of Dr. Lao*, based on the book *The Circus of Dr. Lao* by Charles G. Finney. Tony Randall stars as the title character and additionally portrays six other characters as the citizens of a small western town in the late 19th century are made to realize unpleasant truths about themselves through the good Doctor's circus.

The most moving, heart-rending sequence is when a fluttery, matronly woman visits Apollonius, a blind fortune teller played (of course) by Randall, who is accursed always "to speak the absolute truth." The woman, who had entertained notions of remarrying or striking oil, listens to her future quietly, irrevocably dashed to pieces by the seer. In slow horror she realizes that, when he says there will be no new men, when he says that the land she purchased in hope of finding oil would yield nothing, he speaks the hideous truth.

And then he quietly, sorrowfully, but implacably passes judgment on her life by concluding, "You will turn to dust, and be forgotten. And for all that you have accomplished in your life, good or evil — you might just as well have never lived at all."

That's part of the fun of working within a mythic universe such as the *Star Trek* universe or the Marvel or DC universe.

Something with an established history and a following that considers the stories to be more than just stories. As much as I enjoy the books that I've written or am writing that are all mine, both published and not published, I also get great satisfaction out of producing things like my current *Star Trek* novel that explores the previously unrevealed history of Commander Riker and Deanna Troi.

Because for some readers, they're not going to read it and say, "Nice story." Instead they'll say, "Ohhh! That's what happened! That's how they met!" For those people, it's more than just a story. It's a series of events that actually occurred, somewhere in the great myth-mind of *Star Trek* history, and I'm simply reporting on it.

But Joe Shuster was more than a reporter. He, along with Jerry Siegel, was a newsmaker. Whereas Bill Mantlo or I can hope that we're remembered, Joe Shuster guaranteed that he will be. He'll be remembered by people who never even heard of him, because he co-created Superman. Even though DC endeavored to take that away from Siegel and Shuster in 1947, the corporate entity couldn't succeed in doing that. The annual stipend 30 years later was simply a monetary acknowledgement of that.

Siegel and Shuster created something that was greater than themselves. The two teen-agers from Cleveland were concerned about their lives. Superman's concerns were, and are, on a galactic (if not universal) scale. And, eventually, Superman, strange visitor from another planet, would belong to the world.

But Siegel and Shuster belonged to Superman.

(Peter David, writer of stuff, is heading out to San Diego this week. He will see all of you — or will have already seen all of you there — or — oh, skip it.)

Historical Notes:

1) *As of this writing, Bill Mantlo is still alive, but mentally incapacitated. They say that where there's life, there's hope. But sometimes where there's life, there's also great cruelty.*

SECTION 6

Keep On Trekkin'

I didn't realize I had done enough articles on *Star Trek* alone to warrant a separate section for it.

Then again, I shouldn't be surprised. *Trek* has always been a major part of my life, going all the way back to seventh grade. I've met my life-long mate and life-long friends through *Trek*. My *Trek* novels have gotten me more fans, notoriety, creative enjoyment, best-seller credits, and a lot of money. In short, *Star Trek* did everything for me except put hair on my head — and with the latter, at least Patrick Stewart made being bald OK.

So — a whole section for *Star Trek* then. It's entitled.

IN SPACE, NO ONE CAN HEAR YOU LAUGH (Oct. 12, 1990)

Humor in *Star Trek*.

Having a character get raped in *Atlantis Chronicles* drew little response. But every single month one of the most hotly debated issues in the comics I write is whether I should be allowed to be funny in the *Star Trek* comic book that DC publishes.

How much humor is too much humor? Where should I be allowed to use shtick and where not? I'm not taking *Star Trek* seriously, I'm told. I'm not being true to the spirit of the original series.

Anyone watch the original series lately?

Funny stuff. Genuinely funny stuff.

This was back in the days when *Star Trek* was, well, a TV show. When they went to planets populated by Roman gladiators or gangsters. When Spock and McCoy would engage in verbal byplay, insulting each other in order to cover the fact that they liked each other and hated to admit it. When Spock would quote statistics to the fifth decimal point, analyze confrontations with unknown beings by declaring that they had recited "Very bad poetry, Captain," or sanguinely inform Kirk — in the process of disguising himself as an SS trooper — "I have always thought you would make a most convincing Nazi."

This was back when every reading was off their scale, back when it was like nothing they had encountered before, back when We Were Right. "We" being the United States, of course.

Vietnam killed *Star Trek*. Killed the humor. Killed the fun, as it did for so many other things.

Kirk, Spock, *et al.* supposedly obeyed a Prime Directive that told them not to interfere. You remember. It was the thing they always quoted just before Kirk ignored it. That's because, at that time, *Star Trek* was the 20th-century American in the 23rd century. Noble. Proud. Right. Americanism was so right that they had the Constitution on other worlds, for heaven's sake. We Were Always Right.

Then *Trek* ended, and Vietnam wound down, and when, years later, *Next Generation* appeared, well, it reflected the new America. Tentative. Cautious. Don't get involved if you can at all avoid it, because we might screw up, just as we did in Vietnam. We Americans, as a people, still aren't comfortable with ourselves. We like the British much better than we do ourselves. That's why we lionize their comics, and put a British guy in charge of the *Enterprise*.

We are so paranoid as a nation that we actually discuss whether people should be prohibited from burning the flag. We're so insecure that we can't take the criticism that that act implies.

And boy, we can't take a joke.

At least, not when it comes to *Trek*. When Shatner told fans to "Get a life" on *Saturday Night Live*, it struck too close to home for too many people.

Star Trek V was brutalized by the majority of fans and by the critics. Now, was it "that bad"?

Well — No. Not *that* bad. I mean, *Darkman* was much worse, and a number of critics embraced it.

The main thing that people seemed to attack *Trek V* for — and the same thing that many attack the comic book for — is that it seemed as if those involved didn't take *Star Trek* seriously.

I can't speak for Shatner, of course, because he's not here, but I can take a guess about him and I know about myself, and that philosophy is this — sure, I take *Trek* seriously, but only to a degree. I don't take it *that* seriously. I take it as seriously as I do *The Hulk*. It's entertainment. It's fun. I like to have fun with *Star Trek*. Call me crazy, call me a fool, but I happen to think that something that was designed for entertainment should be entertaining.

And I try to be true to the spirit of *Star Trek* as I see it. I try to produce stories that are in the style of the original series. Not in the style of the new series, because the styles are very different. *Next Gen* is very much the post-Vietnam style and, for that matter, it also carries with it the trauma of being an icon. An institution. *Next Gen* carries the weight of all the fans' expectations on its back and considers that to be a very serious responsibility. *Next Gen* is a very serious program.

How do we know this? There's one major clue.

Music.

In the original series, practically every scene was scored from beginning to end. Not *Next Gen*. When you're watching Serious Drama, there's rarely incidental music. That's too trivial.

Think about it. *Trek* fans can hum the music of the approaching Doomsday Machine; that haunting string music (Vulcan harp?) when Amanda pleaded with Spock to save Sarek; that zippy jig when Kirk pursued Finnegan; that musical sting when Kirk stopped McCoy from saving Edith Keeler — on and on.

There are many things to remember from the original series. For that matter, there are many things to remember from *Next Gen*, as well, because both shows have so many things that they can do, so many elements they can hook you with. Acting. Music. Sound effects. Special effects and visual effects. "Time Squared" made no sense? Didn't matter. Great visual effects. "Sarek" was a rehash of "Journey to Babel?" (Vulcan ambassador comes aboard *Enterprise*, falls ill, and crew member risks own life to save him.) Doesn't matter. We have the great acting of Mark Lenard and Patrick Stewart.

What've we got in the comics?

Music? No.

Visual effects? Not that pack the same punch as TV, no. Besides, when people read the comics, they spend most of the time trying to determine whether the likenesses are consistent. You think anyone tunes in *Next Gen* saying, "Let's hope that Riker looks like Jonathan Frakes this week?" "Let's hope they got the bridge right"?

Acting? Only what the readers can conjure in their minds upon reading the words.

Sound effects? Silent medium. Again, lacks that TV punch.

Make up? Come on. We have an audience which is used to seeing Nightcrawler or The Hulk every month. If Ensign Fouton, the tall, skinny blue alien, appeared on the TV show, fans would be singing praises about the make-up required to give him life. In the comic book, the most response we've had to something visual was R.J. Blaise, and she was human! Exotic aliens and civilizations don't have the same effect on comics fans as it does when they see the same thing on the series.

Face it, the comics can't possibly work as well, on all levels, as the TV series — both old and new — do.

Except for one thing: humor.

We can be as funny as the original series. All we have to do is keep Kirk, Spock and McCoy — and their knack for banter — in character. Or, if we're going for situational gags, put them in potentially fun environments such as the gangster planet in "Piece of the Action." (Hmmm. Maybe we'll send them to a planet that holds a *Star Trek* convention. That's a thought.)

I have all the elements of the original series in the comic book. Space battles. Character interaction. New worlds and new civilizations. And humor.

But the humor stands out, in comparison to the new series, because it doesn't need special effects or music to carry it off. The humor works as well in the comic book as it does on TV and in the movies. Because it does, that's what people remember, above and beyond every other element in the comic book. And because it's what people remember, they tend to forget everything else.

If you study what is generally considered to be the best of the original series episodes, "City on the Edge of Forever," you'll be amazed at the dazzling number of jokes and humorous situations. But that's considered to be one of the most dramatic. Yet if "City" had never been written, and I (through some burst of inspiration) had tried to write it for the comic book, I'd be criticized for throwing in stupid bits about Spock catching his head in a mechanical rice picker.

Or if I wrote a comic book where Spock and Kirk are trying to break out of a prison cell, and Spock is stepping on Kirk's back during these endeavors, calmly chatting while Kirk is in agony (because his back is covered with whip scars) — why, I would be accused of making light of a serious situation.

Or if I tried to dump 1,771,561 tribbles on Kirk, well — forget it.

The comic book is attacked because of the one thing it does as well as anybody. Because that one thing is no longer in style. *Star Trek V* took *Star Trek* with the same degree of seriousness and, well, fun, that the original series took. But *Trek V* didn't know that Vietnam, 25 years of analysis, and the generally serious tone of *Next Gen* would cause humor to fall out of style.

I will admit that things have gotten a bit better in the humor department for *Next Gen*. Like the episode when Howling Mad Murdock became Holodeck-Mad Murdock, anything with Q or Mrs. Troi, and a handful of others. But there's no steady interplay or repartee to continually provide a smile, a chuckle, or a leavening of an otherwise deadly situation. That sort of interplay lives only in the *Trek* movies and the comic books, where it continues to catch all sorts of flak. And it lives on in the reruns, of course.

Perhaps some people would be well served to review those episodes and pretend that 25 years of back-breaking pretention hadn't gone down. Remember what it was like when it was fun. And realize that that's the spirit of what I'm trying to capture in the comic book. The fun.

I *thought* that's what it was all about.

• And now a public service announcement. In an earlier column I mentioned that the Beat Brothers, producers of the "Seduction of the Innocent" CD, were looking for musically or performanced-inclined comics professionals to contribute to a new record project entitled Notes from the Comic World.

Since then, I've gotten a number of calls asking for specifics. If you are a comics professional (don't try this at home, kids) contact John Christensen at the Beat Brothers, 4067 Hardwick St., Suite 279, Lakewood, Calif. 90712. Phone number is (213) 664-9436.

*(Peter David, writer of stuff, welcomes comments c/o **CBG**.)*

Historical Notes:

*1) There was a fellow working at Paramount who took a particular dislike to me personally and my work in general — probably because I laughed in his face when he said that the Gold Key **Star Trek** stories was the ideal level to which Trek comics should aspire. We'll call him "Arnie."*

*Unfortunately Arnie was Gene Roddenberry's **aide de camp**, and was in charge of approving my comic book work. When my stories came in, I was told (by observers) this fellow's attitude was, "Here's Peter's latest story. Let's see what's wrong with it."*

*He did everything he could to convince Roddenberry that I was out to destroy **Trek**, and he was quite successful at it. One of the tools he used was the preceeding column; without ever showing it to Roddenberry, he told Gene that I had publicly attacked **Trek** and stated — get this — that I wrote better **Star Trek** than Roddenberry. He managed to so thoroughly poison Roddenberry's mind against me that Gene would never speak to me, and I never had the chance to tell him, face to face, all that I owed to his series.*

Arnie was subsequently fired when Gene died. But I will never, ever forgive him for his actions.

POST-GENE (Nov. 29, 1991)

Bob Greenberger called my wife and said he'd heard I was knocking at Death's Door. Myra said that it was more like I was playing handball on Death's Stoop, which is probably the more accurate.

It was kind of like having a college curriculum of illness-majoring in bronchitis, minoring in pneumonia, with the extra credit of a week's worth of 103° fever. Fortunately they gave me enough medication so that I was completely doped up (casual acquaintances would not have been able to tell the difference) and served a helping of threats: the doctor warned that, if I didn't get better, they'd hospitalize me. I hate hospitals. I hate IVs and those stupid gowns and the total lack of control over one's existence. I am terrified of dying in a hospital. I want to die in a Porsche.

At any rate, I am much better now. My thanks to my editors for staying off my back while I was flat on it, and also for the nice flowers from the *Hulk* and *X-Factor* offices.

In fact, I recovered sufficiently to fulfill my obligation of attending — albeit it with a limited schedule — the Dreamwerks convention in Harrisburg, Pennsylvania. This was, naturally, the first *Star Trek* convention I attended since the death of Gene Roddenberry.

Fans seemed pensive. The question on everyone's minds, the question that was asked of all the guests, was this: What's going to happen to *Star Trek* now that Gene Roddenberry is gone?

Now, I'm not connected with the TV show or the movies. My guess is worth no more than anyone else's, and less than some. But, here's what I think is going to happen in regards to the TV show and movies:

Nothing.

Look, Gene's death — while a loss to many fans, an unhappy event for his family and friends, and sad to me since I owe so much of my career to the existence of *Star Trek* — did not exactly come as a surprise to anyone who was up on recent events. He'd had heart trouble, at least one stroke, was wheelchair-bound in all his recent public appearances, and was 70 years old. Not to sound cold, but he was not in good health. It wasn't the kind of death that takes your breath away and sends you into shock, like Carol Kalish's was.

The mark of a good executive is that, if he goes off to lunch and gets hit by a truck, he has matters well enough organized and subordinates well-versed enough in the ins and outs of the company so that the business can go on without a hitch.

Roddenberry was, as near as I can tell, a good executive in that respect.

From all reports, Roddenberry's day-to-day involvement in *Next Gen* had diminished consistently over the past year or two. The program was pretty much in the hands of executive producer Rick Berman who was more recently aided by Michael Piller. In recent months — again, from what I understand through sources — Gene didn't have much to do with the series at all. He simply wasn't up to it.

But now, with Roddenberry gone, fans seem concerned that *Trek* is going to change substantially. I do not share this concern. It's not like Berman and Piller have been aching to turn the *Enterprise* into a space-going cat house, or want to transform the Federation into galactic warmongers, and the only thing stopping them was Gene. One can presume that, if Gene hired them, it's because they were people who shared his views of what *Trek* was supposed to be.

If anything, *Next Gen* leans towards overcaution.

Storylines and events of more daring occur in an average episode of *L.A. Law* or *China Beach* (now in reruns on "Lifetime") than in the average *season* of *Next Generation*. It's been that way even with Roddenberry's token-to-nonexistent participation, and will probably stay that way.

The reason for this is that no one is quite sure just how the *Trek* phenomenon came about, but they do know they've managed to capture, for a quarter of a century, lightning in a bottle. No one wants to be the cluck who does something that dislodges the cork and lets the lightning escape. So they proceed with extreme wariness, and as a result, the characters have not substantially grown or developed since the pilot episode, with the possible exception of Worf. Data is no closer to understanding humans than he ever was; Riker's still a stiff; anytime Troi is in danger of getting a good scene, it goes to Guinan; Picard is still imperious although Patrick Stewart's acting elevates the character somewhat; Geordi has trouble with girls and Bev Crusher keeps trying to say something significant to the Captain but never does. This is characterization?

I think I can safely predict that Geordi will not, out of frustration, turn to alcohol; that Riker and Troi won't get married, and so on. I mean, it took them five seasons to get around to doing something fans had been asking to see since the first season — a major crossover with the original series. I foresee no dramatic changes in the future.

As for the movies, Roddenberry did not write, direct, or produce any *Star Trek* movie, nor had he even been much involved, since the first one. In fact, he strongly disagreed with the direction the films were taking — which did nothing to stop them from becoming more and more popular with the fans (with the exception of the beleaguered *ST 5*). The fans are attentive and respectful of Roddenberry's philosophies but, on the other hand, they know what they like. And now Ralph Winters is producing the *Trek* films as *Trek VI* looks forward to its opening date of Dec. 6. (It was moved up from Dec. 13 so as not to go toe-to-toe with *Hook*. That's fine by me. It was bad enough when *Star Trek: The Motion Picture* opened on Pearl Harbor Day, inviting jokes about major bombings. But opening *Trek VI* on Friday the 13th? C'mon.)

What would *Trek* be like without Roddenberry? Guys, we've already seen *Star Trek* without Roddenberry. For quite a few years there, while Gene was producing TV pilots that didn't sell, and Leonard Nimoy was loudly proclaiming in print I Am Not Spock (I keep waiting for the sequel titled, *Oh Hell, I Admit It, I'm Spock. For $4.5 Million, I'll Be Carmen Miranda*), *Star Trek* was doing just fine, thank you. Conventions were a tremendously booming business, packing in as many people as the fire marshals would allow, and *Star Trek* novels and reference works were selling to appreciative, eager audiences. Because *Star Trek* transcended its origins, becoming a massive social event, then business phenomenon, and now moving into the realm of cultural mythos.

The only place where Roddenberry's death may make a major difference is in the licensed product, such as novels and comic books. The Paramount licensing division is populated by people who are generally reasonable and sane. However, there were certain middle-management individuals, working directly for Gene Roddenberry, who were also part of the approval process and had a rather — odd — philosophy of what comics and novels should be like. One individual in particular, who shall go nameless, would make such pronouncements as, "Captain Kirk is no longer interested in pursuing relations with women" or "This story proposal will be too complicated for fans to understand."

However, in order to give his curious opinions the force of law, he would always make sure the memos carried Gene Roddenberry's name on them. The individual knew that his own opinions could be laughed off as totally ludicrous, but no one was going to muck with Roddenberry. Even though all involved were certain the memos *couldn't* be coming from Gene (since they were frequently inconsistent with things he said in person) they still carried his name. And Roddenberry, busy with the TV show or his own ill health, simply didn't have the time to get involved or do more than quickly initial memos.

That practice of affixing Gene's name is, of course, no longer feasible. And as a result, it's possible that some of the more oppressive strictures placed on the licensed material might evaporate. That would be nice to see.

Licensed material aside: Will there be TV or movie *Trek* without Gene? My guess is yes, for so long as such endeavors generate money for Paramount. In the long run it doesn't matter even if the basic philosophies *do* change. They could do a new series where the Federation crumbles completely and everyone is at war with everyone else. Sure, it would be nothing like *Trek* is now, but *Trek* now is nothing like it was and fans still accept it, because it says *Star Trek* right in the opening credits and that must, in the words of Captain Picard, Make it So.

As for Gene Roddenberry — I mourn his passing, but only to the degree that it affects those who love him. I'm much more interested in celebrating the legacy he's left behind: millions of fans, American heroes of almost mythic stature, and a lot of new lives, including the three in this house who came about because their parents met at a *Star Trek* convention.

And just remember —

Star Trek fans do it on Impulse.

(Peter David, writer of stuff, remembers thinking, "Boy, I wish I could find some way of just taking a week or two off from writing." Thus proving once again that you should beware of what you wish for, lest you get it.)

Historical Notes:

1) The "nameless individual" mentioned above is the selfsame "Arnie." As mentioned, he was fired. He still goes around to conventions, though, saying that he should be running **Star Trek***.*

NOT IN ANY STORE... (Feb. 5, 1993)

"We'd like to know if you'd be interested in going on a *Star Trek* special on QVC."

The phone call was from a collectibles company in New Jersey. Among the various paraphernalia they offer for the consumption of consumers everywhere is a host of *Trek* merchandise: autographed plaques, sweatshirts, jackets, etc., *ad infinitum*, and, for some, *ad nauseam*.

For those whose lives are devoid of cable (the TV bonanza, not the steroid-pumped cyborg), QVC is a home shopping network — although not to be confused with the Home Shopping Network. A series of products is paraded before your wondering eyes, all of which can be yours with a simple phone call and an accommodating charge card.

Of the two major shopping channels, QVC is the more low-key. Items are trotted out, discussed, demonstrated, lauded for periods of time. Then they're put aside, only to be returned to at a later time.

If it were a Disney ride, it would be the Peter Pan ride. Home Shopping, by contrast, is Space Mountain — items hurl on and off screen, sometimes with breakneck pace. And if an item isn't moving, they start slashing the price. If you're a daring consumer, you might hold off, hoping that the price gets whacked down to something that you'll chortle over to your grandchildren. Of course, you could wait too long and then the product's sold out. But if you buy too early, you kick yourself if the price drops five minutes later. It's the closest television comes to simulating bungee jumping for viewers.

Still and all, whatever the cosmetic differences, there's a basic philosophy — hawk stuff to the viewers.

My job, if I decided to accept it, would be the equivalent of the color commentator. A QVC spokesman would handle the actual merchandise peddling. I, the *Star Trek* "expert" of the moment, would talk about *Trek* in general and, when appropriate, place the items in something resembling a historical context.

Although I was surprised to "get the call," as it were, I was not wholly unprepared. They'd used other authors before. They had also used a series of *Trek* actors parading across the screen.

Frankly, I'd considered the entire display rather insipid. In many cases, actually embarrassing — watching the *Trek* actors smiling fixedly, responding to vapid questions, and trying to feign interest in a variety of chachkas. I thought it rather silly, even undignified.

And I knew that I would never, ever, lower myself to participate in such a display of naked commercialism.

So when the guy called from New Jersey and said, "Would you be interested in going on a *Star Trek* special on QVC?" I was prepared with my very arch, dignified, "I can't be bought" reply.

Which, for some odd reason, came out, "Yeah, sure. Sounds cool."

Mr. Dignity. Mr. Self-Control.

Now in self-defense, it wasn't quite that abrupt. And I also went through a lengthy self-rationalization process, making the following points to myself:

• The *Star Wars* collector's special with Mark Hamill QVC had done a couple months back had been rather worthwhile. Hamill acquitted himself well; the interviewer really knew his stuff; and some of the products really were attractive. During that special, I myself had purchased a hardbound signed edition of the Archie Goodwin/Al Williamson *Star Wars* comic strips. So it was possible to do one of these things and not feel like a schmuck.

• If I were on the program, they'd offer my hardcover *Trek* book, *Imzadi*, as one of their items. So I would have something personal I could discuss.

• I had plenty of sales experience. I was sales manager for Marvel for five years, remember. Selling came naturally to me; hell, if I could sell *Obnoxio vs. The X-Men*, I could sell anything. (As a digression, I will never forget the time back when Marvel had monthly fan press conferences which I ran, and then-assistant-editor James Owsley described *Obnoxio vs. The X-Men* in the following manner for the fan reporters: "Written, pencilled, inked, and lettered by Alan Kupperberg. Yes, it's untouched by human hands.")

• It was going to be on from 1 to 3 a.m. Eastern Time. The reason was that it was really directed at people on the West Coast, where it would be on from 10 to 12 at night. It meant that I could get some experience conducting myself on a live TV broadcast in relative privacy. It was very short notice (I presumed that their efforts to get someone else had fallen through — and as it turned out, I was right. Originally, they wanted Chris Claremont). It meant that there wouldn't be any advertising of my appearance because there wasn't time. So if I didn't open my mouth about it (aside from telling a few friends and co-workers), the odds were that hardly anyone I knew would see the damned thing. If I screwed up in some manner, no one would know or care.

• I was not required to sit there and tell people that this stuff was going to have some sort of collectibles investment value. This was fortunate because I didn't think they ever would, frankly, and there's no way I would have told people that. As it turned out, QVC has a strong policy *against* billing things as potentially increasing in value. Apparently (they claimed) one has to have a collectibles license or some such in order to make such statements, and QVC doesn't have one. They can say that something is cool looking or a "must have" item, but they can't and won't say, "If you buy this now, it'll go up and up in value." So that made me more comfortable with the whole notion.

• The money they were paying for the appearance wasn't a fortune, but it wasn't anything to sneeze at, either.

• Isaac Asimov had done tire commercials. Hell, if it was good enough for Asimov —

• I figured I could get a column out of it.

So there I was a few days later, having been picked up from my hotel (where I had checked in merely a few hours earlier and made a futile attempt to get some sleep) and was now being whisked to the QVC broadcast facility in West Chester, Pennsylvania.

They had told me I should wear a jacket and tie. I told them to buzz off and wore jeans and a sweater. At 1 in the morning, they're lucky I didn't show up in pajamas and bathrobe.

My driver was the fellow from the collectibles outfit who had contacted me in the first place. I expressed to him my concern that I might say or do something inappropriate, but he didn't seem particularly disturbed by the notion. Maybe the lateness of the hour was of comfort to him as well. Also, it seemed unlikely to them that I could be a bigger disaster than one high-profile actor had been when he had done a QVC appearance for them.

As the salesman had described the items in detail, the actor had said — on the air — "Wow, this stuff is really overpriced."

Now *there* was a ringing endorsement. On the one hand you can admire his candor; on the other, that wasn't exactly in the spirit of the agreement he'd made with his sponsors. The collectibles guy, who had presumably paid big money for the actor's time, said drily, "Yeah, we sure got a lot of bang for our buck out of *that* appearance."

The QVC studio bore something of a resemblance to Mission Control. Over half of the auditorium-sized room was taken up with operators (you know, the kind who are always "standing by now") at computer screens, taking orders from customers. This was only one bank of operators, it turned out, with other groups scattered throughout the East Coast. This, combined with the automated service wherein you don't even have to talk to a human being to buy things (the ultimate dream for agora- and xenophobes), makes QVC an organization designed for sucking away money second only to the IRS.

The other half was filled with the actual broadcast mechanism. Now, in the days before my appearance I'd been watching a lot of QVC to prepare myself.

(Indeed, it was during that time that I really began to understand QVC's allure. Nothing bad ever happens there. It's not like CNN, with its parade of worldwide disasters. Or like the networks: There's no obnoxious sitcom kids. There's no talk show hosts discussing bisexual bigamist husband/wife beaters. There's no Amy Fisher or Buttafuocos.

There's just — folks selling stuff. And there's no pressure, particularly if you're one of those people who gets cold sweats when a salesman comes over in a store and says, "May I help you?" It's all soft-sell, (at least on QVC), and you can always walk away from it. It's peaceful — almost hypnotic. As opposed to the depressing world depicted on most other stations (Nickelodeon and Disney excepted), the absolute worst thing that ever happens on QVC is that they sell out of something. And I seriously doubt that any viewer out there has ever been watching QVC and screamed something like, "Edna! They're out of the salad shooter!" and subsequently blown their brains out because they couldn't cope. I mean, if there *were* people like that, we'd be hearing about it on CNN.)

During my several days' worth of viewing, I had counted four different sets. What amazed me, upon my arrival at the studio, was the economy of space and ingenuity involved. The sets were not scattered throughout, which would have required multiple camera and lighting set-ups. Instead all four sets were together, mounted on a giant turntable, quartered by walls. When it was time for a set change (usually when embarking on a new sales program — an hour of jewelry, for example, followed by an hour of cameras) they just rotated the turntable. Presto. Cameras and lighting remained the same.

The fellow who was going to be my "host" was named Dan Wheeler. As opposed to the fellow who interviewed Hamill, Dan was not any sort of long-time SF or *Trek* aficionado. Rather, his bosses had simply said to him, "We've decided we're going to have you run the late-night *Trek* programs."

Not being a fan is hardly a criminal offense. But when you're supposed to be selling the stuff, it is something of an inconvenience. So Wheeler had been gamely immersing himself in 25 years worth of *Trek* history.

In person, Dan Wheeler comes across as a guy who's genuinely trying to do his job, and honestly trying to have on-air conversations that will, hopefully, educate both himself and the viewership.

That's in person. However — as I subsequently saw when I watched not only myself on tape, but author Mike Friedman in a later appearance — on the airwaves Dan appears condescending, even patronizing. His ignorance of his subject matter seems magnified (although having him read off cue cards with catastrophic typos such as "the Kingdom Empire" instead of "the Klingon Empire" certainly doesn't help).

All I can say is that, working with him both backstage and on camera, he sure didn't seem that way at the time. He didn't seem patronizing to me — a bit perplexed and overwhelmed, maybe, but not patronizing. I can only guess that it's something he has to work on.

The up side of Dan's relative ignorance was that it made me look better. My knowledge of *Trek* is somewhat modest compared to more avid fans; next to Dan, I looked like a walking encyclopedia.

Moments before I went on I kept muttering to myself, like a mantra, "Don't screw up, don't screw up." (Actually, I used a stronger word than that, but this is a family publication.) But as with most things in life that you're apprehensive about, most of the concern is in the anticipation. Once I was out there and discussing things that I was comfortable with, I felt a bit more at ease.

Still, it was difficult to get any real sort of dialogue going, because the bottom line is that this two-hour stint wasn't really a talk show. Wheeler could never ask a follow-up question, because the format called for one question, one answer, followed by five minutes of selling stuff. That's what QVC exists for, after all — to move product, not chat with the guest. It's an uneasy mix at times.

We took calls from viewers. Some of them were genuinely fans of mine and familiar with my work. Others — quite understandably — had never heard of me before that night. They were the ones who were politely befuddled when Dan asked, "Do you have any questions for Peter David?" because, of course, they didn't. Those were the moments during which I felt the most uncomfortable.

But it didn't last long, because, as the night (or morning, I suppose) wore on, I started to get punchy. You think drinking and driving is a dangerous combination? Try live television and sleep deprivation.

At one point they were hawking sets of uncut trading cards. I personally see no use for them, but by that time I was on autopilot and my old sales reflexes started to kick in. I actually heard my own voice saying, "Why yes, in fact, you should buy two sets of these, so you can frame one side with the pictures out and the other side with the text on display!"

It got stranger. Later a woman who had ordered those selfsame trading cards got on the air and asked, "Do these come with the hologram cards as well?"

I waited for Dan to reply. He was the authority on the products, not me. I was just the color commentator.

Wheeler's smile was still in place, but he turned to me and I could see in his eyes that he simply had no clue. Dead silence. I hadn't spotted any in the sheets, and then I thought of the old adage — "If you can't dazzle them with your intellect, baffle them with your bull."

"No, and here's why," I said, speaking with authority. "The hologram cards are printed with a completely different process, on their own separate sheets and in much smaller quantities. They're not intermixed on the sheets."

It seemed reasonable. Maybe it was even right.

"Oh," said the woman over the phone, sounding a bit disappointed.

And, having no idea where to go from there — to Wheeler's utter shock — I burst into tears.

"I'm sorry!" I sobbed. "Oh — *Goddddd*. I'm so *sooorrryyy*!" I doubled over and wailed into my hands.

I held it for a couple of seconds and then immediately snapped back to normal, thereby erasing any thought that I had sincerely broken down, but doubtlessly confirming the opinion of the people at QVC that I was out of my mind.

We moved more than 300 copies of *Imzadi*. I admit to being disappointed with that number, although I like to think that if they'd been autographed we'd have sold more (because of the short notice, there hadn't been time for me to sign them, although I had offered to do so)

So they were offering unsigned copies at list price, and anyone who was interested knew perfectly well he or she could go down to his or her local bookstore and buy it for less. Still, at least people now have a face and a demented persona to put with the name, and perhaps they'll check it out at their local bookstore.

Overall it was a bizarre experience.

And I'd never do it again.

Unless — y'know — they asked —

(Peter David, writer of stuff, can be written to c/o To Be Continued, P.O. Box 239, Bayport, New York 11705. Write before midnight tonight and get a set of ginsu knives.)

Historical Note:

1) I haven't been invited back to QVC, although others have. I think I make them nervous.

SECTION 7:

The Silver Scream

When I was a kid, my father, Gunter, was a reporter who would occasionally review movies. When it was an appropriate film, he'd bring me along. After the film, we'd go back to the office, and he would sit at his typewriter and pound out a review, and I'd sit at a typewriter and write mine.

My father is no longer a reporter, but I'm still writing reviews.

Generally I stick to genre films. Most of them I have not included here, because, frankly, I didn't think they'd be of much interest.

Several did not wind up on the cutting room floor, however, for two reasons: either because they addressed themes beyond a simple movie review or because You Guys Asked for Them. One of them, a disemboweling of the beloved *Wizard of Oz*, is easily the most asked-for column in terms of seeing it reprinted.

(Actually, it started out as a comedy routine in my occasional stand-up comedy forays.) It was the third installment of *But I Digress*, and put the column on the map.

The other "asked for" column was my analysis of *Alien* [3], mostly because my convincing explanation that it was all a dream helped console people who found the wretched exercise to be utterly without merit and ruinous of the previous two films.

PAY NO ATTENTION TO THAT FAN BEHIND THE CURTAIN (Aug. 10, 1990)

What I really want to discuss is *The Wizard of Oz*, but if I just do that, Don and Maggie Thompson will croak, because it's not comics-related. So we'll start with comics and wind up with *Wizard*. I tell you now, because, unless you know where I'm headed, this column will seem to ramble even more than it usually does.

The most frequent types of letters we get to *The Incredible Hulk* (from Hulk to Oz — how *will* he do it? Stay tuned.) are villain letters. For every letter that asks when Betty will return or when Rick Jones is coming back or whatever happened to Thunderbolt Ross' body — for every one of those letters, we get 10 or 20 saying, "I want to see The Hulk fight the Abomination/Rhino/Absorbing Man/fill-in-the-blank."

I always read these letters (I read all fan mail to all the comics I write) and at first I wondered, "Why? Why do readers ask for that?"

For example, The Hulk has fought The Rhino in the past and beaten him. And you know what? If he fights him again, he'll beat him again. You *know* he'll beat him again and again and again, because it's The Hulk's book. When someone shows up in The Hulk's comic book, The Hulk beats him. It's written in stone. It's a given.

Who likes reading a story where they know what's going to happen? Comics readers, apparently. I couldn't understand what the big attraction was. Certainly there was always the question of How Would The Hulk Beat The Rhino This Time? There are infinite variations on that, and I thought perhaps the attraction was that readers wanted to see what new and interesting ways the writer could come up with to beat up villains.

But that sounded limiting and dull. And besides, let's face it, no matter how you dress it up, all hero-villain fights are going to boil down to one thing: The hero hits the villain until the villain stops moving. The end.

Where is the commentary on the human condition in that? Where is the dramatic tension? Where is the passion? Where are the sales? Well — through the roof, actually, at least in regards to that last question. Which means that not only do the fans know what they want, but they're laying down serious bucks to get it.

In later years, however, my opinions have changed somewhat, as I've come to realize that comics fans are no different than anyone else in their tastes.

As I write this, movies with Roman numerals in their titles seem to outnumber non-numeraled films. Sequels, all over the place. Even non-sequels are sequels; every critic in America is under the impression that *Dick Tracy* is a sequel to *Batman*. Certainly they've been comparing the two, as dissimilar as they are, as if the same creative personnel were involved.

It's the comparison, I've come to realize, that makes things fun for the comics fan. This time The Hulk beat The Absorbing Man by doing this; last time he beat him another way. Fans gets a kick out of it.

Movie critics (and, to an extent, movie audiences) get a sinister kick out of it, however. Comics fans seem satisfied with fundamentally the same story, with only the most minute of twists and turns. That's why it's tempting for writers to get lazy and why we have to keep trying not to.

Moviegoers, however, are rarely, if ever, satisfied. Moviemakers find themselves in a bind: If they do a film that's just like the first one, they get slammed for rehashing. If they do a film that's drastically different in tone and style — which is creatively more satisfying — then they get slammed because the elements which attracted viewers in the first place are no longer there. And they refuse to judge the film on its own terms.

Occasionally, moviemakers luck out. *Lethal Weapon II*, everyone loved. But *Back to the Future II* was panned, as was *Indiana Jones and the Temple of Doom* — films which had many merits, the greatest of them being that the filmmakers had the guts to try something different from the parent film. And, boy, did they get ripped. Made money — tons — but got ripped.

Curiously, *BTTF III* and *Last Crusade* were well-received precisely because they were very similar to the first ones. I tend to think that the darker middle films were there to break ground and give a more serious underpinning to the characters.

But no sequel, to my knowledge, has ever been as lambasted, torn to shreds, and generally villified as *Return to Oz*.

What? Never heard of it? Only vaguely familiar with it? I'm not surprised.

Probably one of the best live-action FX film Disney ever made, *Return to Oz* was mercilessly shredded in the press. Critics actively warned parents not to let their children see it, to stay away from this damaging film.

Reviewers said it was much too terrifying for small children, apparently oblivious of the fact that Margaret Hamilton had been scaring the stuffings out of two generations with no discernable damage.

There were even loopier critiques than that. *Return* was attacked because it didn't have Judy Garland. Because there were no songs.

What *did* it have? Well, a Dorothy who was the right age, for one thing. Brilliant and seamless special effects (no visible strings holding up the lion's tail here). Dazzling claymation by Will Vinton. Dozens of positives, all overlooked, because of the Garland film.

Virtually all of the film was drawn from the Oz books, as well as the entire visual look, as *Return* chronicled Dorothy's struggle against the Nome King. The only holdover from the Garland version was having parallels between Oz and the real world.

In *Return*, the Nome King has a parallel in a psychiatrist who (paralleling the King's motives) is out to "help" Dorothy to forget Oz. The doctor's head nurse becomes, in Oz, the evil Mombi. An ethereal, mysterious patient becomes Ozma. Orderlies who wheel a hospital gurney become the dreaded Wheelers.

But they take it further than the first film's simple "this person is that person." The doctor's shock therapy machine (with which Dorothy is threatened but from which, ultimately, she escapes in the nick of time) becomes Tik Tok of Oz. Dorothy's room in the hospital is #31, the same number as the door behind which Mombi keeps —

Never mind. Effects and subtleties aside, *Return* is, in every way, superior to *Wizard of Oz*. Even the story is far superior. In *Return*, Dorothy is a mover and shaker. She makes plans and strategies, executes them, outthinks extremely formidable adversaries, and is, in every way, a superb and admirable heroine.

133

By contrast, Dorothy in the first film is a perpetual victim. She is swept along by the tide of events. She counts on her friends to protect her. She never plans, merely cries and desperately wants to return to a land where she can live in black-and-white and be assaulted by pigs. Oh, sure, she defeats the wicked witch, but it's by accident. She was trying to extinguish the Scarecrow.

And that water bit! Talk about *deus ex machina*! In *Return*, the Nome King's defeat is excellently set up. In *Wizard*, there is no hint whatsoever that the witch is vulnerable to water. Sure, we all know it now, but, boy, is that a bad piece of storytelling.

Let's face it. *The Wizard of Oz* makes no sense at all. Of course, neither does *Total Recall*, but no one's ever going to release a special 50th anniversary videotape edition of *Total Recall* (call it a hunch).

Who's the worst witch in *Wizard*? Not the one from the West. At least she's up-front. She wants to kill Dorothy and get the slippers. You know where you stand with her.

It's the one from the North: Glinda the bubble-head, who pretends to be Dorothy's friend. A careful viewing of the film reveals Glinda either is a total moron or simply a nasty customer.

We know Glinda's a few yellow bricks shy of a load from the moment she shows up. Her first words to Dorothy: "Are you a good witch or a bad witch?" All right, a fair question. But when Dorothy says she's not a witch, Glinda then addresses the same question to the dog. This woman can't recognize a dog? You can't be serious. And don't say there are no dogs in Oz, because The Witch of the West knows Toto for what he is immediately.

It gets worse. The Wicked Witch shows up, and Glinda removes the formidable ruby slippers from the dead witch. Does she put these magic talismans on herself to battle The Wicked Witch? No! She puts them on the *non*-witch from *Kansas*!

Why? The only reason I can think of is this: Have you ever rented bowling shoes? They always feel creepy, and sometimes there's stuff growing in them. And that's shoes worn by mortals. Can you imagine shoes worn by a witch, for who-knows-how-long? We know witches aren't big on personal hygiene; if they wash, they'll melt. The only way I'd put on those ruby slippers is if they came with industrial-strength Odor Eaters.

So Glinda sticks these disgusting, unclean pumps on poor, helpless Dorothy. And then Glinda delivers the strangest line of the movie to the Wicked Witch: "You have no power here. Begone," etc. This statement is not refuted by the evil one.

I don't get this at all. She has no power in Munchkinland? She's surrounded by 3 million Munchkins who have just learned this bit of information. Bam. Film's over by reel two, as this powerless, green-skinned crone is battered to death by the Lollypop Guild and danced on by the Lullaby League.

But no, the Munchkins are in on it with Glinda — either stupid or vindictive. Probably stupid. Dorothy is given simple traveling instructions: "Follow the Yellow Brick Road." She even says it to herself a few times to get it down. What happens? There's a damned Munchkin stopping her every two feet repeating it to her, apparently concerned she can't remember five words in sequence. They think she's as stupid as they are.

Probably she is, because she never realizes that the whole film is an arbitrary, pointless exercise on Glinda's part. Why didn't Glinda tell her the shoes would bring her home? "Because she wouldn't have believed me."

Was anyone besides Dorothy taken in by this? I mean, come on. She was standing in Munchkinland, in color, surrounded by little people and witches, having been swept there by a tornado. Does anyone think that if Glinda had said, "Try banging the shoes together," Dorothy would have said, "Hah! You expect me to believe that! I'll walk, thanks?"

I think not. I think Dorothy's suspension of disbelief was pretty much over the rainbow by that point, thank you very much. Call me crazy, but I think she would have given it a whack.

No, she wanted Dorothy to learn a lesson. What was the lesson? This: Never dream. Never travel. Never envision that which you do not have or strive to acquire more than is immediately available, because, if you don't already have it, maybe you didn't need it to begin with.

Right. We don't need to travel to the stars or seek new technology or dream of going over the rainbow. Stay at home, dwell in sepia tones, and be content in a colorless world where an old bat can come along and have your dog gassed. What a great message.

The message of a benevolent person? A sane person? No. Glinda was demented at best or at worst just plain buck-stupid.

In *Return to Oz*, Dorothy dreams of another land, learns it exists, and at the end of the film is a whole, confident, and happy individual. In *The Wizard of Oz*, Dorothy dreams of a better place, learns that her dream is a pointless exercise in futility — that maybe she didn't really need it to begin with — and goes back to dwell in a dreary land that I wouldn't wish on my worst enemy, much less a beloved heroine.

You tell me which film is better.

See? From The Hulk to *The Wizard of Oz*. It was easy. All I had to do was click my Reeboks three times.

(I feel constrained to point out that there are all kinds of real reasons why the script for *Wizard* is the way it is. Multiple drafts by half a dozen writers, for one thing. Also many people, far more scholarly than I, have written all kinds of interpretations — such as that the "own back yard" speech was actually a cloaked plea for isolationism, since the United States was contemplating entering World War II. This column is not out to explore any of that, but merely to entertain. For those interested in pursuing the matter, there are a number of excellent books on the subject, including the actual script complete with excised scenes. And while you're at it, rent *Return to Oz* on tape. Don't watch it on the Disney Channel. The morons edited out the really scary parts.)

*(Peter David has never missed an airing of **The Wizard Of Oz** for two decades and yet saw it through entirely new eyes, when his 9-year-old daughter asked why Dorothy didn't simply turn the stupid hourglass over to buy herself more time. And he realized that, not only didn't he have an answer, but it had never occurred to him before. If anyone out there has an answer (aside from the obviously lame "It was too heavy" or "It was stuck"), send it to him c/o **CBG**. That and any other questions, except for when is The Hulk going to fight The Rhino?)*

THE PERFECT SUPER-HERO FILM OF ALL TIME (Oct. 5, 1990)

I have finally seen the first absolutely perfect costumed super-hero film. It is called *Darkman*.

And what makes it perfect is the last line.

Now let me make it clear here: "Perfect" is not, in this instance, to be considered synonymous with "good." Or "quality." "Perfect" is not defined herein as "in a state of undiminished or highest excellence." No, I'm speaking of my directory's first definition: "Complete of its nature or kind."

The nature of this kind of movie is standard super-hero comic book. Other films have come close — but they haven't had *everything*. They haven't been complete. Somewhere, in some aspect or other, they've been lacking.

What's ironic, of course, is that *Darkman* is not based on any specific comic-book hero, although he's pretty much a combo of The Shadow and The Avenger, both from pulps, with Swamp Thing's origin thrown in for good measure, to wit: A scientist runs afoul of some bad guys and gets himself and his lab blown up. However, due to a homegrown skin project he's got cooking, he's able to reconstruct faces, including the bad guys' and his own. Swathing his face in bandages and a coat and hat Lamont Cranston left sitting around, he seeks vengeance. No specific hero, but an agglommeration.

Because of that, *Darkman* is the first film, as I have said, to feature absolutely everything you find in your standard comic book. Everything. Even including the last line.

I will endeavor not to blow any major plot points along the way, but if you're skittish about this sort of thing and intend to see the film, then stop here; otherwise, onward:

Darkman features all of the following, whereas other super-hero or comic-book films have featured only some:

• *Constant Movement without Regard to Dramatic Pacing*. Standard comics must have something happening every single page, i.e., someone's getting hit, someone's in jeopardy, or someone's in motion. Exposition is usually given on the run. Talking heads are anathema. In *Darkman*, either the plot is barreling forward with the speed of a freight train, or else the camera is. Sam Raimi, who came up with what can laughingly be referred to as the story, also directed as if he'd been taking No-Doz and washing it down with Jolt.

Batman, *Turtles*, and most others feature some great action sequences, but there are also long moments when absolutely nothing is happening. Ain't no butlers reminiscing about young master Bruce in this film, baby. Only *RoboCop* matches *Darkman* for sheer kinetic lunacy.

• *Villains Who Are Evil Because They're Villains*. *Darkman* comes dangerously close to blowing it on this with a real estate-developer villain who actually tries to explain himself. Fortunately, though, there's Larry Drake of *L.A. Law* present to more than make up for it. You think Benny Stolwitz has mental problems? You should see the nut Drake plays in this one. Drake's villain is relentlessly sadistic, right down to his hobbies. He's nasty and nauseating because he's nasty and nauseating. All his henchmen are, also.

Superman missed the boat on this with Luthor, as did *Batman* with The Joker — in both cases, they have much too much style. We find ourselves drawn to them. How many people came out of *Batman* saying that The Joker was the better role? Everybody. Drake's character exists only to be a bastard. We know nothing about his background, nothing of his family, nothing of what made him the way he is. He's there to do hideous things and get clobbered by *Darkman*.

Again, *RoboCop* does manage to match it with the unrelenting nastiness of Clarence Boddiker. Actually, what amazes me, now that I think about it, is that the producers of *Batman* thought they were doing something clever in having The Joker figure into *Batman*'s origin. Villains were also responsible for the hero's origins in *RoboCop*, *Swamp Thing*, and now *Darkman*. This seems unique to movies since, in the comics, origins always seem unrelated to any sort of major villain. Common thugs have figured in more frequently.

• *A Nifty Secret Headquarters*. Gotta have a secret HQ. Ya got your sewers; ya got your Fortress of Solitude. Here's where *RoboCop* missed the boat. He had a cage in police HQ where he could eat babyfood. That doesn't cut it, sorry. *Darkman* has a lab in a deserted warehouse with patched-together computer equipment, giving the entire thing an air of a funky Batcave, cobbled together during a rummage sale. Considering the hero got his duds out of a dumpster, it's consistent.

• *Bad Transitions*. Nowhere do you see worse transitions than standard super-hero comic books. And no super-hero film can beat *Darkman* for this. Every other super-hero film features standard cuts. Not this one; *Darkman* actually has a sequence where a woman sees her boyfriend's lab blown up, freezes in that position, and then the background shifts to put her in a cemetery while the camera reclothes her in black. It's supposed to be clever, but it's just awful, which is what makes it authentic.

• *Angst*. You didn't have angst until the Marvel Age started, but now everyone's got it. There's no angst in *Superman*. There's no angst in *Swamp Thing*. There's a little in *Batman*, but by the end of the film, our hero has a babe that loves him, a city that adores him, a mansion, a neat cave with lots of equipment, a great car, and he's nailed the guy who killed his folks. The only things he doesn't have are his plane and a costume that lets him turn his head. Not the stuff of drama.

This is where *Darkman* lays its strongest claim to perfection. The hero questions his motives and his sanity in clear, no-nonsense, histrionic dialogue that you never hear outside of, well, comic books (He actually exclaims, "What have I become?" There's a phrase that I myself certainly utter at least once a day.)

• *Everything Is Spelled Out*. In *Batman*, you're left to ponder just how together Bruce Wayne is. He's wrapped so tightly that, despite his statement to Vicki that she "got in," we still don't really know him by film's end. *Darkman* doesn't have this problem. Not remotely. Not only, as noted above, does he frequently and loudly question his sanity, but Raimi insists on hitting us over the head with it. When *Darkman* is getting upset, the camera zooms in and out and all kinds of bizarre images flash all over him, just to make sure you know *this guy's around the bend*!

• *Ludicrous Implausability, Especially During Fight Scenes*. You thought having The Joker shoot down the Batwing was absurd? Get this: Darkman feels no pain, literally. This is supposed to explain how this guy can be dangling from a tow cable of a helicopter, moving at about 60 miles per hour, get smashed through the window of a skyscraper, and be utterly uninjured. Legs, arms, internal organs — everything's intact. Even his wit — he utters a funny exit line before being hauled skyward once more.

• *Damsel in Distress*. Well, they all have that. But there's one thing that *Darkman* has that the others don't, although RoboCop is pretty close. And that is that all important last line.

• *The Hero Must Utter His Name Near or at the End of His Origin*.

Think about it. Ben Grimm didn't say, "I've been transformed into some kind of — of orange rocky guy!", because "Orange Rocky Guy" won't look good on a pair of Underoos. Nah. He said, "I'm some sort of — Thing!" Catchy.

Heroes are always naming themselves in bursts of inspiration. Villains, too. Frequently, they have names that already are three-quarters of the way to being a *nom de guerre*, and they only have to change a syllable. For example, if Marvel's editor-in-chief were bitten by a radioactive bird from the Bronx and as a result sprouted feathers and a beak, he could easily stand on the roof at 387 Park Avenue South and shout, "Once I was ordinary Tom DeFalco, but now I am — Duh Falcon!"

But in movies, super-heroes always seem self-conscious of their names. Also, when they *do* say their names, it's not at the end of the film. The only film where the timing of it was correct was *RoboCop*, and when he turned in response to the question of his name, he said "Murphy." This was a nice twist on the old line, and it showed that he had recaptured a bit of this humanity.

Batman, on the other hand, seemed self-conscious about his name, and his *gadgets'* names. The batmobile, batwing, batcave, batsignal and batarang were never identified as such. He only referred to his own name but once, and that wasn't at the end of the film (which was, to all intents and purposes, his origin). We had deafening church bells and a dramatic shot, but no "I'm Batman." That was in the first 10 minutes.

(Actually, I'd always thought it would have been fun if Batman — who was new at this, remember — had inadvertently done what *RoboCop* deliberately did. You know — "What are you?" "I'm Bruce Wayne —no, wait. Damn. I did it wrong. Well, guess I'll have to drop you." "Aaaaahhhh!")

Now Darkman — well, he's obeyed every other tradition/cliché of comics, and this one is here, too, in all its glory. The final line, spoken with proper angst as he melts into the crowd, giving up his old life and girlfriend: "Call me — Darkman."

Actually, more likely, next summer we'll be calling him: *Darkman II.*

*(Peter David, writer of **Hulk**, **Dreadstar**, and **Star Trek**, got up on the wrong side of the bed this morning.)*

Historical Notes:

*1) No **Darkman II** has surfaced. However, there was a six-issue series published by Marvel in 1993 that was quite good.*
And talk of a TV incarnation of Darkman persists.

CUTTING UP WITH EDDIE (Jan. 18, 1991)

In Hollywood, there's a popular euphemism for saying that someone doesn't like a script or a movie. They don't say, "I don't like it." They say, "I'm sorry, I just didn't get it." The former, you see, implies some sort of failure on the part of the movie maker. But the latter implies a failure on the part of the viewer. As in, "If I were only a smarter or more perceptive person, I would have understood what you, in your genius, were doing." It's all polite nonsense, of course. They just didn't like it, period.

So I read my local newspaper's review of *Edward Scissorhands*, and the reviewer hated it. He made that quite clear. He flat out didn't like it. The basic thrust of the review was, "Here's a guy with scissors on his hands, and what does he spend the movie doing? Making sculptures out of bushes and ice. How stupid." He didn't make the film sound remotely appealing.

Then James Fry, whose opinion I respect (how can you *not* respect someone whose mascot is the Robot Monster?) said that *Edward* was an absolutely beautiful, touching, wonderful film and that I had to run right out and see it. So I ran right out and saw it.

Turns out James was right. If you have not yet seen *Edward Scissorhands*, then you must. Here is a film that is more visually staggering than Burton's previous effort, *Batman*, because, rather than millions of dollars being spent on creating Gotham (when, if you wanted a gritty, dirty city, you could easily have filmed in Manhattan at night and gotten much better effects), *Edward* creates a world that could only exist in films.

Imagine, if you will, a suburban never-neverland. A dazzling array of tract houses, differing from each other only in their choice of cotton-candy pastel colorings. And at the end of the street of the development there just so happens to be this massive, overgrown castle on a mountain where a mad scientist (played by Vincent Price) lives. Throughout the film, no one ever comments on this. No one ever complains about the creepy house. It's simply accepted, and the acceptance adds to the discordance.

From this house comes Edward (played to perfection by Johnny Depp), an unliving being created from a robot skeleton by Price, who dies before he can finish his creation and attach hands. Ghastly white with puckered lips and a face scarred from accidentally touching it with his "fingers," Edward views this bizarre world through the eyes of an innocent. And he begins to create sculptures from the local bushes.

It is at this point that I began to understand the reviewer's problem. It was a reverse on the old Hollywood bit. Instead of not liking a film but simply claiming they "didn't get it," here was a reviewer who clearly didn't get it but instead stridently stated that he didn't like it.

The young son of the Avon lady who takes Edward in comments several times how one karate chop from Edward's hands could send someone's head flying. That's obviously what the reviewer wanted to see. If Edward had patrolled the city at night, looking for crime, that would have been fine. Or if it had been a film in the vein of *Nightmare on Elm Street*, that would have been even better.

Edward Scissorhands is *not* a film about a guy with blades on his wrists who wastes two hours of screen time making sculptures. It's about an artistic soul trapped in a hideous body, whose only means of self expression — his blessing — doubles as his curse. The blades help him carve beauty, but he can't touch beauty. Backed up by Danny Elfman's mournful score, it's a wonderful film.

I would not advise taking small children to it, which I saw a number of people doing. My 9-year-old handled it just fine, although she was in tears by the end because "it's so sad." My 5-year-old, though, would have seen Edward as terrifying, not sympathetic, and would not have liked it at all. I don't mind films that scare kids (à la *Return to Oz*, as I've said in the past) as long as they can easily relate to the protagonist. That's not going to happen here. So be warned.

So fascinated was I with *Edward* that I did some digging into the origins of the movie and found some interesting facts. As is typical of Hollywood, *Edward Scissorhands* went through a staggering number of changes before winding up on the screen. It took Tim Burton years to sell it, and I've managed to unearth some of the earlier concepts that simply never flew. I list the earlier titles here, along with brief synopses, to give you an idea of how Hollywood forces compromise and bends the artistic vision. In Burton's original story concepts, Edward wasn't bereft of normal hands. Instead, he was a misfit in other aspects:

Edward Sphincter Hands: Beginning life as an anal retentive comic-book editor with a hands-on approach, Edward becomes so unpopular that he moves to Hollywood and lands a job approving *Star Trek* comics and novels for Paramount. When this doesn't pan out, he goes to medical school and becomes a successful proctologist.

A biting satire, executives were concerned that the hero was just too darned unlikeable. So Burton changed it to:

Edward Swizzler Hands: Edward is the world's greatest bartender, learning his trade from an older, wiser bartender. This got into development, with Ted Danson and Tom Cruise attached, but the failure of *Cocktail* killed this plan. Burton went back to the drawing board and returned with:

Edward Shvitzer Hands: Set in a steamroom, Edward is a Hispanic attendant who is really God. This actually went into preproduction, with Rene (*Hill Street Blues*) Enriquez in the lead, until someone pointed out that this was just like *Steambath*, by Bruce Jay Friedman, which was a play and also aired on PBS. Tim Burton reportedly complained loudly, stating that no one went to plays, no one watched PBS, and who cares about a script by "some stupid *Star Trek* writer" (apparently confusing him with Michael Jan Friedman).

It was at this point that Burton, starting to get frustrated, zeroed in on his own sense of the absurd regarding the project and tapped into it. Having fixated, for no discernable reason, on having a protagonist whose name ended in "Hands," he began experimenting with the concept of having something other than normal human hands at the end of the character's arms. He started out with:

Edward Bear Hands: It was here that Edward first became an artifical being. Here, though, he was created by Disney Imagineers and had little Winnie the Pooh toys on his wrists instead of hands. The toy tie-ins seemed perfect. However, the whole project received protest from Christopher Milne, son of A.A. Milne, and rather than risk bad PR, Burton came up with:

Edward Glad Hands: Edward has Glad sandwich bags instead of hands. Studio execs, though, were concerned that kids might start using plastic bags for toys and could suffocate. Frustrated and deciding to go strictly for laughs, Burton turned to:

Edward Shpritzer Hands: Set in the time of vaudeville, Edward is a comedian who, through a tragic accident, ends up with seltzer bottles in lieu of hands. However, he becomes a tremendous hit and ends up rich and running a hotel in the Borcsht Belt. This was almost a go when Patrick Swayze expressed interest but then he decided on *Ghost* instead and the project fell apart.

By this point, Burton decided to take all the elements he liked best: The artificial life. The sense of absurdity. Something other than normal human hands for his protagonist. And he created:

Edward Switzerhands. This draft was almost identical to the final version, except Edward had Swiss army knives instead of hands and spent much of the film opening bottles of wine. There was concern, though, that it would be viewed as a film promoting alcoholism.

So Burton sat there, looking over the story and staring at an artist's conception of his lead character. He envisioned ditching the corkscrew and having just blades, but worried about comparisons to Freddie Krueger or Wolverine.

So he substituted scissors.

The rest is movie history.

*(Peter David, writer of stuff, will explain next week how, through casting confusion, **The Terminator** almost featured Danny DeVito in the title role rather than Arnold Schwarzenegger, and how that led in turn to **Twins**. See you next time — at the movies.)*

ALIEN 3, PEOPLE NOTHING (June 26, 1992)

In order not to disappoint those of you who haven't seen *Alien* ^{3} (or, as I like to call it, *Alien 3, People 0*) and, therefore, have to skip the column this week, I'll warm up with this utterly irrelevant but nonetheless enchanting anecdote, so that you won't walk away from this issue feeling cheated. Feel free to keep on reading until I say otherwise.

I got a call from Harlan Ellison the other day, who not only confirmed my observation in the column from issue #969 that smokers were going to have a new rallying cry thanks to *Basic Instinct*, but informed me that he had encountered it personally.

You see it coming, don't you?

Harlan was in New York, having attended a memorial service for Isaac Asimov, at which Harlan was one of the speakers. It was later that night and Harlan, hungry, decided to stop at a pizza joint and buy a slice. So he's standing there in the pizza place, about to start eating, and a woman right next to him opens up her pocket book, removes a package of cigarettes, and lights up.

Now this was one of those small joints that opens right out onto the street. It would have been no effort for her to puff to her heart's content a few feet away, but instead she lit up illegally inside.

"Excuse me," said Harlan, "but this is an open-air restaurant. Would you mind taking that outside?"

Apparently having just seen *Basic Instinct*, she looked at Harlan smugly and said, "What are you going to do? Arrest me for smoking?"

Harlan didn't arrest her.

Instead, Harlan plucked the cigarette from her mouth and dropped it in her pocketbook — where it promptly worked its way to the bottom and, still lit, began to ignite the contents.

The woman shrieked, madly trying to salvage the interior of her pocketbook and she took a swing at Harlan. She missed him clean, and Harlan, referring to his slice, said, "Look, sweetheart, if you want to wear this pizza, just keep right on swinging."

Did anyone leap to her aid? Hell, no. This is New York. Besides, I figure the place was filled either with non-smokers who were thinking, "Yes! Yes! Way to go!" or smokers who were thinking, "I'm not messing with *this* nut."

The woman left in a huff with smoldered pocketbook, scorched dignity, and probably headed straight home to write a really angry letter to screenwriter Joe Eszterhaus to complain that she tried his stupid line and it didn't work.

Me, I think Harlan should get together with Tony Randall, who (so I heard) on a *Tonight Show* appearance warned some massive wrestler sitting next to him to extinguish a cigarette and, when the guy wouldn't do it, put it out for him. I bet Harlan and Randall could exchange some terrific anti-smoking war stories.

So here we are, well into this week's installment, and now it's time to move on to *Alien* ^{3}. **Spoiler warnings abound**. If you keep reading, and the movie is ruined for you, don't come whining to *me* about it.

When I saw the first two *Alien* films, there was a moment in each of them where my opinion of them solidified. I remember them quite clearly.

In *Alien*, it was when the crewmembers of the *Nostromo* who had not yet been devoured were trying to decide what course of action to take, and someone made the reasonable suggestion that they man the life boats and get the hell out of there. And we were told that isn't possible; the escape pods didn't have sufficient seating capacity for an evacuation.

That little revelation jolted me right out of the picture. I envisioned the screenwriter sitting there, fingers poised over the keyboard, thinking, "Why don't they just leave? Well — uh — not enough room on the escape pods. That's good."

No, it's not good. It's not like we're talking about a crew of a thousand. The crew, even intact, numbered less than a dozen. And there was no emergency evac procedure to handle that paltry total? I didn't buy it for a second.

So by the time we got into later stupidities, such as Ellen Ripley (Sigourney Weaver) risking the life and limb of herself and the remains of the crew to search for the cat, or the *Nostromo's* self-destruct mechanism with its triggering device in the core of the ship (rather than the logical place, which would be next to the exit door of the escape pod; you know — start the countdown, hop in the pod and leave), I was so detached from the film that I was laughing all through the climax.

The point in *Aliens* where I made my decision on the film was midway through, after the marines had just gotten their butts kicked in their first encounter with the aliens. At first Private Vasquez (Jenette Goldstein) wants to go back in and slug it out again, but Ripley calmly says, basically, "I say we get out of here and nuke them from orbit. It's the only way to be sure."

It's a sensible moment, a logical moment. It's everything the first film lacked. And even better: The other marines echo the sentiment. The fact that they *don't* manage to return to the ship is due, not to stretches of credulity, but a perfectly believable plot moment with an alien warrior trashing the drop ship.

So I liked *Aliens*, starting with that moment. Liked it a lot.

Then we get to the third film.

Ripley is the sole survivor of an emergency crash landing on prison planet Fiorina 161, caused by an alien face hugger, or huggers, trying to penetrate the sleeping capsule. Where the face-hugger came from, we haven't a clue. The queen left eggs behind, on the *Sulaco*? When? The face-huggers were cracking the capsules? How? They couldn't break through the glass specimen casings they were enclosed in in *Aliens* until Burke (Paul Reiser) released them. One would think the sleeping tubes would be even tougher material.

Still reeling from all this nonsense, I haven't even begun to consider that the prison planet she's landed on makes no sense. Here's a Company so rapacious that it thinks nothing of abandoning or killing its *own employees*, but it *is* willing to go to the expense of sending out a semi-annual supply ship to keep two dozen double-Y chromosome losers happy.

No, I'm sitting there, still incredulous that Newt — who Ripley risked life and limb for — is dead, virtually making the last half hour of *Aliens* moot. I'm also angry that Hicks is dead, aborting a promising character relationship with Ripley before it even got going. So there's Ripley at the funeral —

And her nose starts to bleed.

That was the moment — the moment I thought, "Oh, terrific. She's got an alien gestating in her. Not only is everyone on this stupid planet dead, but Ripley's going to die, too."

I was 99% certain, and it was finally confirmed for me beyond any shadow of a doubt when the alien warrior got upclose and personal with her and then left her alone.

It's not a good sign when a movie is that predictable 15 minutes in. The whole trick to movie making is *looking* like you're going to be predictable and then coming up with twists and turns so that the outcome is utterly unexpected but at the same time completely logical.

A^3 does not make that effort. A^3 makes very little effort about anything. In the first two films there was some attempt to give all the supporting players some degree of personality, so that, when they inevitably became alien-chow, their deaths meant something. Not so this time. Aside from the fact that, with all their heads shaved, all the prisoners look remarkably alike, they never rise above the position of cannon fodder. Their deaths are meaningless.

There are only two characters who seem to have any depth at all.

One is the doctor, played by Charles Dance, who dies shortly after a roll in the hay with Ripley (thereby perpetuating the filmic notion that any time Sigourney Weaver takes her clothes off trouble ensues).

The other is Charles S. Dutton, who plays the religious spearhead of the convict group. But even his character is reduced to delivering a supposedly rallying speech that is more notable for its profanity than its uplifting spirit. Bill Murray's "It just doesn't matter!" oratory in *Meatballs* was more moving.

Originally, the script called for Dutton's character to sacrifice himself and Ripley to escape — until Weaver took it upon herself to insist that Ripley be offed.

I will admit that such an approach is a nice twist to the type of "Hollywood ending" so neatly skewered in *The Player*. But I question the timing; *after* Ripley has survived two previous films, *that's* when they go for a downbeat ending? She makes it through all that only to succumb at the end? It makes the first two feel like exercises in futility.

What I have to give the creators of the film credit for is nerve — more guts than brains, really. Most of the script's text is eminently forgettable, but the film has far more subtext than either of the previous two entries. Whereas the first film was essentially a space-going haunted house story and the second a military operation with maternal overtones, A^3 has the audacity to try to produce a two-hour religious metaphor.

One doesn't usually come out of an SF horror film discussing theological symbolism, but A^3 is replete with it. When Ripley first shows up, the religious converted convicts view her with suspicion and fear. As well they should. In most theologies, women represent two things: They bring ruin upon man (Lilith, Eve, Pandora) or they are the lifebringers, the providers of salvation (Mary).

The lifers assume that Ripley represents the first instance, and they're not incorrect. After all, shortly after Ripley shows up, all hell breaks loose in the little hell they've created. In this scenario, the alien becomes more than just a marauding force. It's the incarnation of evil itself: a dark, slavering Satan figure, punishing the convicts for their crimes.

But as the film progresses, Ripley takes on the second religious female persona: the bringer of life. For Ripley has an alien growing inside her — and not just *any* alien, but a queen. Whereas in *Aliens* it was one mother (Ripley on behalf of Newt) versus another (the Queen, protective of her eggs), this time they are united, albeit unwillingly. Thus Ripley fills multiple functions: would-be savior of the human race and surrogate mother to yet more aliens.

And, boy, does director David Fincher feast on this notion. Because Ripley isn't just *any* old savior. She's the Messiah. I mean, even this humble Jew picked up on that.

Humanity has, to all intents and purposes, evolved into the soulless, heartless "Company." Its activities and disregard for human life have caused all the problems in the first two films.

So Ripley, basically, dies for our sins. Just to jackhammer the point home, Fincher presents us with a final view of Ripley plummeting into the purging flames of an inferno (Hell?), her arms outstretched in perfect evocation of the crucifixion. In so doing, she takes the newborn queen with her, thus saving humanity from —

Well, from nothing, actually. If the Company really is that hot to have an alien, it can just hie itself back to the original derelict ship that Crewman Kane discovered in the first film. Presumably it was far enough from the colony to escape the nuclear blast that climaxed *Aliens*. After all, it had eluded detection for a couple of decades. The Company would then have thousands of eggs to choose from. To quote Ren and Stimpy, "Happy Happy Joy Joy."

With this utterly pointless and futile death of a heroine who deserved so much better, I was watching the film and was reminded of the Harry Chapin song, "30,000 Pounds of Bananas," in which a doomed trucker's brakes go out on a run to Scranton, Pa., and he hurtles to oblivion with the title fruit as cargo. There's a line which goes: "And he said, 'God, make it a dream!' as he rode his last ride down."

That's what I felt like — trapped in a high-speed vehicle (a climactic and confusing chase through endlessly spinning tunnels, for example, induces vertigo rather than tension) — and I sent out a prayer that perhaps this could all be a dream.

It's rare that I would be happy about the notion of blowing off a whole film by wishing for the hoary cliché of one of the principals waking up. But A^3 undercuts *Aliens*, which I enjoyed immensely. If I have to sacrifice one film or the other, I'll ditch A^3 in a heartbeat.

And it's so easy to do.

In fact, A^3 makes *more* sense if it's a dream — because then, as with *Total Recall*, you don't have to worry about lapses in logic. Since when do dreams make sense, after all?

Better than religious symbolism, I can easily paint all sorts of dream symbolism to "prove" A^3 was a figment of Ripley's imagination. The film was Ripley's every nightmare incarnate. How does Newt die in A^3? She drowns. This is an obvious dream allusion to the sequence in *Aliens* where Newt (Carrie Henn) is up to her neck in water and subsequently kidnapped by an alien. Ripley gets there just in time to see the head of Newt's doll sink below the water. After the autopsy in A^3, pretty much the only thing left intact is Newt's head.

• In *Aliens*, Bishop is impaled by the Queen (checkmate). In A^3, it's Hicks who dies by being impaled. Same death, different guy. Coincidence? I think not.

• In dreams you frequently have no true sense of where you are. Locales shift with dizzying speed and with no rhyme or reason. That happens throughout A^3. Ordinarily one would have to chalk this up to bad directing — but, if A^3 is a dream, then the liability is actually a plus.

• Ripley parades around nude in the sickbay without overmuch concern. Commonplace in dream circumstances.

• She has sex with the doctor for no particular reason other than that he's there. Reasons don't matter, if it's a dream.

• Look at the last lines of *Aliens*, for heaven's sake:

Newt: Ripley — can I dream now?

Ripley: Yes, honey. I think we both can.

There you go. She says it right there. She's going to dream now.

• Compare it to the final words of A^3, which is a recording of Ripley's final log entry on the *Nostromo's* escape ship. From the way the shot is framed, it's clearly supposed to be originating from the ship that Ripley crashes onto Fiorina 161. Now, why in hell would the voice log from the *Nostromo* be on an emergency escape pod from the *Sulaco*? It makes no sense whatsoever — but, if it's a dream, *it doesn't have to*.

Please, someone at 20th Century Fox — consider this as a possibility. Otherwise, the only thing that really makes sense is that the prisoners were double-Y chromosome guys. Because you come out of the film saying, "Why? Why?"

*(Peter David, writer of stuff, is curious if — in Don Simpson's book — being critical of **Alien** ³ means that Peter David is, in fact, jealous of those involved.)*

TURKEY HERO (Oct. 30, 1992)

When you look back at 1992 and are asked what movie best epitomizes what the literature of heroic fiction in general and comic books in specific is supposedly about —

What are you going to reply? The chances are that most people would kind of shrug their shoulders and say, "*Batman Returns.*" I mean, what's the alternative? "*Captain America,*" newly released on videotape? Hardly.

The thing is: There is a movie currently out that is a far better exploration of the nature of heroes, which is what most super-hero comics are supposed to be in the first place.

That film is the aptly titled *Hero*, currently on view at a theater near you. And I would be inclined to say that *Hero* should be required viewing for all people currently participating in the super-hero genre of comic books. Because it's a fabulous treatise on the nature of heroes and a reminder of just what the comics we're producing should be about.

Dustin Hoffman is a down-and-out loser named Bernie Laplante. Facing a certain prison sentence, a frowning ex-wife, a sure-to-be-disillusioned son, Bernie remains resolutely unlikable.

Many critics have compared Laplante to Hoffman's Ratso Rizzo from *Midnight Cowboy*. That may be off-base; if you're looking for comparisons, you might choose Hoffman's Raymond from *Rain Man* who, because of his mental condition, is incapable of learning and changing and growing.

Likewise, no matter how many people try to help him, Bernie continually watches out for himself above all others. He regrets his apparently inevitable prison term, but one senses that, given the exact same set of circumstances, he'd find himself right back in front of the same judge awaiting sentencing.

And then fate literally throws an opportunity to elevate himself directly into Bernie's path — a crippled jumbo jet which, one night, incredibly (and in unlikely fashion) crash-lands on the road mere feet in front of Bernie's car.

And Bernie saves the day.

He's not happy about it. He crabs all the way. He drags passenger after passenger to safety, unable to ignore their pleas for help — including cutesy-named TV reporter Gail Gayley (Geena Davis) — and the entire time curses himself out for what he perceives to be his weakness of character.

He subsequently disappears into the night and ultimately is more than happy to distance himself from the entire incident. When he makes half-hearted attempts to tell people who know him about his adventure, the notion that he would act heroically is dismissed out of hand. ("It's against your father's religion," his son is informed by his ex-wife, played by Joan Cusack.) Bernie is more than happy to let it drop — until a reward of $1 million is offered to the unknown hero that the media refer to as "The Angel of Flight 407." But before he can claim it, someone beats him to it: A homeless man named John

Bubber (Andy Garcia, resolutely bland in the role. Oh, what Scott Bakula or William Hurt could have done with it), who was the only one who listened to Bernie's tale, steps forward and takes credit.

Bernie rots in jail while Bubber becomes the toast of the town. And then things *really* get involved.

Hero gets tremendous mileage out of a simple premise that has been explored in such diverse vehicles as *Mr. Smith Goes to Washington, Amazing Fantasy* #15, "The City on the Edge of Forever," and *Quantum Leap*. That notion is that one person can make a difference: that anyone, no matter how humble, has it within him/her to do great good, if presented with the right set of circumstances.

This was the sort of thing that Frank Capra, with such films as *Mr. Smith* and *It's a Wonderful Life* (both starring quintessential Everyman Jimmy Stewart), excelled in. Stewart's desperate filibuster in *Mr. Smith* remains one of the great movie moments and the purest definition of the little guy rising to heroic status.

In *Quantum Leap*, time traveler Sam Beckett's actions have far-reaching consequences: Convince a teen-ager in the 1960s that life is worth living, and in the 1990s he makes the breakthrough that results in a cure for cancer.

"City on the Edge of Forever" explores the downside of that equation: Edith Keeler has qualities that make her special and important, but those very qualities are what doom her, because World War II was not the time to promote the notion of "peace is the way."

And, of course, *Amazing Fantasy* #15, in which Peter Parker learns that not only can one person make a difference, but that people have an obligation to try to make that difference, if it's at all within their power to do so.

The thing about Peter Parker is that there was so much about him not to like. Indeed, he's the kind of kid that most other kids who were typical readers would have, under ordinary circumstances, distanced themselves from in school. Think about it: He wore glasses, neatly pressed pants, and sweater vests.

He was a brain — the kind of guy who wrecked the grade curve.

His aunt babied him and he let her.

He whined constantly about all his problems.

He never, ever wanted to go out and have a good time.

Instead, he was studying constantly.

He wasn't on any teams.

Let's face it. Peter Parker was not the sort of guy whom anyone would have been friends with in real life.

But Stan Lee and Steve Ditko created a hero whom, nevertheless, we rooted for. We liked him (no small feat) not in spite of his failings, but because of them. Because we were able to relate to his struggle against tremendous odds and, ultimately, we admired him for his resolute ability to pick himself up, no matter how many times he got knocked down, and keep coming back.

We were pulling for him.

We feel the same about Bernie Laplante. Here's a guy whom, quite simply, you should not trust. Someone who, in the midst of performing a heroic deed, stops to filch a woman's purse. A criminal, a lousy husband, a crummy father teaching his son the worst possible lessons he can.

Yet we find ourselves attracted to, and amused by, the perversity of his nature. Deep within Bernie — so deep that it's invisible to everyone he knows — is a streak of heroism. And we sense that he knows it, too, and is embarrassed by it.

It gives us a subtext (and the wonderful thing about subtexts is that they can be anything to anyone) in which all of Bernie's griping is a cover for this truly admirable individual that he has secreted within him. Nobility is a drawback in his line of work (selling stolen goods), and so he does everything he can to bury it away from all eyes, including his own.

But when the crunch comes, the hero within him blossoms forth. Unlike George Reeves' transformations, in which he would leave all hints of the meek and mild Clark Kent behind in an alley, Bernie is incapable of checking his ignoble baggage and instead carries it on the plane with him, grousing through his bravery. It makes him all the more likable and accessible for the viewer, because now we're in on the "act." He can complain all he wants, but we're in on his deepest secret now.

And so we like him.

The stained hero, the hero who's apparently unheroic in many ways, has been very much a part of the super-hero scene ever since the debut of *Fantastic Four* #1.

Before that, the civilian identities of the heroes were either ciphers or had one attribute (Clark Kent was mild-mannered, Bruce Wayne was a millionaire playboy). And the heroes were men (mostly) who used their powers for right because (in circular reasoning) they were heroes. And the villains used their powers for evil because they were villains. And the villains were as imperfect as the heroes were perfect.

But then in the early '60s we got The Fantastic Four who fought all the time (as opposed to other teams where everyone got along famously) and then the prototypical reluctant hero, Spider-Man.

Now, though, we're in the 1990s. Anti-heroes abound in comics. The problem is, a lot of creators have got the "anti" part right — but they're totally missing the boat on the "hero" part.

It's easy to create someone who's unlikable. That's a snap.

The much harder task is to create someone who's unlikable that the audience then likes, not only in spite of the character, but in spite of themselves.

Stan Lee and Jack Kirby and Steve Ditko pioneered the comic-book concept of the flawed hero. But now, like a photocopy of a photocopy, we're losing sight of what made the hero work in the first place. Instead we're developing a series of characters who have the flaws but none of the truly noble qualities that would make them admirable.

It could be argued that making protagonists imperfect makes them human. Granted. But what makes them protagonists is that they try to overcome those imperfections and rise to heroic heights. The reader identifies with, and admires, the striving.

But instead, in comics, we now have some characters who not only do not strive to overcome their flaws, but instead, in fact, revel in them. Their morals are nonexistent, their actions repulsive.

What makes them heroes? Nothing readily apparent. Indeed, when young fans are asked what they like about these characters, they are unable to cite anything that relates even vaguely to simple humanity.

Instead, in many instances the only thing that counts is body counts. What makes a hero a hero is not something as apparently immaterial as bucking the odds, both physical and personal. Instead, the more popular a hero is is based on how willing he is to kill and just how many people he manages to off.

What a great message to send to readers. Instead of giving them characters that appeal to the best part of human nature, we give them characters that appeal to the worst.

And there's no epiphany. No moment of heroic impulse.

Jefferson Smith, confronted by the political machine that is out to crush him, realizes that his responsibility is to the people who sent him to the Senate and knows that he must take action. The heroic impulse.

Peter Parker, confronted with the burglar who murdered his uncle, realizes that he can never stand by again. The heroic impulse.

And young Bruce Wayne — well, he's grist for an entire column in and of himself. So we'll leave him for another time.

And then there's Bernie Laplante, who seems more concerned about his expensive shoes than about the lives of the passengers. But we know that, deep down, it's just another excuse to avoid the heroic impulse that he reins in. And then that impulse can no longer be hidden, when a frantic young boy pleads with Bernie to save the boy's father, still trapped in the plane.

Bernie looks down at him, seeing something of his own son in the boy's face, and finally gives in to the heroic impulse.

We applaud this moment. We applaud him: the all-too-fallible human, elevated to a moment during which he can accomplish great things. During which he can take actions that will serve the greater good.

Too many "heroes" of the comics are losing touch with that humanity. Their personal struggles seem capricious. And the villains they struggle against have motives so obscure, plans so oblique, that it's hard to remember that humanity has anything at stake.

We've got to go back to giving readers characters with ties to humanity that the readers can relate to. Giving them stories that can make them feel good about themselves.

It would take effort. Effort of — dare we say it? — heroic proportions.

Ultimately, one hopes that it will be worth it.

*(Peter David, writer of stuff, highly recommends **Cerebus** #162 to anyone who has ever had a bone to pick with Gary Groth. Dave Sim, in a three-page essay, neatly eviscerates Groth's world better than I've ever seen it done before in response to a Groth editorial about Sim. Groth may want to return to attacking the deceased in the future — it's so much safer.)*

SECTION 8:

Pros, Cons, and Fans

First and foremost, I produce comics for myself.

I write them to please and entertain me. My hope is that the books will then find enough readers with similar sensibilities.

There are some who are casual readers. They are interested in the adventures of their favorite heroes, have little or no knowledge of the people who actually produce the things, and could take or leave comic books depending on their mood.

Then there are the fans, the ones who know everything you've written, are eager to find out what you've got coming up, and have a better memory of your character's history than you do.

Fans are not of one mind. They will argue furiously, for hours on end either in person or by letter or by computer, over what is good and what is bad. Rarely is there any middle ground. Anything worth arguing over is worth arguing over to extremes.

I have had, in my day, quite a lot of interaction with fans. I started out as a fan, working my way "up, " as it were. It literally seems only yesterday that I was on the other side of the autograph table, hoping to "connect" in some way with a pro or learn the mysterious, carefully guarded secrets for breaking in. I have tried to keep those days in mind when I meet and greet the fans at conventions.

Conventions. Now there's something else entirely. I've attended conventions where only three people showed up. I've been to cons that were crammed with thousands of people. Conventions where fans have stood in line for hours to get me to sign stuff and conventions where the only noise was the sounds of crickets chirping in the vicinity.

My experiences with fans and conventions have been as varied as the fans and cons themselves.

Here are some of them.

TOXIC WASTE SYNDROME (Feb. 22, 1991)

A little convention-going can be a dangerous thing.

When I attend conventions, I do so primarily because I want to. I want to meet the fans, talk with them, find out what they're thinking, and give them previews of things that are coming up.

Certainly I, and most other comics pros, don't do it for the money. Unlike movie and TV actors, by and large we don't collect fat appearance fees (*Star Trek* actors can command thousands of dollars.) Unlike baseball players, we don't charge for autographs. Granted, we might make money selling artwork or, in my case, novels or old plots, but that's peanuts compared to what we could make if we just stayed home and worked.

And there are occasional perks — sometimes expense-paid trips to interesting cities, although usually you don't get out of the hotel, and a convention in Boston looks pretty much like a convention in Seattle from inside a Holiday Inn.

And there's the pure ego-gratification of having people walk up to you and tell you you're great. Of course, it cuts both ways — one convention was highlighted for me mostly by the impressive number of fans stopping by only to ask me directions to the Todd McFarlane signing.

Mostly, we're there because most of us were fans before we became pros and remember what it was like to be on the other side of the table. We want to try to give back some of what we've received over the years.

The last thing I want to do is hurt people's feelings, and yet it has now come to my attention that that might be precisely what I have done or am doing. I'm there because I like the fans, not because I'm out to insult them. Yet, apparently, a little insult — even unintended — has far stronger legs than a lot of good intentions.

Recently a fan characterized me in an APA (Amateur Press Association) as being "in real life — an unrepentant piece of toxic waste fit only for contempt." What prompted such ire? It turned out that, according to the writer, I had been rude to him at a convention. Rude and condescending.

I was dumbfounded. I don't go to cons to be rude and condescending. What was it that I had said specifically?

He couldn't remember. It had been three years ago. Three *years* ago. Talk about carrying a grudge.

It also made me wonder whom else I might have offended and angered as a result of personal appearances, but I was simply unaware of it, because they had never bothered to set it down in writing. They were merely grumbling to themselves, "Peter David, what an idiot." Or perhaps I had even said something that made them feel bad about themselves — had made them feel small. I never would have wanted to do that. That's not how I would have wanted a pro to make me feel when I was on the other side of the table.

So, first — a blanket apology to anyone whom I accidentally offended or angered at a convention. Whatever I said was not intended to hurt anyone, and, if it was taken that way, I'm terribly sorry.

Now to study the matter of how things I say might get misconstrued, or how my personal conduct may rub people the wrong way. (To a certain extent, observations herein might apply to other comics creators as well, but I leave it to them [and their own columns, *ahem*] to agree, disagree, or ignore the following):

When I do a convention appearance, the most common way I have of interacting with the fans is when I'm sitting behind a table. If I'm lucky, there are a steady stream of fans with comics and books for me to sign and a large number of folks hovering around, interested in discussing this, that, and the other thing.

This sort of set-up can lead to a number of potential points of irritation, and, if we're all aware of it, maybe people will get less bent out of shape:

1) *Eye contact*: The first thing you've got to remember is that I'm trying to do two things at once: sign my name over and over again while holding a conversation. Frequently, several conversations. In America, generally, when we talk with someone, we make eye contact. Difficult to make eye contact when you're (a) looking down at comics you're signing and (b) being addressed by several people.

So it occurs to me that, as a fan, if I were talking to someone and they weren't "bothering" to look in my direction, I might subconsciously feel as if that person weren't really paying attention to what I was saying. That would annoy me.

2) *Answers sound rehearsed or tired*: Believe it or not, by 3 in the afternoon, the chances are extremely good that you're not the first person who's asking if The Hulk is going to physically change into Bruce Banner again (no, he's going to look like that all the time now) or if I've ever considered writing a script for the *Next Generation* (I did, they rejected it, and I turned it into *A Rock and a Hard Place*).

Despite my best efforts, despite the smile that is solidly affixed to my face, I might wind up sounding as if I'm sorry you've asked this question and for goodness' sake leave me alone already. I'm sorry. It's nothing personal. I really do want to answer your question. I really do want you to know what's going on and what's coming up. That's what I'm there for. But after a long day, and especially if it's the second or third or, heaven help us, the fourth day of a convention, I can start to get punchy. You would, too.

3) *I look annoyed because you ask what I do and who I am*: Generally I bring with me, or the convention has made up for me, a name card that sits on the table and reads: "Peter David, writer of *Hulk, Star Trek*, etc., etc." And I'll have various novels of mine sitting out, as well. So, if someone comes up and says, "Who are you and what do you do?" I'll try to smile and reply. But I'll be thinking, *Read the sign, jerk*.

Or they'll hold up a copy of one of my *Trek* novels and say, "Did you write this?" And I'll say, "Yup," but I'll be thinking, *No, the other Peter David wrote it, whatta you think?* (Note that asking about whether I wrote the David Peters-credited Psi-Man books is an eminently legitimate question. Of course, by late in the con, I've answered it 30 times [see above]). And I'm not a good enough actor to cover what's running through my mind — so, if someone approached me and couldn't be bothered to read a sign and put two and two together, I might have conveyed an air of mild aggravation.

147

4) *I don't take what you say seriously*: It's very difficult to have a lengthy, serious discussion at a convention, because there are so many people crushing forward to gain your attention. So, whenever a subject is broached, I generally keep my approach to it light, airy, and quick. I have to keep things moving because, if there's a crowd, I have to keep the crowd moving. As a result, I may wind up brushing off something that you take very, very seriously. That's unfortunately the reality of a busy convention.

If you spot me sitting at a table and there's no one around, and there's something of importance you wish to discuss, then I'm amenable to it. But be sensitive to other fans who just wanna get their books and comics signed.

5) *You stop me while I'm in motion and I'm short with you*: Keep in mind that, if I'm moving, that means I'm going somewhere. To a lunch appointment or the bathroom or to make a call or even just to have a few minutes to myself. That's not the greatest time to come up to me with your complete run of my work on *Spec Spidey*.

6) *I tell you to take your comics out of their Mylars before I sign them*: I actually had one fan at a convention say to me, "What, you're too busy to do it yourself?" And my response was a rather short-tempered, "No, fool, I'm afraid I'll snag the comics on the tape." Which I was. But I shouldn't have called him a fool. But he was.

Best way to get a lot of copies signed: Open every single one up to the page you want signed and hand them to me in a stack. I can shoot right through them in no time flat, when they're presented in such a manner.

7) *I tell you your samples suck*: Invariably, would-be writers or artists come up to me and want to show me samples of their work. I'll always look at them, with cautions to the writers that this is only going to be a quick skim of their work and cautions to the artist that, not being an artist, I'm really not qualified to give in-depth analysis.

I'll try to be as nice as I can about it but, if I think your stuff really bites it, I'll tell you so. Be aware that (a) it's only one person's opinion and (b) I'm not criticizing you as an individual. It's nothing personal. I'm criticizing the work. I will be honest with you, though, so be prepared for that if you ask what I think. And, if other people are standing around snickering as I tear your work to ribbons, well, that's your problem, not mine.

Also be aware that, if you really have your heart set on making it in any creative endeavor, you're going to be criticized along the way by people of far more import than a two-bit comics writer, and far more viciously. If you can't take it, you're trying to break into the wrong profession.

8) *I don't remember you from the last time we met*: I'm terrible with names and faces. Always have been, always will be. And that's aggravated by the fact that I meet thousands of people over the course of years of convention-going. We may have had one of the most insightful and meaningful discussions of your life last year, but, I'm sorry, I'm just not going to recall it. That doesn't mean it wasn't important to me at the time. It just means I have a lousy memory.

9) *I insult you to your face*: No, I don't. What I may do is reply in a tongue-in-cheek manner and you misinterpret it.

I'm always kidding around with my friends, and people who have known me for years are aware of that. The entire comics profession is very much a give-and-take, spar-and-punch arena, the industry equivalent of moose butting horns. And when I'm at a convention, I immediately regard the smiling faces grouped around my table as a group of friends, temporary and transient as they may be. I let down my hair (what there is of it) and kid around, as I would with any other gang of pals. As I might at a party or social gathering.

But I now come to realize that perhaps that isn't a proper approach. That kidding-around jabs, which would be taken in stride by one of my peers, is taken too much to heart by a fan who says to himself, "Peter David insulted me! I never did anything to him! And I was such a fan of his work! What a creep!" That I was a fan so relatively recently and still possess some degree of that fan mentality so that I feel as if I'm with "my" guys when, in fact, there simply can't be that kind of "equal" relationship, because I'm a pro now.

Maybe I should, for all time, put aside that aspect of my personality that is the fan persona and just instead be very serious, very thoughtful, and very distant.

Not say much beyond "Why, thank you" and behave in a complete, polished, professional manner.

Hmm.

Naaahhhh...

(Peter David, writer of stuff, hopes to see you at upcoming conventions and hopes that he has shown that even toxic waste can repent.)

HOTEL HELL (Feb. 7, 1992)

(**Historical Note**: *As is alluded to in the first paragraph, an article titled "Xenogenesis" ran in two issues of* **CBG**. *It focused on the shocking and abysmally rude behavior of some fans toward some pros at conventions, up to and including a fan tossing a cup of warm vomit onto a writer the fan did not care for.*)

I, as were most (I would imagine) of *CBG's* readers, was appalled at the litany of appalling, spiteful and downright vindictive behavior on the part of various fans throughout the years, as portrayed in Harlan Ellison's scathing "Xenogenesis."

Perhaps part of it, at least in Harlan's case, is that some fans "know" what a dirtbag Harlan Ellison is. They've heard stories, tales, innuendos. Whether these stories about Harlan have any basis in fact is, of course, besides the point. Rarely have they ever met him, chatted with him, or suffered any sort of abusive acts at his hands. But, heck, just because hearsay isn't allowable in a court of law, that doesn't mean it's not good enough for the real world, right?

So those fans who think they know Harlan Ellison for what he is lie waiting in the high grass, anticipating their moment to get back at him. Or cheer or encourage others to "get" him. Hell, I've already mentioned how, when I first started this column, I asked people about subjects they'd like me to talk about. And several people wrote to me saying, "Do a column that rips apart Harlan Ellison." These people didn't know Ellison is a friend of mine. Maybe they wouldn't have cared if they had known — or instead would have assumed that there had to be something wrong with me.

Go figure.

At any rate, my professional career doesn't stretch remotely as long as Harlan's — nor, for that matter, as long as any of the careers of the people mentioned in "Xenogenesis." Perhaps familiarity, or presumed familiarity, breeds far more than contempt. Perhaps it breeds overt hostility. So look what I have to look forward to. Thus far, however, my career is still young enough that I haven't yet become the target of the sort of behavior cited in "Xenogenesis." Sure, there's been the occasional rude fan, but then, again, I run into plenty of rude people outside of conventions.

In fact, I recall the fan who sought me out at a recent convention and said, "I wanted to apologize for something I said to you at a convention three years ago." He seemed really eaten up about it. The fact that I didn't remember him or what he had said, and barely even recalled the convention, was all secondary to the guilt that he was carrying which had magnified an off-hand joke into some sort of massive insult over which I was, no doubt, still nursing a grudge.

So, yes, I've encountered the occasional rude fan, but none who have crossed the line into maliciousness or vindictiveness. Wow. Just think what I have to look forward to. I have, I'm embarrassed to say, no real fan-related true horror stories.

No, all of my horror stories of my convention going history have to do with hotels.

Hotel horror stories.

Get a bunch of fans together and swap those for a while. You will quickly develop a litany of incompetence, rudeness, thoughtlessness, and just plain poor organization. With horror stories of fan behavior, you could argue that these are fans who cared too much, to the point where they lost all sense of reason and proportion. Hotel horror stories, on the other hand, are invariably tales of hotels run by managements that simply didn't care.

I don't want to name the hotels, because, for all I know, managements have changed over time. And if a convention is advertising a con at that hotel, I don't want people saying, "Oh, I'm not going there; Peter David wrote what a lousy hotel it was." That wouldn't be fair. So the stories are true, but the names have been omitted to protect the innocent.

When I was growing up and first seriously getting into fandom, I lived about 20 minutes outside of Philadelphia and attended a number of SF cons there.

I will never forget the year that there was a science-fiction convention booked into a Philadelphia hotel, and the hotel double-booked the Shriners in at the same time. Booked the same convention space, the same hotel rooms — everything. My understanding was that the SF fans had booked the space first; no matter. The hotel gave preference to the Shriners. Function space was cut down to a fraction of what had originally been promised. Not only that, but several friends and I were among dozens of fans who arrived at the hotel to discover that our hotel rooms were already chock full of Shriners. We stood there, waving our confirmation slips, and the desk people shrugged at us. A hotel three blocks away was designated as the overflow hotel, and we had to haul all of our luggage and material to the other hotel.

Three blocks may not sound like a tremendous inconvenience. The problem was that a friend of mine, Dave Klapholz, and I were entered in the costume competition Saturday evening. (Cut me some slack, OK? I was 19.) We were entered as characters from *National Lampoon's Bored of the Rings*. Dave was Goodgulf the magician, and I was the Ballhog. The costume competition, naturally, was at the convention hotel, but there were no changing facilities there, so we had to get into costume at the overflow hotel and hoof it.

Words cannot relate the experience of walking down the darkened streets of center-city Philadelphia, bouncing a basketball and dressed head-to-toe in a black bodystocking, gym shorts, and a T-shirt that read "Villanova," the chill wind cutting through my tights, accompanied by a guy wearing swirling blue robes, a tall pointed hat, and a glowing neon necktie that read "Wilt Thou Kiss Me in the Dark, Baby?" Cop cars slowed down, and muggers left us alone because they were laughing too hard.

Perhaps the crowning indignity was all the Shriners pointing and saying, "Look at all the weirdly dressed geeks." I was a teen-ager in costume. They were middle aged men wearing fezzes. What was their excuse?

There was a convention another year that occurred right at the time that the Army/Navy football game was in town. At least we had our rooms that time, but the hotel was also chock full of Navy guys rooting for their team. By and large they were polite and even mildly interested in the convention. They behaved like officers and gentlemen.

That was before the game.

When they came back from the game, it was the evening, and Navy had won. The Navy guys had their girlfriends with them, and liquor was flowing freely. The hallways were filled with drunken, carousing people. (To be fair, it was mostly the girlfriends who were drunk. The Navy guys were busy trying to corral them, but it was tough work.)

Hotel guests who were neither Navy nor fans complained loudly to hotel authorities, who immediately swung into action. Except, as far as anyone could see, the servicemen and girlfriends were still gallivanting about. So what did the hotel do to assuage angered guests? Yes, that's right. They shut down all the SF room parties.

Fans sitting quietly in rooms, folk singing in low voices, were told by hotel officials to shut it down, while all around the Navy partying continued until all hours. To the best of our knowledge, hotel security either never did anything to slow down the Navy parties or else cautioned them but never tried to enforce it. But, boy, they had those discussion groups about Marion Zimmer Bradley, or the video-watching parties (where the strongest thing being served was Mountain Dew) shut down tight as a drum by 10 p.m.

Of more recent vintage was the convention I brought my entire family to. What a marvelous place that was. The soda machines on every single floor were devoid of soda (not as a result of demand; they were empty from the moment we got there and never got restocked). They botched our room reservations so that the connecting rooms we were supposed to have with the kids became rooms across the hall from each other. This became particularly pertinent, when the fire alarm went off around midnight and they emptied the hotel: The girls had bolted their door, and our pounding on the door wasn't rousing them (the ringing phone finally did.)

Apparently a smoke detector had gone off somewhere in the hotel, but the system was malfunctioning and they had no clue as to *where* in the hotel it had gone off. So people froze in the lobby for close to an hour while the fire department checked over every single possible location, before they finally discovered — nothing.

I was told the food in the hotel restaurant was quite nice. I can't swear to it personally; we never got so much as a glass of water, much less a menu. After several requests to the hostess that a waiter be sent over, we were ignored for a solid half hour before getting up and leaving in disgust. The hostess said to us, "Wait, I'll get someone!" as we walked out the door.

I've been to hotels which mysteriously shut down the pool for "repairs" for the duration of the convention. This has happened enough times to make me feel that it's far from coincidental. I've been in hotels where the ventilation system pumped heat during the summer and cool air in winter, both into function rooms and hotel rooms, and no matter how much you begged and pleaded with the management, they could not or would not stop it.

Billing can also be a challenge. There was the hotel which, after one convention stay, sent me a number of threatening letters, promising to charge me for the hotel bedspread that I had allegedly stolen from the room. I tried pointing out to them repeatedly that the only bed we had in the house was a kingsize, and the room I'd stayed in had a single bed in it; what was I going to *do* with one of their cheesy bedspreads, even if I *had* stolen it? Which, of course, I hadn't. They tried to tack the charge on my credit card, and I informed the credit card company that it was not a permissible charge, so they refused to let the hotel do it. So the hotel threatened to take me to court. I said, in essence, "Take your best shot." I never heard from them again.

Then there was the hotel that tried to charge me $73.71 for a call to — I swear to God — Thailand. I told them I knew no one in Thailand. No, no, they swore. There was the record of the charge, right there on my bill. It was, they told me smugly, irrefutable. I endeavored to refute it by pointing out that the records indicated the call had been made the morning of the day that I had checked in — but I hadn't checked in until the afternoon. It still took another 15 minutes to straighten it out, and the whole time they acted as if I were trying to pull something. Maybe they'd been talking to the bedspread people.

There have been plenty of decent and even superior hotels, of course, just as there have been plenty of decent and even superior fans. But I still have, to this day, a napkin from the coffee shop of that Philadelphia hotel that double-booked us with the Shriners and shrugged off our confirmed reservations. The napkin carries the then-current motto of the hotel, referring to how dependable their services were: "The Best Surprise is No Surprise."

(Peter David, writer of stuff, hopes that everyone had a safe and trouble-free New Year's Day.)

FANS: THE NEXT GENERATION (April 3, 1992)

I seem to have picked up, what is to me, an odd additional vocation: Dispenser of wisdom (or whatever semblance there is of that rattling around in my head) to today's youth.

On several occasions now I have found myself speaking to classes of children throughout the range of primary and secondary schools. It's a rewarding experience, and, if any comic-book creators out there are ever afforded the opportunity to do so, I highly recommend it.

However, in addition to being rewarding, it can also be extremely nerve-wracking. Much more so than when I go to talk at a comic-book convention. In those instances, I can be reasonably assured that the people seated in front of me in whatever auditorium or speaking room I happen to be in are, in fact, genuinely interested in who I am and what I might have to say.

There is no such guarantee at a school. In the average public school, kids have no say in what they do or where they go. They are shuffled here and there, and everywhere else. Every minute of every day is dictated for them. So when the kids are trotted in for you as you're wedged in somewhere between the mysteries of mixed fractions and lunchtime, you're not entirely certain just how you're going to be viewed. Source of information? Source of amusement? Source of curiosity?

Do the kids know what you do and — even worse — do they care? If kids aren't interested in you, they're not terribly good at covering it up. They haven't developed the adult ability to smile and keep the eyes focused while the brain vegges out. No, kids are obvious about it if you're boring them. They shuffle their feet, they fidget, they look at the clock (repeatedly), they chat with the kids behind them. If you tell a joke that isn't funny, don't count on polite laughter. Nothing but dead silence, broken only by the loud tick of the clock hands on the wall that the kids look at again. If you figure that your prepared text isn't going well and you're going to throw the floor open to questions, be careful. There may wind up being nothing on the floor except old chewing gum wrappers.

If you can draw, the odds are that you won't have a problem. As long as the school has provided you with a drawing surface on which you can display your talent, you're going to do just fine. Kids will be endlessly fascinated as characters materialize out of nowhere before their very eyes. You'll have them eating out of your hand. They're sure to shout out suggestions of what they want you to draw, so I would suggest you brush up on your renderings of Ninja Turtles and Bart Simpson.

If you're a writer, however, it's another matter entirely. Not only do you not have a built-in visual aid, but you're dealing with a student body that progressively shows less and less interest in reading *anything*, much less comics. So you have to develop a method that will capture their attention visually if you really want to be effective — especially when you're dealing with the younger crowd.

For what it's worth, here's what I do. My dog-and-pony show, as my wife calls it. This method works fairly well up through sixth grade and has thus far been a real crowd-pleaser.

My tools are a chalkboard and chalk. First I greet the kids. With kindergarten through second grade, this is a genuine ritual, in which I will say, "Now, you're the sixth graders, right?" A huge chorus of "Noooooo!" responds. Puzzled, I'll say, "What — you're fifth graders?" "Noooooo!" And so on, down to the actual grade level, at which I'll express incredulity because they look so big. They're very kindly disposed towards me after that.

I tell them right up front, "I do not pencil the comics. I do not ink them, color them, letter them" (they don't necessarily know what all these terms mean yet, but at least I've got their interest). "I write the comics. Who wants to see how a comic book gets made?" This will generally get me a sea of raised hands.

If you try this and members of your audience don't raise their hands, tap on the mike and say, "Is this thing on?" or perhaps check for pulses. If they are, indeed, alive and just not responding, excuse yourself for a drink of water, run outside to your car, and leave. If it means losing an honorarium, then lose it. No amount of money is worth this.

(As a side note, I continue to have nothing but respect and awe for teachers. That they can go in there day after day and constantly attempt to find new ways to challenge the students — wow.)

"Who knows what a plot is?" I ask. The older kids generally know. From the first graders I've gotten such answers as, "It's like a plop. A sound."

Indeed, when asking any "Who knows what a — ?" questions, don't let it go on for too long. If five kids in a row haven't a clue, tell them. If a kid is close but not quite right, immediately say, "That's pretty close," and then tell them. Keep it moving.

After defining a plot to the point where they understand it, I say, "I'm going to plot something very simple: a fight." And I write, across the top of the board, "The Hulk hits the bad guy, who falls down. The girl is saved and is happy."

I then explain that this sequence is drawn by a penciller, and I proceed to draw three very large stick figures. For my purposes, this is perfectly fine — indeed, I can even draw silly faces on the figures and get a laugh that way.

I then proceed to "script" it, writing down and numbering the following phrases: "Take that, you rat." "Oooof." "My Hero!" Then I draw the word balloons (the entire time defining everything I'm doing) and number them 1, 2, and 3 to correspond to the preceding phrases.

Having explained the basic concept of scripting as "filling in the words" and "showing where they go," I go on to the lettering phase, where I now write the appropriate dialogue in the balloons. For the younger kids, I skip the numbering concept and just write the dialogue in the balloons to begin with. No need to overly complicate it.

This is when the fun begins. Because now I explain that a person named an inker goes over the pencil lines and makes the drawings seem life-like by adding thick pen lines. I, of course, can't use a big thick pen on the blackboard. So instead, to bring the drawings to "life," I'm going to need some help.

I ask for volunteers and select a Hulk, a villain, and a girl (a.k.a. a damsel in distress or a heroine, depending on the age group). I take great pains to pose the kids in the same manner as the drawings (explaining why a fully outstretched punch looks better than a shortened one — that kind of thing). I always make sure to pose the girl so that her fingers are interlaced and to one side of her head as she looks on adoringly.

Then I have each of the kids say their dialogue out loud in rapid succession, and sometimes even have the audience say it along with them. And that gives them a quick, painless, and totally involving idea of how a comic book is made and what goes into it from my point of view.

One additional wrinkle: For the younger kids, instead of starting off with this demonstration, I instead give out comic books (for them to keep). I can then go through the comic book with them and explain to them different terms, like thought balloon, word balloon, caption, splash page, etc. I keep a large stock of *Little Mermaid* comics on hand. You just have to be careful that you don't lose control of the audience by doing this. On the other hand, it's an excellent way of keeping them *under* control, by making them uniformly look at page one, then turn the page, and so on. After showing them this finished comic book and explaining some basics, I'll continue with a shortened version of the "plotting" presentation.

At this point I'll generally open it up to questions, and by then the kids are pretty much involved in the whole process. They will ask a variety of questions, and of course the trick is that, even when you've heard the question many times before, you want to make your answer sound fresh.

Some of the more frequent questions:

• "How much money do you make?" Instead of telling them that (which really isn't their business) I'll describe to them the page rate system and tell them the starting page rates. Even that relatively measly sum draws amazed gasps (since, of course, they usually have maybe a buck or two in their pockets at most).

• "How long have you been writing comics?" (About six years.)

• "How long does it take you to write one?" (A plot, about two to three hours. Script, about four or five. But I'm always thinking about new plots and ideas.)

• "How long does it take a comic book to be made?" (With luck, no more than a month for a monthly title.)

• "Where do you get your ideas?" (From what's going on in the world, so read those newspapers and watch the news, kids.)

• "What's your favorite comic book you've written?" (*Atlantis Chronicles*, which usually gets blank stares. That's OK; I get that from fans, too.)

• "What's your favorite comic book that you like to read?" (*Groo the Wanderer*, which also frequently gets blank stares. Sorry, Sergio and Mark.)

• "How fast do you type?" (Since typing is being taught earlier and earlier in school, they're really interested in my answer to this, which is between 100-120 words per minute. It's the only answer I give that draws audible gasps from the teachers.)

Then there are some of the more unusual questions — questions which I will have no idea where they came from, but will occasionally reveal something about the questioner. Generally these come from the second grade and under set (the sequences in the film *Kindergarten Cop* in which the kids say things totally out of left field are absolutely dead on). Questions such as:

• "I have some comic books at home." (Yes, I know that's not a question. They just want to get up and tell me what they're thinking about. After all, it's only fair. I told them what was on *my* mind.)

• "What did you have for breakfast, and what are you having for dinner?" (I told him I'd had a buttered bagel for breakfast, and I didn't know what I was having for dinner. I asked if he was inviting me over. He said no. Darn.)

• "Would you sing a song?" (The principal explained to me that, to them, I was a celebrity, and a celebrity sings and dances. So I did the first five bars of "Be Our Guest." Jerry Orbach need not lose sleep.)

• "What do you spend more time doing: Writing comics or playing with your children?" (Boy, was this a sharp question. And the little boy who asked it had such a look of concern on his face that I strongly suspected he got a good deal of "Not now, son, daddy's working" at home. I told him what's nice about my job is that I can work during the day and be there for my kids when they come home. But the truth is that there are many occasions where my work runs over into time that I should be spending with my kids, including evenings and weekends. I gotta watch that.)

And the best question you can get from any kid at any grade level: "When are you coming back?"

That makes it worthwhile.

(Peter David, writer of stuff, smugly points out that he put **Beauty and the Beast** *being up for the best picture Oscar on his wish list, also predicted that "Be Our Guest" would definitely be nominated for best song, and suggested that other* **B&B** *songs might be, as well. Yeah, yeah, sure — he also said he wanted to see Linda Hamilton up for best actress for* **T2**. *And she wasn't. She wuz robbed, ladies and gentlemen.)*

BACK TO THE DRAWING BOARD (June 19, 1992)

(**Historical Note**: *I had related the following story to Dave Sim, creator of* **Cerebus**. *Dave told me that I should run it in my column. For reasons that utterly elude me, I told him I would do so only if he wrote in and asked. To my surprise, he did.)*

OK, Dave. But only because you asked so nicely, you fan boy, you.

My convention artwork story, for the benefit of Dave Sim. Not only was it the first time I really, truly understood the selling power of Wolverine, but it was also the only time I ever attended a convention and wound up doing illustrations — as best as my questionable memory can recall (it was quite a few years ago).

Long before I was doing anything connected with the creative side of comics, I was (as mentioned in other columns) Marvel Comics' assistant manager (and later manager) of direct sales. I attended numerous conventions in this capacity, although my presence rarely created any sort of stir. At one convention, for example, a kid came up to me at the Marvel display table and asked if I drew for Marvel. I said no. Write? No. Ink? Color? Letter? Edit? No.

"So what do you do?" he asked.

"I sell them. I'm in direct sales."

He pondered that a moment, and then handed me a program book and said, "Oh, well — I guess I'll get your autograph anyway." Which was the first time I ever signed an autograph in any capacity for Marvel.

But that's not the story Dave was asking about.

This incident took place at a smallish convention in Florida. I was attending as the direct-sales rep; Marvel was to have a table set up there with stuff to display. And there was to be one, and only one, Marvel creator in attendance. But it was to be one of the big guns: John Byrne.

I arrived at the convention and was greeted by the news that John, due to illness (either himself or someone in his family, I don't recall which) had been forced to cancel at the last minute. Now there are certainly creators who agree to appearances and then routinely cancel out, but Byrne does not fall into that category. No one questioned that it was utterly legitimate.

This did not particularly mollify the fans, however.

The first hours of the convention were extremely dicey, as fan after fan kept coming up to me, with increasing belligerence, demanding to know where John was, and why I was unable or unwilling to produce him — as if I had him tucked away in a box or perhaps hidden in my sock.

Fans were not taking it well. They had come to the convention to meet and greet John and, even more, to get him to do a drawing. The most often-mentioned were Wolverine and Storm. And when John wasn't there to do the drawings, the fans did the logical thing.

They started asking me to do sketches. They figured, "Well, he's from Marvel; people from Marvel draw; therefore, he can draw." Q.E.D.

Problem is: I can't draw.

I have extremely good visual sense. I can write with an eye toward what will look good. I can imagine, when I write full-script, what something will look like.

But I can't draw. Stick figures and perhaps little sketches of the *Peanuts* characters are pretty much my limit.

So now I was getting to disappoint people twice: first, when I was unable to produce John Byrne, and second, when I was unable to produce drawings for them.

It could have been a lot worse, had not a local artist shown up.

(I tried to get in touch with him so that I could get his permission to use his name in this column, but couldn't locate a current phone number for him. So we'll just call him Dan.) Dan showed up, introduced himself to me, and I eagerly invited him to hang out at the Marvel table with me. Now we had someone who could draw sketches and keep the fans happy. It took a lot of the pressure off me. And Dan, of course, had a chance to shine, because, if John had been there, then Dan would have been eclipsed (as would I, but I would have dearly welcomed some time in the shadows).

Then things got a little weird.

In between sketches, Dan decided to do a very detailed pencil rendering. What he produced was a gorgeous full pencil drawing, on 10 x 15 bristol board, of Alpha Flight — logical enough, since it seemed like something the Byrne fans would snap up. It was really nice work. And Dan tagged it at some relatively nominal price. I don't remember what precisely. For the sake of argument, let's say it was $10.

No one was buying it.

Dan seemed somewhat annoyed. I was, frankly, dumbfounded. It was such a good piece, and the price was low. The only thing I could figure was that, since Alpha Flight was a John Byrne group, fans were only interested in the drawing if John had done it.

In the meantime, there was this one guy who still hadn't quite grasped the fact that I wasn't an artist. And he really wanted me to do a drawing of Storm. He'd keep swinging by and saying, "Draw Storm. Draw Storm."

Finally, utterly sick of him, I said, "OK, fine. Here!"

And I grabbed a piece of paper and inside of three seconds I produced the following:

And the guy stared at it for a moment, and then slid it back to me and said, "Do Nightcrawler."

Well, that was easy. I drew a little picture of an earthworm and labelled it "Nightcrawler."

This created a mild sensation, as a small group of fans, entranced by the silliness of it all, kept asking me to draw a variety of characters that I quickly dubbed the "Ex-Men." The only one that gave me pause was a request for Professor X until I came up with this:

"How much?" people were asking me. "I dunno — a buck," I said, and people actually started reaching for their wallets, before I told them I was kidding and, here, take the stupid things.

Both Dan and I were incredulous that people were snapping up these dumb sketches of mine (admittedly, I was giving them away) and his Alpha Flight drawing remained.

So, as I was sitting there knocking out a drawing of Kitty Pryde as Sprite (yeah, you can guess what I drew) one kid was asking me, "Why is it that Wolverine's claws look different when different artists draw him?"

The kid didn't realize that he had really answered his own question. Different artists have different styles. Some drew them with curves, while Frank Miller, for example, drew those funky razor blades. But I figured that any kid who had to ask that question would be disappointed with a straight answer. He would doubtlessly prefer something that was a "real," continuity-based answer.

"Well," I said, "the fact is that Wolverine's claws are detachable."

"They are?" said the kid wonderingly.

"Oh yes," I deadpanned. "He can put in different things to suit his mood. He can attach curved claws, or flat claws. He could attach a corkscrew. He could even substitute a knife, spoon, and fork if he wanted to."

And Dan, upon hearing this bit of malarkey, took the Alpha Flight sketch which wasn't selling, flipped it over, and, using a chisel-tip magic marker, produced a Feiffer-esque rendering of Wolverine in about 30 seconds flat. It was a parody of issue #1, I believe, of the *Wolverine* limited series — the one with Wolverine facing the reader in a close shot, one hand raised and his claws extended. Except instead of the claws, Dan drew a knife, spoon, and fork sticking out of the back of Wolverine's hand. And he slapped the finished drawing down on the table.

Within a minute, a fan was studying it. He picked it up and said, "How much?"

"Twenty bucks," said Dan kiddingly.

Without a word the fan took out his wallet and pulled out two tens.

Dan and I looked at each other, stunned, as the fan picked up his newly purchased artwork and gazed at it adoringly.

"You know," I said, "there's a really nice drawing of Alpha Flight on the back."

The fan flipped the Bristol board over, glanced momentarily at the Alpha Flight drawing, and then turned it back over so that he could relish his gen-u-ine Wolverine portrait. He walked away with it proudly, and I just know that this guy took it and put it up on his bedroom wall with this chicken-scratching Wolverine shot displayed, and no one ever saw Dan's Alpha Flight portrait again.

But at least Dan made some money off the deal.

And that's the convention story that Dave Sim likes so much.

Now if you're all really good, someday I'll tell you the great Dave Sim anecdote that even Dave doesn't know.

*(Peter David, writer of stuff, intends to do a fairly thorough write-up on **Alien** [3] next week. The discussion of the film's subtext will require talking about the ending, so I give a full week's spoiler warning — if you intend to see the film but haven't before next week's **CBG**. you'll probably want to pass up the next **BID** until you've had a chance to see **Alien** [3].)*

Historical Notes:

1) I have yet to publish the Dave Sim anecdote that even Dave doesn't know.

2) The downside of the above was related to me by retailer John Christensen of "Paper Heroes." At the San Diego Comic-Con, I was signing books, and a kid came up to me with his sketchbook and insisted I draw him a picture. He didn't know I wasn't an artist and, despite my telling him, "I really can't draw very well; I'm not an artist," he couldn't be dissuaded from his course. So I drew him one of the cockamamie "Storm" portraits. What I didn't know was that the kid was devastated by this action, my earlier disclaimers apparently not having penetrated.

*John came upon the kid a short time later. The boy was with his mother and grandmother, staring forlornly at his apparently now ruined sketchbook that some jerk had drawn a cloud in. John took one look, comprehended immediately what had happened, and said to the kid, "You got a sketch by Peter David? **Wow**!" The kid looked up at John in confusion, not comprehending why an adult was expressing enthusiasm for such a clearly amateurish drawing. "He's one of the top writers in the industry!" said John (the kid having no real clue to my identity; he'd just seen a lot of people lined up and figured I was popular). "He never does sketches! You've got something really rare there!" The kid was so brightened that he went away beaming.*

Me, I'm never doing another sketch for anyone under 12.

*3) The review of **Alien** [3] appears in the "Silver Scream" section on page 139.*

PRO/CON (Aug. 14, 1992)

There are no comic-book conventions.

And we could really use one.

This is an odd realization for anyone to come to, but the comics industry is one of the few that does not have a convention in the traditional sense.

Any number of times during my travels — particularly during my days in the Marvel sales department — I would find myself staying at hotels where conventions were being held for various professionals in various industries: Insurance salesmen. Carpenters. Computer programmers. Electricians. Water companies.

Pick a business, any business. And you can be assured that somewhere, at some point, they're going to have a convention.

Any business except comics.

Now this may sound like a remarkably nonsensical statement to you. All one has to do is flip through the pages of *CBG* to reveal dozens, if not hundreds, of comic-book conventions. So how can I possibly claim that they don't exist?

Because those aren't conventions in the sense that I'm discussing.

Carpenters don't have hundreds of fans standing in lines for autographs. Insurance salesmen don't have panels in which they explain what's going to be coming up in the exciting world of insurance to audiences of people not in the industry. Electricians aren't critiquing circuitry designed by would-be electricians, or judging costume competitions with fans dressed as fluorescent bulbs.

When people in these realms get together for a convention, they do so for two purposes. They discuss the advancements and techniques of their industry. And they socialize.

With each other.

At the traditional comic-book convention, on the other hand, comic-book creators are not really there for each other. Socializing certainly can and does occur. Hanging out in the bar (a particularly pervasive pastime at British conventions) or late-night card games are traditional-enough activities at some of the larger cons.

But to all intents and purposes, the comics creators are there for the fans. There to sign autographs and give advice on how to break in and (ideally) smile and be polite. If discussions are held on the state of the industry, they are done so for an audience of fans, which means that not only are the panelists trying to explore a given topic, but they're trying to do so in an entertaining manner so that the fans won't be bored.

I hope none of the foregoing comes across as "anti-fan." But the fact of the matter is that, when the fans are around, comics creators can't always be themselves. Particularly if the comics creator is by nature, for example, a jerk. Because if he or she acts like a jerk in front of the fans, you're going to see computer board postings or letters to *CBG* about it so quickly that it'll make your head spin.

When the fans are around, creators are, to some degree, always "on," any time they happen to venture out. I've had people ask me what's happening in *The Hulk* while I'm in the restroom. I've had would-be writers show me plot proposals while I was trying to have a quiet breakfast — which is why, if I want to be assured of having a meal uninterrupted, I order room service.

Comics creators have to be at the disposal of the fans the entire time. They have to be affable, patient, and, above all, diplomatic. In some instances, creators are representing not only themselves, but a publisher. And if a creator feels harassed and, losing his temper, tells a fan to kiss various portions of anatomy, it not only makes the creator look bad, but it can reflect poorly on the publisher, as well.

I go to conventions for two reasons: to socialize with pros and meet and greet the fans. And the latter invariably takes precedence over the former. Which is fine. The conventions are being held for the fans. It's the fans whose money is supporting the thing. Whose at-the-door admissions are (it is hoped) covering the hotel costs and the air fare for the guests (or at least certain guests) and who then spend money in the dealers' room which not only support the dealers but further augments the convention's coffers, because it charged for the dealers' tables.

What it boils down to, then, is that the creators are under a microscope during the 48-to-72- (and even 96-) hour period of the convention. It's not always a fun place to be. Many times it is, but sometimes it's not.

Comic-book *retailers* have conventions. Except they're not called conventions. They're called "trade shows," sponsored by comic-book distributors for the benefit of their customers. But they're much closer to the traditional idea of a convention, in that you have a professional group (retailers, in this case) getting together, meeting and greeting each other, and attending seminars and discussions about how to improve the art of retailing.

At "trade shows," retailers don't have their customers coming up to them and asking when the next issue of *X-Men* is coming out or saying, "Here, take a look at my collection and tell me how much it's worth."

And the distributors? They have conventions, too. These are organized by individual comic-book publishers, and at these conventions (which are technically called "distributor meetings") the publishers present their wares for the coming year so that the distributors can get a feeling for how to proceed with their plans. They also take the opportunity to have their own get-togethers (sometimes with meeting space provided by the publishers, although publishers are then excluded from these business meetings).

And at these distributor meetings, of course, retailers are not there, complaining about how they want improvements in that distributor's reorder service or wanting to know if they can get a higher discount.

So all the people involved with the sales of the comics have their meetings and try to improve the art of selling the comics.

But the people who actually *make* the comics — writers, pencillers, inkers, letterers, colorists — whenever they're at a convention, they're part of the show. They're whom the fans come to see, and their obligations are to the fans, not to the comics and not to each other.

157

So what I'm saying in my customarily long, roundabout way, is that it would be nice if, just once, that were not the case.

It would be nice if the creators had their own convention. Call it — I dunno — not "Creation Convention," certainly. Maybe "ProCon."

The name is secondary, really, to the concept. And the concept is that the people who actually *make* the comics would have the opportunity to get together and improve the art form.

It's not just the form itself, either. The comic-book creative community has always been a fractious bunch, but in the past there's always been an "us versus them" mentality. When alliances of comic-book creators were formed in the past, they were invariably to present a united front to the publishers.

But now it's gone beyond that. I think of the upcoming San Diego Comic-Con, at which there's supposed to be a panel titled "Do Artists Need Writers?" It was one of the four most-popular panels when SDCC was looking for volunteers; it wound up getting roughly five times as many potential panelists as it could use.

This question, of course, arises from the notorious "Name Withheld" letter in *CBG* that inspired lengthy debate, and one would think that the respective panelists can't wait to tear into a subject that is, at its most basic, inherently silly. Of course, artists don't *need* writers. And writers don't *need* artists (there's this thing called a "book" that some of you may have heard of). I believe, however, that some of the best comics are those wherein a good writer and good artist produce a work that surpasses what either could have accomplished singly.

Unfortunately, we're developing into a society that has no concept of loyalty. A society where "Watch out for Number One" has become not just a philosophy, but the be-all and end-all of existence. The concept of the writer/artist team — in which two people work so well together that, if unleashed upon a project, you can be guaranteed of quality — has become almost an outdated notion.

I certainly think that, to some degree, this column has added to the situation. "Why do you hate John Byrne?" the fans ask. Well — gee. I don't. "When are you going to attack Image again?" I'm asked. Well — gee. Not to sound disingenuous, but I thought I was simply pointing out when the Image guys were saying what I perceived as thoughtless things, in hopes that they would start giving thought to what they said. (Which, by the way, has worked to some degree. Notice that I haven't written a word about Erik in a while. He hasn't said anything thoughtless. Although the same cannot be said of — nah. Why get into it?) The thing is I never perceived it as an attack. But others have.

I think a creators-only convention is just what the creative community could use. Something where all the creative personnel get together. Where workshops are held, discussing the fundamental dynamics of storytelling. Discussing the most effective way to exaggerate human anatomy for storytelling purposes. The best brushes to use in inks, the best pens for lettering. A pro is a pro is a pro, but there are people in our industry who are unquestionably more talented than others. I'd attend a writing seminar spearheaded by Neil Gaiman in a heartbeat. Any inkers out there who would pass up a couple of hours of learning tips from Terry Austin? Anyone going to give a miss to a humor seminar from Sergio Aragones? Who would stay away from a keynote address by a Will Eisner or a Harlan Ellison on what's right or wrong with the comics industry today?

Do artists need writers? Rather than putting five panelists in front of an audience of fans, wouldn't more be accomplished by devoting several hours to it in a seminar room, with (I know it sounds quaint) chairs pulled in a circle? Followed by a volleyball game or leaping into a pool?

The problem is, of course, who would sponsor it? When distributors or publishers put together their various shows and meetings, there's always something to be gained from it: "something" being, bottom line, money. Better-educated retailers are better customers. Distributors who are wined and dined and impressed by upcoming projects mean higher sales.

For ProCon, there's nothing for anyone to turn a buck from. It would be held purely for the nonsensical concept of good relations and good comics.

Which means that creators would have to do it themselves. Creators would have to pay registration fees that would go toward covering the costs of the convention. Someone would have to organize the thing and handle the money.

And for pity's sake, don't look to me to do it. I can't even organize my desk, and I can't remember the last time I correctly balanced my checkbook. It'd have to be someone whom everyone knows and who is relatively trustworthy. Me, I'd suggest Star*Reach. It reps a few dozen comics creators already, and it's been around for a while. (Geez, Mike's just going to love it when he reads this. "You want me to organize a *what*?!")

In keeping with that train of thought, we would have it in California — preferably in Anaheim. There are lots of creators out there, there are plenty of cheap airfares to Los Angeles, and me, I'm a sucker for Disneyland any day.

We'd need start-up costs; that much is certain. Hotels want deposits up front. Costs of people invited as speakers would certainly have to be covered. We'd have to be sure that there was enough money in the kitty to get things started and keep things going. The idea is that enough creators would attend that registration fees would pay back those who put up money in the first place. And if not — well, hell, it's a business expense. That makes it tax deductible.

If someone reputable will organize the thing, I'll put up $500 to start. Anyone care to match it?

(Peter David, writer of stuff, saw the world's worst ad placement on his way to Con-Version in Calgary. He was on a Delta flight bound for Salt Lake City [making a connection there], trusted wife Myra by his side, when he showed her an ad for Alamo car rental in the in-flight magazine that read, "Wouldn't You Rather Be in a Cadillac Right Now?" Myra took one look at it and said reasonably, "Of course not. We're 32,000 feet in the air. If we were in a Cadillac, we'd drop like a rock. I'd much rather be in an airplane." Now there's logic you can't argue with.)

Historical Notes:

1) If I had to pick one column to cite as having done the most good, it would be the Pro/Con column. Nine months later, Pro/Con was actually held. Neil Gaiman spoke about writing, Will Eisner discussed storytelling. We didn't have Terry Austin, but we did get Dick Giordano. Dave Sim spoke about self-publishing. Despite some pros loudly proclaiming that they saw no need for such a thing, we had well over a hundred people attending. There was certainly room for improvement, but it was widely considered to be a smashing success. Never have I felt more gratified than when Pro/Con came to fruition. More are being planned even as we speak.

THE *BID* POLL (Dec. 4, 1992)

(**Historical Note**: *A weekly news magazine ran a poll, looking to get a feeling from members of the public as to what they thought the next century would have to bring in terms of science, religion, the world — whatever. I decided to do something similar in* **BID** *except, of course, I focused on comics. That, and I tried to limit it to the next decade. I have deleted the initial poll form, since the questions are repeated for each answer. Since it required two columns to run, I've also dropped out the bridging section that summarizes the first half.)*

Douglas Kass, the author of the notorious **Barron's** article that set off a firestorm of negative publicity for Marvel — even though it was loaded with misinformation — was one of the earliest respondents to the "Future of Comics" survey. On his poll, he jotted down the question, "Are we having fun yet?"

The answer is, yes, we had a lot of fun.

From the tongue-in-cheek nature of the survey, I wasn't certain how many people would take it seriously enough to respond. The answer was: 219. For a first-time effort that doesn't result in plaques, awards, banquets, or anything except a few laughs and some intriguing insights, we here at *BID* were extremely pleased with the turnout. Heck, I thought if we topped 50, we'd be lucky.

Apparently there are quite a few folks out there who want to be able to look to the future and say, "Ha! I saw that coming back in 1992."

Here, then, are the responses, compiled by the intrepid Myra with the use of Survey Tabulator, software from issue #9 of *Big Blue Disk*. We present, in each case, the total number of responses and the percentage they represent. In several instances, the percentages will add up to more than 100%, since multiple responses were available for some questions.

Some of the replies were — curious. There was the fellow whose responses were primarily anti-Japanese and anti-Semitic. And then, of course, there was the respondent who wrote "Who cares?" to *every single question*. Imagine spending 29¢ to mail that in. It's rare that you find apathy quite that contentious.

Any entry that got more than one vote is listed, as well as some of the more interesting single-vote getters. My (inevitable) comments follow some entries.

Here we go:

Ten years from now

1) *The No. 1 Comic book company will be:*

Marvel	95	(43.38%)
DC	39	(17.81%)
Valiant	23	(10.50%)
Doesn't exist yet	20	(9.13%)
Image	13	(5.94%)
Dark Horse	11	(5.02%)
Malibu	2	(0.91%)
Tundra	2	(0.91%)

Single votes were also recorded for, among others, Fantagraphics, Blue Sky Blue, Archie, and a merger of Marvel and DC.

What was entertaining about this particular entry was the large number of people who have started their own comic-book companies and declare that, 10 years from now, they'll be on top. This can be attributed either to wishful thinking or just hoping to get a plug for their company. I didn't list most of these — except for Blue Sky Blue, which is the vision of Jo Duffy. Having read the first issue of *Nestrobber*, BSB's first title, I figured — why not?

Marvel's 43.38% draw is interesting in that I believe that's right around where its current market share is. Valiant placed a solid third. What's intriguing is Image's low posting: Even though it currently hovers between the #2 and #3 slots in ordering, its draw in the poll is significantly lower than DC and Valiant and only marginally higher than Dark Horse — even if you combine it with Malibu's numbers.

The reason for this becomes quickly apparent in the second question:

2) *The following company (or companies) will no longer exist*:

Image	136	(62.10%)
Valiant	74	(33.79%)
Dark Horse	32	(14.61%)
DC	21	(9.59%)
Marvel	12	(5.48%)
Innovation	9	(4.11%)
Now	7	(3.20%)
Comico	6	(2.74%)
Eclipse	6	(2.74%)
Fantagraphics	5	(2.28%)
Malibu	3	(1.37%)
Disney	2	(0.91%)
Archie	2	(0.91%)
Personality	2	(0.91%)

What's fascinating about the results on this one is how they run so contrary to (a) current ordering practices and (b) attitudes towards Marvel. Whereas many older fans in particular (and we'll see later that most of the respondents were older) are quick to bash Marvel's various titles and business practices, there seems to be no question as to the popularity and effectiveness of both.

Image's long-term health, on the hand, has the dubious honor of being one of the few instances where a majority of respondents agreed on something (as opposed to a plurality).

Now — y'see — if I were *really nasty*, I'd say that the creators at Image might want to have someone start writing their résumés for them. But — I'm not *really nasty*.

3) *The top selling comic book will be:*

Doesn't exist yet	94	(42.92%)
X-Men	26	(11.87%)
Spider-Man	19	(8.68%)
Superman	11	(5.02%)
Batman	11	(5.02%)
Next Men	7	(3.20%)

Spawn	4	(1.38%)
Harbinger	2	(0.91%)
Legion of Super-Heroes	2	(0.91%)
Cerebus	2	(0.91%)
Hulk	2	(0.91%)
Lobo	2	(0.91%)

Single votes were also recorded for, among others, *New Warriors*, *Nestrobber* (gee, I wonder who voted for that one?), *Jughead*, *Sandman*, *Doom Patrol*, and *Captain America*.

Apparently this question was answered with an eye towards the transitory state of the market. Although *X-Men* and its various spin-offs has been a (if not the) top-selling comic book for the past decade or so, that does not seem to be a guarantee for its future. Just over 12% foresee *X-Men* maintaining its rarified status. Instead, it would appear that the readership is eagerly awaiting the coming of a title that will claim leadership in the marketplace. Had I known that "Does not exist" would score so well, I would have placed a back-up question for everyone who answered that way, asking, "Who do you think will be publishing it?"

Unfortunately, the survey program is not sophisticated enough to be able to ask it for cross-correlation. But if we look at the closeness in percentages of the #1 responses for both questions (1) and (3), we can surmise that respondents probably figure that Marvel will be publishing it — whatever the heck it turns out to be.

Gentlemen and ladies: Start your creative juices flowing. The readership is awaiting your efforts.

4) *The following character(s) will have died and been replaced by someone else bearing the same name:*

Iron Man	126	(57.53%)
Robin	113	(51.60%)
Punisher	97	(44.29%)
Captain America	89	(40.64%)
Superman	67	(30.59%)
Spawn	65	(29.68%)
Wonder Woman	54	(24.66%)
Spider-Man	44	(20.09%)
Batman	33	(15.07%)
Wolverine	23	(10.50%)
Hulk	7	(3.20%)
Flash	6	(2.74%)
Green Lantern	5	(2.28%)
Lobo	3	(1.37%)
Thor	2	(0.91%)
Archie	2	(0.91%)
Daredevil	2	(0.91%)
Aquaman	2	(0.91%)

Single votes were also received for, among others, Clark Kent, Swamp Thing, Dr. Strange, Warlock, Grimjack, Quicksilver, Jean Grey, Aunt May, and Barbie.

Barbie?

The clear message from the foregoing is that Jim Rhodes, who currently sports the armor of Iron Man, would be well-advised not to start reading any continued stories.

What is unsurprising is that the top respondents have already done the replacement shtick before. Apparently respondents are of the opinion that, if a gimmick is done once, the odds are that it's going to happen again. (Hell, in *Iron Man* it's already happened *three* times, pingponging back and forth between Tony Stark and Rhodey.) Considering the track record of the comic-book companies, I'd be hard-pressed to disagree.

But — Barbie?

At any rate, since DC and Image are going to do crossovers, and since Superman is dead and since Spawn has been dead since the beginning and since they're only separated by one percentage point in the poll —

Perhaps DC and Image might want to consider swapping the characters. Have Superman be reincarnated as Spawn, and have Spawn start wearing the Superman outfit. You have to admit it certainly has the merit of being unexpected.

Barbie? Geez —

5) *The following person will be the editor-in-chief of Marvel Comics (should there be a Marvel Comics):*

Mark Gruenwald	49	(22.37%)
Fabian Nicieza	28	(12.79%)
Peter David	28	(12.79%)
Tom DeFalco	19	(8.68%)
Jim Shooter	12	(5.48%)
John Byrne	12	(5.48%)
Chris Claremont	10	(4.57%)
Rob Liefeld	8	(3.65%)
Bob Harras	8	(3.65%)
Mike Carlin	6	(2.74%)
Who cares?	6	(2.74%)
Todd McFarlane	3	(1.37%)
Paul Levitz	2	(0.91%)
Name Withheld	2	(0.91%)

Single votes were also noted for, among others, Joey Cavalieri, Al Milgrom, Roy Thomas, Scott Lobdell, Jim Starlin, Stan Lee, Alan Moore, and Renee Witterstaetter.

So it would seem that Marvel's current second-in-command is being given the nod for the big chair in the 21st century. Fabian put in an impressive showing, and as for all those who voted for me — gee, thanks, but I think not. That's *one* headache I definitely don't need.

6) *The following person will be the editor-in-chief of DC Comics (should there still be a DC Comics):*

Mike Carlin	37	(16.89%)
Paul Levitz	36	(16.44%)
Jim Shooter	30	(13.70%)
Peter David	17	(7.76%)
John Byrne	10	(4.57%)
Tom DeFalco	9	(4.11%)
Who cares?	7	(3.20%)
Rob Liefeld	6	(2.74%)
Joey Cavalieri	6	(2.74%)
Chris Claremont	5	(2.28%)
Mark Gruenwald	5	(2.28%)
Bob Harras	5	(2.28%)
Todd McFarlane	3	(1.37%)
Frank Miller	2	(0.91%)
Denny O'Neil	2	(0.91%)

Single votes were also recorded for, among others, Fabian Nicieza, Marv Wolfman, Ross Perot, Archie Goodwin, Neal Pozner, Mike Eury, Karen Berger, Howard Stern (!), Len Wein, and Katie Main.

Whereas Gruenwald has a clear lead in the field at Marvel, it seems Carlin and Levitz will be slugging it out. Certainly Carlin's overseeing the successful Superman renaissance has to weigh well in his favor; then again, Levitz has the seniority and the business savvy, enabling him to see editorial concerns from a variety of angles. It'll be interesting to see how this plays out. Not to mention the strong interest respondents seem to have in seeing Shooter running the place.

What I found interesting was Joey Cavalieri's performance. Joey was barely mentioned on the Marvel side, but garnered six votes here. It makes you wonder whether people think he's going to jump back to DC or are simply unaware that he's currently with Marvel.

7) *The following person will be revealed to be the Anti-Christ:*

Rob Liefeld	78	(35.62%)
Todd McFarlane	20	(9.13%)
Tom DeFalco	14	(6.39%)
Peter David	12	(5.48%)
Jim Shooter	11	(5.02%)
John Byrne	10	(4.57%)
Bill Clinton	6	(2.74%)
Respondent	3	(1.37%)
Fabian Nicieza	2	(0.91%)
Gary Groth	2	(0.91%)
Tony Isabella	2	(0.91%)
Ross Perot	2	(0.91%)

Single votes went to, among others, Mike Carlin, Mark Gruenwald, Paul Levitz, Erik Larsen, Superman, Lobo, Damien, Rich Buckler, Dave Sim, Sam Donaldson, Pat Buchanan, Sinead O'Connor, George Bush, Macaulay Culkin, and Cat Yronwode.

I must admit, I was amazed by the results on this one. I mean, let's face it: Considering that I've seen Tom DeFalco blamed for everything short of JFK's assassination, I thought he had a lock on this one. But he drew less than 7%. Considering the acrimonious departure from the mutant titles by such worthies as Claremont and Byrne, I thought Bob Harras would draw his share. But he got *no* votes at all. Hell, Bill Clinton got six votes, and he wasn't even on the ballot. Three people tagged themselves as the Anti-Christ. But the winner —

Rob Liefeld? Of all people, *Liefeld*? I never expected that. Apparently readers are of the impression that *Youngblood* surpasses bad and is, in fact, one of the seven signs of the Apocalypse. Either that or someone spotted a "666" on Rob's forehead and word has spread.

The suggestion is that, to 35% of the respondents, Rob represents something that they really don't like. What that might be, I leave to you to figure out. Certainly if one clear-cut conclusion can be drawn from this, it's that Rob is desperately in need of better public relations.

8) *The following title(s) will probably be just about hitting the stands.*

Youngblood #4	108 (49.32%)
An X-Men title that doesn't yet exist	103 (47.03%)
Cerebus #300	68 (31.05%)
Ms. Mystic #8	36 (16.44%)
Tom DeFalco's Two Fisted Adventures #6	6 (2.74%)

What we have to wonder here is whether Rob's inability to turn a monthly book out on anything less than lunar eclipse frequency prompted people to decide that he's the Anti-Christ — or whether it is, in fact, the nature of the Anti-Christ to drive people nuts by turning a comic book out late. (In which case the comics industry is breeding ground for an army of Anti-Christs, I should think.)

As for Tom DeFalco — well, it's nice to know he'll have something to keep him busy, what with his not being editor-in-chief any more.

9) *The standard Marvel comic book is 32 pages for $1.25.*
Ten years from now, should there still be Marvel comics, the standard one will be:

32 pages	99 (45.21%)
24 pages	53 (24.20%)
16 pages	38 (17.35%)
48 pages	20 (9.13%)
64 pages	3 (1.37%)
A disc	3 (1.37%)

(There were seventeen other votes for various page lengths.)

And will cost:

$2.50	80	(36.53%)
$3.95	40	(18.26%)
1500 Yen	16	(7.31%)
$1.75	12	(5.48%)
$2.95	4	(1.83%)
$4.95	4	(1.83%)
$5.00	4	(1.83%)
$2.00	4	(1.83%)
$10.00	3	(1.37%)
$1.00	2	(0.91%)
$1.25	2	(0.91%)
$1.50	2	(0.91%)
$3.75	2	(0.91%)

Single votes were also recorded for, among others, $3.25, $5.95, and $3.50.

So it would seem that the future Marvel package would be 32 pages for $2.50 — a 100% increase over the next ten years — and getting nothing in addition in terms of editorial matter — unless, of course, Marvel expands on the present 22 pages of story and art by cutting back on advertising revenue (yeah, right).

Make more, get the same. I guess it's better than pay more, get less. And, speaking of people who pay more:

10) *If Warners ever unloads DC Comics, it will probably be bought by:*

The Japanese	67	(30.59%)
Marvel	37	(16.89%)
Jim Shooter	24	(10.96%)
Disney	22	(10.05%)
Ross Perot	11	(5.02%)
Image	7	(3.20%)
Seduction of the Innocent	4	(1.83%)
Krause Publications	2	(0.91%)
Ted Turner	2	(0.91%)
Malibu	2	(0.91%)

Single votes were also recorded for, among others, Murphy Brown, Three X-Editors, Archie Comics, Dave Sim, Eastman and Laird, and Nabisco.

One reader remonstrated me for saying "The Japanese" rather than "A Japanese company." I dunno — I think either way gets the point across.

Will DC be sold? It wouldn't surprise me. Although some of the responses were gag possibilities, the top vote getters don't seem like entirely unlikely purchasers to me.

Who knows? Maybe they'll be bought by Ron Perlman, so that the former *Beauty and the Beast* star doesn't have to deal with fans who keep asking, "I hear you bought Marvel comics." Instead of saying, "No, you have me confused with Ron Perelman," he can reply, "No, you're mistaken, I bought DC."

11) *The majority of comics will be produced by:*

Writer/artist teams	170 (77.63%)
Writer/artists	42 (19.18%)

A thumping majority let it be known that they think that teamwork is the way to go. And of that majority, almost none of them withheld their names.

12) *The majority of comics produced will feature:*
Characters owned by the publisher and produced as straight
work-for-hire (example, Marvel):   121 (55.25%)
Characters owned by the creator and published by someone
else, wherein the publisher assumes most of the risk
(example, Epic):   42 (19.18%)
Characters owned by the creator and published by someone
else, wherein the publisher is essentially a hired hand
(example, Image):   40 (18.26%)
Characters owned by the creator, published by the creator
(example: *Cerebus*):   13   (5.94%)

So it would seem that a majority of the respondents believe that the status is going to remain fairly quo. That, combined with the notion that Marvel will be the #1 publisher and that the majority of comics will be by teams, makes the futurescape of comics look very similar to the present.

All of which ties in with the notion that Image will fold its tent.

There's nothing like consistency of vision.

13) *Check off all of the following which will actively be used as marketing gimmicks:*

Trading/Holo cards	135	(61.64%)
Signed ltd. edit.	134	(61.19%)
Prebagged comics	129	(58.90%)
Hologram covers	129	(58.90%)
Foil covers	121	(55.25%)
Multiple covers	114	(52.05%)
Talking covers	108	(49.32%)
Flexidiscs	97	(44.29%)
Scratch & sniff	96	(43.84%)
Pop-up books	6	(2.74%)
Floppy disks	4	(1.83%)
Holograms	4	(1.83%)
Multiple endings, same story	3	(1.37%)
Virtual reality	2	(0.91%)
#0 Origin issues	2	(0.91%)

Single votes were also received for, among others, covers but no pages, lower prices (oh, dream on), recycled comics, multiple editions of the same story, but with different artists (now there's a thought), and — of all things — dinner with the artist.

That last idea could be dangerous, considering that dinner with some of the artists I'm acquainted with might not only prompt the lucky fan to stop buying the artist's comic book but might, in fact, drive the fan out of comics collecting altogether.

As for the rest of it, it would appear that the majority of readers cannot envision a time when cards, bagged comics, etc., have gone the way of the dinosaur. People seem resigned to these and various other gimcracks — with more to come.

Ask a DC rep about goldfish covers sometime —

14) *Check off all the following places that you think Seduction of the Innocent will be playing:*

Street corners	92	(42.01%)
San Diego Comic-Con	76	(34.70%)
Chicago Comicon	71	(32.42%)
The Disney Channel	47	(21.46%)
Atlanta Fantasy Fair	44	(20.09%)
Great Eastern Conventions	38	(17.35%)
Caesar's Palace	36	(16.44%)
Dragon Con	29	(13.24%)

Single votes were also received for WonderCon (where they've actually played) and the Sci-Fi Channel.

Well, it looks as if a considerable percentage of the fans are still hoping for a SDCC/SOTI reconciliation — although a larger number are anticipating Bill, Miguel, Chris, Al, and Steve playing on street corners, perhaps hoping to scrape together airfare to San Diego next year. Not a pretty picture at all.

Give while you can, folks. It's a terrible thing to lose one's mind.

15) *The year 2002 will seem most like:*

Space: 1999	64	(29.22%)
John Byrne's 2112	39	(17.81%)
2000 AD	32	(14.61%)
Spider-Man 2099	24	(10.96%)
Jack Kirby's 2001	23	(10.50%)

Single votes were also received for *Blade Runner, Terminator,* 1992, *Max Headroom,* and *Clockwork Orange.* The fact of the matter is that the guy who said "1992" is probably the most correct. I'm curious as to whether those who voted for *Space: 1999* did so in the belief that we'll have Moon colonies — or in the belief that we're all going to turn into really bad actors.

16) *In the year 2002,* **Spider-Man 2099** *will be in:*

The 3/$1 box	106	(48.40%)
2099	49	(22.37%)
2109	31	(14.16%)
2100	17	(7.76%)
2101	14	(6.39%)
2105	7	(3.20%)

Yeah, well, screw you. What do *you* know, anyway?

17) *I think my comics will be worth more ten years from now than they are now:*

Agree	154	(70.32%)
Disagree	60	(27.40%)

18) *I think the bottom is going to fall out of the collector's market:*

Agree	126	(57.53%)
Disagree	90	(41.10%)

I found questions #17 and #18 combined to be the most fascinating contrast. I would have bet money that whatever the majority held on the first question, they'd go the opposite way on the second. But instead the majority (although not the exact same majority) agreed with both.

What this would indicate is that, although the majority of collectors believe that the bottom will fall out of the market, they are laboring under the belief that *their comics will be immune* — that whatever it is that crashes will not have an impact on their own collections.

Several people who agreed with both statements went out of their way to explain the apparent discrepancy by stating that they collected only Golden and Silver Age comics, which they seemed to regard as the blue chip stocks of comics speculating. Buyers, it is assumed, will be demanding early issues of *Action* long after *Supreme* has lost any meaning other than being a popular dessert suffix.

Who knows? Maybe they're right. They better hope they are — because otherwise there's a very large speculators' market out there that is kidding itself to degrees previously undreamt of.

19) *Ten years from now, the average reader will be buying comics:*

To read the stories	130 (59.36%)
To look at the artwork	62 (28.31%)
For collectible value	50 (22.83%)

I had intended for people to check only one. Quite a few checked combinations, however. And someone else pointed out that saying "the average reader" tilted the question towards a reading response; the more correct phrasing would have been "the average consumer."

Ah, well. It's my first time. Be gentle.

20) *But I Digress* will be:

A fond memory	92 (42.01%)
Written by me	78 (35.62%)
Written by Shana	26 (11.87%)
Drawn by Todd McFarlane	13 (5.94%)
An unfond memory	6 (2.74%)

I tend to side with the folks who think it'll be a fond memory, as I have great difficulty envisioning my doing this column 10 years hence. Then, again, when I first started it two and a half years ago, I figured I'd go six months at the most. So I guess you never know.

Shana, in the meantime, buoyed by the positive response to her first column and pleased at the 26 people who see her as taking over this thing, is working on more columns. With a several years' head-start she should be able to get quite a few ready to go.

And, as for the wiseguy who said he thought Shana was ghosting them for me now, why I oughta —

I am

20-something	99 (45.21%)
30-something	69 (31.51%)
40-something	21 (9.59%)
teen-something	21 (9.59%)
Over 40-something	3 (1.37%)
Kid something	1 (0.46%)

Pretty good turnout for the under-30 crowd. Maybe it bodes well for the percentages of voting in this country at election times. A consciousness-raised, activist generation is certainly to be hoped for.

I buy comics:

Combo of story/art	122	(55.71%)
Mostly for the story	76	(34.70%)
Investment value	44	(20.09%)
Because I'm a Marvel Zombie	11	(5.02%)
Mostly for the art	9	(4.11%)
Because they're written by PAD	2	(0.91%)

Judging by these responses, I find it fascinating that most publications that revolve around the comics industry and the salesworthiness of comics are focusing on the artist, sometimes to the exclusion of the writer. Based on the way many comics are listed, with the beginning and ending issues of an artist's tenure spelled out in detail — to the degree where one forgets that a writer was involved at all — it's pretty clear that those listings are of little use to those 20 and up. And, of course, it's the 20s and up who have all the money — not teen-agers.

Tying in with the voting that comics will be produced by writer/artist teams, those who purchase comics for the combo of story and art seem to be sending a definite message — one that, as a writer, I'm quite happy to hear.

And as for the two people who say they buy stuff because I write it: Bless you. The checks are in the mail.

I am:

A fan	163 (74.43%)
Inigo Montoya. You killed my father. Prepare to die.	40 (18.26%)
A professional in the comics industry	31 (14.16%)
The pirate king	8 (3.65%)
The president of Marvel	2 (0.91%)
The very model of a modern major general	2 (0.91%)
An editor at *CBG*	1 (0.46%)
Mark Gruenwald's father	1 (0.46%)

A number of people checked both "fan" and "pro," and in the majority of those instances they were people who ran comics shops. I guess they feel that, even though they're in the business, they're still fans at heart. Next time I'll make a separate one for "work in a comics shop."

You wouldn't think that "Inigo Montoya" would be such a common name, would you?

Interestingly, neither of the people who said they were the president of Marvel was actually Terry Stewart. The individual who claimed to be an editor at *CBG* was not Don or Maggie Thompson. However, the fellow claiming to be Mark Gruenwald's father was, in fact, Mark Gruenwald's father. And, although there should be confidentiality in this balloting, I'll go ahead and say that, yes, he voted for Mark as editor-in-chief of Marvel. Wasn't that nice?

I thank you all for participating in this exercise of democratic silliness.

We'll check back next century and see how we did.

And I realize only now that for the last "I am" question, I should have added as a possible response, "outta here." Ah, the missed chances —

(Peter David, writer of stuff, was born September 23, 1956. That's in response to the individual who ran an ad in the CBG personals column inquiring. If we ever find out why there was interest, we'll let you all know.)

Historical Notes:

1) Batman, who was picked by 33 voters to die and be replaced, has, in fact, been crippled and replaced. Interesting considering that Denny O'Neil masterminded the removal of Tony Stark from the Iron Man armor and his subsequent replacement by Jim Rhodes. Everyone else remains intact thus far — but they're watching their backs.

I HAVE IT ON RELIABLE AUTHORITY (Jan. 8, 1993)

It would seem that the pages of *Comics Buyer's Guide Price Guide* will be carrying a new column — or rather, a revival of an old one from *Comics Collector* — called *Ask the Experts*, in which fans will be invited to write in questions that will be answered by pros in the industry. The esteemed Don and Maggie asked if I would be interested in contributing to it, with the first question being "What is a day in a writer's life like?" which had previously been answered by Marv Wolfman. (The Marvelous One's example was sent along.)

Now I figure, what the heck, I'll probably participate. I mean, heck, I'd donate a kidney, if Don and Maggie asked me to (not one of *my* kidneys, mind you).

But it occurs to us here in the skyscraper headquarters of *But I Digress* that experts' answers frequently pale compared to the *thousands* of experts out there in the world of comics.

Yes, I'm talking about those authorities who wander through comics stores or conventions or letters columns, giving the latest inside information that they *swear* is absolutely true.

Undeterred by facts, they cite mysterious sources and claim full knowledge of the innermost workings of every aspect of the comics world.

My personal experience goes as far back as Marvel's premature release of the *Return of the Jedi* movie adaptation to the direct market, an act which — according to a number of "confirmed" rumors floating through the grapevine — so infuriated George Lucas that Marvel fired nine people in the sales department as a result.

At the time, the Marvel direct-sales department consisted of exactly three people: Carol Kalish, Sandy Schechter, and me. So if Marvel had fired Carol, Sandy, and me, that was three. They could have fired the VP of sales, so that would have been four. Possibly they could have fired Publishing VP Mike Hobson, Editor-in-Chief Jim Shooter, and the editor of the comic book (Archie Goodwin, I think). That's seven. To fill out the "confirmed" nine, they might have had to start firing people in subscription.

No one was fired over it, of course. Which didn't stop people from calling me with consoling messages, since they'd heard about the Lucas-ordered head-rolling.

And it goes up to the most recent "confirmed" rumors that "Peter David had Larry Stroman fired off *X-Factor* because he hated Stroman's art" (yeah, right) and the widely reported "Dale Keown was fired off *Incredible Hulk* because he's working for Image" (when in fact Dale resigned from the title weeks before Marvel even knew about *Pitt*, citing "burnout.")

So I think it would be much more interesting if, instead of reviving *Ask the Experts*, the *CBG Price Guide* gave the comics-collecting Cliff Clavins of the world their own forum, and introduced:

"Ask the Self-Proclaimed Experts"

We asked Mort W., largest customer of "Comics Whiz-Bang" in Freehold, N.J.:

"What is a day in a writer's life like? What hours does he work? Where does he work? How does he go about putting a comic book together?"

Mort replies:

Well, I'm glad you asked me that, because I heard from this guy who's dating Peter David's wife's manicurist.

On a typical day, Peter David wakes up, like, 10 or 11 o'clock in the morning. He's got a butler who's just like the one in *Arthur*, and the bath is already drawn with a croissant and two eggs over easy by the side of the tub. He never has to worry about his kids, because they're all off at boarding school, except for the baby and they have a nanny who takes care of her. His wife is a casting director and so she's hardly ever home.

He goes to his office at noon.

He's got this big studio custom-built behind the house with a jacuzzi and hot tub. There he calls up — let's say, on *Hulk*, for example — he calls up his editor, Bobby Chase. And Bobby, he tells David what that month's issue is going to be about. Like, "This month you have to do a story that brings back The Juggernaut." And then David writes a story that's, y'know, a page or two long that says, "The Hulk runs into The Juggernaut and they have a big fight, while stuff happens with Betty and Rick and Marlo back home." It's real loose. And then the artist writes the rest of the story, does all the artwork, and writes the dialogue in between the panels. The artist then sends the art pages to David. Then David retypes the artist's dialogue and draws in where the balloons are supposed to go, maybe adding a word here or there. By this time it's maybe 3 p.m., and he knocks off for the day.

Oh, they pay him by the page. I hear, like, $500 a page or something.

From that money, he hires someone to write *But I Digress* for him. And he farms out the novels, too.

* * * * *

We asked Sam M., largest customer of "Another Dimension" in Albany, N.Y.:

"How does the editorial process work at Marvel? How do comic books get published? How does the approval systems work?"

Sam replies:

It all goes through Tom DeFalco. Everything. Every word. Every syllable. DeFalco reads every plot and demands changes. And every single change is for the purpose of making the story worse, because he's so jealous that everyone writes better than he does that he wants to tear them down. DeFalco reads all the scripting that comes in and changes the word balloons and sometimes mixes them up. You know when you think there was a production error? It wasn't a mistake. DeFalco insisted it be put in there on purpose, just to make the comic book look bad.

DeFalco knows that everyone hates big crossovers, but he insists that Marvel keep doing them because he hates the fans, because he knows the fans don't like his work and he wants to get back at them.

And DeFalco promised all the guys at Image big raises and their own imprint and everything, and then went back on the whole deal, and that's why they went off and created Image. And now Marvel's market share is down to, like, 3%, and I hear they threatened to fire DeFalco unless he lets Marvel Comics be good again. So you might see some improvement.

But don't count on it.

* * * * *

We asked Taylor S., the largest customer of "Comics Cascade" in Seattle, Wash.,

"Who's the hardest working man in comics today?"

Taylor replies:

Joe Duffy. He's doing this self-publishing "Blue Sky Blue" thing. He's working his butt off. And I have tremendous respect for him after the job he turned in on *The Punisher*. He's the hardest working man in comics, definitely.

I hear in his off-hours, he's having an affair with Terry Austin — 'cause I hear she was real upset when Chris Claremont married some guy.

* * * * *

We asked Jack B., publisher of *Just the Facts, Jack* comics newsletter, whether Superman is indeed going to come back grim and gritty, or — as John Byrne was wondering — whether "anyone outside

Peter David really think(s) the resurrection will leave us with a Superman noticeably different from the one we know so well."

Jack replies:

Well, y'see, that's the question that the people at DC are asking themselves. What they're trying to figure out is, just who *is* the Superman that we know so well?

I mean, when I think of Superman, I think of the guy I grew up with, who was so noble and so pure that he swore that he would never, ever, kill anyone or anything.

But other, newer readers — they know the Superman who took it upon himself to execute three Kryptonian villains. Oh sure, you can argue that that story was done so that Superman's code against killing seemed to have come from somewhere rather than out of the blue.

Then again, I seem to recall something about a commandment (one of 10, collect 'em all) about not killing. A shame that His Word wasn't good enough for the hero who was once the highest moral bastion in comics.

Even though Superman ultimately decided that the killing wasn't justified, hundreds of thousands of Vietnam-War protesters (for example) were able to make that same statement without having killed someone themselves. Some became fugitives from justice rather than take a life, even though it would have been government-sanctioned. The Amish (as another example) won't fight at all, under any circumstances.

Saying "I'll never kill again" isn't remotely the same as saying, "I'll never kill." The Superman I always knew never had to make that distinction.

If you want to look for the corruption of Superman's moral high ground, if you want your precedent for a grim and gritty Superman — someone who killed when he felt it was warranted — you don't have to look any further than right there, at *Superman* #22. And as soon as the people at DC manage to figure out what the Superman "everyone knows" is, they can determine which way they'll go from there.

Who wrote that "Superman kills" issue?

Wait, lemme check —

It was —

Whoops. Next question.

* * * * *

Zack S., largest customer of "Comics Arena" in Ft. Wayne, Ind., was asked: "What's the best way to break into Marvel Comics?"

Zack responds:

The better you are, the less chance you have. They're not looking for really talented people.

There's this policy in force now. They're not hiring anyone that's really good, because they figure that any really good people will wind up going to work for Image. They're terrified of Image. They've already decided that they're not setting up at any conventions that Image is set up at.

And they figure: Why give anyone any sort of exposure so that they can then get real hot and work for Image? So what they're trying to do is lower the talent pool. They're hiring only guys with real lame styles who don't know how to draw anatomy and don't draw backgrounds. And if there's any shred of decent pencilling on the page, they hire bad inkers to come in and wreck the stuff so that it looks even worse.

That way they figure that they won't give Image any new talent to raid, and they hope that that'll make Image go away.

So if you're any sort of decent artist, you should be trying to break in at DC, because Image doesn't care as much about them yet. Don't bother with Marvel.

The only way to get in at Marvel is if you grease DeFalco's palm. Then he'll get your stuff shown around, and maybe even get you a decent inker assigned.

Where'd I hear that from?

I know this guy who knows this guy who spoke to a guy named Sam in Albany — and, believe me, nothing goes on in the industry that this guy doesn't know.

(Peter David, writer of stuff, once again makes more friends in the industry.)

Historical Notes:

1) The joke about my wife's manicurist is based in fact. Myra handed me a copy of **Imzadi** *to autograph one day. She told me the request had come from her manicurist. It seemed her manicurist's cousin had told a friend that she could get a signed copy of my hardcover* **Trek** *book because of this family connection. And I said, "Wait, let me get this straight. Somewhere out there, there's a guy who tells his friends, 'Yes, that's right — my cousin is Peter David's wife's manicurist.'" For some reason that struck me as incredibly funny.*

COMICS ARE A RIOT (Feb. 19, 1993)

No kidding around this time.

No fooling.

This time I'm serious.

This time I'm scared.

Because I was at the Great Eastern Convention in New York this weekend, folks, and I saw some behavior that is starting to become all too typical.

Behavior more appropriate to, oh, piranha converging on an unsuspecting bather. Behavior that had previously been limited in the human world to rock concerts or soccer games or (on a daily basis) the floor of the stock exchange.

I'm talking about the behavior on the part of some fans that transformed crowds into mobs.

Screaming, shouting, pushing, shoving.

It used to be that way at Great Eastern Cons at the Ramada Hotel (formerly the Penta, formerly the Statler Hilton). The situation was a fire marshal's nightmare, particularly as the day of the comic-book megastar dawned. Certain creators who are the comic-book equivalent of rock stars drew in tons (literally) of autograph seekers. Lines stretched up and down aisles, around corners, choking off exits, choking off air. Comic-book conventions became endurance tests; more fun was had by victims of the Spanish Inquisition than by fans who wanted to perform the apparently simple act of walking down an aisle but were unable to do so.

Various conventions began handling the situation in a variety of ways. San Diego had several floors to spread hot creators over, to avoid congestion. Chicago spread creators out through several rooms and even into tents — along with a highly criticized, but nevertheless mob-preventing, tactic of handing out time-coordinated tickets (and the rock-star-creators helped by limiting people to one signature per person, no ifs, ands, or buts).

And Great Eastern, realizing that crowding into the Ramada was creating a dangerous situation, relocated into the spacious Jacob Javits center. By any stretch of the imagination, that vast arena should have been sufficient.

It was not.

Oh, the dealers seemed to have enough space. But in the areas where the "hot" folks were set up, it was insanity as usual: staggeringly long lines in confined areas that led to congestion and short tempers.

Even that, though, could have been dealt with. But nothing could cope with the mob mindset of the crowd which, at several times during the convention degenerated into loud, raucous, shoving masses of human flesh.

I was staked out signing books at the *Comics Buyer's Guide* table, generously accorded space there by Don and Maggie (since, before I found them, I wandered around aimlessly with no clue as to where — if, indeed, anywhere — I was supposed to be). The people waiting for me to deface their comics with my signature were orderly by comparison with the crowds in some other parts of the convention. But on Saturday, particularly, they had a hard time grasping the notion of remaining single file. Fans were crowded in three and four abreast.

At one particularly horrendous point, there was a boy about 10 years old or so. Comics in hand, he was trying to move forward as much as the line would allow him (since people were, as mentioned before, four across, it made it that much more difficult for anyone to leave, once I'd signed their comics for them).

I saw the boy start to make headway — and then two "adults," each about a foot taller and at least a hundred pounds heavier, came in from either side. The boy's head was at their shoulder level and, to my horror, their shoulders converged on the boy's skull, starting to crush it in between, as they obliviously tried to get to me.

I leaned over the table, reached into the crowd, grabbed the boy by the shirt, and pulled him forward. I signed his books for him and then made sure that he got out of there safely.

(The next day we were far more on top of it. Maggie, who missed her calling as a bouncer, made damned sure that people remained single-file, ordering people back into place when they showed signs of repeating the previous day's threats to life and limb.)

My problem in such situations is that I'm torn between trying to be accommodating (chatting with the fans, not setting tight limits on the numbers of books I'll sign) and trying just to get the job done. I'm paranoid enough to feel that it doesn't matter if I sign 3000 signatures and talk to 1000 fans; the one guy to whom I say, "Sorry, I just finished, I really have to go now," or "Look, I can't sign fifty copies of *Spider-Man 2099* #1. I'll do a few, but that's it," is going to be the guy who goes around to all his friends or writes letters to fanzines saying, "Yeah, I met Peter David — what a jerk! He wouldn't sign my books."

But the absolute low point of the convention came Sunday afternoon. I'm still unclear as to precisely what happened. What I do know is that it occurred at one of the "rock-comics star" tables. At various times during the day, the occupants of that table had given away single editions of various "hot" comics, and it had been those charitable notions that had caused the loud, raucous feeding frenzies to which I alluded earlier.

But those had been isolated incidents. On Sunday afternoon, however —

It's hard to say exactly what happened.

As is usual at disasters, accounts varied wildly. The one most often repeated was that one of the creators started actually throwing "hot" comics into the crowd, thereby instigating a wave of pandemonium that would only have been surpassed if, say, Michelle Pfeiffer had shown up in full Catwoman regalia, climbed up on a piano, and started doing a striptease while singing "Makin' Whoopie."

Another version was that it was announced that a lot of "hot" comics were about to be given away free, and the crowd surged forward, waves crashing against the shore.

Perhaps the two accounts aren't mutually exclusive — perhaps the announcement was made, the crowd went berserk, and (in self-defense) the star creators started throwing the comic books into the crowd (the way that you've seen burglars in movies distract deadly guard dogs by tossing hunks of raw meat).

What everyone seems to agree upon is that the unruly mob (although, as Don Thompson pointed out, have you ever seen a *ruly* mob or even the word "ruly"?) went crazy. No swimmer with an open vein had ever attracted more enthusiastic sharks than the announcement of free "hot" comics being distributed to people in the crowd.

The other thing that everyone seems to agree upon is that the security guards at the Javits Center converged on the scene, broke up the mob, and shut down the table. End of giveaways. End of convention display. Great Eastern was only lucky that the guards didn't shut down all the neighboring tables, as well.

Ladies and gentlemen: This type of behavior was (to use Daffy Duck's favorite word) despicable. At one point earlier in the day, when the crowd was getting excessively uncontrolled, I actually shouted at it to knock it off. Anyone who knows me will tell you that I don't need such trivialities as bullhorns in order to make myself heard. It actually worked for a little while — until the flying comics incident precipitated near-chaos. If it hadn't been for the Javits cops, I hate to think what would have happened.

Now that we've had a few days to compose ourselves; now that you're reading this column at your leisure (perhaps in your living room or den or lying in your bed or sitting in your office or on the toilet or perhaps lining your birdcage with it, stopping briefly to see if there's anything of any importance to skim before Tweety relieves himself); now that, in short, we're all calm —

I'd like to say something.

I'm not talking to all of you, of course. Hopefully, you know who you are.

Let me put this just as straightforwardly as I know how:

They're just **comics**, *OK?* ***Get a grip!***

They're funny books! Some of them are better done than others, but the bottom line is, they're all flights of fancy! They're air! They don't mean anything aside from a few moments of diversion from the everyday and humdrum.

They're not gold bars. They're not diamonds. They're not stocks and bonds. They're not kruggerands. They're not the Treasure of the Sierra Madre or the Maltese Falcon.

They're *comic books*. They're black-and-white or four-color ravings, produced by people who are paid fabricators. They're made from pulped trees. They have no permanence! No matter what you do, sooner or later, *they will crumble and rot and go away*, OK?

By and large, they chronicle the adventures of wish-fulfillment, steroid-cased, outsized, costumed bozos.

They are not to be taken seriously.

They are subjected to insane inflated prices, driven there by: greedy speculators; money-grubbing retailers and distributors; pandering creators; profit-motivated publishers bent on developing newer and newer gimmicks to cover a fundamental lack of substance; ignorant fans who are incapable of grasping the simplest law of supply and demand no matter how often it's explained to them in words of one syllable; and media flacks who delight in beginning story after story with the words, "Remember those comic books your mother threw away? Well, now they're worth thousands of dollars!" thereby pouring kerosene onto the raging fire of speculation.

In the cosmic scheme of things, they're meaningless! We used to buy them, roll them up and shove them in our back pockets.

And there is no comic book in this world — *no* comic book, be it silver, gold, platinum, or puce; bagged or unbagged; hologrammed, holofaxed, holofixed, holocaust; laminated or unlaminated; embossed or flat; Image, DC, Marvel, Valiant, Dark Horse, anything — that is worth the risk of a single injury to a single person.

The concept that a comic-book convention, which should be a wonderful introduction for kids to the dazzling and varied world of comics collecting — where a kid can meet and greet the creators he's always admired and ask questions and feel that much closer to the (to him) magical process that brings super-hero adventures to him every month and perhaps even fantasize about a time when he'll be on the other side of that table, signing autographs or drawing sketches for kids that are the age that he is right then — the concept that such a convention should ever become a dangerous place, where young fans risk life and limb and might be trampled by alleged "adults" trying to get a hundred copies of the latest "hot" comic book signed so that they can tack on a few more bucks to the selling price —

It is intolerable.

Intolerable.

And we should not suffer it to continue.

(Peter David, writer of stuff, can be written to at To Be Continued, Inc., P.O. Box 239, Bayport, N.Y. 11705.)

Historical Notes:

1) In the same issue, Don and Maggie ran a proposed list of convention rules to avoid such a debacle recurring. Some cons have already adopted it.

2) Image representatives have continued to throw comics into crowds.

3) One comic book writer/artist did an interview in which she spoke very harshly about the above, stating that maybe Peter David didn't take his work in comics seriously and maybe to him they were "just" comics, but she took her work very seriously and was very dedicated, and so forth. I can only say that she missed the point — namely that comics aren't worth getting killed over — but she's never brought it up to me directly, so I never told her.

SECTION 9

On The Road Again —

I'm out doing conventions or store appearances on the average of once a month. During extended sojourns, I keep diaries of my trips, and have — on several occasions — reproduced them in the column. If nothing else, it's a painless way to keep current with the column as I travel about.

I've done write-ups on trips to WonderCon, San Diego, Glasgow, Los Angeles, and Romania. I've incorporated the best of them here — moments when I saw or experienced something that, I think, made that particular travelogue moment of more than passing interest.

TO LIVE OR DIE IN L.A. (May 31, 1991)

Monday, April 30: Look outside my window in room 833 of Ma Maison in L.A. I love the smell of Hollywood in the morning. Smells like tinsel. A city that's a writer's dream, because people live their day-to-day life here in a perpetual state of unreality.

The city revolves around "The Business": eats, sleeps, and breathes it. It invades every aspect of the citizens' lives. Everything follows scripts, it seems, as evidenced by Kirk Gibson's movie-style home run a couple years back in the World Series. People rise and fall within eyeblinks; careers turn on a dime. Real life never moves with the kind of helter-skelter twists and turns that you find in the movies — except that the movies reflect the energy and insanity of "the business" of Hollywood: what Paddy Chayfesky called "The Boredom-Killing Business."

I grab a croissant for breakfast across the street at the humungous Beverly Center mall, then head over to Paramount Pictures, to be the guest of George Takei who is busy filming *Star Trek VI*.

Up until the moment where they give me the drive-on pass and wave me through, I am certain that something will go wrong. I park and head over to Studio 5, go through a massive door informing me that this is a closed set, and enter the world of the 24th century. George (who knows me from our co-writing last year's *Trek* annual) comes over to meet me, smiling. He's looking extremely spiffy in his Starfleet uniform, so energetic that I briefly ponder (not for the first time) the national obsession with criticizing the original *Trek* on the basis that the leads are older, as if aging were a criminal offense.

I am constrained not to discuss major plot elements or surprises that have not been publicized. It would be, to my mind, an inappropriate response to being invited to the set. However, it has been reported any number of places that this film will feature Captain Sulu of the *Excelsior*. George is wearing his rank and command well, clearly taking pride in the progress of this character in whose skin he has lived for a quarter of a century.

They're busy lighting the *Excelsior* bridge, and George points and says, "There's someone who's a crew member that you might recognize." I look where he's pointing and I recognize the individual immediately — another cast member from the original series whose involvement I had heard nothing about. I will not mention identities, since no one has mentioned it publicly yet, and I won't be the first. But it's this kind of attention to continuity that gives me a positive feeling about the film.

I meet Nick Meyer, serious and intent on his work, totally focused and puffing on a cigar. He reminds me a bit of Harlan Ellison. I'm impressed by his command, his easy knowledge of scholarly works, and his ability to trade 2000-Year-Old-Man routines with me. Also meet the producers of the film, and everyone is polite, friendly, and interested. All of this seems to indicate a positive working atmosphere.

Major plot turning points are played out, with much attention paid to such atmospheric elements as the bridge crew reacting to things Captain Sulu says and does. A particular speech about loyalties prompts Meyer to speculate that there will be tremendous divided response when it plays across the screen — half the fans will love it, the other half will hate it. I can't wait to find out.

Meet and chat with Mike Okrand, the Klingon-speech authority who is tutoring the Klingons in proper enunciation. Also encounter, to my surprise, Scott Leva, a young actor and stunt man whom I remember very well from the days when he was one of Marvel's Spider-Man character actors. First Jonathan Frakes is a Captain America, and now Scott graduates to a starship bridge, although in a small role as a crew member. Am now thoroughly getting into the magic of Hollywood.

Days before, I had completed a screen adaptation of a novel of mine, *Howling Mad*, the producers of which I'm meeting with on Tuesday to get their feedback on my first draft. Now I'm imagining being on the set of that movie, watching actors speak my words. Hollywood, like Bali Hai, seems to call me.

George and I eat lunch at the commissary, and he brings me up to date about a film he made last year. Originally entitled *Blood Oath*, it's now been retitled *Prisoners of the Sun*. George stars with Bryan (F/X) Brown and plays Baron Takahashi, a cousin of the Japanese emperor, and to attempt to summarize the complex and multi-layered plot would not do it justice. Suffice to say that it opens June 14 in New York and L.A. and a week later in Atlanta, D.C., Boston, Chicago, Seattle, and San Francisco. George hopes that the *Trek* fans will take an interest. So do I. He's a very talented actor and a nice guy, and I'd like to see the film succeed.

Check out the costumes and make-up. Three long racks of costumes, densely packed. It seems you could clothe half of Rhode Island with it. I'm like a kid in a candy store (or, for that matter, myself in a candy store). I'm getting more and more into the Hollywood experience. I'm buying into the fantasy.

I wander the set of a Klingon cruiser, sit in the command chair, bark orders in Klingonese. I study carefully the dedication plate for the *Excelsior*, situated just to the right of the main viewscreen and laugh hysterically at the gag tossed into it (presumably by Mike Okuda). It's a quote from a very well-known SF film.

They're shooting again. George has to turn briskly in the command chair, but it's clumsy and shakes. A stagehand lies just below camera range and helps push the chair so George can pivot authoritatively. I'm going to be impossible to see *Trek VI* with — I'm going to laugh in all sorts of places for no apparent reason.

I learn that Kim Cattrall was on the set earlier, but I didn't get to meet her. It's probably better that way; I think she's really cute and I would've just stood there and stammered. David Warner shows up in Klingon makeup.

But he's wearing a T-shirt, jeans, and a checked bathrobe. He looks like a Klingon Arthur Dent.

I'm in *Trek*-fan heaven, welcomed into the real unreality. When I finally leave, it's a genuine effort. I drive back to the hotel, still radiating the glow of witnessing the glorious illusion of moviemaking in action. What a great town. I get back to my hotel and there's a phone message from the *Howling Mad* producers. They must want to confirm our breakfast meeting tomorrow and tell me how much they like my script. I call them.

They hate it.

They hate it.

They hate it.

They hate the scenes.

They hate the pacing.

They hate the characterization.

They hate it.

They like a couple of point-of-view shots.

Otherwise, they hate it.

I'm caught completely off guard. My mind shuts down. My nice, comforting room irises out, and, instead of a thought process, there's just a dull buzz, like a hive or a lost phone connection.

They hate it.

They hate it.

They hate it.

I've failed.

The phone is still to my ear, and the only thing I can think of is winding the cord around my neck. My hands grip the receiver like a life preserver, but my life preserver is telling me they're disappointed.

175

Where's the imagination that was so prevalent in the book? Where's the invention, the interesting characterization? Scenes are unfocused, the story doesn't flow, the character transitions are unconvincing.

They hate it.

I'm nothing.

They didn't say I'm nothing. *I* did. Or rather, some voice in my head, all the insecurities I always carry around with me, leaping out of my personal Pandora's box, invading every facet of my confidence, eroding it, butter on a skillet just melting away.

Just like that. So easily.

Because I'd bought into the Hollywood unreality, because I'd let down my guard, because I'm not on my home turf — all of it and all of the usual defense mechanisms for coping with rejection were given the day off, and now they can't get back to rescue me from the mire of my own insecurity.

From somewhere in the receiver they're asking me if I still want to have breakfast the next morning. Right now I'm thinking about vomiting, not eating, and I mumble something semi-articulate and hang up.

They hate it. I've failed.

Hollywood has abandoned me. No tinsel, no patina of success, no unreality. The real world has thudded down on me with jackhammer force, because I've so built myself up that, when I fall, it is so much further to fall.

I call my wife. I call a close friend. I sound like I'm talking from the other side of the grave. I sound like someone just died. Someone did.

They try desperately to cheer me. I try to sound like they've succeeded, but I'm just a black hole, sucking in the light of friendship and encouragment and giving nothing back.

Because that voice in my head whispers, "She's your wife, he's your friend. What they say doesn't count, because they like you, and that colors their perception of your work. But the movie producers, they're the ones who really count."

They hate it.

I've failed.

Suddenly I just want to get away from Hollywood, from the business. For starters, I don't want to be in California. Or in this country or on this planet.

No Hollywood success story. No movie-like twist. I've failed.

I've got to get out of the room, which now seems like a coffin. The mall across the street is still open. I go out the front of the hotel, and they're filming a movie. It's the last thing I want to see. I'm sick of movie sets, of movies, of me. I'm sick of it all.

And yet, masochistically, I summon up enough energy to ask a young crew member what they're filming. It's a film for the USA cable channel. That's nice. I smile gamely, turn towards the street, miserable and soul sick.

And the crew member says, "Do I know you?"

I look back at him. "I write comic books," I say cautiously.

He points and says, "You're Peter David!"

I am stunned, shocked. A different kind of shock, like a flashbulb going off. "You know me?" He knows me from New York, from a comic-book store I occasionally went to. His name is John Minardi. He's a grip (a lighting man) on the film. He's been here for a year. And he's a fan.

A fan of my work.

He waxes enthusiastic about my comics work, about my novels. He tells me how much he likes my work, how good my work is. He quickly summons a co-worker and introduces me, and the co-worker is also a fan.

And I drink it in, greedily, hungrily. He doesn't know, doesn't have any idea how much I'm taking this in. How much I needed to hear this, right at this moment, at the lowest I've been in ages.

He's read, as near as I can tell, most of my work, although because of the higher price-tag he hasn't picked up my latest *Trek* book, *Vendetta*, yet; but he assures me he will.

Then he has to get back to work, and I head into the mall, and now my confidence is seeping back with every step, John Minardi — a relative stranger — having pried open the door. The grip who helped me get a grip.

So they didn't like the script. So it's just their opinion. They're just people, and, as William Goldman has said, no one in Hollywood knows anything. I knew it would have to be rewritten. All scripts are. I can handle it. I can handle anything. And if they decide to go with another writer, well, it's their loss.

Just their opinion. And, right now, I'm clinging instead to John Minardi's opinion.

I buy cookies, a new necktie, and a copy of *Vendetta*. I go back to the hotel and hand him the book, already signed, with simply the word, "Thanks," above my name. He has no idea why I've done this, and I can't tell him, because I'm just so damned happy he was there that, if I try to let him know, I'll crack.

A fan. The gods of Hollywood reached down and put a fan there, right in my path. Ironically, I needed to hear the words of a stranger. Like Blanche DuBois, I depend on the kindness of strangers.

What a plot twist. If it happened in the movies, I would say it was contrived. But Hollywood justifies all things, mixing movie moments into reality and smiling at the way it all comes together.

I head upstairs to write this column and get a decent night's sleep (since I have a busy day tomorrow), stopping only briefly to brush some tinsel off my shoulder.

(Peter David, writer of stuff has nothing more to add.)

STAND AND DELIVER (Sept. 18, 1992)

Continuing assorted ramblings about the San Diego ComicCon:

"Do Artists Need Writers" is, indeed, one of the most popular panel topics — so much so that it's scheduled twice, for Thursday and Saturday. As noted previously, I had volunteered to be on it but was told that they had more people than they needed. This does not deter a variety of people from asking me why I wasn't on it — a couple in a fairly challenging manner, as if waiting for me to say, "I didn't have the guts." I am undeterred, however, from actually attending the thing.

The place fills up in short order, I see Todd McFarlane up there but register mild disappointment that John Byrne, announced as a panelist, is not there. I was curious to see whether Todd would have the nerve to try a repeat of the "my pal Johnny" shenanigans he pulled in Atlanta at Dragon Con. Also on the panel are Mark Bagley, Bill Willingham, Steve Gerber, and Doug Murray as moderator. I do not envy Doug his job. Indeed, he's a braver man than I; had I been offered the moderator slot, I would have turned it down.

Sitting next to me in the audience is Marvel Editor Craig Anderson. The place becomes packed pretty quickly. The person largely believed within the industry to be "Name Withheld" strides in and takes a seat in the audience. The whole business promises to be interesting.

At first the thing threatens to degenerate into a "Kill Todd McFarlane" session. Todd gives a five-minute speech explaining what he wants from life. In essence, he states that all he wants is to do the best job he can, and he's satisfied with that. That he knows he'll never be a great writer and it doesn't bother him and he doesn't see why it should bother anyone else. That he's happy being the best he can be. That all he wants out of life is to be happy and do work that makes him happy, and even if he was producing a comic book that sold 5000 copies, he'd still be happy because that's how much he loves comics.

This gets some applause.

A person in the audience subsequently raises his hand and asks Todd something to the effect of, "I have a question about characterization, pacing, and subtext. Specifically, I'd like to know if we're going to see any of that in your work any time soon." This draws louder applause but negative reaction from Todd supporters. The whole thing is starting to seem like Jets vs. Sharks.

Todd, utterly unfazed by the assessment of his creative abilities, points out the commercial success of his work as an indication that he must be doing something right. He also makes the odd analogy that *Terminator 2* is no *Gandhi* but just because the former made a lot of money doesn't mean that it was a bad film. The reason the analogy is odd, of course, is because no one claimed that just because something makes a lot of money, it is automatically bad. Rather, the argument was that just because something makes a lot of money doesn't make it automatically good, or even defensible.

The questioner (or it might have been another audience member by that point — my tape is garbled) subsequently utters a profanity generally associated with copulation. Todd chides him for using "the 'F' word." This is a bit amusing, since in a just-published interview with Todd, every fifth word out of his mouth is "the 'F' word."

(Todd remains to me a fascinating study in contradictions. In that same interview, he makes a point of saying that, as a penciller, he would never try to tell the writer what to do. He feels it isn't his place to do so. That as a penciller, his job is to do the art, and he isn't going to start telling the writer how to write any more than he expects the writer to start telling him how to draw. From our year and a half on *The Hulk*, I can personally vouch for that. But in the pages of *CBG* some months back, the linchpin of his "Respect" piece was how irked he was that no one ever asked his advice on what made books sell. So why was it any more his "place" to tell sales and marketing people how to do their job than it was to tell writers how to do theirs? But I digress...)

Steve Gerber makes the fairly accurate point that complaining about artists who write ignores the fact that in comics, there are many writers-by-trade who are turning out substandard work. I find this indisputable. Just as there are many artists recycling hot art styles, there are many writers recycling stories that have been around for years. Too many people are only able to point to comics as their literary influences, and that is unfortunate and limiting.

Bill Willingham, on the other hand, contends that, by and large, a story produced by a writer and artist cannot possibly be as good as something produced by someone with a single vision — is indeed, that a single vision is the best.

One would be hard-pressed to refute such a viewpoint when one thinks of such talents as Will Eisner or Frank Miller. Then again, neither Stan Lee nor Jack Kirby has ever surpassed Lee/Kirby. And, hey — I liked *The Black Dragon*. I'm enjoying *Next Men*. But I'm sorry — none of it sings to me the way Claremont/Byrne *X-Men* did.

I'm old-fashioned enough to believe that two heads can genuinely be better than one and that, if you get a good writer and a good artist together, they can produce something that is truly greater than what they can accomplish individually. The simple concept of people pulling together for a goal is not only what the era of super-heroes was founded upon (can you say "Siegel and Shuster"?), but, indeed, is the notion upon which this country was built. (I apologize for the effusiveness; TNT recently ran *1776* and I'm always like this for a few weeks after seeing that film.)

For a time, Mark Bagley almost seems under siege. Stating that he himself feels he doesn't have any stories to tell, he is instead genuinely happy to be teamed with good writers so that he can be part of a group effort. That he, as an artist, feels elevated to a degree by linking up with a talented writer. He seems almost defensive for having that worldview, and not surprisingly so; in today's climate, there's almost an attitude that there's something "wrong" with an artist who has no interest in writing. That such an artist is somehow inherently inferior to another artist who does write, or at least tries to.

Forty-five minutes into the session, I feel the desire to open my mouth and make a fool of myself welling up within me, beyond my control. Hoping that someone will dissuade me, I turn to Craig. "Should I say something?" I ask, hoping he'll say, "I'd stay out of it if I were you." Instead Craig says, "Go for it." Terrific.

My hand goes up, joining the dozen others in the audience.

But eagle-eyed Todd spots me immediately, leapfrogging over Doug Murray's authority as moderator and calling out something like, "Yes! My friend, Peter David, over there!"

I stand up slowly, and am startled and disconcerted by the fact that the place has suddenly become very quiet. Every video camera in the place is now aimed squarely at me.

Everyone's waiting for me to say something, which is interesting, considering I hadn't thought out what I would say. They're probably expecting me to launch an attack on Todd, in keeping with the impression everyone seems to have that I'm Anti-Image, Rah-Rah Marvel.

I never realized before what a sense of security being up on a dais presents. It's as if the physical positioning automatically lends authority to your words. Speaking from the audience, with no microphone and no overview, I feel more vulnerable. Doug offers me a mike, but that offer had not been made to anyone else in the audience, so I don't feel I should take advantage of it.

In the back of my mind, I hear the five-note "Man With No Name" Clint Eastwood music. I have no idea how long I was quiet.

Seems like forever.

I don't remember exactly what I said. No doubt it's on video tape. Maybe in recounting it, I'm unconsciously adding things I wish I'd said, or certainly adding more eloquence than I probably displayed off the cuff. But I believe it went something like this: "It seems to me that a creator has a responsibility, both to himself and to his audience, to be trying to improve himself constantly. To be reinventing himself. To live by the credo that 'Good enough never is.' And the moment a creator decides, 'This is the best that I can do, and I'm happy with the best that I can do,' then that person is no longer a growing, developing creator. Instead, he's in a kind of creative spin cycle. That a creator can never be completely satisfied with anything he's done but, instead, must always want to improve himself.

"In that vein, I do not see how any rational person can possibly protest, if someone who previously was a penciller wants to write, as well. I have no problem with that at all. What I find disturbing is the notion of people who take on writing, and not only do not have a clue as to how to write, but — even more disturbing — show absolutely no interest in learning. Such an attitude displays a contempt for writing and not only is limiting to the artist-who-would-write, but ultimately is unfair to the audience.

"Harlan Ellison espouses the philosophy, 'Beware he who writes more than he reads.' I think it's important that anyone who writes take it upon himself to devote at least as much energy to learning how to write as he did to learning how to draw.

"Otherwise he has no business saying he's a writer of any kind."

This draws some applause. Steve Gerber says that he agrees with me 100%. Todd says nothing in response. Taking a guess, I think he thought I was going to launch some sort of personal attack, and when he didn't get it, wasn't sure how to reply.

Sorry if I disappointed him.

Later, I attend the Eisner awards. As I anticipated, any category that I'm in that Neil Gaiman or *Sandman* is also in results in a nod to Neil. I'm annoyed with myself, having failed to try to get Neil to go double-or-nothing on our chocolate chip cookie bet from the **CBG** Award.

I have a program in front of me, on which I've checked off my guesses as to who would win, and then the actual results. I'm running about 75% right. We get to the final category that I'm in, which is Best Writer/Artist or Writer/Artist Team. I've already checked off Frank Miller as my guess, although I'm thinking that maybe Dave Sim and Gerhard have a good shot, since *Cerebus* has been nothing short of brilliant this past year.

There are six writer/artists nominated, vs. three writer/artist teams. Based purely on the math, odds are 2-to-1 that a writer/artist is going to win.

When they announce that Dale Keown and I have won for our work on *Hulk*, I sit there in absolute shock. My jaw is somewhere in my lap. Roxanne Starr, seated next to me, shoves at me to get up there and accept the award.

It's the second time in the same day that I try to say something when I hadn't prepared anything. I spend most of my time praising Dale. It's only afterward that I kick myself for not having mentioned *Hulk* editor Bobbie Chase ("What would you think of working with this guy?" asked Bobbie three years ago, showing me sketches that Dale had done of The Hulk, Bruce, and Betty), whose nomination of the work had gotten us up there for consideration in the first place.

To me, winning the thing represents something of a vindication of my entire position of a writer-artist team still being a worthwhile contribution to the comics field — particularly since we beat out six writer/artists.

I have no idea how seriously anyone takes these awards — but I know that I take them very seriously. Afterward I get Will Eisner to sign the back of the plaque. He tells me he thinks it's a little silly, since no one will know his signature's there.

"*I'll* know," I reply.

And now you will, too.

At first I felt a little depressed, since the award was for a team that no longer exists, since Dale decided to leave. But then I start to cheer up, deciding that it's a nice way to close the book on a creatively rewarding association. It's a physical reminder of the validity of the notion of writer/artist teams.

And lastly, I think of the Image guy who, as one of his arguments for getting Dale to break the team up, convinced him that *The Incredible Hulk* was a dead-end career track that would never get him any recognition. So now Dale has a plaque that proves how utterly off-base that statement was.

I love a good team.

Now if only there was a decent one playing baseball in New York —

(Peter David, writer of stuff, wants to thank the Academy —)

CASTING ABOUT (April 2, 1993)

The casting office is fairly small. Black-and-white glossies of hundreds of actors line the walls and the floor, a permanent smiling audience.

The actor who has entered is a little taller than I am, and quite a bit slimmer. He is dressed in crisp black slacks and a black shirt buttoned to the neck. He has curly hair, a beard, and a face that is rugged, if not classically handsome. The casting director turns to me as the actor sticks out his hand to shake mine firmly. "Peter David," says the director, "this is Ron Perlman. He'll be reading for the part of Caliban. Ron, Peter here is the writer."

"A fun script," says Ron Perlman, in the voice that caused millions of female hearts to flutter for three years as Vincent, the man/monster hero of *Beauty and the Beast*. "I enjoyed it. Nice job."

Yes, that's right. Undaunted by the fact that I got my teeth kicked in last time, I have once again made a foray into the jungle of show business. It's turning out a lot better. It's also a lot weirder.

Long-time readers may remember my previous, disastrous, brush with Tinsel Town two years ago. At that time, my novel *Howling Mad* had been optioned by a movie producer who had (obviously) liked the book enough to give me money for movie rights. Not enough, however, to want to use any shred of the book's actual plot. An associate producer, working with several other associates, developed a treatment for the film that bore no resemblance to the novel, even in name. They then handed it to me and said, "Write a script based on this."

I did as I was told, figuring that, hell, they're the movie people and are far more experienced in these things than I. This, unfortunately, ignored the admonition of writer William Goldman, who claimed that, when it comes to movie making, "Nobody knows anything."

This was certainly borne out when I finished the script, turned it in, and promptly had the associate producer's boss reject it in its entirety, ripping it (not to mention my self-esteem) into small, bloody ribbons. Galling was the statement that the script's major fault was that the story lacked the invention displayed in the novel. Gee. Imagine that.

Eventually all the associate producers who developed the misbegotten treatment were fired. At the point at which the option eventually expired, the entire company was expiring along with it. This made two movie producers who became involved with me and paid for it with the life of their company. (The first was some folks who had optioned *Knight Life*. Their only claim to fame was that they produced the "Ernest" movies — you know, *Ernest Saves Christmas* and the like. At the point at which their company imploded, they were contemplating trying to turn my King Arthur Returns novel into a vehicle for Jim "Ernest" Varney, with Varney himself as Arthur. To quote either Doctor Zachary Smith or ship's counselor Deanna Troi, "The pain — the pain — "

So, thus far, my experiences in Tinsel Town had been less than glittering. However I am nothing if not — well, stupid, I guess. And, when the opportunity presented itself to dabble once again in movies, I opted for it.

This time, however, things developed a bit differently. Rather than working with a property that I had developed myself, I was flown to Los Angeles by an outfit called Full Moon Entertainment. Having obtained (through means too torturous to go into here) one of several scripts I'd written through the years, Full Moon CEO Charles Band decided that I'd be the perfect writer for his next major Blockbuster release.

When I say "major Blockbuster release," by the way, I'm referring not to the film's quality, but rather its method of distribution. Full Moon has carved a niche for itself as one of the major suppliers of films designed straight for video release (as opposed to films intended for theatrical release but which never quite make it, such as the wretched *Captain America*).

Its output is a variety of science fiction, fantasy, horror, and comedy. Full Moon's backlist includes such films as *Doctor Mordrid, Robojox, Dollman, Demonic Toys, Dollman vs. the Demonic Toys* (crossovers are everywhere these days), and — most importantly for my purposes — *Trancers I, II,* and *III*.

The first *Trancers* film, written by no lesser talents than Danny Bilson and Paul DiMeo (of *Rocketeer* movie and *Flash* TV fame), chronicled the battle by future cop Jack Deth (played by Tim Thomerson) against zombified creatures called "Trancers."

There had been two more since then, and Charlie Band had decided that I would be ideal to write *IV* and *V*. They flew me out there and I pitched a variety of ideas. One of them involved refashioning the Trancers as a vampiric race on another world. In order to save costs (a major Full Moon priority), the whole thing was going to be filmed in Romania, so, unsurprisingly, that was the concept they liked the best.

Having had projects blow up in my face before, I decided not to say anything publicly until matters were further along. Now, though, the scripts are done and approved, the director assigned, and I'm once again in Hollywoodland living the show-business experience. If it falls apart at this point, it will take the company's falling apart to do it — which, admittedly, isn't unprecedented for me.

The week before I came out, I spoke with the director, Dave Nutter, who sought my input for casting. "You know who we should get for Caliban (the main villain)?" I told him. "The guy who played Lex Luthor on the *Superboy* TV show."

"Sherman Howard?" he said. "I'll put him on my list."

So now it's several days later and here I am. I spend much of my first day in L.A. whipping the scripts into final draft form (or at least as final as these things ever are at this stage) and holding an informal read-through with star Thomerson to get a feeling for what lines he's comfortable with and what lines he'd like to see changed. As I sit at a desk crammed into a converted film-editing room, pounding away at my laptop, Dave calls on the intercom and says, "Come on up to the conference room."

I go upstairs and see that Lex Luthor is standing barely two feet away. He smiles pleasantly, which makes me nervous as hell, considering that, every time I've seen him smile in the past, it invariably meant the beginning of some nefarious scheme.

The experience gives me my first concept of what power is like, Hollywood style. I idly mention someone whom I'd like to see considered for a role, and a week later the actor has shown up. It's a heady feeling. At the same time, it gives me the slightest glimmering of how easy it is to get swept away in all of this.

Here's a nothing writer (by Hollywood standards) asking to see someone, and, poof, there he is. How much greater a power trip is it for studio executives who can pick up a phone and "order in" some major name as casually as an ordinary mortal would call out to get a pizza delivered. It strikes me as a truly miserable way for an actor to lead his life: having to bend one's schedule, one's entire existence, around the whims (sometimes capricious) of Those in Power.

Talk about power, though. The power wielded in a casting session is truly astonishing. That, and the bizarre feeling of watching talented folks take the cold words that I've written and breathe life into them.

Actors fly in and out with blinding speed. They vary wildly in temperament and style. Some are confident enough in their interpretation of the character that they just jump into it.

Some have their entire audition pieces memorized. Others glance at the script for occasional confirmation. And one actress has to look down at every single typewritten line before she delivers it, making it an achingly long audition.

Some ask for input as to what we want to see in the character. Some immediately launch into the piece, while others take time to get loose, get into character, get into "the mood." I don't perceive any particular approach being "better" than any other. Whatever works.

Jackie Earl Haley reads for a supporting part and puts so much energy into it that it seems as if he's going to blow holes in the wall.

The actor who played a supporting role in *Lethal Weapon 3* reads Caliban with gusto and comes close to going over the top without actually hopping over. He speaks in a thundering voice that makes my little fantasy script sound like Shakespeare. I can't believe it; I barely recognize my own dialogue.

An array of females read for the part of a slave girl pleading for her life, some of them so heart-wrenching that a couple of times we're almost moved to tears. And what makes it truly wrenching is that, naturally, they can't all be hired.

At least Full Moon and its casting people have tried to make the processes as painless as possible. I've heard stories about auditions held in stark rooms, with the casting people seated behind a large table like some sort of inquisition. The casting room at Full Moon is carpeted, pleasant. Dave Nutter, the casting director, and I lounge on couches and chairs, and there's very much of an open feeling. Dave is uniformly complimentary — even to the achingly bad actress. Coming in and performing at the drop of a hat — trying, within the space of five minutes, to get a roomful of utter strangers to *like you*, is brutal enough. No need to make it a hostile environment.

I'm thrilled and amazed at the high caliber of actors who are parading through the door. I mean, this is not an actor's dream job. The money is underwhelming. The features are for the straight-to-video market, which is not exactly high-profile. And the shoot is going to be in Romania. There's not a lot of upsides to it.

I'm told times are difficult. That jobs and money are scarce, and the talent is willing to go where the work is. Nowhere is this more driven home than when Perlman walks in. I have friends — not to mention a wife — who would kill to be standing as close to Perlman as I am at this moment. I resist the urge to drop to the ground and shout, "*We're not worthy*!" I also resist the urge to ask for an autograph for my wife, because I figure it would be a *faux pas*. (Dave later tells me that Perlman would probably have been happy to oblige, so now I feel like a total jerk.)

I tell Perlman as much as I can about Caliban, and, when he does the reading of it, he is as wonderful as one would imagine. He starts out reserved but then builds in intensity, becoming more and more forceful. A wonderful reading. A great performance.

One of many. One of so many I see over the course of several days. It heightens my respect for actors. It seems a harsh process to undergo, this auditioning — yet a successful day for an actor is one in which he can subject himself to it several times. Because that increases the odds that he or she might get a job — increases the odds from "none" to "slim," but increases them, nevertheless.

As of this writing, I have no idea who will end up with what part. I can't believe that a deal could be worked out with Perlman, who, as far as I'm concerned, would be ideal; then again, I can't believe that he came in to read for it in the first place. And I did get to watch him perform one of my characters, even if it does wind up being just for five minutes. I can only hope for more.

Then again, Hollywood runs on hope.

*(Peter David, writer of stuff, is impressed by how cynical children are getting these days. The family was watching **The Wizard of Oz**. When Dorothy uttered the famous line, "Somehow I don't think we're in Kansas anymore, Toto," 8-year-old Jenny responded with an acerbic, "D-uh!" Another movie moment shot to Hell.)*

Historical Notes:

*1) None of the actors mentioned above were cast (with the obvious exception of Tim Thomerson as Jack Deth). The part that Ron Perlman and Sherman Howard were being considered for went to Clabe Hartley of "**Posse**." The part Jackie Earl Haley read for so well was played by Mark Arnold of "**Teen Wolf**." The film is currently scheduled for January release, and frankly I now have difficulty seeing anyone other than the actors who were cast playing those roles.*

CRIPPLED CHILDREN (July 9, 1993)

Concluding the printing of my journal from my sojourn to Romania for the filming of *Trancers IV* & *Trancers V*:

When last we left me, I was in the middle of an elaborate practical joke in which we had convinced one of the actors that I was Romanian, and I had just shared in a meal prepared in questionable fashion by the crew consisting of questionable fish caught from a questionable lake.

May 17 — No sign of food poisoning. I lucked out.

As Vlad-the-Romanian, I climb into the morning van to the studio. Laughlin and his girlfriend, Sharon, are waiting. The Romanian driver says something to me in his native tongue. I reply in Romanian that my book is mineral water. We're on our way.

The driver pushes matters through the ride, tossing occasional comments my way. I pull replies off storefronts and billboards. He asks me something. My answer: "Milk products." That sort of thing.

The shooting day progresses, and I'm still Vlad. Tim Thomerson is playing along with particular enthusiasm, engaging me in my broken English conversations and loudly denouncing me "behind my back" (since, presumably, I can't understand him) as "a weird mother__."

Finally, director Dave Nutter, having gotten Laughlin's main scenes out of the way, helps me spring it. Now we find out whether he knew or not.

With camera rolling after a completed take, I step onto camera with Laughlin. Dropping the accent, I say, "So did we fool you? Or did you know all along?"

He stares at me uncomprehendingly. I know in a heartbeat that we got him. He is unquestionably a talented actor, but nobody is that good that he could fake that stunned an expression. He is utterly shocked.

The crew is howling. Laughlin doesn't understand what the hell has happened to my accent. He tells me later that for an instant, he was convinced that nobody on the entire crew was actually Romanian, so confused had we made him. "I'm the writer," I tell him. The camera's rolling. He starts to laugh in amazement — he can't believe that this elaborate a gag has been staged purely for his benefit. "Was Sharon in on this?" he demands. No, she is in the next room, watching the monitor with her jaw around her ankles.

He takes it extraordinarily well — much better than I would have, in all likelihood. Especially when I make it clear to him that it was nothing personal. The gag, which just sort of evolved, would have been pulled on whatever actor had been brought in. He also seems, to me at least, a lot more relaxed the rest of the shooting day. All in all, a very worthwhile practical joke, because no one was hurt by it and it pulled a lot of folks together.

The kicker is that I learned later that Sharon had said to Laughlin, "You know, I'm not sure if I like Tim. He's being very mean to Vlad."

Joe, the make-up guy, helps me out so that I finally meet F. Murray Abraham, who says I should call him Murray. "Not F?" I ask. No. Murray. I tell him I write comic books. He tells me that his son is a comic-book enthusiast. I offer to sign a comic book to his son if I can have my picture taken with him. No sweat.

I go over to the set for *Nostradamus*. They have a library set that has to be at least five times the size of our library set. It's amazing what $20 million can do. I give him the comic book, sign it to his son (Hey, maybe he's reading this. Hi, Mick. Your dad's a really nice guy.), get my picture taken with Murray, get yelled at by the assistant director because I didn't ask his (the A.D.'s) permission to come on the set. I tell him I didn't know and I'm sorry. He says I should have asked his permission. I tell him I didn't know and I'm sorry. He says I should have asked his permission. By this point I'm ready to knock his block off, because how many times am I supposed to apologize? Now I know what $20 million can get you besides great sets: bitchy assistant directors.

Back on our own set, we film a sequence where a time-warping watch that Jack Deth wears backfires on him. Ideally, it slows the rest of the world down, while Jack remains unaffected. In the previous three films, it's been done by overcranking the camera so Jack moves in slow motion, while the rest of the world comes to a halt.

Catering to Tim's gift for physical comedy — which he never gets to display as Jack Deth — I flip-flop it. In the scene, Jack is faced with a group of enemies and activates the watch. He moves in slow motion —

And his enemies are unaffected. As Tim moves at a snail's pace, the others circle him in befuddlement. "Is this some bizarre attempt at levity?" asks one in confusion. Since they're moving at normal speed, they knock him out with no problem. Tim does the longest collapse into unconsciousness in film history. With music and sound effects, it should be a high point of the film.

I have dinner with Laughlin and Sharon. They're really good kids. Laughlin was in one of the best scenes in *Unforgiven* — the sequence where the first of the two cowboys that Eastwood has been hired to kill is gunned down. It's an unforgettable scene. As the young cowboy lies dying, his friend makes a desperate attempt to aid him. The friend is Laughlin, the one who was shouting, "Don't you shoot me, you bastards!" as he rushed to aid his friend as best he could and wound up having him die in his arms. Very emotional.

Most of his *Trancers* work is done. I may not see him again while in Romania, but we part friends — although if we're on the same set on another film, I'll probably be watching my back —

May 18 — An off day. I spend a portion of the day shopping with the aid of a guide assigned by the production office. His name is Adrian. Adrian brings me to various stores in Bucharest. I can't find anything made in Romania. Turkey, England, Italy, yes, but not Romania. Adrian tells me I wouldn't want anything made in Romania, so shoddy is the workmanship.

Adrian dreams of taking his wife and child and moving to America. He tells me that, if he could spend the next five years of his life in the United States, he would die happy. It's a remarkable comment on his desire to get out of Romania. We drive past people lined up about 30 deep — for milk. There's another line elsewhere of similar length, for bread. I can walk into a 7-11, in and out, in two minutes, buying whatever brand of milk or bread I feel like, and these people have to devote as much as five hours to a similar purchase, with no choice. Here it is. Your bread. Your milk. What *kind* of milk or bread? You're kidding.

It harkens to another conversation I had with another young employee, Dragos, two days previously. He's 20 years old. He's an artist who loves to do fashion designing. He wants to come to America to make his fortune. But he's stuck where he is. He estimates the cost of an air ticket, plus visa, will take him about 10 years to earn. By that time he'll be 30: not quite as easy to start a new life as when he's 20. And he needs someone to sponsor him. In America, people dream of fame, fortune. In Romania, people dream of America. One major step removed, a photocopy of a photocopy. The picture that much faded, its definition vague.

He asks me, out of curiosity, how long it takes me to earn $1000. I lie, telling him I have no idea. "Six months?" he asks. I nod, knowing that the true answer is more like a fraction of that time. I try to explain that even though pay is higher in the States, everything costs more, too. That doesn't seem to matter to him. Maybe he can't quite comprehend it. All he cares about is his dream — a dream he very likely will never achieve.

I want to tell him I'll help him. Write a check to cover airfare and visa. Say that I'll sponsor him. I could help him. I could do it in a heartbeat.

But then there's Adrian and his family or any of the half-dozen other Romanians I've spoken to — who have expressed similar desires. How can I say, "I'll help this person, but not that one"? Feeling as if I'm carrying a guilty secret, I tell him that I hope it all works out for him.

It serves as a reminder of how lucky I am. I've reached a certain station in life because of happenstance. I have a God-given talent, and I was born in the right place at the right time. Right now in Romania there may be writers and artists who could leave in the dust everyone currently working in comics. Talented people, dreaming of fame and fortune. And all they will ever have are dreams.

May 19 — I'm spiralling downward, from people with hopeless dreams to people with no dreams.

We have moved to our first shooting location, and there are no chairs anywhere for the cast. I commandeer a driver to take me to a department store, where we can buy some folding chairs.

Outside the department store, I spot a beggar. Not a "homeless person" or an "indigent" or any name that takes the sting out of it: a beggar. At first I don't comprehend what I'm seeing. The old man is wearing his shirt open and appears to have a flesh-colored snake around his shoulder, moving and twitching spasmodically. My guide is not getting too close. I stay back, pull out my camera and zoom in so that I can understand what I'm viewing.

Most of his right arm is gone. The bare flesh is flapping around like a bony kite stuck on a tree. I'm on autopilot. I snap his picture, feeling unclean, and go over and put 500 lei in his box to try to wash myself.

We go into the department store, take the escalator to the third floor. As we pass the second, I can't believe what I see.

A child, a girl, somewhere between 5 and 8 years old, is following her mother, calling after her. Her skin is dark. She might have been beautiful, if given a chance.

She is on her knees. Walking on her knees.

Sort of.

Her legs don't bend back. They are bent forward, at the knees.

Her body is teetering at about an 80-degree angle, like a Gumby or a collapsing marionette. She half-pulls, half-shuffles along, sliding on her calves.

My guide sees what I've spotted. His face is impassive.

"What the hell is wrong with her?" I whisper. Grasping at the only explanation I can, I say, "Chernobyl?"

"Gypsies," he replies.

I don't understand and tell him so.

"You see a lot of gypsy children like that," he explains. "When they're a few months old, sometimes their parents break their knees or their elbows, or put out an eye. They figure it will help them make more money when they beg."

I nod.

We are looking at chairs, but I'm picturing a child who looks like my 8-year-old daughter, walking on reversed knees, calves scraping along the floor making sounds like sandpaper.

We are buying the chairs, but I'm picturing a baby who looks like the smiling one waiting for me at home, howling as a mallet or a sledge hammer or maybe a jagged rock shatters her joints.

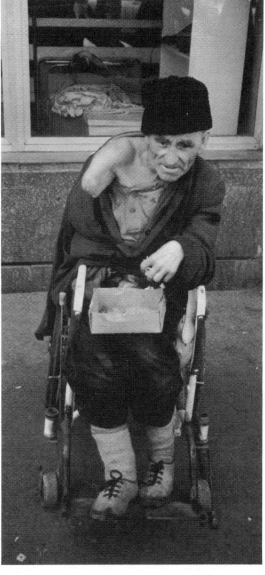

We get the chairs and go out a different exit. There's another gypsy child, begging. A boy. His legs go the wrong way. I'm in a Stephen King novel and can't close it. I take his picture from behind, unable to face him.

I buy a case of Coke for the cast, get back into the van, and almost break down.

I return to the set but am unable to remain. I can't get into filming make-believe. A number of off-duty cast members are going into town. I go with them.

We see no more Roger Cormanesque children. But there is one boy, begging, who is being yanked to his feet by his father, yelling at the boy and clearly prepared to cuff him because, however much money he might have taken in to that point, it obviously wasn't enough.

Clabe Hartley, who portrays our main villain, is watching. Clabe has a stone-cold dangerous stare. Clearly he's considering whether or not to make a move. Clabe's in terrific shape, versed in various fighting techniques; he could take the guy apart. The problem is that Clabe would wind up in jail, and the child would wind up in traction or on a slab when his father got through taking out his humiliation on the boy.

I'm not sure whether the father is aware Clabe is observing him. Perhaps he is, because abruptly he settles for yanking the boy to his feet and dragging him away. Clabe paces him for half a block, moving like a panther, still weighing options, before slowing and turning away.

There's nothing he can do.

Nothing anyone can do.

The boy was walking properly and had two eyes and two ears. I find myself wondering whether he still will meet all those conditions tomorrow.

Thoughts of concerts and practical jokes and nice dinners and the magic of movies are a million miles away. I wish I were a million miles away, as well.

God, get me the hell out of here.

May 20 — I watch my last day of shooting. A major sword duel is fought between heroine Shaleen (Terri Ivens) and villainous Lucius (Mark Arnold). It's breathtaking. As the actors go through take after take, they reach deeper into hidden reserves: grunting, howling, almost cursing as they slam together, swords clanging. Mark Arnold's Lucius is smug and assured, Terri Ivens' Shaleen feral and dangerous. It's a good match. If I hadn't written the script, I'd say it could go either way. At one point, though, Mark's sword slips and scrapes Terri's fingers. A halt is called as an essentially unhurt Terri is patched up, but Mark looks grief-stricken. After all, the Brandon Lee tragedy is still fairly fresh, and avoiding accidents is high on everyone's minds.

I see my first dailies. "Dailies" are supposed to be film that was shot the previous day and viewed the next shooting day. But because film is being shipped to Los Angeles for developing and then being returned to Romania, the process is just a tad longer. "Tri-weeklies" would be more like it.

Nevertheless, I'm impressed by what I see. Adolfo's meticulous lighting has paid off. The lighting is moody and consistent. And the sets don't look like sets. They look like rooms.

In short, the whole thing is starting to look like a movie.

Who would've thought it?

I have dinner with the cast this night, since it's my last night with them. They've developed into a solid family unit. They are working extremely well together. Not a single one is copping an attitude. It's good to see that happiness.

I needed to see it.

But it doesn't make the wrong-legged children go away. I don't think anything ever will.

May 21 — I have plenty of lei from my *per diem* left over, since I hardly spent any of it. The producers have told me that it's mine to do with as I wish; they don't want or need it back. I can't transfer it to U.S. dollars, so I start giving away huge tips to various folks in the hotel. They're gaping as I'm handing them thousands of lei and saying, "Here. Take it." It's useless to me, and, besides, you're not allowed to take more than 5000 lei (about seven bucks) out of the country.

I have a suspicion I'm handing these people as much money as they make in a couple of months.

At the airport, they run a metal detector rod over me. It stops at my wallet, and the security guy taps my side pocket, indicating I should remove it. "That's not metal," I say quietly. He taps it again. I pull it out and hand it to him. He flips through the billfold, finds maybe 200 lei. He makes a sound of loud annoyance. Obviously, he was hoping to find more. I'd heard that security guards at the airport regularly pocket any money over the 5000 limit. Sorry I couldn't oblige.

I sleep on the plane and dream of crippled children.

(Peter David, writer of stuff, can be written to c/o To Be Continued, Inc., PO Box 239, Bayport, N.Y. 11705.)

SECTION 10:

And Now for Something Completely Different

All right, I admit it. I didn't know where the hell to stick these entries. They were too warped to fit into any general category, but I didn't want to leave them out simply because they couldn't be pigeon-holed. If this were Jeopardy, they would be under "Hodgepodge" or "Potpourri" or something like that.

(Although, when it comes to Jeopardy categories, I've always liked James Fry's rendition of himself as a Jeopardy contestant, confidently encountering his dream category: "Alex, I'll take 'Things Only I Know' for $200.")

The artwork for the "Disney Heroine" roundtable came from Richard Howell, my collaborator on *Soulsearchers and Company* from Claypool Press. The artwork for "Take Your Daughter to Work Day" was by my 8-year-old, Jenny, to give it that authentic feel.

AN ANIMATED DISCUSSION (Jan. 1, 1993)

Snow: Well, this is all tremendously exciting. Every decade or so, the nice folks at Disney sponsor a get-together with all the lead actresses of recent animated features. This gives us a chance to chat, exchange tips on how to clean house —

Jasmine: Allah, give me strength.

Snow: — and, overall, just get to know each other as girls.

Belle: Women.

Snow: Since I was the first full-length Disney heroine, they generally ask me to moderate. And I'd like to welcome this year's guests — Princess Jasmine from *Aladdin* —

Jasmine: Is this going to take long?

Snow: Belle from *Beauty and the Beast* — and congratulations again on that Best Picture nomination.

Belle: Thank you. We were robbed. Losing to a cannibal — now, what does that say about society and its priorities? In the words of Sartre —

Snow: And, of course, Ariel from *The Little Mermaid*.

Ariel: It's exciting to meet you, Snow.

Snow: Thank you. Uhm, you're dripping on my clean floor.

Ariel: Oh. Sorry.

Snow: We *were* also going to be joined by Olivia Flaversham, the plucky little heroine from *The Great Mouse Detective*. But we had a bit of a mishap, because *someone* on the panel couldn't control her rather large kitty cat.

Jasmine: Look, I already *said* I was sorry. I'm no happier about it than anybody else. If the damned invitation had said there were going to be mice running around, I wouldn't have brought Rajah along in the first place. OK? Let's move on.

Snow: I must say, before we start, that I admit my breath is a bit taken away by the changes in clothing styles for Disney heroines. With your little harem outfit, Jasmine, and you, Ariel, with your — shells — and both of you with all that skin hanging out: It seems a trifle — what's the word?

Belle: Sluttish?

Ariel: Oh, well, thanks a lot! Big talk from someone whose idea of a good time is sitting around in an apron talking to sheep.

Belle: You talk to fish.

Ariel: But they talk back.

Snow: Actually, I was going to say "daring" rather than "sluttish." But this really brings us to our first point of discussion: Namely, what do you think our role in movies today should be?

Jasmine: I'll tell you what it *shouldn't* be. It shouldn't be sitting around waiting for someone to "take you away from it all." I mean, come *on*. Could you see me singing, "Some day my prince will come"? Ack ack ack.

Snow: You don't have to stick your finger down your throat and gag, Jasmine. It happens to be a lovely song.

Ariel: Jasmine's right. Life isn't something that happens to you. Life is what you make happen. You have to take control. That's what I did.

Jasmine: Me, too.

Belle: So did I.

Jasmine: Oh, sure. Right.

Belle: I did! Really!

Ariel: Sure you did. First you walked around town, looking down your nose and talking about how provincial all these hard-working villagers are and how there has to be more to life than that. If Cruella de Ville had sung the exact same thing, people would have said it was the most arrogant song ever written.

Belle: But —

Jasmine: And, while you said you want more out of life, you didn't *do* anything to get it.

Belle: Yes, I did! I gave up my liberty, sacrificing for my father! I promised I'd stay a prisoner in the Beast's castle, forever!

Ariel: Uh huh. And how long was it before you went running out the front door saying, "Promise or no promise, I can't stay here another minute?" A week? A month? A year?

Belle: Uhm — well, actually — about three, four hours, maybe. But there are such things as promises made under duress, and they're not always binding. Perhaps it's Machiavellian, but even so —

Jasmine: Well, *there's* a woman of her word. Some heroine.

Snow: Ladies, I think we're getting off the topic.

Jasmine: Me, I defied my father. I had the guts to go against what he said and run off.

Ariel: Your father. Heh.

Jasmine: What's that supposed to mean?

Ariel: The two of you with your fathers. You defied yours, she sacrificed for hers. And you've both got these roly-poly, cute, comedy-relief fathers. Me, I've got the King of the Sea for mine. He throws around energy bolts and can bench press a whale. I'm the only one with real guts here.

Belle: More guts than brains, that's for sure. Cutting deals with the Sea Witch. *There* was a smooth move. Obviously, if you'd ever read anything by Marlowe, you'd've realized the folly of that.

Snow: Belle, who are all these people you're talking about?

Belle: Authors. Playwrights. Philosophers. Crack open a book, why don't you? You, too, Miss Turkish Trunks. And you too, Fishy.

Ariel: I read books. Human books.

Belle: Oh, right. You can't remember tough words like "feet" and you don't know why fire burns. How'd they miss having you on *Jeopardy*, I wonder. Oh, and here's a news flash for you: It's a fork, OK? A *fork*. You eat food with a fork. You don't comb your hair with it. If you combed your hair with it, it would be called a *comb*, not a *fork*. All right, Einstein?

Jasmine: Some of us have royal duties to attend to and don't have a lot of time for books.

Belle: That is *so* typical. You three are just typical elitist examples of the societal class structure. All of you, born to royalty. Bored children of privilege.

Snow: But you're royalty, too! At the end of the movie, you married — uh — what *was* his real name?

Belle: I — don't know. Besides, I was talking about being born to entitlement. You lived your lives in castles, children of kings and queens — or at least kings, since there never seem to be any queens in Disney films. So you endured a couple of days of hardship, dabbling in the sort of life that I lived every single day, before you settled down with your prince. It's disgusting. Particularly you, Ariel, who totally subverted everything you were in order to be part of her man's world.

Ariel: Oh, yeah? You looked pretty comfortable strutting around in that big yellow gown at the end. I didn't see you fighting to remain a peasant.

Belle: That's all the underprivileged masses are to you, aren't they? Peasants. The Proletariat. In the words of Karl Marx —

Ariel: Oh, Lord, here she goes again.

Snow: Actually, this presents us with a topic that might not cause such bickering: Namely, what do you look for in a prince?

Ariel: Well, for me, it was love at first sight. I watched him dancing, and talking, and — I just knew.

Jasmine: "I just knew. I just knew." A guy flashes a smile and a royal title at you, and you get mushy. Love at first sight is a convenient excuse not to think.

Snow: Some of us, Jasmine, are fortunate enough to meet our prince and be drawn to him immediately. Others of us turn princes into kitty treats for our tigers.

Jasmine: Some of us, Snow, *prefer* thinking. Ariel, your prince was heroic enough, but about as thick as a brick.

Ariel: Why, you —

Jasmine: And you, Snow: You barely even *spoke* to the guy. How could you *possibly* have known he was the man for you? What about him could *possibly* have drawn you to him?

Snow: If you want to know why I love him so, it's in his kiss.

Jasmine: *That's* where it is?

Belle: You're really pathetic, Snow, you know that? Not that I can stand Ariel or Jasmine, but Eric defeated Ursula, and Ariel went off with him. Aladdin defeated Jafar, and Jasmine married Aladdin. But the dwarves —

Snow: Dwarfs.

Belle: Whatever — risked their lives for you — they adored you — and then some jerk prince comes along, gives you three seconds of liplock, and you abandon the dwarves —

Snow. Dwarfs.

Belle: *Whatever!* — and go riding off with him. What an ingrate.

Snow: *Sniff.*

Ariel: Oh, great. Now you made her cry.

Jasmine: She's a big girl. She can take it.

Ariel: That's about the kind of empathy I'd expect from someone who walks around in her pajamas all day.

Jasmine: Fish Face.

Ariel: Baklava Breath.

Belle: Ah, the upper class, displaying their typical —

Ariel and Jasmine: Shut up!

(*A young blonde girl enters.*)

Eilonwy: Excuse me? Am I too late for the meeting?

Snow: Who (*sniffle*) who are you?

Eilonwy: I'm Eilonwy. I'm a princess.

Belle: Oh, terrific. Another example of the —

Jasmine: I'm warning you, Belle, Rajah's still hungry.

Snow: I'm sorry, dear. You're who?

Eilonwy: Princess Eilonwy.

Snow: Well — I don't know who sent you here, but this is for Disney heroines.

Eilonwy: But I *am* a Disney heroine. I was in *The Black Cauldron*.

(*Blank stares from everyone.*)

Ariel: The what?

Eilonwy: Based on "The Chronicles of Prydain" books —

Snow: Books? Belle, I hate to ask —

Belle: Oh, right, now they come groveling.

Jasmine: Rajah! Time for din —

Belle: OK, OK. It was a fantasy series by Lloyd Alexander.

Characters TM and © 1992 Walt Disney Productions

Eilonwy: Right! And I was in the movie!

Jasmine: What movie?

Eilonwy: Oh, come on, didn't *anyone* see it? 1985? 80 minutes long? Supposed to usher in a new era of Disney animation?

Ariel: Actually, *my* film did that.

Jasmine: Oh, aren't we full of ourselves?

Eilonwy: Sword-and-sorcery epic? There was me and Taran the assistant pigkeeper, and Fflewddur Fflam —

Jasmine: You *must* be joking.

Snow: No, wait! I remember now. I got a ticket for an advance screening. But I was busy that night, so I sent Happy instead.

Eilonwy: What did he think?

Snow: He *hated* it. I've never seen Happy complain that much — or at all. But he just kept talking about how awful it was. Grumpy finally had to slap him.

Eilowny: That's not fair! We were ground-breaking!

Belle: Poor spoiled princess, just like all the others. Boohoo —

Jasmine: That's it. *Rajah!*

Rajah: Rawwrrrrrrr!

Belle: Eeeeeekk!

(Sebastian walks in)

Sebastian: Ariel, da king wants to know how long — eeeepp!

Rajah: Raarrrrrr!

Belle: Let me out! *Let me out!*

Sebastian: Ohhh mon!

Ariel: Put him down! I *mean* it!

Jasmine: Pajamas, huh?

Snow: You know, these discussion groups used to be fun. Me and Cindy, we'd sit and chat for hours. Sure, Aurora would keep dozing off —

Belle: Shut up! Knock off that high-pitched little-girl voice! It's making me nuts! And get me the hell out of here!

Snow: Well, I hope you'll all join us for our next discussion group.

Sebastian: Arrrieelll!

Rajah: *Chomp* *Chomp*

Ariel: Jasmine! Make him spit him out! Right now!

Snow: It's going to be called, "Life's a Bitch, and So Am I." Participants will be Lady from *Lady and the Tramp*, Perdita from *101 Dalmatians*, and Georgette from *Oliver and Company*. I'm sure the fur will really fly. Thanks for coming. Hi ho hi ho —

Rajah: *Urrrp.*

*(Peter David, writer of stuff, thanks Paul Dini for his contribution to the foregoing silliness. Also, Paul pointed out the Disney in-joke in **Aladdin** that almost no one spots: When the Sultan is seen playing with stacking toys, one of the toys on the left hand side is clearly a figure of The Beast. Sneaky, sneaky Disney —)*

Historical Notes:

1) I got a call from Dave Seidman at Disney Comics when this came out. He said, "I just want you to know, everyone here thought it was hysterical. Uhm — you weren't planning on working for Disney again any time soon, were you — ?"

WHAT THE DICKENS? (Jan. 22, 1993)

Well, I've just had the pleasure of seeing noted actor Patrick Stewart performing one of the best pieces of science fiction I've ever seen.

Not *Star Trek: The Next Generation*, of course. No, most episodes are little more than wastes of Stewart's time and talent. No, I'm talking about that science-fiction classic that has been part of world literature since the middle of last century. Yes, that's right: *A Christmas Carol* by master science-fiction writer Charles Dickens.

What's that you're saying? *Christmas Carol* is not science fiction? It wouldn't make anyone's list of top ten SF stories?

I don't see why not.

I've been doing a lot of thinking about *Christmas Carol* lately. In preparation for taking the two older children to see Stewart's one-man performance on Broadway, I read them the entire text over a week. It helped remind me of how my perceptions of the story changed over time.

When I was a child, for example — and my main exposure to the story was *Mr. Magoo's Christmas Carol* — I didn't understand who the story was about. Not what, but *who*.

Just as I thought that Disney's *Mary Poppins* was about the title character, when, in fact, it was really about the father (he's the one who changes, after all), I thought *Christmas Carol* was about Bob Cratchit. I found Bob and his family — and most of all, of course, Tiny Tim — to be far more accessible. This despite the fact that, in the book, Cratchit is merely one of a number of richly drawn and detailed denizens of Scrooge's world, along with Fezziwig; nephew Fred; Scrooge's lost love, Belle; and so on. A less important facet, in fact, considering that Bob's not even named in the text for the first half of the book, but merely referred to as "the clerk."

Nevertheless, Scrooge was to me, just as he was to Tiny Tim, merely a monster. I thought that the main reason for the visitation of the four ghosts was to change Scrooge, but with the ultimate goal being the saving of Tiny Tim's life, not Scrooge's soul.

It may well be that with recent feature film adaptations of the story, featuring such recognizable characters as Mickey Mouse and Kermit the Frog in the role of Cratchit, a new generation of viewers might get the same impression.

Which is fine. Children find their own entry points into stories.

But as adults, we should understand that *Christmas Carol* is, of course, one of the great SF stories — speculative fiction, if the "science" aspect is too stringent for you — of all time.

Now, we know it's not a psychological horror story. That implies that maybe it really happened or maybe it was in Scrooge's mind.

But that doesn't hold up. Scrooge, in his forays through his life, becomes privy to all sorts of information that he could not possibly have had. I doubt that he was familiar with Cratchit's family, and I'm positive that he could not possibly have known the friends of his nephew, Fred — yet he meets them on his sojourn and everything he encounters is borne out. No, beyond question — it happened. But *what* happened?

You could claim it was a simple ghost story. And, if the entire tale had revolved around Ebenezer being terrorized in his house by the ghost of the deceased Jacob Marley, I might swallow it.

But the vast majority of *Christmas Carol* involves a plot device that is so much a part of SF that to classify it as anything other than SF would be an injustice.

That plot device, of course, is time travel.

All three of the Christmas spirits take Scrooge on journeys through time and space. Christmas Past takes him on a journey from his childhood to a point a mere seven years previous. Christmas Present, although ostensibly the spirit of the here-and-now, in fact time jumps all over the next 23 hours. (I mean, if he were genuinely the ghost of Christmas Present, and *only* the present, he would merely have been able to show Scrooge what was going on at 1 in the morning, which was when he showed up.) Not only that, but he can see events a year down the line, as he (correctly) predicts that Tiny Tim will not be alive to see another Christmas.

Christmas Yet-to-Come, obviously, takes him to the future — a future that includes the death of Tiny Tim and Scrooge's own unmourned demise.

And if time travel isn't enough to claim *Christmas Carol* for the realm of SF, the latter two spirits don't merely travel into just *any* future. Instead, they actually explore parallel universes — alternate time lines, if you will — because the Christmas day presented by the spirit to Scrooge is not the one that actually occurs. The Cratchits feast on a substantially larger bird than they had originally eaten, and Scrooge is present at his nephew's Christmas gathering, when, in the original time line, he had been absent.

And as for Christmas Yet-To-Come, we know — because Dickens tells us so — that Tiny Tim did *not* die. And, presumably, when Scrooge did eventually kick off, there were plenty of people who were choked up about it, rather than the London folk who previously greeted the news with *sang-froid* and chilly dispatch.

But now, of course, we have a problem.

Having made the assertion that *Christmas Carol* is SF, we cannot stick with the assumption that the ghosts are merely ghosts. Because then we're introducing elements of unexplained fantasy, and that doesn't really work in the world of SF.

What we *do* have is the credo that any science, if sufficiently advanced, will seem like magic to people who don't understand it (which is certainly the only hope in hell that *Star Trek: The Next Generation*, with its replicators and holodecks, its transporters-with-no-receivers, and its faster-than-light drive that defies Einstein's theories, could possibly have, if it's to be classified as SF).

If we say that the ghosts are just ghosts, then it's mere fantasy.

But what if — what if —

There were no ghosts.

Not ghosts in the way that supernatural literature would describe.

What if, in fact, it *were* a sort of psychological thriller — but steeped in science fiction?

What if the ghosts did not come from an outside agency but were, in fact, created by Scrooge himself?

But how? How would that be possible?

Get ready. The Marvel Zombies are going to love this.

Ebenezer Scrooge was a mutant.

Before you start screaming, stick with me on this one.

Scrooge's main power was a combination of time travel. He also had the power of telepathic projection, projecting images of his own devising and also from history or literature.

The quickest way to attack this argument is to say, of course, "Well, hell, if he had this power, why didn't it manifest until he was old? And why, for the first time, on that particular Christmas Eve?"

Ah, but it *did* manifest much earlier on. We can infer a couple of examples and at least once — as I will now describe — we see it directly.

When he visits himself as a young man, alone in his boarding school, he suddenly spots "a man, in foreign garments: wonderfully real and distinct to look at" standing at the window. The man is identified as Ali Baba, and a host of other literary figures parade past.

Notice the utter lack of qualifiers. Dickens doesn't say that Scrooge *thought* he saw them or *fancied* he saw them. In fact, Dickens goes out of his way to note how real they are — as real, one would surmise, as the Spirits. Scrooge recognizes them as he would old friends. Obviously, this image projection was routine in his youth, so routine that it didn't strike him as out of the ordinary to see it.

His power increased as he got older. Marvel tradition has it that mutant powers don't fully kick in until adolescence. That's how it was in Scrooge's case.

Here's where we get into inferences — but Dickens was nothing if not a meticulous storyteller, and the way in which he does not explain certain aspects of the tale would seem to be red flags to the reader.

Before our eyes, the child Scrooge ages. His stature changes, but his environment does not. It would seem that he is destined to spend another Christmas in his miserable boarding school.

But wait! In runs, totally unannounced, his little sister. Her mission, she announces jubilantly, is to take young Scrooge home. She bubbles:

"Home, forever and ever. Father is so much kinder than he used to be, that home's like Heaven! — And you're to be a man! — and are never to come back here — !"

Her comment about his becoming a man is a clear reference to the fact that he's hit puberty. There is the clue that he's now an adolescent, with his mutant power manifesting at full strength.

But what's even more important is the timing of it all. Just when Scrooge's power really kicks in, suddenly — with no explanation whatsoever — Scrooge's father abruptly undergoes a change of heart.

Why?

What in the world could have motivated Papa Scrooge to do such a massive turnaround?

Dickens never says. No hint is given. He's just "so much kinder," and that's that.

Then again, Dickens doesn't *have* to spell it out, does he?

Someone undergoing a change of heart — just in time for the Christmas holidays?

It's too obvious.

Scrooge "scrooged" his own father.

Obviously, Scrooge's power is governed to a large degree by his subconscious. This would be consistent with Dickens' description of a man who was not given over to flights of fancy (his parade of literary figures notwithstanding).

Subconsciously, Scrooge was sick of his dreary life. Subconsciously, Scrooge wanted to do something about it. And, subconsciously, Scrooge did.

We have no idea whether Papa Scrooge was visited by the same sorts of manifestations that Ebenezer eventually visited upon himself. It would seem logical. It's clear that *something* happened to make Papa Scrooge see the light. And the immediate beneficiary was prodigal son Ebenezer, who came home for the holidays, never to be exiled again.

But as Scrooge grew older — as his attention turned toward money and greed — his heart hardened, and his power darkened. He became, you should pardon the expression, Dark Scrooge.

Another Christmas, and, bang, someone else in Scrooge's life "saw the light." His beloved Belle dumped him at a time of year when most people are in a festive mood. What could have been the catalyst for such a decision? Could it have been "ghosts" which showed Belle an endless future lifetime of being shackled to the money-hungry miser? And could these visions have prompted Belle to decide that she could — that she was, in fact, well-advised to — seek a husband elsewhere?

Maaaaaybe.

But now, now we get to the latter years of Scrooge's life. Although on the surface he is happy, his subconscious dwells on the fact that his life is, essentially, meaningless. He has no one. He loves no one. No one gives a damn about him — least of all himself. The cocky certainty of "Dark Scrooge" gives way to his deep-down awareness of his own mortality.

Inwardly, he starts to realize that something has to change.

And his power starts to stir.

It's seven years before the start of *Christmas Carol*, and his subconscious realizes that Scrooge is going to have trouble changing, because his partner, Jacob Marley, is cut from the same cloth. Even if Scrooge did undergo a change of heart, Marley would probably tell him he'd lost his mind — maybe even convince him that it had all been a dream.

So he has to get Jacob Marley to change first. It's consistent, after all; most of Scrooge's life, his power has functioned to change the people around him rather than he himself.

It's right around Christmas, the time of year when, for whatever mysterious reason, the mutant power of Ebenezer Scrooge is at its strongest.

Some manifestation of his power leaps out (probably while Scrooge is sleeping) and Jacob Marley suddenly finds himself face-to-face with some sort of bizarre apparition. Perhaps another deceased financier of their mutual acquaintance.

And it backfires — because Marley has a heart attack. He dies shortly thereafter — on Christmas Eve, in fact.

I can just see it: "Jacob Marley, you will be visited by three ghosts — "

"Accck!" Thud.

"Or — maybe not."

Yes, once again — far too many times for coincidence, by any rational stretch of the imagination — something major happens in Scrooge's life right at Christmas. Dickens doesn't say that Marley was visited by ghosts — but by this point, certainly we can't turn our thoughts away from the inevitable conclusions.

Deep, deep down where the aspects of Scrooge's mind that control his power lie, Ebenezer is horrified and shocked that his power has brought about the death of his partner. The power hides away, safe and sound.

But Scrooge's inward body clock ticks away and, year upon passing year, the concerns as to his own mortality become stronger and stronger.

And finally, finally, his subconscious can take it no longer. That part of him that manipulates his mutant power decides that enough is enough. Ebenezer Scrooge will be made to face directly, for the first time since he was a very young boy in that drafty, broken-down schoolhouse, the images and temporal powers that his mutant mind can bring forth.

It will happen — big shock here — on Christmas Eve.

And Scrooge will be the better man for it.

Just think, boys and girls: If Charles Dickens were writing now, instead of then, and whipping this story up for Marvel —

You just *know* what the title would be.

Yes, that's right. Not *A Christmas Carol*, no. We'd have seen Patrick Stewart performing in —

The Uncanny X-Mas.

God save us, every one.

(Peter David, writer of stuff, will next theorize how Mary Poppins was actually a Time Lord, and her carpet bag was actually her TARDIS, which would explain how it was able to transport her [the umbrella was just a prop] and how she could fit so much stuff into it, and — eh, maybe not.)

TAKE YOUR DAUGHTER TO WORK DAY (May 28, 1993)

Michelle Weizel   April 29, 1993
Mrs. Rosetti's class   Fourth Grade

For "Take Your Daughter to Work Day," my dad took me to where he works with the American Justice Alliance. That is where my dad works because my dad is a super-hero. He has been a super-hero for a very very very very long time.

He was not always a super-hero. He was a super-hero for a while and then he stopped being one when I was born. But when I was one year old, my ma was killed by bad guys and my daddy says he learned that day that he could not not be a super-hero because he always had to fight bad guys.

He also says that he is waiting for mommy to come back from the dead. I wish he would stop saying that. It's a little creepy. He says he is sure it's going to happen, but I don't think so. And he tells my teachers that at the parent-teacher conferences because he doesn't like going to them, and he always tells my teachers, "Maybe next year my wife will have come back from the dead and she'll come instead of me." I know he is still doing it because my teachers point at me and whisper big words like "cycletherapy," whatever that is, and how I'm going to end up riding one or something like that.

My dad's name is Wylie Weizel. That is his plain name. But when he was a teen-ager he got some kind of powers from something nuclear. My teachers say that nuclear stuff kills people. My dad says that teachers don't know anything about it and that nuclear stuff is really good for you. I don't know for sure. I guess my daddy is right. But I still think he shouldn't have big bunches of his hair falling out all at once like that.

His super-hero name is Wild Weasel. I think it's a silly name myself. I told him so once. He told me that he had to call himself that because it was so close to his own name, and when you have an own

194

My Daddy
Wild Weasel
By Michelle
Weizel

name that could be made into a super-name real easy, you're supposed to do it. He says it's a rule or something. I don't know. In the comics, Clark Kent doesn't sound like Superman and Peter Parker doesn't sound like Spider-Man, and people seem to like them just fine. Daddy says I'll understand when I get older.

The American Justice Alliance is a group of heroes like daddy, except I don't think most of their names are as silly as "Wild Weasel." My daddy and I always have breakfast together. Today he made me french toast. Sometimes he makes me scrambled eggs or eggs sunnyside up. He says breakfast is the most important meal of the day. He also likes prune juice.

He is always smiling and joking and being so nice. Which is why what happened when he took me to work was so weird.

Daddy put on his costume. I think his costume is kind of silly but not as silly as his name. The silliest is his mask, but he says he needs the costume because he has to "get into character." I'm not sure what that means, and he had trouble explaining it. He drove us to work in this special car he drives called the "Weasel Whacker." He says that it's called that because he uses it to whack criminals. But one time he had some of his super-friends over for a party, and they were making jokes about it when daddy was out of the room. I heard them from upstairs. I didn't understand the jokes, and when I came down and asked about them his friends got all red and said it was nothing. That it was "the drinks talking." I didn't know drinks could talk.

Daddy said today that he was on monitor duty. It's kind of like being paid to watch television all day, except there's nothing on that's any good. He took me to AJA headquarters which is this big place inside of a big cave. You take an elevator to get down to it. The elevator plays music. I didn't recognize the song. He said the person who sang the song is dead. I asked my daddy if he killed him, but my daddy just laughed.

Daddy took me to the monitor room. It's a big place with all these TV screens. There was all kinds of things on them like streets and ambulances and stuff. My father said it was important to watch because it was real life. He got a little mad when I told him that Nickelodeon was better, and he said he didn't know if he wanted me watching "Salute Your Shorts" any more because it was stupid. I thought sitting around watching TV with nothing good on was stupid, but I didn't say so.

What was weird was that daddy acted like himself when it was the two of us. But then another of his super-friends came in.

He was this big guy who can make wind come up from nowhere. He's called Major Blow, although sometimes daddy makes jokes about that too that I don't understand. But he says them kind of softly to himself, so I don't think I'm supposed to understand them.

Anyway, Major Blow came in and said something about daddy being "stuck with" monitor duty. And daddy started talking real strange. He didn't act like himself at all. He started snarling and bending over and waving his claws. And his eyeballs disappeared and got all white, and he started using silly words like "Fraggin'" and "Holy Spit" and something that I didn't understand at all but which sounded kind of like #*@&! I think all of them were supposed to sound like dirty words, but they just sounded silly.

And then daddy started fighting with Major Blow, which was really silly because they're supposed to be on the same side.

Daddy said something about "needing a workout," and Major Blow said, "You had this coming a long time," and they started jumping around and blowing and weaseling and things.

They wrecked up some stuff and what was really weird was that they kept talking the whole time. Whole sentences and stuff. I don't know how they managed to do that, because I've seen fights at school between some of the bigger boys, and they don't talk. They kind of grunt and slap at each other and push and shove, and the most they ever say is, "I'm going to tell." So it was a weird fight.

I started to cry a little, and my daddy and Major Blow saw, and they stopped fighting. And my daddy said, "You made her cry!" And Major Blow said that my daddy had made me cry, and called him another one of those "cycle" words, and they fought a little more. I said I didn't know why they were fighting. My daddy said it was to fill up time and to show how their powers worked. It seemed silly to me.

Then we heard a real loud noise. My daddy said it was the alarm. That there was a bad guy doing something real bad, and they had to go stop him. Major Blow said I should wait in the cave, but daddy said I was supposed to go with him to work, and this was part of work, and I should go.

So I went.

We went in this real fast jet and got to the place where the bad guy was. He was in this big building which my daddy said was a bank. There were lots of policemen outside, and they acted like they didn't know what to do at all. My daddy and Major Blow said that they would handle it, and the policemen looked real happy. I don't understand why, because I thought it was the policemen's job to arrest people. If I had a job like that, I wouldn't be happy having someone else doing my job for me. I think that's lazy. Daddy says that's the way it is.

The policemen said there were people still inside who the bad guy said he was going to hurt. And then someone got thrown right through a window. Major Blow saved them. Then another person got thrown out the window, and this time my daddy saved them. Major Blow said that with all these people being thrown out of windows, the bad guy was probably "The Defenestrator." My daddy said "fragging" and other silly words again. He was snarling a lot and kind of drooling, like he was real crazy. But at one point he winked at me. I think it was to let me know that it was all pretend.

Then daddy and Major Blow ran towards the bank, yelling and shouting and blowing. I ran after them. Major Blow blew open the bank doors, and there was The Defenestrator. He was very big and very mean looking. He talked real loud, and he didn't have any eyeballs either, just like daddy. Except his eyes were red.

And his face was solid white, like a clown's, but he looked a little scarier.

They started to fight. They talked a lot, too.

I didn't want to get hit by any of the flying things, so I hid behind a desk. There was another little girl there. She was very pretty. She had black hair. She smiled at me and I smiled back.

I asked her who she was. She said her name was Stephanie.

She said she was here for "Take Your Daughter to Work" day. I asked if her parent worked at the bank. She said, "Kind of. He's robbing it." I asked her what it was like having a bad guy for a father.

She told me about what it was like at home, and it sounded pretty much like what we had, except her daddy likes cereal in the morning. Also sometimes she has to be by herself at home because her daddy is in jail. But that's usually only for a short time, because he breaks out a lot.

She got a little mad when I told her that my daddy was Wild Weasel and that he put her daddy in jail sometimes. She said that when good guys fight bad guys it isn't fair. Because the good guys gang up on the bad guys, and that's not right.

I couldn't say she was wrong, because my daddy and Major Blow were ganging up on The Defenestrator. That was two against one. That didn't seem fair.

So I walked into the middle of the fight and told them to stop. That it wasn't fair and that they should fight one against one. And Major Blow and my daddy got all red, and The Defenestrator laughed and said I was right. Daddy said this was grown-up stuff and I didn't understand. I said he was the one who taught me about fair is fair.

So my daddy fought The Defenestrator by himself and got thrown out a window. And then Major Blow fought him and he got thrown out a window, too.

And Stephanie and her daddy escaped.

Major Blow got even madder than ever, but my daddy said they'd get him next time. Major Blow said he thought that my daddy should never have brought me and that "Take Your Daughter to Work Day" was stupid and said he was glad he didn't have any children. And daddy said something about being glad too and something about a jean pool being glad, and then they fought some more.

Daddy took me out to Friendly's for dinner. He wasn't in his costume any more, and his eyes were back, and he wasn't drooling or anything. And he asked me if I wanted to be a super-hero when I grew up. And I said no. I told him I want to be the person who fixes windows after fights. I think I can make a lot of money. He said I was probably right.

At night, after he tucked me in and read me a story, I snuck out of bed and called Stephanie, because she'd given me her phone number. We're going to play together this weekend. She says her daddy has a neat make-up case that he lets her borrow sometimes.

I can't wait.

(Peter David, writer of stuff, thanks Mrs. Rosetti for sharing her class essay with him. Unfortunately, the other essay she sent, "My mommy goes to make a porn movie," will not see print any time soon.)

SECTION 11:

Social Studies

or
Don't Know Much about History

Every so often, I take off on a flight of social consciousness and try to write about things that are actually happening in the world outside of comic books (yes, there is such a thing). Most of the time I manage to make it relate in some distant manner to our collective industry/hobby. On occasion I make no such effort at all, and at those times I depend on my editors and readers to indulge me.

Several times I teed off on George Bush and Dan Quayle. These garnered some of the nastiest responses of anything I've ever written — particularly when I dared to question Desert Storm, anti-abortion rallies, and other touchy subjects. I was going to include some of them, but, in reading them over now, they are among those columns most hurt by the passage of time. With no immediacy, they also have little bite.

Don't worry, though. I'm sure that, in the columns you're about to read, you'll find *something* to get upset about.

AUNTIE VIOLENCE (April 19, 1991)

I can't wait to see if the inevitable next edition of the Teenage Mutant Ninja Turtles video game, in addition to The Shredder (or as smaller kids pronounce it, "The Sweater"), Rock Steady, and other comic-book and cartoon enemies of the Shell Shockers, will feature an appearance by the Turtles' newest and potentially most deadly foe — The People Who Assume I'm an Incompetent Parent.

Their names are irrelevant, as are the names of whatever organizations they've created, thrown together in basements or living rooms furnished with plastic-covered furniture. Of late they seem to be mostly women, although that gender is not a requirement. And they've been around certainly for as long as I can remember.

They are clever; you must give them that. In the past they've managed to outwit Bugs Bunny, take the fight out of Race Bannon, and blow Space Ghost right into null space. And now: They've set their sights on the Multimillionaires of Mayhem, the Toitles.

There they were: two women with the exact same kind of expression worn by the head of "Parents against Funny Cartoons" who made a brief appearance on *Tiny Toon Adventures* protesting the violence of the "Anvil Chorus" (right before she got smeared by an anvil — wish fulfillment in action). They managed to bag some airtime on *Entertainment Tonight* so that they could launch an assault against the "excessive violence" in the subterranean world of the Turtles.

They say they're worried about what children might learn from the Turtles, we are told. They're concerned that kids might pick up violent ways from the Turtles. They will be encouraged to take action against their playmates and karate-chop them to kibble. And so the Turtles must be stopped.

Their main ire was aimed towards the new Turtles film (which I have not yet seen). Actually, it was backlash from the first one which, again, drew charges of being much too violent. No blood was shed, of course. No gore splattered across the screen. But it was too violent for the children.

And makers of the new Turtles film stated how they had made sure to tone down the Turtles for their latest screen venture. They wanted to make sure that protesting parents didn't have to be worried that children will be corrupted and badly influenced.

My question is — which children?

The children of the protesters? Of course, as parents they have the right to prevent their kids from going to see a Turtles film. They have the right to make sure their kids don't watch the Turtles cartoon show. Or buy the cereal or the frozen pizza. If I were going to lodge a protest against anything, it would be against the Turtles' dessert pie, which is not only an assault against aesthetics, but looks like it has snot coming out of it.

And these women, with my blessing, can stop their own kids from ingesting or digesting Turtles to their heart's content. I acknowledge this.

What *they* do not seem to acknowledge is that I have the right, as a parent, to bring my kid to a Turtles movie and let her watch the chop-socky action. They assume that any competent parent would agree with them — and, if the parent doesn't agree with them, then the parent must be incompetent and protected from him/herself.

Or perhaps they're concerned that my 9-year-old daughter is going to go out after watching Turtles and beat up on their kid. Maybe it's first-strike mentality: Stop violence at its source (TV, movies, etc.) and we can eliminate *all* violence in children.

Protesting parents will occasionally cite studies that show kids watching, say, *GI Joe*, then picking up guns and playing *GI Joe*-like games, and claim cause and effect. On the face of it, it seems simple enough logic: no more *GI Joe*, and therefore no more violent play. If children are shielded from such "entertainment," they will be nice and polite and never get into any sort of physical trouble.

Unfortunately, this logic fails to pass what I refer to as the Yeah? So? test. This test functions as follows:

Statement: "Children watch the Turtles and start doing kung fu stuff."

Response: "Yeah? So?"

Statement: "Well, don't you see that it means that kids will start jumping around and acting like the Turtles? That they'll play violent karate games?"

Response: "Yeah? So?"

The attitude is that violent play is learned from Turtles. Or GI Joe. Or Bugs Bunny.

It's not. *Method of play* may be learned, yes. But violence — that cuts far more deeply.

What was playing in the Triplex during the French and Indian War? Was John Wilkes Booth chowing down on Twinkies before he killed Lincoln? Did Saddam Hussein watch a videotape of *The Terminator* 20 times before he launched missiles or assassinated citizens? What was on the tube when Cain killed Abel?

If it's not Turtles vs. Shredder, or GI Joe vs. Cobra, then it's cops and robbers or cowboys and Indians.

You can argue that violence is part of our society. You can argue that violence is an inherited trait. You can argue the whys and wherefores of violence, write entire papers on it, make a career out of analyzing it. But arguing that TV, movies, books, etc. *cause* violence is specious. It is, to my mind, unfounded.

Some of the most violent, most obnoxious children I know have parents who make it a point never to let those kids watch Turtles or "junk" and discourage any sort of violent play. It's as if the violent energy, unable to channel itself, explodes out of every pore into malicious mischief.

I know one woman who survived the concentration camps of World War II and was so anti-war and anti-tools of war that she never bought her son anything remotely resembling a toy gun. So what happened? The kid would pick up a broom or a mop, aim the handle at his friends, and shout, "Bang! Bang!"

You think kids are taught violence by the Turtles? What about when they see adults eagerly discussing boxing or hockey brawls or war? Enjoying it, revelling in it. Maybe the Turtles say that fighting is cool, but so do adults, and I have a sneaking suspicion that the adults have more influence than Turtles do.

I have never forgiven the protecters of morals for "protecting" me from my favorite Saturday-morning shows when I was a kid: knocking all the cartoon super-heroes off the air and replacing them with puerile shows like *Hong Kong Phooey*. Carving the action out of classic Warner Bros. cartoons, a maneuver I still don't comprehend, because the parents who want the mayhem out of Bugs Bunny cartoons *grew up with that mayhem*. So what are they saying about themselves? That the mayhem unhinged them? Then we shouldn't listen to them because they're crazy. That the mayhem *didn't* unhinge them? Then what are they complaining about?

If I was going to complain about violence at all, it would be that there's not enough. If there's anything I find offensive about the entire concept of comic-book violence, it's that it shows actions without consequences. People get punched and spring right up, cartoon-like, with no effect.

If we're doing our youth any disservice, it's depicting scenarios where we don't show what really happens when someone gets injured: clean and tidy brutality. (Which is why I always enjoyed *Remington Steele*. When Steele made the mistake of punching someone in the jaw, he would invariably clutch at his fist and curse himself out for doing so. And for good reason.)

But you don't see people lobbying to see more blackened eyes and bloodied noses. No one goes on *Entertainment Tonight* and states that the next time Leonardo hits someone in the head, we should show that individual suffering a concussion. No, they are saying that the violence should be toned down to an acceptable level.

Acceptable violence. Is that like acceptable deaths? How much violence can we live with? More to the point: How much nonsensical railing against the entertainment media are we supposed to live with?

Cartoons cause violence. Comics cause violence. Books, magazines, radio shows, television, records, rock concerts, all cause violence. And they should all be stopped.

I got one for you: Some nut goes on TV and claims that, throughout the history of humanity, millions of people have been maimed, tortured, and killed in the names of various gods. Therefore, organized religion should be abolished in the United States.

Oh, the hullabaloo we'd hear about that! And rightly so. This country was founded on freedom of religion. To try to eliminate it strikes at the core of what America is all about.

Of course, it's also about freedom of expression, just as much as religion. And that that annoying freedom of expression extends to movies, TV, books — and even Turtles.

Totally awesome, dude.

*(Peter David, writer of stuff, was once watching **The Agony and the Ecstasy** on TV, and his youngest daughter asked what the film was about. He replied, "It's about an artist named Michelangelo." "Oh, I know about him," she said. "Really? What do you know about him?" he asked. And she replied sagely, "Michelangelo is a party dude."*

BOY TOYS (Dec. 20, 1991)

The wonderful thing about being an adult is that, when you walk into a toy store, you don't have to ask your parent's permission to buy something.

It's great. I see little boys tugging on their mother's sleeves or skirts, using that magic word with startling rapidity when just the night before at the dinner table, they couldn't remember it to save their life. "Please," they beg, "please, please, please, pleezpleezpleez — "

There are the little boys grasping towards the new line of X-Men toys. Toys where they can don a clawed glove to be like Wolverine or a Cyclops mask with working visor (although whether the visor will, in fact, contain the power of a force beam is subject to debate; there's nothing on the box about it).

However, I don't pay as much attention to the little boy toys (except when it's something I want, of course). With only female-type offspring in my brood, my Hanukkah want-lists (generously provided yearly, and even semi-annually, by my daughters) are generally filled — not with super-hero *chachkas* — but with the latest in Barbie fashions or Pretty Pretty Princess or something else packaged in pink and lavender.

(At least this year I can be grateful that the license we all thought was dead, but which has now returned from its little plush grave, did not make the David family cut. Yes, there were no requests at *casa* David for the new line of "Care Bears," and I tend to think this does not bode well for the manufacturer. Why? Because my kids want *everything*. Whatever commercial hits the airwaves, one or the other of the two older girls invariably says, "Oh, Daddy, pleeeeease!" When the commercials for Care Bears come on, my kids go to the kitchen for a snack. No, it does not bode well at all.)

However, this year, upon perusing the toy store aisles and noticing such intriguing oddities as that, in the new action figure line based on *Hook*, the captain of the title has his hook on the wrong hand, I began to take notice of something that was really rather interesting.

Actually, the only reason I took notice of it was because my wife pointed it out to me. She reminded me of something that we, as young people and teen-agers of the 1960s and '70s, and parents of the '80s, had been fighting for during those decades. A small but determined battle that seemed, at the time, to have a great deal of merit.

It was something that we had been acutely aware of when our first child was born and we were determined to carry through on the concept that she could grow up to be anything she wanted to be.

Now let's be honest here. This philosophy is far more important to parents of girls. Because, you see, parents of boys know that, in today's society, the odds are much greater that their child really *can* grow up to be anything he wants. But parents of girls, when they say this to their kids, are whistling in the dark. The fact is that, although great progress has been made, girls really *can't* grow up to be whatever they want, because a society run by males won't let them.

But no parent wants to say to his or her daughter, "You can be whatever you want, within limits." So instead parents do what they can to try to make this prediction as true as possible. And generally, they start young. The first vow that is made is that their kids will be raised in an atmosphere that is entirely free of gender bias.

The problem is there's only so much you can do. You can be supportive of your daughter when she wants to play in the local softball league. You cannot wince, if your son wants a doll.

(When I was a kid and *Mary Poppins* was in the theaters, I saw that Sears was offering a neat-looking doll of her. Already a budding Disneyana fan, I asked my father about it, and he looked at me in horror. "You want a *doll*?" he said, staring at me as if I'd just sprouted antlers. And I quickly said, "Who — me? No. Of course not. I just thought it would make, uh, a nice present for Lori Kane [the little girl who lived two doors down]." My father nodded, relieved albeit still a bit suspicious. I'm half-tempted to call him right now and say, "Hey, Dad! I just bought the fashion doll of Belle from *Beauty and the Beast* and I keep it in my display case in my office, next to my Ariel doll! Guess that means I'll grow up to be a sissy, huh, Dad?! Bwwwaa-ha-ha!")

Where all this is going is that, as a parent, one wonders when the toy companies as a whole will catch up with this forward thinking. Toys that don't bludgeon children into accepting pre-determined roles have been something that parents have requested for decades.

Judging by our recent stroll through Toys-R-Us, it ain't going to happen anytime soon.

What I discovered, with my wife pointing out some of the greatest offenders, was that toy manufacturers are helping to determine for us just what precisely is expected of specific genders, virtually from the moment kids become self-aware, through to when they're teen-agers. Many toys give very precise outlines of what is expected and what is acceptable.

Now, granted, there are tons of early-learning toys that are designed to stimulate the senses, prime the imagination, and stir the child further to new intellectual heights. But most of these toys are much more easily found in small specialty stores located in larger malls. The places where the real action is — Toys-R-Us, Playworld, Kay-Bee — these places are the domain of Fisher Price, Playskool, Little Tykes, Tyco, and the like. And these companies, through packaging and design, are gearing many of their products into stereotyped and "accepted" roles.

The first thing you notice when inspecting toys with an eye towards role control is the basic coloring. Now, we're all used to Barbie toys being packaged in pink and purple to a degree where — when you see them all lined up in an aisle — you have to fight back a gagging reflex.

But the color coding extends beyond that. Because what you don't notice immediately is that "boy" toys are consistently packaged in strong, vibrant, primary colors. We're not talking about limiting it to the traditional "blue for boys" motif. No, all the most powerful colors of the spectrum adorn boy packages: patriotic red, white, and blue, followed by vigorous yellow and green. Red, yellow, and green are colors of command. Don't believe me? Check out a traffic light. Not only do the boxes carry these colors, but frequently the models on the boxes are wearing clothes in similar hues.

Boy's toys are dynamic, forceful, take-charge colors. Girls, on the other hand, have all their toys packaged in pink, lavender, and other soft, non-dynamic, non-threatening, non-take-charge colors.

And then there are the *types* of toys.

To clarify here: when I discuss "girls' toys" vs. "boys' toys," I'm differentiating based on the clearly intended market. Girls' toys not only have the color coding, but also have a little girl demonstrating the toy on the box; Boys' toys have little boys doing the modeling. The usage is obvious. Of course, you can buy boy-packaged toys for your girl and vice versa. But we're discussing *intent* here. Besides, what if you want to give it as a gift for someone else? Are you *sure* how they'll react if you give a "boys'" toy to their little girl, or vice versa? Probably not — and why take the risk?

They start you when you're still in the crib, and, coincidentally, the discrimination is the most outrageous at a time when the kids are youngest. Playskool manufactures, for six-months-and-up little girls, "Baby's First Purse." Pink, of course, with various teething rings and such in the shapes of keys and all the other things you'd find in a typical purse. (Although my personal favorite object, a teething tampon, is mysteriously absent.)

OK. Fine. Women carry purses. So what does Playskool offer as the equivalent for boys? The logical thing would be "Baby's First Wallet," right? Or perhaps "Baby's First Briefcase?"

Uh uh. Little boys get "Baby's First Doctor's Kit."

That's laying it on the line early on, ain't it?

If that were isolated, it would be one thing. But it carries through, all through the developmental years.

Is your little girl trying to learn to walk, and you want to get her a walking toy? One of those things with handles and wheels for her to push? Then you're invited to buy the Playskool Steady Steps Grocery Shopping Cart or the Fisher-Price Walker Stroller to push your baby doll or the Fisher-Price Pick Up and Go Vacuum cleaner. If you're a boy, however, then you get the Playskool Walker Firetruck (which admittedly does feature a woman seated in the passenger seat of the Firetruck waving; God forbid she should be driving, though), or the Fisher Price Pick Up and Go Dump Truck.

So let's see what we've got so far: Boys become doctors or truck drivers or firemen. Girls become mothers and shoppers and clean up. Now there's progress for you.

OK. Now your kid's a toddler. A toddler girl can play with Fisher-Price's Toddler kitchen. The male equivalent? The Toddler Basketball and Toddler Bowling.

Kids are a little older? Getting underfoot in the house, and you want them to play outside in the sandbox? Want to buy something more elaborate than the standard pail-and-shovel? Once again, your little girl can thrill to the Fisher-Price Sand Kitchen, with various kitchen utensils to scoop and mold sand sculptures. What does your little boy get? The Fisher-Price Sand Workshop with toy power tools.

Actually, tools and workshops are the biggest male-only domain of children's toys. There were about six different variations on carpenter's tools, tool belts, and other woodworking or home repair implements, and every single one of them was packaged solely for boys: a smiling, blue-and-red clad boy standing there proudly wielding his little tools, sometimes accompanied by beaming father. The only manufacturer who allowed a female to appear on any package was Little Tykes. Its Little Tykes Tool Pouch featured a grandfather smiling down at his woodworking grandson. The Little Tykes Measuring Set, similarly packaged, actually featured a mother, smiling down at her woodworking — son. Daughter? Get real.

Your kid ready for building toys or those snap-together building bricks? Tyco makes Building Superblocks in blue and red for boys to build houses and trucks. Girls get lavender blocks to construct a teen bedroom. Thus we perpetuate that the domain of the male is either out on the road or anywhere or even building houses, but a female's domain is the bedroom. Or is that all? Heck, no. Lego packages red, white, and blue Legos for boys to construct buildings. They also package purple and pink Legos for girls to construct the one place females are allowed to aspire to, aside from the kitchen, supermarket, and bedroom: a shopping mall.

The environment of the shopping mall is an extremely popular one. Once your child is older and ready for games of more sophistication than "Rock 'em Sock 'em Robots" (all boys pictured) or "Pretty Pretty Princess" (all girls pictured), young ladies can actually have their choice of mall games directed at them. Pressman gives us Electronic Mall Madness, while Tyco graciously produces Meet Me at the Mall. These are typical "girl" games.

What's a typical "boy" game? Milton-Bradley's Hero Quest, an adventure game with nary a female in sight. The message is clear: Boys go on grand adventures seeking treasure and bring it home so that girls can spend it at the mall.

Are *all* kids' toys like this? No. For example, Avco produces Dr. Mickey's Medical Kit, a Disney tie-in featuring a box that has a little girl on one side and a little boy on the other. The box can be displayed either way, and in the store we went to they were side-by-side.

Fisher-Price produces My Pretty Purse for young girls, and for little boys, My Shaving Kit. That seems equitable to me: I don't think a kit for little girls to pretend shaving their legs would really sell all that well, and, besides, it's better than purse vs. doctor's bag. Speaking of doctors, Fisher-Price also makes a Medical Kit where, believe it or not, a girl is pictured using a stethoscope on a boy. Labelling it "Medical Kit" rather than "Doctor Kit" dodges the entire issue, avoiding the boy=doctor, girl=nurse and, instead, concentrating on the notion of treating the sick.

Interestingly, although females are generally not allowed to invade male toy domains, boys are sometimes allowed into girl places under the right circumstances. Little Tykes also makes a playset called a Party Kitchen, and naturally there's a little girl in there slaving away making a meal. But, lo and behold, there's a little boy also pictured on the box. Not that he's being much help, but at least he's there, rather than sitting in some sort of living room playset shouting, "When's dinner ready?"

Also Fisher-Price makes a Laundry Center. Now get ready for this: The girl is depicted doing the wash, but amazingly, the little boy is there, big as life, doing the ironing.

As for the startling amount of Marvel Comics-oriented toys on the market, such as the X-Men Danger Room playset — there are *no* little kids depicted on the box. This might be to try to make the toys as broad-based as possible in their appeal. Then, again, it might be so that adult comics fans buying them for themselves might not feel self-conscious.

Of course, the bottom line is I'm not making any startlingly original observations here. None of this gender-instruction is new. It was pointed out 30 years ago. So were the dangers of smoking. At least with cigarettes there warning labels, and advertising was banned from TV. With toys, by and large, a girl's place remains in the kitchen, bedroom, and mall, and a boy's place is anywhere he wants to make it.

(Peter David, writer of stuff, also remembers the time when daughter Shana — 5 years old at the time — only wanted a doll of the "Rainbow Brite" character named "Indigo" for her birthday. My wife and I went to the toy store to buy it and found, to our surprise, that our child had zeroed in on the one doll in the toy line that was black. Being white, my wife and I kind of looked at each other, and my wife said, "Well, here's a good test. Are we really liberal or not?" We bought the doll, although the cashier whispered to me, "You know, they make white ones, too.")

HERO TODAY, GONE-O TOMORROW (March 13, 1992)

One of the most often-repeated observations being made of late is that heroes in comics have changed to their very core — and not for the better.

There have been, to my mind, three stages of comics heroes so far. The first was the Element Age, so-called for two reasons: It encompasses Golden and Silver Age, and the heroes of the time were elementary. Their purpose was clear. Their morals were spotless. If there were any initial flaws in their characters (Batman originally killed people and was hunted by the police, notions that were clearly ahead of their time; relatively quickly, he stopped packing guns and became an extension of the Gotham police force), they were done away with. Oh, maybe The Spectre was creepy, but he pretty much had God backing him up, so it was OK.

Perhaps it helped that, at the time, there was such a clear and present evil in the world — namely the Axis powers. The good guys of fiction had to be *that good* because the bad guys of reality were *that bad*. Heck, perhaps it's no coincidence that, as America moved into the '50s, comics heroes lightened up more and more. Superman and Batman, notably, had less and less of an edge to them. But they were still morally stand-up guys.

Then we moved into the second heroic age of comics, which can only be termed the Marvel Age, because the angst-ridden characters were so closely associated with those published by Marvel. The tortured Thing, the hard-luck Spider-Man, the Thunder God who could command elements but not a woman's heart — they wore their difficulties on their sleeves and were extremely appealing to readers. Teen-age readers in particular, who are, by definition, little more than angst on two legs.

The emotionally plagued heroes became so popular that DC even endeavoredto graft angst onto its own characters, which is like trying to parallel park an 18-wheeler into a space large enough for a VW: You can do it, but the final result isn't going to be pretty.

An outgrowth of angst was "relevance." Excessive agonizing about their own problems began to wear thin, so heroes began agonizing about the problems of society, as well.

And then we rolled into the third age of heroes, the age that I refer to as: The Mess Age.

Why? Two reasons.

First, because heroes went from having problems to being complete societal messes. The heroic community of the Mess Age includes among its membership: alcoholics, drug addicts, emotional cripples, psychos, and mass murderers.

Second, because the more popular a hero is seems to be directly related to how much of a bloody mess he can leave in his wake.

Look at Superman, for heaven's sake: once upon a time, the icon of perfection and flawlessly moral behavior. But in *Dark Knight* he was portrayed as a puppet of the American government, a mindless object of scorn. In his own title, he carefully and deliberately killed renegade Kryptonians and agonized over it for months afterward.

And Batman, Superman's long-time pal? He became dementedly single-minded, alienating Kal-El and Dick Grayson and going through kid sidekicks as though they were potato chips. (The last thing you want to do is *really draw attention* to the fact that Batman routinely engages in child endangerment, as Bob Ingersoll has pointed out. But that's precisely what DC has done.)

Jailing bad guys was no longer enough. Their bodies piled up like cordwood, as The Punisher, Wolverine, Lobo, and their brethren cut a bloody swath through the legions of the nasty. The line between heroes and villains has so blurred as to be invisible. Not only are the most popular heroes guys who you can't count on for rational and just behavior — they're not even people you'd want to share a cab with.

Why has this happened? Why is the notion of a hero with a stable moral center — a hero who is heroic — suddenly so *passé*?

Look around you.

Art reflects society, and at this point society is extremely aware that many of its heroes are hardly paragons of purity. Each new revelation, each new sordid action, each new headline that's splashed across supermarket tabloids or ballyhooed on the evening news rips away at the fabric of heroism in this country.

A recent local newscast led with politicians hurling racial epithets and closed with covering a new sport: nude Bungy jumping. Personally, I think they should have combined the two stories: Any politician who's into nude Bungy jumping would get *my* vote. It beats heaving on the Japanese Prime Minister.

Where do we look for our heroes? Who have our heroes been in the past?

Sports figures? Magic Johnson recently played what will probably be his final game, voted to his position by fans who didn't care that he hadn't played a single game this season. And he responded with a bravura performance that earned him the game MVP award. He deserved the accolades, and it added to his rightful stature as a heroic figure.

But what can't be ignored is that he became exposed to AIDS through sexual conduct that was — to put it delicately — not thought out. If he'd had the moral center that heroes are "supposed" to have — the moral purity that people wax nostalgic for when they speak of the current crop of the comic-book Mess Age — he wouldn't have been sleeping around in the first place. The one who's really heroic is his wife, who is standing by her man rather than, say, appearing on *Oprah* and complaining about his less-than-sterling conduct.

What's heroic is that Johnson has tried to turn his own misfortune into the potentially life-saving message of "heterosexual transmission of AIDS is a real threat." We can hope that will pierce through the notion of "Yeah, but it couldn't happen to *me*" that pervades our population.

Then there's Mike Tyson. Here is a man who beats people up for a living. Who has a history of violence in and out of the ring. Who raped a young woman that the defense was so desperate to discredit that they put forward the notion that she was sexually hyped up from listening to rap music. (Thank God I wasn't on the jury, because my doubtlessly audible "*Aw, come on*" would not have endeared me to the judge.)

But each day, when he was escorted to and from the courthouse, the path would be lined with well-wishers and supporters. Even after the conviction, his old neighborhood of Brownsville clung to Tyson as a hero through and through. Jesse Gibson, 38, told one reporter, "He's a great guy who got a bum deal — anytime somebody looks up to somebody, they want to break him down." Other residents echoed the sentiments. "He was made an example of," said Lyman May. "Now they can show you another black man who has failed," who pointed out that Tyson failed where the white William Kennedy Smith succeeded.

(To my mild surprise, there hasn't seemed to be all that much emphasis on the notion that Tyson was given unfair treatment because of skin color. Actually, you can look at the Tyson case from the other angle: Tyson's accuser, a black woman, succeeded in making herself a credible witness, whereas by all accounts, Smith's accuser, a white woman, did not. So what does *that* say about race relations?)

So, to some, Tyson remains a hero, while to Judge Patricia Gifford he is simply another criminal for sentencing. Again, I'm no lawyer, but I've been wondering: Maybe they should have tried an insanity defense. My (limited) understanding of the law is that it has to be proved that you understood you were committing a crime. I'm convinced Tyson did not, and still does not, understand.

Let's face it: The guy's not a rocket scientist. For the past 10 years he's been consistently told that sometimes it's OK to beat people up, and sometimes it's not (as opposed to the average child, who is told it's *never* OK). Not only that, but his own testimony makes it clear that he doesn't think of women as people, but rather sacks of meat to be grabbed and used. Hitler thought of Jews not as people, but as subhumans, and nobody thinks Hitler was a candidate for the mental health poster boy. Tyson is hardly Hitler, but his grasp of male-female interaction is certainly not the societal norm.

Or maybe it is. Maybe he just personifies what all men secretly think, especially when hormones first kick in. But whereas other men clean up their act, Tyson never did. Never had to. And now he'll probably be slapped away somewhere, which is good, because he's a rapist and dangerous. But it's sad, too. Especially to those people who held him to be a hero because he was black and uneducated but still successful. Because they could aspire to that, too. But who wants to aspire to being a jailed rapist?

More heroes. Look around. Who are the traditional heroes?

Policemen? By and large hardworking and dedicated. But look at the travesties over the years. The police corruption in New York and Philadelphia. The brutality of some L.A. cops immortalized on videotape. Who can overlook the notion that the Milwaukee police stumbled over a blood-covered boy who had escaped the horrors of Jeffrey Dahmer — and when Dahmer told the cops that it was just "a lover's quarrel," gave the hysterical boy *back to Dahmer*, who killed the kid in short order. And went on to kill four more, after the police should have stopped him.

Astronauts? Anybody heard from the space program lately? No one notices astronauts any more. Most kids don't know the significance of the names Armstrong, Aldrin, and Collins. And NASA is the outfit that blew up the *Challenger*.

Doctors? Once they were almost godlike beings, typified by the fatherly, all-knowing Marcus Welby. Nowadays, though, doctors have to be just as worried about malpractice as they do about their patients. House calls are a thing of the past. We desperately want to trust our medical practitioners — but everything you read and hear makes us afraid to do so.

Soldiers? Absolutely heroic — and yet look what this country did to the returning Vietnam soldiers. Indeed, they might have been the very first of the heroes to be pilloried by changing societal mores. Like Rip Van Winkle, they returned to a country that was not what they left behind. The lionizing of Desert Storm participants, while a tribute to people who did their duty, comes across like a nation trying to assuage its guilty conscience over the lousy treatment of the Vietnam vets.

Our nation's leaders? Living or dead, they're objects of attack. George Bush, without the winds of war puffing his sails, finds himself becalmed on the seas of America's financial frustration and despair.

And whether you're John F. Kennedy or Bill Clinton, your sexual exploits — in the eyes of the media — take on far more import than your political agenda or the desire to do right by your constituents. I wonder why Clinton hasn't tried to attack the focus on the Gennifer Flowers business by claiming that it's a conspiracy to bring down the uppity white man. After all, Clarence Thomas pushed his way past sexual harrassment charges by claiming it was a plot to bring down the uppity black man.

The Supreme Court? Now there's a group of people who used to be my personal heroes — until the make-up of the court changed, and it went from being a body of justices out to protect free expression for the people, to being a group out to protect people *from* free expression.

Firemen? Well, uhm. Hm. OK. Firemen. Nobody badmouths firemen. Ultimately, no one cares what firemen do in their private lives or what their motivations are in their chosen line of work. You're just so damned glad to see them, if your house is burning down, that, unlike the Bridge over San Luis Rey, what brought them to this moment in time is of no consequence. Thank heavens they're there. Firemen, America's last undisputed heroes.

But they're outweighed by the battlefield of destroyed individuals that, back in the Element Age, were held up to the heroic ideal. We've become a country that knows entirely too much about entirely everything, and as a result we're basically cynical and mistrustful. Perhaps that's why we love the Olympics so much — once every four years, we get a set of pristine heroes to enjoy and take pride in. Guys like Team USA or the intrepid Paul Wylie. And the beauty of those heroes is that they'll fade into obscurity or go on nice tours or become announcers — stuff that will do nothing to diminish their places in our hearts and minds so that we can continue to treasure those fond memories without the heartbreak of subsequent disclosures. (Film at 11.)

So why are so many super-heroes cynical, nasty, angry, even unheroic?

Look around, babe. Look at the newspapers. Look at the mirror. Just — look.

(Peter David, writer of stuff, can now be written to directly c/o To Be Continued Inc., PO Box 239, Bayport, N.Y. 11705.)

GAY ABANDON (June 12, 1992)

While I was at Wondercon, Sharon Cho — an agent with Star*Reach productions — came over to the Marvel table, where I had more or less set up shop, and handed me the following letter that she had intended to mail:

"I just read your *BID* (5/1/92), the one that contained a section on *Basic Instinct*. You said, 'But there's nothing in the movie that implies "Gay = Cretin." — *because everyone in the movie is a cretin.*

"Peter, I am gay. I wish we lived in a world where we can write anything or film anything or draw anything without having to think about social ramifications, but we don't. There are a lot of people out there who don't have an open mind, who don't know their cousin is gay, who feel that we should be locked up behind bars 'for our own good.'

"Peter, have you ever stood in line to go into a bar and have a few cars full of men drive by, throwing cans and yelling things like *'Dyke*! Why doncha find yourself a real man!' Or walked down a hallway, passing by a woman whose eyes turn wide at the sight of you, backs up to the wall to avoid your touch, and screams at you to go away after you have safely passed? I have (in a big 'gay-friendly' city), and let me tell you, it shook me up to know that there is such hatred or ignorance in the world.

"Perhaps you're right; just because everyone in a movie or a comic book is portrayed as a cretin, it's OK to portray gays and bisexuals as cretins. But there's a lot of people out there who can't make that jump in logic. It's those people that I'm scared of, the ones that knifed to death an acquaintance of mine who walked out of a gay restaurant, the ones who ignored AIDS because it was 'a gay disease,' the ones like my mother who threw out towels and Lysoled everything after a gay male friend of mine used the bathroom.

"It's not often you, being a white, heterosexual male, experience this type of prejudice. I'm a Chinese, homosexual woman; I get it often enough not to want any justification or excuses for people to hate me or be afraid of me.

"I wish there were more open-minded people, people who can look at things logically like you. But then, you can't always get what you want, right?"

Well, Sharon and I had a couple of lively discussions after that, some of which I'll relate here — not verbatim, 'cause I don't remember every word, but the general thrust.

A lot of what concerns gays about films such as *Basic Instinct* (and, for that matter, women about hard-core porn) is the concept of reinforcement of stereotypes. But I have a problem buying into this concern, for the following reason:

I don't think people are that stupid. Pretty stupid, by and large, yes, but not *that* stupid.

I think that when it comes to matters of sexual persuasion, it's one of those things that adults already have an opinion on (and kids shouldn't be seeing *Basic Instinct* anyway — the "R" in this case stands for "Really Not Kidding"). Either the concept of homosexuality bothers you ("It's a sin"; "It's sick") or it doesn't ("Love is love"; "Who am I to judge someone else?").

On that basis, I don't believe that *Basic Instinct* is going to affect people's opinions, because with something like this, opinions were formed long before the audiences queued up to watch Sharon Stone not wear underwear.

I simply have a great deal of trouble believing that someone who is *not* predisposed against gays is going to come out of that movie saying, "Oh, my God, lesbians are murderers! I had no idea! I'm gonna beat me up some lezzies before they stab me with an ice pick!" Any more so than (to use the other example I brought up) someone who is anti-gay is going to come out of *Frankie and Johnny* and say,

"Wow, you know, I never knew that gay men could be so witty and charming. No more gay bashing for me."

I believe that people pick and choose what they will accept as credible evidence for those things that go to the core of their nature. At this point I'm still not sure where I stand with Bill Clinton or Ross Perot — that's something my opinion can be affected on. But a number of years ago, in an office, I stumbled over a truly hard-core porn magazine — the first such I'd ever seen. I flipped through it, encountered some nauseating images, tossed it away immediately out of disgust, and that was that. I didn't see those pictures and become transformed into a debaser of women. And I don't believe that people are going to see *Basic Instinct* and have their opinions materially changed one way or the other.

Now, of course, the logical way to disagree with me on this point is the way that Sharon did — to say, in essence, "You don't understand. You haven't been there."

My response to that is: Yes. I have.

Surprise.

I have written in the past about how much I hated Verona, N.J., where I spent my early adolescence. I never really made clear why. Now I will.

One of the oldest clichés is, "Some of my best friends are gay." I will go that one better: My best man was gay. A friend of mine, Keith, was the best man at my wedding some 15 years ago. And he was (presumably still is) gay.

But in the years before I got married, Keith and I were friends in Verona, first in junior high and then in the first year of high school.

It was somewhat evident to all concerned that Keith was gay — except to Keith himself. His mannerisms were effeminate, and he never showed particular interest towards females at a time when most guys were following girls around with their eyes leaping out of their heads (remember, minis and hot pants were big at the time). Whenever I'd discuss girls, he'd sort of be politely interested, but that was about it. It wasn't until we were both adults that he admitted to himself, and to me, that he was gay, at which point I told him this wasn't exactly a shock.

But he was, during those middle-school and early high-school years, my best friend. And I paid for that dearly, because everyone assumed I was gay, too.

And, boy, did they let me have it.

If Keith and I so much as walked down a hallway together, the shouts of "Faggots" would be hurled at us. I had almost no other friends besides Keith — no one wanted to be seen with me. All the way into my junior year of high school, I couldn't get a date. What girl would want to go out with me, after all? It wouldn't do her own rep any good, and, besides, if I tried to kiss her or something, I'd probably just be faking it, right?

Then Keith's family moved away, as I entered my sophomore year. That was the worst; then I was totally alone. We'd talk on the phone all the time, but the day-in, day-out reality of life — well, Sharon, no, I've never stood outside a bar and been harassed by cars full of men. However, I did get to kick off my second year of high school with the word "Fag" having been scrawled in big, indelible marker on my locker.

A high school is a very confined, closed social atmosphere in which to have no friends. Yes, it's pretty lousy to be hated and despised for something you are. I can assure you it's also not great fun to be loathed for something you *aren't*. That's one reason I always find it ironic, when the junior-high and high-school-aged kids clamor for my autograph at a convention. Because, when I was their age, they wouldn't have come near me with a 10-meter cattle prod.

Of course, there's plenty of hatred reserved for what one *is*, too. No, I haven't had a woman recoil upon seeing me (well, maybe my wife, first thing in the morning — but that's not the same thing). However, I have had people tell me that they wish my grandparents hadn't escaped Nazi Germany so that I had never been born. I have had people hand me fliers explaining that Jews are secretly running the country and that we should all be exterminated.

Being a white heterosexual male, Sharon, I don't experience your sort of prejudice. On the other hand, you'll never have to deal with one of your daughters asking you how to deal with the fact that a boy she thought was a friend told her that he couldn't stand Jews. (I suggested inviting him over so that I could back the car over him; she worked it out herself.)

Sometimes, I think that's one of the main problems with this country: No one listens or makes any attempt to understand what anyone else is saying, because there's this intrinsic belief that everyone's feelings are unique. This is not true. *Experiences* are unique, yes. But not feelings. Hatred, love, bigotry, jealousy — these are universal.

If John Doe says, "You don't understand, because you haven't been through what I've been through," this misses the point to a large degree. What John is really saying is, "If you'd been through the experiences that I've been through, then you would agree with me." Which, of course, boils down to, "I agree with everything I believe in. And if you were me, you would, too." But because I'm *not* John Doe, John automatically assumes that any disagreement with his point of view comes from ignorance on my part.

But, as noted above, hatred and love are universal. As far as I'm concerned, the reasons for the emotions are not quite as important as the fact that the emotions are being felt. I think there's a lot more common ground between people than people generally believe, if they'd just choose to see it. However, because there's this "You're not me" mindset, those commonalities are obscured and the differences are focused on. In fact, not just focused on but magnified to the point where there are huge chasms between people, and simple common sense gets lost in the shuffle.

"You're not me" proceeds from a false assumption of relevance.

Without this commonality of feelings and emotions, the fictional world of comics (and movies and books, etc.) could not possibly work. We identify with and care about characters because they're experiencing — not necessarily specific incidents that we've gone through — but emotions and feelings that are universal. The details of a busted romance aren't nearly as important as the heartache it brings.

Ironic, then, that we have such an easy time opening ourselves up to fictional characters, but when it comes to fellow human beings, we close up and say, "You couldn't possibly understand."

Eventually, by the way — for anyone remotely interested — my family wound up moving, as well, taking me out of that North Jersey hell hole and transplanting us to Pennsylvania. Things went much better at the high school there. I got dates and everything.

Keith and I got together a few times after I got married, but I sensed he was uncomfortable around me. I think my flagrantly heterosexual lifestyle made him edgy. I called him a number of times over the years, urged him to call me back — but he never did. Eventually I got the hint, which saddened me. I'd resolutely kept him as a friend all during the time that that resolve made me a pariah in our social sphere. So now, when it didn't matter, seemed an odd time to have to let go. But you have to honor the wishes of friends.

Oh — just for the record, I asked Sharon what she thought of the "Daisy Dyke" joke, since all I'd heard from on the topic was outraged heterosexuals protesting on behalf of gays everywhere. She told me she thought it was funny as hell. So there. Nyaaah.

(Peter David, writer of stuff, admits to being annoyed by one thing about **Basic Instinct** *— smokers now have a brand-new smart-alecky comeback, if told that they are puffing away in a non-smoking area. "What are you going to do? Arrest me for smoking?" Terrific. Thanks a lot, Michael Douglas and Sharon Stone.)*

Historical Notes:

1) I heard from a goodly number of people who told me that they'd experienced similar treatment in high school. On the other hand, I never heard from any of the people who tormented me. They probably don't read my column. Or comic books. Or anything.

SESAME STREET AND THE YOUNGBLOOD GENERATION (July 10, 1992)

I've been thinking...

Which is always a dangerous announcement.

I think I'm starting to realize — or perhaps dread — that the current new crop of comic-book "wartists" may not be a simple aberration.

Comic books are now being produced in which the concept of writing is not only secondary; it borders on irrelevance. Nothing is important aside from what meets the eye. And what meets the eye is a series of images (so to speak), not always connected or flowing from one panel to the other, with little or no subtext or even a grasp of what subtext is.

Youngblood makes as much sense if you read it straight through without bothering to turn the comic book over at the midway point; *Spawn*, which looks like some of the nicest Frank Miller work ever, is at least decipherable — but still there's not so much story as big, flashy pictures that are loosely strung together.

Oddly enough, these may sound like criticisms — but in fact, to judge from various interviews with the creators involved, this is precisely what they set out to produce.

This makes a critique tougher. If someone tries to accomplish certain goals, and the critic says "You haven't achieved them," then that's one thing. But the goals of the new crop of wartists are not to produce the types of comics that I'm accustomed to reading — or, for that matter, the type that all the people they cite as influences are in the habit of producing.

That's why R.C. Harvey's concise and incisive dissection of *Youngblood* in *Oh, So?* — as accurate as it was, and I wish to make it clear that I agreed with every word — was also, by and large, irrelevant. It's difficult to hold the new wartists to a critical standard when, as far as they're concerned, those criteria don't apply to them.

In *People* magazine, for example, Rob Liefeld blithely states that such notions as drawing with an eye toward proper perspective (you know — all lines angling to a single horizon line, that sort of thing) doesn't factor into his work. He's something of an anarchist in that regard, we are told. Whether this is because Rob knows correct rules of perspective, anatomy, etc. and simply chooses to ignore them or exaggerate them (which is one thing) or is, in fact, incapable of drawing a proper page of artwork even if you held a gun to his head (which is quite another thing), I don't really know and leave for you to judge.

Todd McFarlane, in various places, has stated that he never reads anything, which your average first-grade teacher would tell you is absolutely crucial, if you want to learn to write. But again it's irrelevant, because Todd has stated that all that matters is that the page look good. That is, above everything, what is important. Words, plot structure — all secondary to the pictures.

Why?

Why, I asked myself, why is it so important to me, but not to them?

It took a long time for me to come to the realization that it was generational. But when I did, what quickly followed was the horrified realization that this might, indeed, be the wave of the future — which is not a pleasant realization at all.

I hadn't really been looking at the wartists in terms of generational divisions, because I'm not much than a decade older than the youngest of them. A separation of 10 years didn't seem to me, at first glance, to be such an insurmountable gulf.

I mean, it simply wasn't, to me, the same thing as when my father would be shaking his head in disbelief to the music of the Beatles or the Stones and saying, "That's not music; that's just noise." The same way that I now look at the wartists' work and say basically the same thing, except substitute "a story" for "music" and "pictures" for "noise."

My God — am I my father so quickly?

Part of what got me thinking along these lines was Don Simpson's *Oh, So?* letter. By and large it was silly, but what intrigued me was Don's equating being concerned with traditional story-telling rules to something as quaint and old-fashioned as a bingo game.

Don may very well have put his finger on precisely what was eluding my understanding. The wartists, despite the relative closeness in years to many of their elders (certainly less than the traditional two decades) really, truly, are representing a new generation of creators.

But why, I wondered. What is it that caused such a drastic difference in priorities in a relatively short amount of time?

One of the most often-cited influences has been MTV. I think that's part of it, certainly. No longer was music appreciated for its lyrics and melodies; with the advent of MTV, songs were defined by the visuals. If heard subsequently on radio, the images that come to a listener's mind are no longer pulled from their own experience. Instead, the listener envisions the "definitive" version they saw on television.

But I don't think MTV did it singlehandedly. You know what I think did it?

Sesame Street.

Sesame Street has been around for more than two decades. It hit the airwaves at a time when most of the wartists (present-day, and up-and-coming) were young enough to be influenced by it (whereas I was already a teen-ager, far more interested in females than large yellow birds).

Sesame Street, with its hypnotic high-speed technique, presented youngsters when they were at their most impressionable with a barrage of images. Its message was anti-intellectualism, anti-thought, anti-patience. Numbers and letters flew at young viewers, assaulting their senses.

The short-term gains were tremendous. Parents were thrilled that their children, at age 3, could recite the alphabet or count to 10. It gave them bragging rights. The fact that a *parrot* could be taught to perform in a similar manner was not taken into consideration.

This put teachers into a tough position. In the traditional school setting, teachers would spend anywhere from a quarter-hour to a half-hour on a given subject, teaching the kids to *think* and *understand* things before they utilized them. *Sesame Street* taught kids to put up fingers in sequence and say "1-2-3-4-5-6-7-8-9-10" before they fully grasped the notion of greater and lesser quantities.

Oh, eventually they would understand — either from school or by continuing to watch *Sesame Street* and eventually garnering comprehension from some of the longer sketches. Nevertheless, the cart had already been put before the horse, and kids were hanging on for dear life.

The creators of *Sesame Street* understood that, before you teach a child something, you have to get the child's attention. The rapid-fire imaging did that. Fine. No problem. Once the attention is caught, it can have very positive value if the avenues are broadened: If parents watched *Street* with their kids or read to them, it was beneficial — using *Street* as a building block. But parents who simply used the show as a hypnotic babysitter ("Here, watch Cookie Monster. Mommy's busy.") left the kids to dwell only on the superficiality. And kids who want all learning processes to be like that machine-gun introduction are going to be frustrated.

And once they were out of the *Sesame Street* years, the *Street* generation could then graduate, yes, to MTV and videos, where it was no longer necessary to do the most fundamental job of appreciating music: namely, listen to it. Music was no longer for listening to, which requires thought. Music was for looking at, and looking requires no thought at all. *Appreciation* requires thought, but with the *Sesame Street*/MTV generation there wasn't time or interest in that — information and visuals came so quickly that there simply wasn't the opportunity to assimilate and understand. Opportunity? Hell, it wasn't even *possible* — the mental equipment wasn't there.

Fast forward now to the era of the wartists. We have creators drawing without truly knowing anatomy and, "writers" producing stories without any comprehension, or even *interest* in, the foundations of story structure. Creators with no patience for the basics, and even outright disdain.

There's nothing linear about *Sesame Street* — it's a hodgepodge with no structure. There's nothing linear about MTV — it's one thing after another, with one thing no more important than the next. And with the emphasis of a series of cool images over the notion of a clear, cohesive story, there is nothing linear about the work of the wartists.

My (Dear Lord!) generation would sit in front of the TV for an hour and watch a one-hour dramatic program. Heaven knows, it might not have been *good* drama, but at least it made an attempt at having a beginning, middle, and end. The thought of watching an hour of fast-moving pictures that required the attention span of a gnat would have been alien to me. But for the next flight of viewers, it's the norm.

It's not limited simply to comic books. Not only did *Miami Vice* make a big deal of incorporating MTV-style editing into the show, but now we have a new series called *Grapevine* which takes it one step further. Not a scene in *Grapevine* exceeds 90 seconds; most of them average around 10 seconds, as the characters talk to the viewer in rapid succession with the flimsy story ping-ponging all over the place.

Then there are the readers of hypertext webs on computers who can read stories that are nothing remotely like standard narrative. In web works such as Michael Joyce's "afternoon," the reader can jump all over the place, keying off whatever catches his/her interest in the narrative, and going off on tangents based on single words or phrases that — when highlighted — cue up entire related texts. It's the ideal work for people who are unable to focus and pay attention to anything.

It used to be that the work being read was the entertainment. No longer. Now the act of reading alone becomes the entertainment. We've taken yet another step away from being able to think about something as a whole. Ideally, readers of hypertext should be able to assimilate all the strands and weave it together into something coherent. That's the ideal, of course.

Granted, non-linear books and movies are nothing new. Woody Allen did it with *Annie Hall*; James Joyce did it with *Finnegan's Wake*. But one must believe that they thoroughly understood the rules before they trashed them — and, besides, their body of work was designed to *make* you think.

Are the wartists concerned about the notion of embracing the "What-you-see-is-what-you-get" philosophy and making it paramount? Not at all. Because not only is it what they set out to do, but they also point to the unprecedented sales figures and say, in essence, "Ha-ha, see? We're right. We're the wave of the future, because our sales are so strong." As if commercial success ultimately proves anything. If we keep with that logic, then *Basic Instinct* is a much better film than *The Maltese Falcon*, because it's made so much more money.

Never mind the thought of producing something that will last. The "now" is everything. As long as it makes money now, as long as it appeals to the commercial consciousness now, as long as it's a success now, then that's all that matters. Cream rises to the top, and wartists perceive themselves as the cream. This ignores the fact, however, that it's milk that builds bones.

The world is hurtling forward at breakneck pace, and the new wave of wartists and their work is only the latest manifestation of a society that values immediate dissemination of information over everything else. Don't dwell on anything. Don't think about anything. Simply look and move on, because something's going to be coming along in the very next second, and if you blink, you'll miss it.

I'm certain, by the way, that there will be people who read this piece and view it as simply an attack on everyone involved with Image (which it's not) instead of an overview of the elements of society that helped form a new breed of audience and creators with wildly different priorities than their predecessors. If the former conclusion is what you draw, then I'll bet that either you're under 30 — or that you wish you were.

Youngblood versus a Bingo game? Well, I've read *Youngblood*. And I've played Bingo. And if you ask me which provides more intellectual stimulation, my response is: N 32.

(Peter David, writer of stuff, says hi to everyone he met at the Atlanta Fantasy Fair and will also meet and greet folks at the Chicago Comicon over the July 4th weekend. Autograph lines will not be linear, but instead cross-hatched.)

Historical Notes:

1) Ohhh, did I hear about this one. Most critics proclaimed that, rather than trying to analyze a societal trend, I was ragging on Image again. Michael Heisler, an Image freelancer, was the most dedicated. He wrote a series of letters, each one wandering more far afield than the one before, embarking on further and further tangents until the original point was hopelessly lost.

Other folks, however, sent me articles from various scholarly journals that addressed all the points that I had made and even drew some of the same conclusions — all, it would seem, without hating Image Comics.

PLANET OF THE APES (April 30, 1993)

"Tragic failures become moral sins only if one should have known better from the outset."
The above quote is from *The Third Chimpanzee* by Jared Diamond, a fascinating book on humanity — where we've been and where we are, in all likelihood, going to wind up.

I finished reading it during WonderCon in Oakland. It was unquestionably the best of that series of conventions I've been to: the best-attended (it seemed) and most enthusiastic.

However, in the course of the weekend I was also witness to, or made aware of, two incidents that directly relate to Diamond's gem mentioned above. Both of them, interestingly, are also germane to comics, as well.

The first was the untimely passing of Brandon Lee.

Lee was in the final week of filming *The Crow*, based on the comic book of the same name. The set had been so wracked by accidents that *Entertainment Weekly* reported that there was talk of "The Curse of *The Crow*." Yet, despite the mishaps, a production coordinator was quoted as saying, "I don't think this is exceptional. We have a lot of stunts and effects, and I've been on productions before where people have died."

The article became eerily prophetic when the term "movie shoot" turned into a deadly literal phrase: A scene being filmed involved Lee's character being gunned down, which in the script was a precursor to his returning to life.

Nowhere was the difference between reality and art more sharply delineated when the cameras rolled, the gun was fired, Lee went down, the director shouted, "Cut," and Lee did not get back up again. The autopsy reportedly found a bullet lodged in him.

As of this writing, although the official ruling was "accidental shooting," there is still much confusion as to what happened and why. Live ammo is not allowed on movie sets, and guns are checked before every scene — and guarded zealously by the prop master.

How did it happen? No one is sure. But one thing seems certain: An actor took a supposedly empty gun and fired a real bullet out of it and someone died. (Unless we're getting into complete *Columbo* territory here, and the bullet was fired from somewhere else at precisely the same moment [*JFK* enthusiasts, take note].)

I am forced to wonder something once again that I've been pondering ever since Jon-Erik Hexum killed himself. What the hell are real guns doing on movie sets?

For those of you who don't remember Hexum, he was a dashing young actor on a short-lived TV series called *Voyagers*. Some years back, he was clowning around on a set and put a gun to his head and pulled the trigger. It was loaded with blanks. He thought that, because it was blanks, they could do him no harm. He was wrong and paid with his life.

And what I started wondering at that point was: If we know that you can die from point-blank range, even if blanks are in a gun — how about six inches, then? A foot? Two feet? What, precisely, is safe?

And now we have actors dying from genuine rounds of ammo. Whether it was deliberate or accidental, two things remain true: Brandon Lee is dead, and, if there had been no real guns on the set, then he wouldn't be. His mother wouldn't be burying him next to his father and, by the time you read this, he would have been a newlywed.

I understand the reasons that they use real guns in movies. They want that effective-looking discharge. They want it to look real.

Well, Carolco studios has got "real," all right. They have footage of Brandon Lee dying. I'm sorry — that's just a bit too real for me.

I know that moviemaking entails risks. Stunt men have died making movies, and of course there was the hideous accident with Vic Morrow and two children during the filming of *Twilight Zone* that resulted in a lengthy trial of the film's director, John Landis. Nothing can be done so that movie making is absolutely safe.

But something can be done to make it safer.

I think it would be an excellent idea if SAG and AFTRA and whatever other movie unions and guilds there are got together and demanded that guns actually capable of discharging bullets under *any* circumstance be banned from movies.

I mean, this is nuts. Moviemakers can fake buildings. They can fake flying men. They can fake the T-1000 Terminator's morphing. They can fake alien worlds. They can fake wind, sea, deserts, snow, ice, earthquakes. They can fake spaceships and light swords. They fake transporters and warp speed jumps. They fake the sound a fist makes when it strikes someone else (unless you really thought that the title character of *Annie* could punch with the same impact noise as Indiana Jones).

Hell, almost everything you see in a movie is fake, including the acting.

So I do not understand how it can be impossible to fake a gun discharging. I just do not. And don't bother trying to explain it to me, because I'm not going to believe it.

Filmmakers are an extremely clever lot, and I'm simply certain that, if they put their mind to it, they could do it.

What would happen if they had to fake the gun discharges while using a weapon that couldn't possibly shoot? Maybe it would cause an increase in budgets. So fine. What's a human life going for these days? An extra ten, twenty grand? Show of hands, everyone out there who thinks their lives aren't worth, oh, fifty thousand bucks. So maybe the lead actors have to live with smaller trailers. Big deal. At least they'll be living.

Or maybe there would be cutbacks on shootouts. Whoa. That should be the worst thing that happens to movie-goers: to be subjected to less violence in the cinema.

Is it *really* that difficult to manufacture a movie-prop equivalent of a cap gun? Is it *really* not worth avoiding potential future disasters such as this one?

All I know is that I have a number of friends who are actors, and I find the prospect of thinking of them getting real guns aimed at them to be an utterly chilling one. I'd like to think they'll realize that no movie in the world is worth dying for, if it can be avoided. And this death, I think, could have been.

If it had been a fake gun, then it would have been a fake death. Any time a real gun is being aimed, a real death is being courted. And if you don't believe me, then run it past Brandon Lee's mom and fiancé.

In some ways, this may sound reminiscent of my earlier column about the near debacle at January's Great Eastern Convention when comics were tossed into a crowd of fans. About putting things in perspective, and how it's just comics (rather than movies) and not worth anyone being hurt. The column which Joe Monks took me to task for, since I didn't specifically cite Image as the instigator.

Well, Joe's just gonna love this.

At that selfsame Wonder-Con, as I was sitting at the *CBG* table thinking about the two members of "Seduction of the Innocent" who were attending Brandon Lee's funeral and, consequently and understandably, were not able to attend (however the remaining performers, plus such pick-ups as Marvel's Don Daley on drums, did a splendid job, although my own guest singing appearance was lousy; I had an off-night and went completely off key, limping through the song and apologizing profusely to everyone afterward), when several people, one after the other, came up to me.

They had looks ranging from astonishment to outrage, and they each said the exact same thing: "Image is doing it again."

I didn't see it myself. But a half-dozen people confirmed it to me separately, which is more than enough for any news story. And what they were confirming was that, at the Image booth, comics were being hurled into the crowd — the convention equivalent of standing at a Michael Jackson concert, pointing to your right and saying loudly, "Hey! Michael! Aren't you supposed to be on stage?"

Fortunately, there was nowhere near the mayhem that came about at the Great Eastern Convention. First, the crowd was smaller. Second, it was a California crowd, as opposed to New York. And third, they were stopped fairly quickly by Image Publisher Tony Lobito or the WonderCon security crew or some combination thereof, according to various sources.

Now, I must take special care to mention at this point that *none* of the Image creators were involved with it. As near as I can determine, they were nowhere around. It was all Image staff people. Indeed, perhaps (and it's just a guess here), they were trying to keep crowd enthusiasm high in the absence of The Gods Themselves.

I have a great deal of trouble believing that they were oblivious to what happened in New York. Part of me wants to believe that they were simply ignorant. I have a far greater suspicion, though, that they were very aware of what happened. They were probably even aware that this column, Don and Maggie, and various *Oh, So?* letter writers have taken them to task.

Which means that they were out to display utter contempt for the opinions of those who are concerned about matters of safety and, by extension, contempt for the safety of those who are their fans.

This isn't like, say, when Marvel has its crazed game-show formats for panels, and Marvel staffers toss comics into the audience. In those instances, the audience is seated and stays so. Anyway, Marvel doesn't have the aura these days of "gotta get it" that Image basks in; besides, Marvel seems to have discontinued the game show stuff, at least at WonderCon. Perhaps it realized the dangers inherent when you get a crowd hyped up. Image, however, apparently hasn't clued into it yet.

The behavior at the Image booth was execrable. Inexcusable. Whatever justifications for ignorance could be pleaded from Great Eastern are long gone. The Image staffers knew perfectly well what was going to happen, when they started tossing comic books into the crowd. They knew people were going to start jumping, shouting, grabbing. They knew damned well that they were playing with fire, and they didn't care. They didn't care.

I have no idea what could possibly drive any exhibitors to so openly flaunt their disregard for safety. At best, they are acting like public nuisances. At the very worst, they are leaving conventions open to lawsuits, should something unfortunate happen. As I've made clear above, mishaps occur even in controlled environments such as movie sets. And the confines of a convention dealers' room, where gullible fans and berserk speculators are being incited to riot, is hardly controlled.

Again, I emphasize it wasn't the Image creators who were involved in this, but rather the staffers. What could possibly prompt Image staffers to behave in this deplorable manner? The answer, perhaps, again lies in Diamond's book:

"(H)umans differ from either common chimps or pygmy chimps in about 1.6% of their (our) DNA, and share 98.4%. Gorillas differ somewhat more, by about 2.3%, from us or from either of the chimps —

"The genetic distance (1.6%) separating us from pygmy or common chimps is barely double that separating pygmy from common chimps (0.7%). It's less than that between two species of gibbons (2.2%), or between such closely related North American bird species as red-eyed vireos and white-eyed vireos (2.9%). The remaining 98.4% of our DNA is just normal chimp DNA — "

Yes, that's right, sports fans. Human beings are, genetically, merely 1.6% removed from nominally dumb animals.

And it may be that there are some members of the species who are even less removed than that.

(Peter David, writer of stuff, has the sneaking suspicion that it is his tendency to write these closes in third person that led to the confused notion that they might be written by someone other than he. That is not the case. It is merely an affectation. These closes are written by me. I write them in the third person to distinguish from the rest of the column. I apologize, if it's caused any confusion.)

Historical Notes:

1) A gun has been developed called a "Non-gun," which emits a flash but does not, cannot, fire. It has yet to gain any widespread use in Hollywood.

SECTION 12:

Useless Stories

The reasons for "Useless Stories" are pretty much laid out in the first installment, so I don't really have to explain them here.

It has been fun, though, to have an outlet for those stories that have no outlet. I like to think that, first and foremost, I am a paid fabricator. Fabricating just for the fun of it comes, sometimes, as a welcome release.

QUANTUM BEAST, PART 1 (Nov. 2, 1990)

I must first make mention of my biggest fan: John Byrne. Anyone can read my column and enjoy it, but only John is so dedicated that he continues to peruse it, week after week, even though the very act causes him to vomit.

Only a real man would endure such physical discomfort to stick with me. And rest assured — should my enthusiasm for this column ever waver — all I have to do is picture John face down at the porcelain life preserver, tossing his lunch while clutching my column, and that image will be more than enough to sustain me.

With that out of the way, we now move into the first installment of an irregular feature of But I Digress, namely:

Useless Stories

For all writers (well, almost all) there are stories which literally write themselves — that spring full-blown into one's mind with a kind of "Eureka" finality, there-it-is, game-set-and-match.

But the simple act of writing a story down isn't sufficient, because the purpose of writing is communication. Putting the story down is only one half of a writer's job — the rest is to get it out to an audience, to share the ideas.

So you have to find a marketplace or a means by which to get the story to readers. In my case, I have a number of directions I can explore — comics, novels, short stories, screenplays (I've written three, none produced) — all of these are avenues I can pursue, with varying degrees of success, in getting stories told. And every so often, I come up with a Useless Story. This is a story which, by its very nature, cannot possibly appear in any of the media stated above. It doesn't mean it's a *bad* story. It's just that no one could possibly buy it. But if it's a story that I like enough, it sits in my head and shouts at me, and I can't shut it up until I tell it to someone.

So I'm telling it to you.

The first germs of it began when I saw a two-hour episode of a certain television series and absolutely hated it. I wanted to do something about it but naturally I couldn't. And then, very recently, I was watching another TV series and suddenly realized that I *could* do something about it. And here's what I did, in a story titled:

Quantum Beast

Dr. Sam Beckett felt the abrupt tingling and sudden disorientation that warned him he was leaping once more. The world kaleidoscoped around him, a shimmering burst of blue, and for one fleeting moment came the customary prayer — *Please. Please, let this be the one that brings me home.* He wasn't certain to whom he was praying or why. Whatever gods there were, they certainly had their own game plan for him and would only return him to the site of the Quantum Leap project when they were ready.

Then reality irised in again, coalesced, and the world reassembled itself into a different time and place.

When someone wakes up in an unfamiliar situation — a hotel, for example — there's always a momentary feeling of confusion. Of trying to get one's bearings. It was a feeling Sam knew all too well. There was the usual flash of despair, as Sam realized that he had not returned to the origin point of the time-travel project that had launched him: the project that had him travelling, always within his own lifetime, always in the bodies of others.

The despair was immediately replaced by puzzlement. The air that hung around Sam was heavy and dank. There was an odd silence, punctuated by — what? A faint tapping of some sort, as if people were banging on metal. It sounded like annoyed tenants, pounding on radiators somewhere, sending a message to some superintendent that heat should be sent up.

Was he in a tenement or something? No. No, definitely not. He was in a room lit only by flickering tapers, and the room was, incredibly, made of rock. He was in a cave somewhere, but *what* a cave: beautifully decorated with an old-world charm, like something out of a fairy tale.

He glanced around, his eyes resting on a small library against the wall. Dickens was there, and Shakespeare. Dante and Chekhov. Playwrights and poets, philosophers and dreamers, the greatest minds and thinkers of humanity were all represented in this bizarre place.

"What the hell — ?" he murmured, his voice echoing softly in the small chamber.

He spun, his eyes searching out a mirror on the wall.

The face of a monster stared back at him.

Sam Beckett jumped back a good five feet, letting out a scream of alarm that, to his horrified ears, was the roar of an infuriated animal. He tripped over a bed and tumbled back. He cowered there a moment, afraid to look, afraid the creature might still be looking back at him.

Slowly he pulled himself up and went again to the mirror. The creature, with long, flowing brown hair and a face like a lion, cocked its head in curiosity.

He brought his hands up to look at them, as well. They were covered with thick fur, and at the end were — claws?

Then he laughed.

"Of course," he said. "It's Halloween or something. This guy's going to a party."

He pulled at the furry gloves and they refused to come off.

He reached up, grabbed his muzzle, and yanked. It felt warm and firm and alive.

He yelled again, this time a full-throated roar of terror.

There was the sound of pounding footsteps, and an instant later a bearded man burst into the room. His hair was tinged with gray, and he was dressed in the same earlier-century style as the body that Sam was inhabiting. He walked with a carved cane.

Sam took a step back, waiting for the man to scream at the sight of him.

"Vincent!" said the bearded man. "What's wrong?"

Sam glanced behind himself, not able to grasp the idea that the creature whose body he possessed had a name. "Vincent?" he said.

The bearded man looked at him with tremendous concern. "Don't you recognize me?" he said slowly. "It's me. Father."

"Father!" gasped Sam. "My God? You mean — " He looked in the mirror again. "I got all this from my mother's side?"

Father went to him and put his hands on either of Sam's muscled arms. "Vincent — please — sit down."

Sam allowed himself to be guided to the edge of the bed, still disoriented and confused. "You're my father —"

"As much of a father as you've ever had," said Father, still sounding worried. "You know that you were found as an infant, abandoned at nearby St. Vincent's hospital, and were brought here."

"Yes, of course, I — " Sam tried to shake it off. "Of course, I remember — Father. I'm sorry, I'm — a little shaky these days," he finished lamely.

And yet Father seemed to accept this. "Of course," he said. "Of course you are. All these months, not knowing. I'm aware of how your concern over Catherine has eaten at you."

"Catherine —" said Sam slowly, still not getting it.

"Catherine Chandler."

It was not the bearded man who had spoken, however.

Al had stepped through a rock wall. He was wearing one of his usually loud suits, this one with dazzlingly glimmering gold trim.

Sam looked up at him with tremendous relief. "Catherine Chandler?"

"Yes, Catherine Chandler," Father said. "Vincent — have you been getting enough sleep?"

"I — feel like I'm dreaming right now," said Sam, looking helplessly at Al. Al flashed a high sign.

"I must admit, Vincent, for a moment I thought that we were going to see a recurrence of the unpleasantness from some months ago," said Father ruefully. "You're quite all right?"

"Fine. Fine, Father. Really. See?" He flexed his muscles. "One hundred percent. Tip top."

Father stared at him as if he'd just muttered an obscenity. " 'Tip Top?' '

"Oh, yeah. I'm fine."

"You usually sound more — I'm not sure —poetic."

Sam blinked and said, "Uhm — Roses are red — grass is green — Catherine's not here — and I feel keen."

Father stared at him long and hard. "Get some rest, Vincent. Please." He eased Sam back onto the bed, turned, and walked right past Al.

Sam snapped back up. "Al, get me out of here!"

"Can't do that, Sam," said Al apologetically. "You know you can't leap until you've accomplished whatever you've been sent here to do." He glanced around. "It's not so bad here. Nice little getaway."

"You can say that; you're a hologram!" said Sam. He walked around the room in confusion. "I don't like the insides of caves! They make me nervous! And that damned tapping won't shut up!"

"This isn't a cave, precisely," Al informed him. "You're under Manhattan."

"Manhattan? "

"Yup. That tapping you hear is their way of communicating, via underground pipes. There's a whole society living under here. You should see it."

"I don't want to see it! This is creepy, Al. This is really creepy." Sam sounded more nervous than Al had ever heard him. Sam held up a hand. "These are claws, Al. I could rip somebody to shreds with these things!"

"You have. Or rather, this guy named Vincent has."

"What?"

Al was busily tapping into the computer back at the Quantum Leap project. He studied the readout on the hand unit. "According to Ziggy," he said briskly, "there was a series of slayings in Manhattan in the late '80s — you're in 1989, by the way — that involved various underworld types being ripped to shreds by something like a wild beast."

"Wild beast," murmured Sam. He stared at his claws in the mirror.

"Newspapers drew a link between those killings to a woman in the D.A.'s office named Catherine Chandler. The problem is, she was eventually found dead, as well."

Sam felt his gorge rising. "Ripped apart?"

"Poisoned," said Al. "Found in her apartment, poisoned. According to Ziggy, that's apparently why you're here. There's a 97% probability," Al looked up, "that you're supposed to save Catherine Chandler."

QUANTUM BEAST — CONCLUSION (Nov. 9, 1990)

And now, another ripping installment of

Useless Stories

Stories that I dreamed up, but couldn't possibly sell anywhere. And this week "Useless Stories" concludes —

Quantum Beast

(Recap: When we last left our time-travelling hero, Dr. Sam Beckett, he had leaped into the body of the man-monster known only as Vincent. His mission: to avert the death of the woman who is Vincent's true love, Catherine Chandler, at the hands of the fiendish Gabriel.)

In the recess of the subway tunnel, Sam peered out from the shadows at the crowded platform. In the distance, but approaching rapidly, was an uptown Lexington Avenue train. The ground was rumbling beneath Sam's booted feet, and rats were scurrying about to get out of the way of the train.

"You can't be serious," he said to Al.

Al, his holographic companion and advisor, glanced once more at the handheld computer interface unit called "Ziggy." Al nodded briskly, taking a puff on a cigar. Al's nonchalance was especially irritating to Sam in many instances, because it reminded him that it was always his butt on the line, not Al's.

"I'm afraid so, Sam," Al confirmed. "It's definitely this Vincent guy's M.O. That's *modus operandi* —"

"I know what it is," Sam cut him off. The train was getting closer. "You're telling me that I'm supposed to ride to the rescue of Catherine Chandler, clinging onto the top of a subway car?"

"That's how he always does it," said Al.

Sam looked again at the oncoming train. He glanced up now at the girdered ceiling. It looked narrow. *Too* narrow. If he picked up his head at the wrong time, he'd cave in his face. Of course, he realized, glancing at his reflection in a puddle, that might be something of an improvement.

"We're in New York, right?"

"That's right, Sam."

"Fine. Vincent can do things his way. I do them mine."

"Sam!" shouted Al, and then he couldn't hear himself as the subway ran over him. Or, more precisely, ran through him. He was, of course, utterly unharmed.

Sam, for his part, strode boldly into the subway car and sat down in an empty seat.

The subway passengers glanced at him. And looked. And stared.

And then they laughed. Or shook their heads. Or made "tsk" noises. Right after that, one by one, they went back to reading newspapers, or chatting with each other. The train started and Sam still garnered an occasional glance. Otherwise, there was no particular reaction.

Al had materialized on board the train and he was looking around in amazed shock. "They're ignoring you!" he said in astonishment.

Sam's leonine lips drew back in amusement. "They're New Yorkers, Al."

"But this Vincent guy is always terrified that someone's going to see him!"

"Beats me why," Sam said in a low voice. "They just assume it's a mask, Al. Or a publicity stunt or a gag."

Al glanced over his shoulder. Seated directly across from Sam was a beefy young man sporting a pink mohawk, red fishnet stocking, white shorts that read "Home of the Big Kahuna," and a black leather vest exposing muscular arms that had "For a good time call JAG-OFFS," tattooed on either bicep. The young man was looking at Sam and shaking his head in disgust.

"Freak," muttered the young man.

Al stared at him in amazement, then back at Sam. "I am in awe of you, Sam."

"Thank you," replied Sam.

A drunk staggered up to Sam and snarled, "Move over, Leo. I wanna siddown."

Sam obediently moved over and the drunk parked himself.

"Who're you talkin' to?" said the drunk.

Why not? thought Sam. "Al," he replied. He pointed. "He's standing right there."

"I don't see him," said the drunk.

"You don't?"

"No." The drunk squinted. "Probably because of the two pink-and-green Sumo wrestlers standing in front of him."

Al rolled his eyes.

* * *

Pain shot through Catherine Chandler, pain that was beyond belief. She clutched at her belly.

Through her haze of agony, she saw the ghostly image of the man called Gabriel standing before her. He nodded briskly. "Looks like it's time, Catherine," he said softly. Evilly.

"Vincent," she moaned.

For a moment — just a moment — she thought she saw a flicker of something else. A man, with short black hair and a cigar — and then he vanished.

Sam stood in front of a huge office building. "This is definitely Gabriel's main headquarters," said Al. "She's up there, all right. She's way pregnant and not in great shape. On the way down, though, I passed at least two dozen security guards, plus cameras. Place is a fortress. Getting in's going to be dicey."

"She's a prisoner there?"

"Kidnapped, yeah."

"That's what I thought," said Sam. He turned and started to walk away. "You head back up, time the contractions, keep an eye on things. I'll handle everything else."

Al followed him, gesturing in confusion. "Sam! Sam, where're you going?"

Sam stepped up to a pay phone. He picked up the receiver, punched in three numbers.

A woman picked up on the third ring. "911," she said.

"I want to report a kidnap victim," said Sam briskly. "Catherine Chandler. I know where she's being held."

Catherine lay back on the delivery table, gasping. Gabriel, the monster, stood by impassively, as did the nurse. The doctor who was to perform the delivery looked up. "There's a problem," he said.

"This is taking too long," said Gabriel icily. "Remove the child."

And then there was a significant look passed between Gabriel and the doctor — a look that, to Al, bespoke volumes.

Al shot out of the delivery room with lightning speed.

"They're gonna kill her, Sam!" he said urgently.

Sam looked at him. "What? Now? But the police aren't here yet!"

"They're going to deliver the baby via c-section, and then they're going to kill Catherine Chandler. It's now or never, Sam!"

With a roar of frustration, Sam charged towards the building.

The great glass doors were locked. Sam didn't even slow down. He brought his arms up before his face for protection and barrelled through. Glass exploded into the lobby.

There was a guard sitting at a front desk, and he immediately leaped to his feet, pulling a gun. He froze as Sam rolled to his feet and faced him. "What the hell — ?" he murmured.

"The police are on their way!" Sam informed him. "There's a kidnapped woman upstairs! You better ask yourself whether your boss pays you enough to risk doing hard time in a federal penitentiary!"

The guard brought his gun up and fired.

Sam was already in motion, dazzled at the reflexes of the great body. He hurtled forward, leaping high over the shot, and slammed into the guard, smashing him to the floor. The guard was unconscious, as Sam pulled the gun off him.

"Guess he *does* pay enough," muttered Sam.

"Maybe he offers a great benefits package," Al suggested.

Sam charged into the nearest stairwell and started up the steps.

On a landing two flights up, Al shouted down, "Sam! Two guards, right here!"

The guards didn't hear him, of course. But they leaned forward, thinking they would have the drop on the intruder when they began firing. Instead they presented perfect targets, and Sam shot both of them with the gun he'd taken off the guard. He shot them in the legs, and they went down, writhing and screaming.

He ran up and past them, stopping only momentarily to relieve them of their machine guns. "This could get nasty, Sam," Al told him.

"Nastier than 'Nam?" Sam asked.

"Could be."

"I'll chance it."

The doctor poised over Catherine Chandler, scalpel ready to slice across her stomach. Nearby was a syringe that he would administer shortly thereafter. Death would be quick and painless.

"Please — don't —" whispered Catherine.

And suddenly a guard burst in. "Sir! We're under attack!"

"Don't do anything," Gabriel ordered the doctor. "I must be here for the birth. I shall return momentarily."

Seconds later Gabriel stared at an array of television screens. *He* was coming. And he was —

Armed?

The beast-man looked up, as if responding to some unseen voice. Then the beast-man raised a machine gun (gun?!) and blew out the TV cameras.

From down below could be heard the sounds of sirens.

"We're leaving," said Gabriel.

Sam burst into the delivery room, cradling an uzi. The room was empty.

"The roof, Sam!" shouted Al. "They're on the roof!"

Sam charged upstairs.

Catherine pitched forward, the pain so overwhelming that she couldn't move her legs any more. Gabriel caught her by one arm, the doctor by the other. A guard was bringing up the rear, and a pilot was revving up the engine of a helicopter that was atop the roof. He was gesturing frantically. Far below he could see the lights of the police cars.

The guard suddenly shouted a warning, as Sam burst out onto the roof. The guard opened fire and Sam ducked behind a vent stack. Bullets pinged off it.

"Run!" shouted the guard. "Run! I'll hold him!" and he continued firing.

Then his trigger clicked on an empty magazine. He ejected it, knowing that there was no way his target could cover the distance in the time it would take him to reload.

The beast-man leaped, arms outstretched, an uzi slung over his shoulder. He landed barely five paces from the astounded guard.

Sam swung an arm up with blinding speed and slammed aside the barrel. His leg lashed out and smashed the guard onto his back. He tried to get back up, and Sam whirled, a sharp kick to the head knocking the guard flat. The guard slipped into unconsciousness.

"*Vincent!*" came the scream.

Sam spun. The helicopter was lifting off. Catherine Chandler was being hauled into the cockpit by a vampiric-looking man who had to be Gabriel. Catherine was fighting back as best she could, her gown billowing around her.

With a roar, Sam charged forward and leaped. His right hand snagged one of the main landing supports. With his free hand he unslung the uzi.

Gabriel's foot lashed out, trying to kick Sam loose. "You can't have it!" shouted Gabriel over the noise of the rotor blades. "It's mine!"

The heel of Gabriel's boot came down again and again on Sam's hand. Al was screaming something and Sam couldn't make it out. Then he realized. The helicopter had swirled sideways and was over the street. He was dangling thousands of feet up.

In the cockpit, Catherine gathered her strength and lunged forward, screaming "Vincent!" Her body hit lengthwise across Gabriel's, blocking Sam who had had, momentarily, a clear shot at Gabriel with the machine gun.

With an animalistic snarl, Gabriel kicked at the uzi, shoving the barrel away. Reflexively Sam's finger closed on the trigger, and a stream of bullets tore into the upper rotor, shredding it.

The helicopter lurched wildly and Catherine tumbled out.

Sam reached out desperately and snagged her wrist just as she fell past. The helicopter skewed, out of control, back toward the roof from which it had come. As they hurtled by, Sam released his grip and he gathered Catherine in his arms, as the helicopter lurched wildly past the roof and kept on going.

Sam landed, absorbing the impact with his powerful legs. He caught a brief glimpse of the helicopter, as it spiralled away and down, down towards the street below.

There were alarmed shouts and then an explosive crashing of metal and a fireball that seemed to leap upward from the street level, as if the gates of hell had opened to receive one of their own.

Sam lay Catherine down on the roof. "Vincent," she gasped. "I knew you'd come. I was not afraid to die, my love, for death shall have — no dominion —"

"No one's dying," said Sam briskly, and he quickly examined her. The baby had to be delivered almost immediately, or he was going to lose both of them. "Breech birth," he muttered. "Damn. Have to do a c-section."

No time. He needed a scalpel to remove the baby, and she wasn't going to make it back down to the delivery room. No time. He needed something sharp —

Something sharp —

He extended a finger. A razor-sharp claw glistened in the moonlight.

* * *

Below the city streets, Sam looked around in wonderment at the assortment of people around him. The underground people, Al had called him. There was the one called Father and a blind woman and an odd young man with blonde hair — all of them, smiling.

And the one with the widest smile, beaming, radiant, was Catherine. She stood next to Sam, leaning against him, cradling her — their — son in her arms.

The bearded man was intoning something about naming. Sam was paying attention as best he could, and then Catherine said to him in a low voice, "Who are you?"

He looked at her in astonishment. "But I'm —" Then he saw the look in her eyes, and he replied softly, "Don't worry. Vincent will be back with you in just a moment, I'm sure. Don't ask me to explain. I barely understand it myself."

"Just tell me your name."

"Sam."

And the old man, Father, was just saying, " — and so, we welcome into our community —"

"Sam," Catherine said loudly.

The others looked at her oddly. "You want to name the child Sam?" asked Father.

She looked up at him, smiling, grateful to be alive. "I can't think of a better one," she said.

And then a world of blue seemed to leap out of Catherine's eyes and surround him, and Sam leaped —

* * *

There was a droning in his head. Numbers.

"Ten — nine — eight —"

Reality spiraled back around him. Sam stood, confused as always. He glanced around.

He was in some sort of control room. Over on the far side of the room were six people. They were wearing silver jumpsuits, looking like giant frozen dinners, and were in suspended animation inside of tubes.

" — seven — six — five —"

Sam looked down at himself. He was wearing some sort of uniform. There was a nameplate on it: Dr. Z. Smith.

The ground rumbled beneath him as a voice said,

"Four — three — two. . . "

"Ooohhhh, boy," said Sam.

Historical Notes:

1) In the first section, reference is made to John Byrne vomiting. The reason is as follows: John had written his very first letter of comment about my column, and it basically said that every week he read **BID** *and every week it made him vomit. Upon reading this, many people thought I would be outraged. Instead I thought it was funny and wrote the reply you see here.*

Since then, the war of words between myself and Byrne has calmed down a bit — especially with the advent of other players in the comics game whom John seems to dislike a lot more than me.

2) Sam Beckett — in Vincent's body — makes use of Vincent's claws. It was pointed out to me that he should not have been able to do this. Well, too bad. He did it anyway.

3) I learned later on that a fan had self-published an identically themed story, likewise called "Quantum Beast." Not only that, she had done a flip-side version featuring Vincent in the Waiting Room. I was unaware of this and was extremely relieved to learn that, other than the basic concept, the events of the stories were nothing alike.

4) At the end, Sam had leaped into the body of Doctor Zachary Smith, just as the **Jupiter II** *was about to launch into her ill-fated flight that would leave the Robinson family "Lost in Space." I spell it out here, because some readers didn't get it.*

WHATEVER HAPPENED TO THE LITTLE MERMAID'S MOTHER (Nov. 1, 1991)

A fish finds that everyone in the MerCity is being very quiet and sad. Everyone seems to be hanging around outside the entryway doors to the great hall of the Sea King, but no one is going in. The fish demands in a loud voice to know what's going on. Another fish starts to chew him out for being disrespectful, and the friend doesn't know what he's talking about. But the Little Mermaid — who is also quite sad, but patient, nevertheless, takes the friend aside and explains to him the significance of this day.

And we flash back to a number of years ago, with a young Little Mermaid — about 6 years of age — and memories of her with her mother, Atlanta. Her mother is young, vibrant, and inquisitive — many of the qualities that the Little Mermaid possesses. She even bears something of a resemblance to the Little Mermaid. Her hair, however, is not red — it is brown. The red hair belongs to her husband, the Sea King — long, flowing red hair, thick red beard — and he absolutely adores his wife. He dotes on her and the children she's given him.

And what is Atlanta's greatest interest? The surface world.

And then, one day, Atlanta is basking on some rocks, enjoying the sun. The rocks are at the edge of a cove that is surrounded by large outcroppings of rocks, forming a virtually private beach.

Unnoticed by Atlanta, there is a young man named Duncan who has seen her and is sketching furiously on a large pad. Then Atlanta spots him and demands to know what he's doing. Nervously, Duncan shows what he's drawing, and Atlanta is struck by the beauty of it. Duncan would love to do more detailed paintings of her, and Atlanta goes to her husband and asks his permission (since Merpeople tend to steer clear of humans, just as a matter of caution). The Sea King is a little skittish about it, but Atlanta sweet-talks him into it.

So Atlanta goes to pose for Duncan, and at one point we see the Sea King watching from a distance. He sees how much Atlanta is enjoying posing for the young artist and even decides that maybe the stories told by his father about how humans were monsters might have been exaggerations. Even so, he still keeps a considerable distance from the cove, and out of sight.

Duncan's paintings become tremendous hits, drawing attention away from another artist, an embittered man named Kole. He is jealous of Duncan's skill and thinks that Duncan is overrated. He probes Duncan about this beautiful model he must be using, but Duncan is tight-lipped, per his promise to Atlanta that he not spread word of her presence.

Atlanta, while posing for Duncan, asks him about the surface world, but more often than not Duncan doesn't even hear what she's saying, since he is concentrating so completely on his work. When Atlanta returns to the MerCity, her daughters ask if they can come along and be painted, as well, but their father absolutely forbids this. But Atlanta says to him, "Look, come and see the latest painting he's working on — it promises to be the most beautiful of all. If you see that and see the quality of what he can do — perhaps you won't be so nervous about it. And you'll let him paint portraits of the girls." He says he'll think about it.

It is the next day. Kole sees his paintings sitting and collecting dust, while Duncan's are commanding large amounts of money. He's driven into a jealous rage and this time follows Duncan, when Duncan heads off to paint. He spies on him from the cliffsides overhead and is stunned when he sees that Duncan has a real-life mermaid posing for him.

Cut to the ocean where the Sea King decides he's going to do what his wife suggested — he's actually going to go up, see the human's work close up, maybe even talk to him. Perhaps a new age of merpeople/human collaboration is dawning.

Cut to Kole, situated on a ledge overlooking Duncan, who is totally involved in his painting. There are a number of large rocks situated on the ledge as well. He resolves to get rid of his rival once and for all and, putting all his strength into it, shoves at the rocks and unbalances them.

Atlanta sees, from the rock she's perched on, what's about to happen and shouts a warning. But Duncan doesn't hear her, because he's concentrating so fully on the painting. The rocks come tumbling down, and a desperate Atlanta launches herself through the air, startling Duncan as she knocks him out of the way. But now, on the ground, she can't maneuver fast enough, and the rocks fall on her.

Her husband, a distance away, emerges from the water and sees what's happened. He screams in horror.

Duncan has pulled Atlanta from the rubble and is crouched over her. From overhead, Kole is shouting furiously that Duncan is next, and he's pushing at other rocks.

And suddenly the sky blackens, lightning cracks across the sky, the sea roils, and the Sea King *looms* out of the water, 20 stories tall, thundering, "*What have you done to my wife?*"

Kole, freaking out, runs like mad, trips, falls, and plummets to his death. Good riddance.

The Sea King now towers over Duncan, taking Atlanta's body in his hands. Furious, he bellows at Duncan, "This is your fault! If you hadn't started with this obsession, she'd still be alive!"

"Don't you think I know that?" shouts Duncan. "It's all my fault! Do what you will!" He bows his head, the unfinished painting of Atlanta next to him on the sand.

And the Sea King draws his trident back to strike, and suddenly the clouds in front of him seem to form into an image of Atlanta as she whispers, "My love, don't let your fury consume you. Don't let it do this to you. Please, please don't let this be the way that I remember you, but instead as the kind, gentle husband I loved."

We angle on Duncan, head bowed, waiting for the end. And then suddenly, the clouds part. He looks up. The Sea King is gone. So is Atlanta. And so is the painting.

There is great sadness in the MerCity when the Sea King returns with the body of his wife. He locks himself into his study. And there he stays for a week. Not seeing anyone. Not speaking to anyone. Finally it is the 6-year-old Little Mermaid, pleading at the door to his chamber, telling him that losing one parent is bad enough — she can't stand losing both of them — that gets him to open it. And when he does, to the shock and horror of everyone, his hair and beard are now dead white — the white that we've come to know. Without a word he embraces his children.

We cut to the Little Mermaid finishing the telling of the story, and the young fish now says that he understands. "Today is the anniversary of the Queen's death, isn't it?" Yes, she says.

And we cut to the Sea King, in his chamber, staring sadly at something, as the Littler Mermaid explains, "Daddy knew that, if he just let his mourning go unchecked, it could have destroyed him. He came back to us. But one day a year, he returns to our mother, and we all mourn her. Because there was so much she could have done, and we mourn our loss." And we pull back to see that he is staring at the unfinished painting of Atlanta as the Little Mermaid concludes, "and the rest of her life that was left unfinished."

BLAST FROM THE PAST (May 15, 1992)

And now, due to absolutely no demand at all, we present another installment of:
Useless Stories

A couple of years ago, as a tie-in with DC's "Invasion" storyline, artist James Fry and I produced one of the single silliest comics it's ever been our joy to put out: *The Blasters*.

The utter antithesis of every serious space-saga ever produced, *Blasters* featured the adventures of humans who had, as a result of alien experiments, developed super-powers. The project was originally developed by James and Robert Loren Fleming. I was brought in and told that DC wanted to go in "a different direction" with them.

I went in a different direction, all right. I went insane. Absurd in-jokes (ranging from *Hitchhiker's Guide to the Galaxy* to *Star Trek* to *Who Framed Roger Rabbit*) were scattered throughout an utterly loopy story and semi-whacked characterization. I knew a lot of people would hate it. Usually I get very concerned about that notion. With *Blasters*, I didn't care.

The main characters were the old JLA mascot Snapper Carr (who could transport by snapping his fingers); Churljenkins, a green-furred cat female; Jolt, who uncontrollably repulsed everyone and everything (kind of like the entire slate of Democratic candidates); Gunther, an alien scientist who tried to alleviate her condition; Frag, a big German guy who exploded into fragments; Dexter, a British guy whose body became round and large, like a mirror, and projected reflected light; Crackpot, a black guy who could talk anyone into anything; Moishe, a small Israeli boy who could spin at cyclonic speeds; and his mother, who had no powers but was the most formidable member of the group because she was a Jewish mother.

So this one-shot special came out, and some people liked it, and some people hated it, and I didn't give it much more thought, because it had been a hoot to work on and that was all that mattered.

Then, a few months ago, I was contacted about the possibility of doing another *Blasters* one-shot. To my mind, there were only two reasons for doing so: to get to work with James again and to see if we could get even more demented than before.

The go-ahead was given, and James and I got together at my house. Our firm conviction about The Blasters hadn't wavered: This group was far too eclectic to try to write anything remotely straight about them. Besides, what was the point? There were lots of straight space adventure stories out there.

Considering the way we'd done *Blasters* the first time, they barely seemed to fit into the present DC Universe at all. And so we decided, hell, let's do something that takes them out of that universe altogether.

And we did, cackling dementedly all the way.

An outline (not a full plot) was sent in, approved at the outset, but then rejected further on down the line, because it didn't fit into the current atmosphere of the DC universe.

We tried to be silly and in-jokey and apparently succeeded beyond our wildest dreams.

Maybe they'll bring in Bob Fleming to go in a different direction with it. That would be appropriate. In the meantime, since I never saw any money off it, I figure it's mine. So you *Blasters* fans (both of you) can thrill to the story you've been saved from, thanks to DC editorial diligence, namely:

The Return of The Blasters
Outline for one-shot
by Peter David & James Fry

Once again The *Blasters* launch into outer-space adventures, this time to save the hapless denizens of an alternate-dimension planet from falling prey to the darksome intentions of an interplanetary menace. Featuring more bizarre riffs, strange attitudes, and insane twists than anyone could possibly expect — or believe, for that matter. At the same time, *Blasters* continues the fourth-wall-shattering, comics-tweaking attitude that had fans all over the country saying, "What the hell is this?"

In recent months, things have gone badly for The Blasters. Since their comic book was not picked up as a regular series, the group broke up and the members went their separate ways, each trying to eke out a living. The smooth-talking Amos, a.k.a. Crackpot, who can convince anyone of the truth of anything he says, is now working as a White House Press liaison. Young Moishe, a.k.a. Dust Devil, is becoming a successful child star, starring as a youthful Captain Kirk in *Star Trek VII: The Voyage Home Alone*.

Others have found employment in the world of comics: Frag, with his exploding abilities, is now a super-villain stunt double (explaining how super-villains always seem to manage to survive the life-ending situations they're in); Dexter is helping Gotham City save electricity by functioning as the Bat Signal; Jolt and Gunther are operating a beauty salon, specializing in producing those weirdo zapped haircuts so popular with such characters as Lobo and Wolverine.

Churljenkins, the rock-and-rolling cat female is currently unemployed, although she has been doing doubling work for Tigra, Catwoman, and the many other feline characters in the various universes. And Snapper Carr has been pursuing, with a singular lack of success, a singing career.

Things change abruptly when Snapper is contacted by representatives from the far off world of Dizz-Nee (the Happiest Planet in the Universe). The reps are under the misconception that The Blasters are, in fact, a singing group, and want them to perform. Snapper, seizing the opportunity, manages to convince the other members of The Blasters to leave their current positions and take their act on the spaceroads.

The Blasters take off, but trouble strikes, when their rented ship goes off course and they fall into a bizarre galactic anomaly called a Kitchen Sink Hole. They drop through the Sink Hole (passing some old webbing that reads "The Spirit") and emerge into a pocket universe (complete with lint.) In front of them is a large world that is being, of all things, pushed along by a small group of super-powered animals.

The Blasters confront the animals, who are revealed to be the SCPA (Space Canine Patrol Agency; one of their members is Krypto, of course, except that Krypto doesn't exist any more, so he'll be wearing nose glasses and a cape with a prohibit slash through the "S" so that no one will know it's him). There is a brief altercation before the SCPA realizes that The Blasters are not their enemy, nor are they agents of He Who Is Their Enemy — namely the planet-ravaging individual known as Galaxis.

The SCPA members have moved their home world, which is called Mort, to this relatively secluded section of space to keep it safe from the anger of Galaxis. Ignoring the fact that this is, of course, preposterous, The Blasters head to the planet surface (noting as they go that the skies are purple) to meet with the ruler of the planet Mort who is, naturally, a talking gorilla. They also run into pastiche versions of the following denizens of the planet Mort: PET (the cats who are pets of the Phantom Zone criminals); Bat-Mite; Super-Turtle; Mopee; female reporters who only dream about unmasking someone; Beppo; whoever else occurs to us. Also, all small children on Mort begin sentences with the phrase "Me am — " and virtually everyone speaks, not in normal conversational tones, but instead in expository dialogue.

It turns out that Galaxis is the enemy of all that Mort stands for. Herein is revealed the Secret Origin of the humongous space-going Galaxis: Eons ago, at the dawn of time, Galaxis was walking home from a movie with his parents, Eternity and Death. And then, to the horror of young Galaxis, his parents were gunned down by Joe Chill.

This so traumatized young Galaxis that, as he grew up, he swore vengeance on the entirety of the universe. But he wasn't sure what form that vengeance should take. And then one night he was sitting in his living room and a planet suddenly hurled through the window and fell into his fireplace, becoming covered with dirt and grit. "That's it!" declared Galaxis. "I shall take planets, and make them gritty!" And so Galaxis travels through the galaxy, taking happy and fun planets and turning them grim and gritty.

The Blasters try to organize the denizens of Mort, telling them that they must take a stand against Galaxis. Mort marshals its collective forces (except for Super-Turtle who's busy eating lollipops), and then Galaxis, in all his towering, grim and gritty fury, shows up. The Blasters and the Morts attack, but all their efforts are as nothing against the World Changer, as he readies his massive Grim and Gritty Ray. He then activates the ray —

And the planet Mort begins to transform. For one thing, it gets an "e" tacked on its name so it becomes "Morte." The SCPA turns into ravenous, snarling beasts. A number of beings are simply too silly to continue to exist — and blink out of existence.

And The Blasters themselves begin to transform, become grim and gritty versions of themselves. Churljenkins starts clawing people and speaking with caption narrative. Amos becomes angry and snarling because he's black. Frag becomes an ex-Nazi alcoholic. Snapper starts snapping necks instead of fingers. Jolt becomes a prostitute, and Gunther her pimp. In one of the most bizarre changes of all, the British Dexter is transformed into — to all intents and purposes — Sandman, using his reflecting power to become a mirror of all the darkness and bleakness in the soul of humanity. In addition his dialogue balloons become white-on-black and no one can make out what he's saying.

The last ones to be affected are Moishe and his mom (since Moishe is the youngest and most innocent, he's the toughest one to change). But it begins when his mom is blown away in cold blood, riddled with more holes than swiss cheese. Moishe runs away screaming, feeling himself also becoming grim and gritty. A 900 number is posted demanding whether or not Moishe should be killed. Moishe runs, screaming, to the office of the Gorilla president and, after narrowly escaping death, discovers a secret lab with a large raygun in a capsule that says, "Enlarging Ray. In Case of Planetary Disaster, Break Glass." Moishe breaks the ray out and turns it on himself, so that he can grow super-huge and confront Galaxis. But just as he activates it, Super-Turtle cruises by and gets caught in the ray.

Galaxis is looking over his handiwork. His job is just about done — and then suddenly to his amazement, he is confronted by the equally towering, super-humongous Giant Turtle Moishe. Giant Turtle Moishe slugs it out with Galaxis —

And the titanic confrontation is witnessed by all the grim and gritty inhabitants of Morte. It is easily the most ludicrous thing they have ever witnessed. They start to laugh uncontrollably, laughter and good humor sweeping the planet. And Dexter absorbs the emotions washing over him, concentrating it and turning the power onto the planet-ravaging Galaxis. Galaxis screams, writhes under the emotional power being turned upon him — and he starts to change —

And he is transformed into — Bizarro Galaxis #1. With a white, fragmented face and a completely new attitude, BG #1 is now determined to bring happiness and fun to the universe. He starts by transforming Morte back into Mort, putting everything the way it was (including reviving everyone who died). He then goes off to spread silliness throughout the galaxy, as the denizens of Mort wish him well.

Having defeated the menace of Galaxis, The Blasters must now find a way to return to their own dimension. The answer to that, of course, is simple: All they have to do is say aloud the word "Sretsalb" — Blasters spelled backwards — and they are magically sent back home. And ahead of them is Dizz-Nee, easy to spot, because it's this big planet with two equal-sized moons positioned at about 11 o'clock and 1 o'clock, giving it the general appearance of a giant stylized mousehead. The Blasters give their first major performance, are a tremendous hit, and launch a new career as a spacegoing rock and roll group.

And then, suddenly —

The comic book ends.

Just for the record, the *Secret Origin of Galaxis* is Part One of James' Secret Origin of Galactus. Herewith Part Two of James' Secret Origin, which explains, among other things, why Galactus had a big "G" on his chest when he first showed up (we would have worked this into the Blasters comic book, too.)

The setting is Stan Lee's office, and Jack Kirby walks in with the pages of *Fantastic Four* #48:

Jack: Here it is, Stan, the latest issue. Story we discussed about the FF fighting someone big and cosmic. Well, here he is.

Stan: This big guy here? With the "G" on him? He looks great, Jack. Who is he? What's the "G" stand for?

Jack: God.

Stan: God?

Jack: That's right, Stan.

Stan: We've got the FF fighting God?

Jack: Well, sure. Big guy, wearing a "G." Shows up on your planet and that's all she wrote. Who *else* is he supposed to be?

Stan: I dunno, Jack. I mean — the FF going up against God?

Jack: Don't count 'em out, Stan. That Ben Grimm, he's a pretty tough customer.

Stan: Hmm. And who's this guy here? on the surfboard?

Jack: That's Frankie Avalon.

Stan: What?

Jack: Oh yeah, trust me on this, Stan. The kids love Frankie Avalon. But I was having trouble with the hair, so I left him bald. Have Vinnie or somebody put that in.

Stan: The FF battle God and Frankie Avalon. Ooookay — if you say so, Jack.

(Peter David, writer of stuff, can be written to c/o To Be Continued, Inc., PO Box 239, Bayport, N.Y. 11705.)

Historical Notes:

1) For some reason that I can't recall, James' fictitious conversation between Stan and Jack did not appear in the column. It sees print here for the first time.

2) I wound up lifting the "Sandman" gag of speaking white on black — and, consequently, being impossible to understand — and using it in the third issue of **Soulsearchers and Company***, wherein we did a full-blown take-off on* **Sandman***.*

SECTION 13

Marking Time

This is one of the more eclectic sections of this collection.

All of the following columns have to do, in some way, with the passage of time. The past or the future. We have the column that marks my first anniversary on the column; my thoughts on getting older; a fictitious look ahead to issue #2000 of *Comics Buyer's Guide*; and a column by a writer of the future, my pre-teen daughter Shana.

Now if you'll excuse me, I'm going to go lie down for a while. This is exhausting.

WILL I DARE TO EAT A PEACH? (Nov. 30, 1990)

So there I was, a year ago, watching *Star Trek IV: The Voyage Home* on cable, and my 5-year-old daughter wandered in.

"What are you watching, Daddy?"

"I'm watching *Star Trek*," I replied.

She plopped down in front of the set and watched along with me for a few minutes as Kirk, Spock *et al.*, went through their paces. And then she turned back to me and asked two words that haunt me to this day:

"Where's Worf?"

Never had I felt quite so old as I did when I heard that question. Because here, genuinely, was the *Next Generation*. To me, the words "Star Trek" will always conjure the first *Enterprise* and its crew. I always refer to the new TV series as *Next Gen*. But to my younger daughter, *Trek* will be epitomized by a Klingon security guard.

Since then, I have become a lot more aware of aging. I'm not talking about the physical aspects, although Lord knows they're there. I'm speaking of the intellectual realization that I'm getting up there in years, although I'm not even 35. I'm older than most of my editors. And most of the fans I interact with were and are shaped by entirely different experiences.

Just as my parents would stare in horror at me, if the name of a 1940s movie star was meaningless to me, so now do I find myself looking through my father's eyes in terror at an upcoming generation who knows nothing of the times I lived through and cares even less.

It hits home even more for me, because I'm in a field of endeavor that so often brings me into contact with people younger than myself — brings me into contact in droves, particularly at conventions. And my own kids are there to provide reminders at home, as well.

Having recently passed my 34th birthday (and received a number of very kind cards from fans, so thank you very much, all) I find myself reflecting on many recent instances when what seems like relative youth becomes instead twisted into the opening guns of Social Security years:

• While we were driving to visit my parents in Pennsylvania, my 9-year-old daughter asked if she could play her New Kids on the Block tape on her cassette player. Before we could tell her that it was fine with us, she added solicitously, "Or, if that's going to bother you, I have a tape of Julie Andrews that you'd probably like better."

I almost drove into a median strip.

My wife and I had grown up with the Stones and Jimi Hendrix and the *Beatles*, for crying out loud: performers who, by their music and appearance, threatened the fabric of society and gave our parents ulcers. To children of the '60s and '70s, New Kids are about as threatening as the Archies. I could easily picture Donny and company performing "Sugar Sugar."

But I'm ooollllddd. I cannot, by definition, like the music that "kids nowadays" listen to. The moment you hit 30, you must gravitate to the Big Band Era or Lawrence Welk. It's expected.

The purpose of music that kids listen to is to shock parents, and, frankly, it's probably causing no end of damage to modern teen-agers that their parents are musically unshockable.

• At the San Diego Comic-Con, there was a nubile young lady who hung around a number of pros. I found out that she was 14. And I thought to myself, *Where was she when I was 14?* Then I realized. When I was 14, she was -6.

• That tastes change in artists and writers is not surprising to me. What *does* surprise me is the vehemence with which they change. Modern young comics fans aren't remotely interested in the creators that I grew up with and yet don't realize that they owe the talents of the current favorites to those artisans of yesteryear.

Readers who picked up Steve Ditko's *Spider-Man* reprints in *Marvel Tales* sniffed disdainfully, in my presence, "This guy draws like Ron Frenz." Where would Frank Miller or Dave Sim be without Will Eisner, yet, out of every 10 readers, how many buy reprints of *The Spirit*, or even know who he is? ("Wasn't he one of the villains killed off by The Scourge?")

• The guy who thought that Napoleon Solo was Han Solo's brother in the *Star Wars* comic book or the girl who thought that Illya Kuryakin was a rock singer.

• The guy who didn't get the ending of "Quantum Beast," because he didn't understand who the "Dr. Z. Smith" guy was supposed to be.

An unrelated aside: At Eaglecon in Philadelphia, a guy came up to me with two fanzines that had appeared earlier this year. To my shock, someone else had come up with the exact same idea I had, "Quantum Beast," right down to the title. It was published out of Colorado, and unquestionably the author beat me to the punch with this, so, if you see it at a convention, you'll know who came first.

The fanzine treatment is somewhat less tongue-in-cheek than mine, and the companion zine focuses on Vincent in the Waiting Room while Sam is using his body. It's the title duplication that really gets me. I should've used my alternate, "Bestial My Foolish Heart.")

• At a costume competition there was a woman in a very tight-fitting black dress. I mumbled, "She looks like Morticia." The guy next to me said, "Who?" Hopefully, this will change when the Addams Family movie with Anjelica Huston comes out.

• Fans debating over all sorts of nit-picking about the new *Flash* TV series. The majority of them, concerned over whether this depiction of The Flash is "serious" enough (people still grumble over the costume, for example) don't recall that the last time The Flash was done live-action on TV, he was part of this godawful special in the '70s that featured a plethora of DC super-heroes, spearheaded by Adam West and Burt Ward as you-know-who. Speed effects were done by having The Flash pose in a running motion and then just vanish off the screen, the sort of cheap-jack in-camera visual effects that are rarely done any more.

• A newscaster, in reference to the current "unpleasantness" in Saudi Arabia and the impact that it's having on oil prices, said, "Americans may have come to terms with the idea that the days of cheap gasoline could be gone forever."

I started laughing. Clearly, the newscaster had to be in his early-to-mid-20s, utterly unaware of, and oblivious to, the gas lines and gas crunch of 1973 and '74. Back then, when prices escalated from about 30¢ a gallon to over a buck, and people had to wait in block-long lines to get it, and locked gas caps and in-the-car gas-tank release buttons became standard issue (no one had them in the '60s) to counter gas siphoning — *that*, Mr. Newscaster, was when Americans kissed good-bye to cheap gasoline.

• The favorite bonding pastime of my generation is to stand around and compare notes on the question, "Where were you when you found out Kennedy was shot?" Several friends of mine were tossing this around at a convention, when a young lady, walking past, overheard this question and said with some surprise, "Ted Kennedy was shot?"

• A friend of mine threw a 1970s Nostalgia party. I was astounded. I mean, the only things to come out of the '70s were gas lines and Nixon's resignation. Otherwise, you can bag the whole damned decade. Just toss it. It was as if everyone was catching their breath from the '60s, and preparing to launch for the '80s: 10 years of treading water.

Yeah, OK, the new *X-Men* came out of the '70s. But what was the hottest-selling title of the time? The biggest thing? Not *X-Men*, kiddo. It was *Howard the Duck.* You can still get big bucks for *Giant Size X-*

Men #1, but how much demand is there for the *Howard* #1, a comic book once so sought-after that store owners were descending on 7-11s and grabbing up every copy they could find?

Shows how much the '70s knew. Either that, or it shows how much damage one bad movie can do to a character.

What's the point of all of the above? Well, nothing, really. Except maybe fans will understand why, for example, I don't take it all that seriously when they tell me that my work on *Spider-Man* was the best ever. Because the best ever was Stan Lee and Steve Ditko, and we've all been spinning our webbed wheels since those issues.

Just starting to feel my years is all. And of course there's lots of people in the business older than I am, who can look at me in the same way that I can look at younger fans and say, "You think you got problems? You think you're so smart? People in their thirties nowadays think they invented introspection and confusion. Why I remember — " and so on.

It's just that somehow, in the war of "Us vs. Them," we're always so surprised to wake up one morning and realize we've become "Them."

(Peter David, writer of stuff, is becoming age-obsessed.)

THE FIRST YEAR (July 26, 1991)

I figured I would do this column for a year.

When the idea was first broached by an anonymous commentator in **Comics Buyer's Guide** and seconded by Don and Maggie Thompson — and then inquired after by any number of friends and business associates — I sat down (since it's easier to type that way) in front of my computer with absolutely no clue as to what I was going to talk about. And now, a year later, I am in the middle of writing the one-year anniversary column with again no clue as to what I'll talk about.

I never really thought I would make the whole year, to be honest. For that matter, I never thought I would be able to write it, week in, week out, come hell or high water.

Actually, the Thompsons did not give me any promise at the time that they would run it weekly, even if I wrote it with that frequency. They simply said that they would do their best. I think part of it was that they didn't want to get readers used to any sort of weekly publication, on the assumption that sooner or later (probably sooner) I would start blowing my deadlines, anyway.

I haven't yet.

I've come really close on occasion. And I've produced short columns and one cartoon column, which required a lot less work, so that I could maintain the weekly schedule. The Thompsons, for that matter, still have not given me any assurance that they will run BID weekly. But there have been times when Maggie has called, warning, "Hey, if you're going to have a column in this week, we're going to have to have it tomorrow." This certainly implies to me that, even though they still haven't guaranteed weekly publication, they've at least grown accustomed to it.

(Usually, by the way, the Thompsons fax me the typeset copy, so that I can proofread it. But, because we're running late this week thanks to the shortened convention and holiday schedule, that's not going to be possible. So if, for example, I type "Clint Flicker," and the appearance of that name makes you scream in indignation due to typos, it's not my fault.)

Mostly, this column started as a challenge I made to myself. I wanted to see if I could turn it out. For example, some of the most exciting writing I had ever read was from collections of columns by Harlan Ellison — as much as I admire his fiction, I think his best work is his essays and commentaries from the several regular columns that he has produced. As a kind of personal challenge, I wanted to see if I could do something like that myself.

The response has been extremely gratifying. Whereas once a fellow professional had told me that he thought it was important to maintain a "curtain" between the comics pros and the audience, a professional distance — rather Wizard-of-Oz-like, I imagine — another has since told me that the advent of my column has helped to bridge that gap between pros and fans, to make the actions of those who create the comics more understandable to those who read them.

I'm flattered by much of the attention that this column has garnered, including compliments from fellow professionals. (One of the first fan letters I got was from Stan Lee, telling me that my column on why writers are scum should have appeared in *The New Yorker*. Yes. *The New Yorker*.) Harlan, whom I was trying to emulate, occasionally calls with suggestions or comments. The many fans who come up to me at conventions tell me they read and enjoy *BID*. It's amazing to me. Give a guy a column and bang, he's, whattaya call, respectable.

Even the detractors have been impressive. There was the guy who, in the course of criticizing *BID* measured the column inches. I mean, that took *work*. And, hey — when was the last time *your* work was characterized as nauseating by a highly recognizable comics pro? Hmmmm? I tend to think that letter was the turning point for this column. People seemed to read that and say, "Wow, there must really be something to *But I Digress*, if it induces projectile vomiting. Usually only your finer rides at amusement parks do that." Yes, it's *But I Digress*, *the* E-ticket attraction of **Comics Buyers's Guide**.

I have been amazed, amused, and even moved by the letters I've been receiving, a number of which I am going to be running over the next several weeks. Some have been argumentative, some thought-provoking, and one of them — as the result of painful confessions made in the course of it — is probably one of the most touching and troubling letters that I've ever received.

I must admit, sometimes it's a little disconcerting. There's still the occasional person who tells me I don't seem like toxic waste (which usually prompts puzzled looks from anyone standing nearby who wasn't in on that column). There are the people who still ask if I'm going to be taking Tony up on his offer and adopting the last name of Isabella. I reiterate: Why whould I want to trade my surname, which is the name of a famous king, for that of a famous queen?

And there are the people who ask me questions that relate to aspects of my personal life, and there's always a momentary flash in my mind of "How did he know this? How does this stranger know my wife is pregnant? How did he know my screenplay was rejected?" And then I realize he must be a reader.

Sometimes, I forget that what I write here, in the privacy of my office, actually goes out and gets read. I mean, I know it intellectually, but the reality of it can throw me from time to time. This column has become such a personal expression of what's going through my mind that week in regard to my life and career that it doesn't occur to me that I'm sharing it with others. As wife Myra has said, it's cheaper than therapy. It's also higher-profile.

But if there's one thing this column has provided me with, it's a sense of appreciation for free speech, for the freedom that was endemic to this country's creation. And, in the year I've been writing this column, the most striking thing I've seen is the downslide in those freedoms.

When I was in high school in Verona, N.J. (a pit if there ever was one, at least at the time), one of the few things they taught us that stayed with me was that the socio-political atmosphere of this country is like a pendulum. That, historically, it swings from liberal to conservative and back again.

I had a great deal of trouble accepting that. Oh, maybe that had happened in the *past*. But here we were just having come through the '60s into the early '70s, and we had a country that was nothing but freedoms.

You could say anything and not fear recrimination. Decision after decision supported a free press. Women had the right to decisions (bad decisions, granted, but decisions) about their own bodies. And people knew that war and slaughter was, by and large, a sad thing.

There is nothing more galling than to realize that a theory you had completely brushed off was, in fact, totally correct. Because if you look at the '90s, you will find that every single one of those major aspects of society is the reverse or in the process of reversing. Freedoms and rights, eroding away, in favor of conservatism and knee-jerk flag-waving.

Many people seem to feel that the greatest political calamity could be President Dan Quayle. I would disagree. I mean, even if that happened, it would be, what, eight years? A couple more, if he came in in the middle of a term? So what?

No, the greatest political calamity is the retirement of the most liberal Supreme Court justice, Thurgood Marshall. I can't blame the man. He's, what, 82? And even with him there, he's consistently in the minority as the court slowly, gently, one soft pin prick at a time, eases its way back into the 1950s.

Adverse rulings have come down on matters ranging from the relatively innocuous (nude dancing) to the matter of being able to discuss options. Ideas. Ideas are being regulated against.

The concept of the Supreme Court issuing a gag order on *any* subject should be antithetical to the First Amendment, and yet that's what's been done on government-funded abortion. And there's more to come; you can bet on that. And we're not talking about an eight-year term. We're talking thirty, forty years or more.

My children are going to grow up in a substantially different atmosphere than I did. Heaven help them. Because the Supreme Court certainly won't.

I didn't intend to get so heavy-handed with this. I suppose it's because in the past year I've seen the country change far more than I have seen the comics industry change. Although I suppose the latter reflects the former, at least in conservatism: retailers and distributors becoming more and more cautious about selling those comic books that aren't guaranteed sellers.

If independent publishers can be perceived as liberals, and Marvel and DC are seen as conservatives, than I guess there is that connection. And, for that matter, comics philosophy preceded the Gulf War in theory and fact. We've got heroes who engage the enemy, do their duty, fight, and win. Yet, curiously, the main villain doesn't really seem to die, and you have to look really hard to see what was accomplished.

A year. I figured I would give up this column after a year.

The heck with it. I'll stick around for a while longer. What're they going to do — take me to court and gag me?

It'll be interesting to find out.

(Peter David, writer of stuff, will make his last public appearance of the summer at a store called Adventure Inc. at 475 Bedford Rd., Pleasantville, N.Y. on Saturday, July 27, from 11 a.m. to 2 p.m. Phone (914) 741-2510 for details. After that, he'll be settling down and waiting for his wife to spawn. Suggested baby names are welcome.)

KID TALK (Nov. 13, 1992)

Well, thus far the response on the turn-of-the-century comics poll has been nothing short of phenomenal. The folks at the Bayport post office have to use a crowbar to jam all the mail into the box. The intrepid Myra is learning the new software I purchased, so that the results can be easily and scientifically tabulated.

And I have been intrigued by the responses we're getting. The most fascinating by far is the overwhelming consensus we're getting on the identity of the likely Anti-Christ. I will admit that Bill Clinton has been putting on an impressive write-in campaign but, thus far, the vast majority of respondents are pointing the finger directly at —

Nah. Why spoil the suspense?

Several people, however, have expressed curiosity about the possibility of this column being written by Shana David, daughter of writer of stuff. A couple have actually asked to hear from my eldest child as to what life here at Ft. Happiness is like. And so I, always looking for an easy out, hereby turn this installment of *BID* over to 11-year-old Shana David, award-winning writer and now columnist (and Don and Maggie have promised not to edit her column for spelling and grammar, so you get a true feel of her ability):

* * * * *

I've heard tell of your suggestion of me writing a column on what it's like being Peter David's daughter. Where the heck did you get the idea that I could write a decent story?! Jeez! Well anyway, here I am Shana David, the eldest daughter of Peter David the writer of stuff. Well that's a nice long title. Maybe I'll use that as a stage name.

Off that subject. It's pretty fun having Peter David as my dad. My friends have fathers with a job that gets them home at around 6. The fathers leave at about 7, so my friends barely ever see their dads. I see my dad almost all the time that I'm home, and believe it or not, I don't get sick of him. I have a strong bond with my dad, that's special to me.

My dad is always home for field trips, and instead of sitting up front with all the other parents talking about cookware, he stays back with us kids. We all tell jokes and ghost stories. Sometimes I think he's even more popular than me. Sometimes he would tell us about upcoming movies, for instance, my class knew about *Hook* and who would star in it, months before anyone else!

He makes me pretty darn popular, giving out comics on Halloween instead of candy, his slogan being, "I'd rather rot kids' minds than their teeth." So therefore, everyone in town knows where I live.

He certainly throws wild parties. At my graduation, he rented a popcorn wagon, like at the circus! Also we had a Karioke machine, basketball hoop, picnic tables, barbecue, and comic books as party favors! Wow, that's a mouthful.

I must admit I do owe a lot to him. He gives me tips on writing, and is supportive of my love of acting. He takes me to Broadway Plays, and discusses them with me. For instance, when I was younger, he took me to *Jerome Robbins Broadway*, instead of a New Kids on the Block concert (A.K.A. New Geeks on the Block). When going to the city, we take trips to the Drama Bookshop. Yay!

Our house is loaded with comics and books. Look in our basement and you'll find large trunks full to the brim with comics. Look in my room, and you'll not only find a mess of clothes, makeup, and old moldy homework, but walls of artwork, boxes of comics, and shelves of Sci Fi and fiction novels. Look in my family's linen closet, and you'll find, well, linen.

It's fun to have my friends come up to me with a copy of *Spider-Man 2099* or of *X-Factor*, asking me to get my dad to sign it. It's weird to know that people stand on long, and I'm telling you long lines to get my dad to write his name. Just the other day I was approached by my friend Donald. He told me that when in 3rd grade, he found out that my Dad wrote comics, he thought it was cool. He never paid much attention to who wrote it, but after he found out about my Dad, he did. Donald told me that he now knows so much more about my Dad now. He said that he would just like to sit with my Dad and talk to him for an hour about, well — anything. I never realized until then how lucky I was, to have Peter David as my Dad, and that I can sit and talk to him almost anytime I want. It seems strange that my boring old Dad could be that popular.

One of the best parts of being "the writer's kid" is free rides in Limousines! Going to store appearances with my Dad is cool. The store owners give me Egg Creams, and the cashiers give me gum. Everyone has to be nice to me, and give me what ever I want. It's the best!

Being a writers daughter, you grow up with different things, for instance, my sisters and I grew up with the phrase "Daddy's on a deadline" which could be interpreted as "Don't bother your father or he'll mash you into the floor." I also grew up in a different environment. I always had much more of an experience with books than other children. For instance, I am currently reading *The Phantom of the Opera* By Gaston Leroux. My father introduced me to good literature earlier than other kids. I was over The Baby-Sitters Club stage, before all my friends. I also learned from him to hate abridged books. Why? I dunno. Ask him.

I don't always read my Dad's books (the answer to the number one question to ask Peter David's daughter). I've read *Imzadi, Q In Law, A Rock and a Hard Place*, his 1st photon book, and his Portuguese copy of *The Swamp Thing* (which I didn't understand in the least). I was always taught to develop my own tastes in reading. I can say, *Imzadi* tied him for 2nd place with Stephen King. I think no one beats Edgar Allen Poe. Even you, Dad.

Believe it or not, my Dad can actually be normal. Not for long, but that's not the point. He helps me with my homework, like a normal parent. Really! And he, ummm, talks on the phone a lot. Call him. You'll see!

He makes me do all that parent stuff, like eating my veggies, and doing my homework, and practicing my bass clarinet, and all that junk. I also sometimes have to do strange tasks, like get my Dad's 5 Catwoman figures out of the trunk, or rearrange the PVC figures.

My Dad can be strange at times, like the day at Atlanta Fantasy Fair, when he bought a 5 foot tall painting of Michelle Pfeiffer as Catwoman. It hangs over the TV set. I'm not kidding!

It can be strange at times, living in a house with 2 phone lines and a Fax line. Some people look me up in the phone book, and they have no idea what number to call! My dad thinks it's normal.

It's really fun when my Dad takes me to conventions. I get to go to the guest banquets sometimes, and that's fun. I like hanging out with my Dad at conventions, and sometimes I go to his panels. They're really fun to watch!

One of the great things my Dad does, is that he lets me read the book before it's in print, for instance I read *Q In Law* in manuscript copy. With *Imzadi*, I was still reading the manuscript copy when it came out in print. I than switched to the book, so I didn't have to keep catching papers as they blew away.

That's about all I can say of what it's like living with my Dad. Also, thanks to everyone who said I should be writing my dad's column. I'll see what I can do about it. All I can say, is that he's a fairly normal dad. NOT!

(Shana David, eldest daughter of Peter David, the writer of stuff, can beat her Dad at basketball any day!)

* * * * *

THINGS TO COME (Jan. 15, 1993)

*(As a bold experiment here at **BID**, we have decided to withhold the column intended for the 1000th issue of CBG and instead go straight to the column for the 2000th issue of **CBG** — which, by our rough calculation, will see print some time in the year 2012. Once we actually get to 2012, we will then run the column originally slated for the 1000th issue—currently in a time capsule buried in the back yard—to serve as a testimony to the current state of affairs.)*

BID: Good day and welcome to the 2000th issue of **CBG**. As a special treat for you today, we have an interview with the hottest creator of comics today: Gabriel Jones, the creator of — among other things — Flagman, the best-selling comic-book hero of all time. Gabriel, how are you doing?

Jones: Terrific. It's great to be here.

BID: Gabe, it's phenomenal the amount of stature that you've achieved in the industry, when you've been in it such a relatively short time. How old are you, anyway?

Jones: 19.

BID: 19. That's really hard to believe.

Jones: OK, OK. I'm 19 next June.

BID: And yet *Flagman*, published by Marvel Comics under its DC Comics imprint, has already made you a multi-millionaire.

Jones: It's amazing, I know. And nowadays, being a multi-millionaire really means something. It's not like the old days when I was born, when the Democrats were running the show for a brief time. Thank God that whole thing self-destructed and we got the country back in GOP hands, heading in the right direction.

BID: So tell us about Flagman — the genesis of the character, that sort of thing.

Jones: Well — I hope this doesn't sound too manipulative, but, frankly, I sort of created the character based on all the things that make a character hot today. First and foremost, of course, was to make him a cowboy.

BID: Well, of course. That's almost a given.

Jones: I mean, c'mon. If a new comics title today isn't a western, romance, or science fiction, you can pretty much forget it.

BID: Of course. And since you're looking to tap into what makes a book hot, that's also why you made him a pacifist.

Jones: Absolutely. He never kills anyone. If he's in a fight, he sticks strictly to passive defense maneuvers and never throws the first punch. A character of high moral standings and ethics: That's what the people want to read about.

BID: And yet he's incredibly promiscuous.

Jones: Well, now, that's one of the remarkable contradictions about this country, isn't it? On the one hand, you have the highbrow morality preached by the government. On the other hand, the simultaneous development of the AIDS vaccine and the ready availability of the male birth control pill, both of which came around at the turn of the century, increased the amount of sexual activity in this country a thousandfold. It was like a volcano had been capped for a while and suddenly unleashed. Naturally, you want your hero to reflect the times.

BID: And when you developed Flagman, the deal you cut with Marvel was —

Jones: Oh, industry standard. The usual 50/50 split of all income generated through all forms of sales, both print and electronic. Plus merchandising, dramatic rights, all that sort of thing. And, of course, when I decide to leave the character, I choose my own replacement and continue to act as creative overseer — and, of course, continue to earn half of all money brought in on the character.

BID: Sounds like a good deal. Do you work with an editor?

Jones: "Editor" isn't really the right word. The correct term is "liaison." She acts as my traffic manager, making sure that the final product gets to the printer and also to the data base, so it can be properly distributed.

BID: I still think the electronic dissemination of comics is among the most fascinating developments in the past few years, don't you?

Jones: Well, it was only to be expected. Downloading the comic book from a central base and paying for the download — and the best thing is, when you read the comic book one time, it then automatically erases. Prevents that annoying pass-around aspect.

BID: It was also the final nail in the coffin for the entire comics-as-collectibles notion.

Jones: Pardon?

BID: You don't know?

Jones: Know what?

BID: Not too long ago, one of the main audiences for comics were speculators who would buy comics and then hoard them for resale value.

Jones: Get outta here! Really?

BID: I'm surprised you don't know. It's fairly recent history, relatively speaking. At any rate, the bottom fell out of the entire speculation thing about 1994. A whole bunch of retailers went belly up, which resulted in the bankruptcy of one of the major distributors. That was around the time DC was sold to Marvel—before that, it was jointly owned by Warners and some Japanese investors, having dissolved the DC corporation a year or so before that. Big shake-ups. For a while there, it looked like Image might buy DC first. It had a massive cash infusion since it abandoned the direct market and signed an exclusive distribution deal with a national chain of retail stores. But it had backed off DC at the last minute and Marvel got it.

Jones: Yeah, well, who cares? That's history, over and done with. What's now is what is.

BID: So how do you go about putting together a comic? I'm sure all our readers would like to know.

Jones: Well, you see, I've got my computer set-up right here. Let's take this sequence I'm working on right now, where Flagman is about to have a shootout with the bad guy.

BID: But he'll only shoot the gun out of his hand.

Jones: Oh, of course. Now, I need a decent shot of Flagman squinting against the sun. So I access my art file, calling up head shots. There, that's a good one. Now I add some of the options: Beard stubble. A bit more squint. Now, let's angle the face a little — maybe about, oh, 11 degrees to the right. There, you see? It sounds like only a little, but it makes a ton of difference. Now, we add shading. The sun's overhead, and his hat is acting to block it, so we should be shading the upper half of his face.

BID: Readers, although you can't see it, you should be aware that Gabe is making all this happen just by touching the screen.

Jones: Of course. The touch-sensitive screen is standard now. I mean, c'mon. What'd you *think* I was going to use? A mouse? Get real. So there's the basic art. Don't need much dialogue here, but this is the slightly tricky part. Once I've activated the dialogue mode, I have to watch what I say, because the computer will automatically enter whatever I say. Once I was dialoguing and my girlfriend came in, and she was feeling frisky, and — well, Flagman was suddenly saying a lot of things like "Oh God, yes!" and "More!" in the middle of a poker game. Which kind of made sense in context, but it was still a little weird. So anyway, here we go. Dialogue mode on: "Draw, fella." Dialogue mode off.

BID: And there the words appear on the screen, already ballooned off.

Jones: Right. Now, that was the last panel on the page, so I'll color the whole page now. Hold on. There. Done.

BID: That took no time at all.

Jones: Well, most of the colors are already predetermined. The coloring program just makes adjustments for things like shading, light source — that sort of thing. Only stuff that really needs much involvement from me is crowd scenes, where I indicate what I want emphasized, so the computer knows what to highlight and what to do as knockouts. You have to let the computer do it. With more than 900 colors on your pallet, there's just no time to make all the decisions yourself.

BID: I'm kind of curious about the actual art selection process. You didn't draw that picture yourself.

Jones: No, of course not. I couldn't draw to save my life.

BID: Then where did the original illustration come from?

Jones: The original? Who knows? Some pencil jockey did it years ago.

BID: And you just copied it.

Jones: Well, I didn't *just* copy it. I tweaked it a bit, put it at a slightly better angle.

BID: Yes, but still —

Jones: I mean, why in the world should I have to sit and draw something? A face is a face, a body is a body. I have more than 8500 different pieces of art in my art file — and that's just for figure work, not counting all the elements I combine to create backgrounds. And the best part is it's an ongoing project. If I find in some old comics other drawings that I like, I just use the scanner, feed them in, and capture the basic linework.

BID: But isn't that essentially theft?

Jones: Of course not. It's swiping. It's hardly anything new. In the old days, there were pencillers who would draw whole comic books composed of nothing but swipes. All this is is the next logical step in the evolution of that practice. Technology didn't invent the practice. It just perfected it.

BID: But doesn't that limit the scope of what you can do?

Jones: Not at all. There's thousands and thousands of different combinations. In fact, it gives me *more* variety than in the old days, when you'd have pencillers drawing the thing. Because either the pencillers would work within the bounds of their own abilities, which means that they could only go so far and no further. Or they would swipe — except that they had to do it clumsily, instead of with the computer perfection that I use.

BID: So, in other words, what you're saying is that the penciller is obsolete.

Jones: Oh, absolutely. Excess baggage. Why in the world any writer would need a penciller is beyond me.

BID: That's kind of ironic, really, that you'd say that. For example, a mere thousand issues ago, back in 1992, the biggest debate was who was more important to a comic book: the writer or the artist.

Jones: That's certainly a dumb debate. Then, again, who can figure out the older generation? Hold on a second.

BID: What did you just do?

Jones: Well, that was the last page I needed to finish for this issue. So I modemed the whole thing to my liaison at Marvel. She'll handle it from there.

BID: So how long does it take you to put together a complete, 32-page comic book?

Jones: From start to finish? About, oh, a day or so.

BID: And for a fan to read it?

Jones: About, oh, two or three minutes.

BID: Doesn't sound like there's that much writing involved.

Jones: "Writing" is almost as obsolete a term as "penciller." What I am is a storyteller. Except I tell stories using pictures. Today's audience doesn't have time to linger. It's not like the old days, when you could kick back and watch a slow-moving film like, I dunno, *Die Hard II*. People don't want to get into a story. They want the story to get into them. Oh, great!

BID: What?

Jones: Coming up on the screen — it's fan letters for *Flagman*.

BID: For which issue?

Jones: The one I just finished.

BID: Finished just now? A few minutes ago?

Jones: Right.

BID: You weren't kidding.

Jones: Nope. Now, if you'll excuse me, I gotta get started designing the splash page for the next issue. I think I'll start with a Liefeld pose or maybe Kirby or maybe — yeah, I'll mix and match.

BID: Thanks for taking the time to talk with us.

Jones: Think anyone will read this? If you'd like, I can do some illustrations to go with it. Won't take a second —

(Peter David, writer of stuff, congratulates all the folks at Krause Publications for reaching the 1000 mark. So — what have you done for us lately?)

SECTION 14:

Fillers — Lists, Songs, and Barf Bags

When you're turning out a weekly column, there are going to be times when you have no time. When you're on the road or on vacation or ill or — well, it could be anything.

At the same time, though, you don't want to ruin your streak of not missing an issue. You want to have something in there. And that's where the fillers come from.

I've chosen not to run the surrounding matter in each one where I quickly explain why I'm crunched for time that particular week. I didn't think that people reading this book would really want to read a litany of excuses, one after the other.

They fall into several categories:

A) "Top Ten Lists" — The Intrepid But I Digress Staff (IBIDS) (T.J. Burnside, Tom Chafin, Myra David, James Fry, Rosie Ianni, Jeff Jonas, Pat O'Neill) once jammed over a New Year's Eve and produced a whole bunch of David Letterman-esque Top Ten lists. One of them remains, to this day, one of the most notorious items ever to appear in *BID*.

B) "Barf Bags" — During a trip to a comics convention (San Diego, I believe), several other comic folks and I got on a plane to nowhere. That is, the plane sat on the runway for hours on end due to engine problems. As hour turned to hour and children on board got crankier and crankier, I desperately grabbed an airplane vomit bag, scribbled a face on it, turned it into a hand puppet and started entertaining the nearest dissatisfied munchkin.

Archie Goodwin then took a bag and drew one of his Archie faces on it. Other artists on the plane followed suit. Within a short time, everyone (OK, not everyone, but lots of people) was using the bags as puppets and cackling dementedly. Which just goes to show the lengths to which desperate people will go to kill time on the tarmac.

This incident, however, was the beginning of my Barf Bag handpuppet collection, as I acquired them from artists throughout the industry. I still collect them, and fans occasionally hand me blank airsick bags for material.

I've selected a few of them for inclusion here, plus a couple that haven't run before.

A health note: I have since learned that airsick bags are lined with disinfectant chemicals on the inside, so actually using them as puppets — while harmless in the short term — isn't something you should make a habit out of. Particularly if you're a frequent flier.

C) Song Lyrics: I don't know why. Somewhere along the way I started running song lyric parodies. So sue me.

D) Artwork: Richard Howell once stepped into the breach and drew Ariel, Sebastian, and Flounder desperately vamping during a week that I was so ill that I couldn't write. Also, I once came up with a wacked idea for a cartoon which I asked James Fry to draw.

Gordon Purcell

Randy Zimmerman

Charles Truog

Paul Dini

Sergio Aragones

Scott Shaw

Dave Gibbons

Don Simpson

Neil Gaiman

Bill Neville

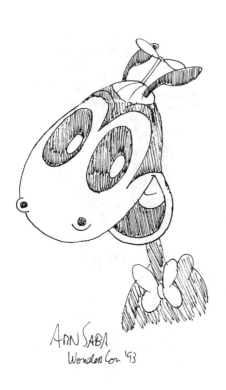

Arn Saba

Dave Sim

242

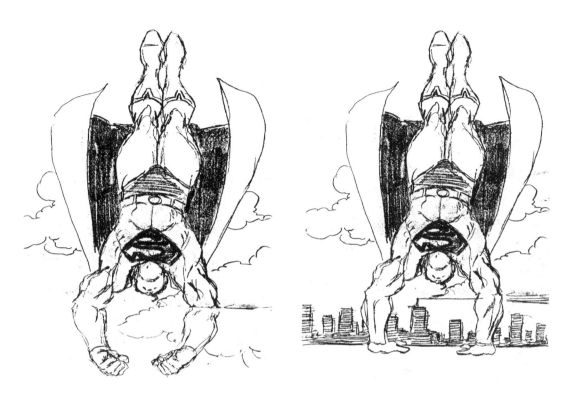

George Perez

Rick Schmitz

Ernie Chan

The Top Ten Things That Fans Have Actually Said to Me at Conventions and Store Appearances:
(Nov. 16, 1990)

10) I just love your work on *Strikeforce: Morituri*, Mr. Gillis.

9) Are the comics you write going to be worth anything?

8) My sister passed gas at dinner last night.

7) I don't buy *The Hulk* because everything Marvel publishes sucks.

6) John Byrne is waiting outside in the parking lot for you. Ha ha. Just kidding.

5) Do you draw *X-Men*? Do you write *X-Men*? Do you know who The X-Men *are*?

4) How did it work when Todd McFarlane wrote *The Hulk*?

3) I don't care *how* old you were when it came out. Autograph my copy of *Avengers* #1.

2) How can you *not* remember me? We discussed comics in the hallway outside the Copper Room at the 1986 San Diego Comic-Con. My hair was longer then.

And the Number One thing someone actually said to me:

1) Who the hell are you supposed to be?

Top Ten Ways You Know Your House Is Haunted: (Jan. 25, 1991)

10) The walls bleed.

9) A doorway to Hell opens up in your basement.

8) Your cat looks at you with glowing eyes and says, "Hey, I got your Tender Vittles right here, pal."

7) The skeletons in your closet ask for more hangers.

6) Your living room furniture rearranges itself — and looks better than the way you had it.

5) The only station your cable box picks up is Channel 666.

4) You're getting junk mail addressed to "Mrs. Muir or Current Occupant."

3) The eyes in your painting move — from room to room.

2) You open the refrigerator, and a sepulchral voice intones, "Zuul can't be here to take your call; please leave message when you hear the tone."

And the Number One way you know your house is haunted (drum roll):

1) An evil hypnotic lawn jockey does rap numbers in your front yard.

Top Ten Unused Ideas for Super-Pairs (Feb. 1, 1991)

10) Blood & Guts
9) Crime & Punishment
8) Death & Taxes
7) Fluff & Fold
6) Bagels & Lox
5) Scratch & Sniff
4) Arts & Entertainment
3) T & A
2) Curl up & Die
And the Number One unused Super-Pair:
1) Rack & Pinion

Historical Notes:

1) Malibu actually did do a series called "Blood 'n' Guts."

Top Ten Rejected Disney Characters: (May 10, 1991)

10) Donald's pervert cousin, Peeking Duck
9) Puke Green (with or without Dwarfs)
8) Winnie the Poof
7) Slimy the Slug
6) Goofball the Drug-Pushing Dog
5) The Little Slut
4) Fryer Rabbit
3) Prince Swarming
2) Chip & Dip
And the Number One rejected Disney character:
1) Daisy Dyke

Historical Notes:

1) Did I hear about this one. "Daisy Dyke" became the official symbol of BID's total political incorrectness. Letter writers, who proclaimed that they themselves were not gay, nevertheless protested on behalf of lesbians everywhere. Others wrote to me accusing me of being homophobic, a bigot, insensitive, and so on, and demanded that I apologize.

I never did.

Because the thing they didn't understand, of course, was that it was not an attack on homosexual women, but rather a joke at Disney's expense, considering that the company works so hard to make its characters squeaky clean and non-controversial.

The real kicker was that it wasn't even my joke. One of the other IBIDs came up with it and asked whether I wanted him/her to write in and take the heat off me. I said, "Absolutely not." First, I had no intention of giving any of my attackers the impression that I was running scared and looking for a scapegoat. And second, it's my column. I take full responsibility for anything that runs.

2) I finally got around to asking a lesbian acquaintance of mine what she thought of the joke. She said she thought it was funny as hell.

3) Thank God none of the protesters knew, apparently, that "Poof" (as in "Winnie The Poof") is British slang for a male homosexual, or I'd never have heard the end of it.

TopTen Really Annoying Complaints from Users of the Emergency Alert System: (July 19, 1991)

(**Historical Notes**: *That's the service with the commercial that has the elderly woman calling, "I've fallen and I can't get up." My hypothesis was that some lonely seniors call up with other, less life-threatening complaints, just because they're bored.*)

10) My son never calls.
9) My daughter is still single.

8) I can't program the VCR.

7) I can't reach the toilet paper.

6) My dentures are stuck in the glass.

5) Mom's on the roof and we can't get her down.

4) Quayle is an idiot.

3) I'm not going to pay a lot for this muffler.

2) Nobody wants to look at my surgical scars.

And the Number One really annoying complaint:

1) It's fallen, and it won't get up.

Top Ten List of Things This Column Should Not Deal With:

10) Religion.

9) Abortion rights.

8) My audio tapes proving Don Thompson's torrid 12-year affair with Louise Simonson.

7) David Duke: America's last hope.

6) Why you always wake up in the morning with that dried crud in your eyes.

5) Tom DeFalco: The Man, the Myth, the Moustache

4) How to handle uncontrolled flatulence gracefully.

3) The Holocaust: Hoax — or evil Jewish scheme?

2) The link between reading *CBG* and abnormally high occurrences of rectal itch.

And the Number One topic this column should not discuss:

1) The large number of parking spaces with wheelchairs painted on them — which are never, ever occupied by wheelchairs.

(Sung to the Tune of "Be Our Guest." Author Unknown) (Jan. 29, 1993)

(Musical intro)

(Spoken) Mesdames et monsieurs, it is with deepest pride and greatest pleasure that we welcome you to yet another one of our theme parks. And now, relax, let us sell you a churro, as the Disney Company happily empties — your wallet.

Be
Our
Guest, be our guest;
Put your paycheck to the test;
When it comes to making profits,
Michael Eisner is the best!
Dollars here, dollars there,
Yen and francs are everywhere!

With each film (it's not surprising)
Comes a flood of merchandising!
Dolls and toys! Belle and Beast!
And Gaston (though he's deceased)!
Buy them all, or your kids will not let you rest!
True, this recession's tragic,
But we'll use our magic,
Re: Our guests, oui, our guests, be our guest!

To get in
For one day
Thirty dollars you will pay
It's a figure which increases, as inflation has its way.

You must drink!
You must eat!
Or expire from the heat!
We don't worry 'bout recession,
Since we own ev'ry concession!
Buy a nice souvenir,
'Cause a gift shop's always here!
And they're not very discreet; that we can say!
The chachkas may be crappy,
But the guests are happy,
Oui our guests

(Looking stressed, screaming children at their breasts)
See our guests; oui, our guests; be our guest!
(Michael Eisner solo — slowly, with feeling)
Life is so unpleasant
When you're poorer than a peasant.
I'm not sane without a plane to call my own.
Ah, how I adore being so wealthy,
Tokyo just called; they need a loan.
This massive corporation,
Richer than a sovereign nation,
Moving assets that can redefine immense!
Now you ask where does the money come from?
Tourists who dress funny!
They roll in and spend their money!

It's a guest, it's a guest!
Buying all that we suggest!
Thank the Lord, here comes a horde
With folks back home to be impressed!
Buy that shirt, if you please,
Because money grows on trees!
And who cares if what you're doin'
Leads you to financial ruin!
For your kid, for your tot,
Those dumb mouse ears must be got!
And you'll watch
Your net income become distressed!
If real mice could talk,
They'd say to buy our stock
For you our guest

(You our guest, you, our guest)
You, our guest!
Be our guest,
Be our guest.
Our resorts, they are the best.
It's ten seconds
Since we made another million
(We're obsessed!)
EuroDisney's a mess,
But we'll still buy CBS,
And the company keeps growing
What a bottom line we're showing!
We'll

En-
Large!
We'll expand!
Kings will bow to our command!
When we buy the world that's when we'll take a rest!
Each new theme park expansion
Buys a brand new mansion!

Be our guest!
Be our guest! Be our guest!
Please, be our guest!

The Lord of Time (Feb. 26, 1993)

(Sung to the tune of Billy Joel's "The Longest Time." Lyrics by Peter David.)

(Lots of "oowas" and such should be tossed in to make it really effective.)

Whoah-oh-oh-oh
For a Lord of Time!
Oh-oh-oh
For a Lord of Time!

When I next return from time and space,
I might have a somewhat different face.
Don't start debating;
I've been off regenerating.
That only happens for a Lord of Time.

When I fight my enemies again,
Master, Dalek, or the Cybermen,
It won't surprise me,
When they do not recognize me.
That is a hazard for a Lord of Time.

Whoah-oh-oh-oh
For a Lord of Time!
Oh-Oh-Oh
For a Lord of Time!

Be it body five, four, three, or two,
Inside I'm still Doctor you-know-who
When change is urgin',
I don't call some plastic surgeon.
No one does a face job like a Lord of Time.

When I opt to trade in some parts,
I say to myself,
"Hold on to your hearts."
Each time I seem younger than before.
If this keeps up much more
I'll wind up wearing Pampers.

I don't know where all the time has gone.
Seems like yesterday the show came on.
I keep on travelin',

Although my scarf's unravelin'.
I just get off on being Lord of Time.

Year in, year out, year without end,
I've traveled alone
Sometimes with a friend,
Stewardess, savage, robots, and boys,
And now they're action toys
You can find in your K-Mart.

Don't know how much longer I will last
Maybe someday my time will have passed.
Until that day comes
I'll keep on dodging ray guns
And go on living as a Lord of Time.

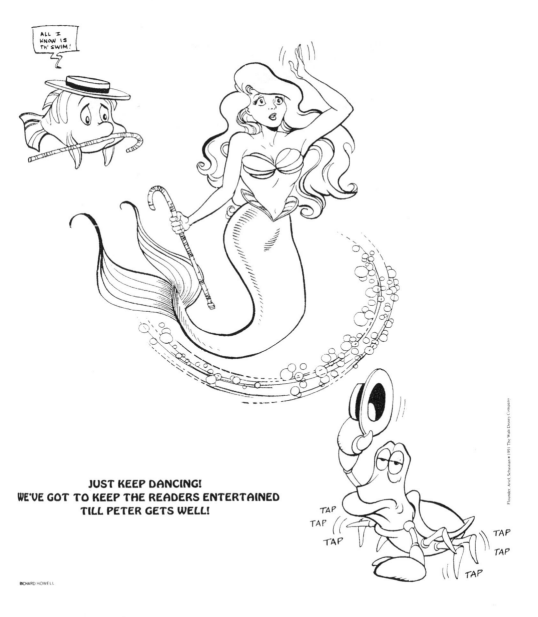

RICHARD HOWELL

CONVENTIONAL DAYS

(Set to the tune of "Arabian Nights." Lyrics by David Seidman.)

"Oh, I come to a land filled with heroes in tights
And they call it the WonderCon.
Where they'll show you some books
that'll fill you with frights;
It's barbaric, but hey — it's *Spawn*.
When the pros from the East meet the fans from the West
And a band named Seduction plays,
Then there's no time to spare, hop aboard US Air,
'Cause it's time for conventional days.
Conventional days! At conventional noons.
Fans are snubbing Dave Sim, as they swarm to Ron Lim
And watch foreign cartoons.
Conventional days gave me trembling and fear.
I'll watch panels until I am ready to kill.
But I'll come back next year."

Final Digression:

It has been three years, and I have yet to have anyone identify himself or herself to me as the person who suggested I write a regular column. If I ever *do* ever meet him or her, I'm not sure whether I'll thankor slug the perpetrator.

Index

Phoenix 113
Piece of the Action 124
Pied Piper, The 73, 74
Piller, Michael 126
Pini, Wendy and Richard 64
Pinocchio 55
Pinter, Harold 92
Player, The 140
Playskool 201, 202
Playworld 201
Poppins, Mary 191, 194, 201
Post, C.W. 110
Postcards from the Edge 22
Pournelle, Jerry 119
Pozner, Neal 162
Presley, Elvis 54, 57, 58
Price, Vincent 137
Pro/Con 156, 158, 159
Professor Moriarty 53
Pryor, Richard 94
Psi-Man 147
Psylocke 61
Pulitzer 86
Puma 20
Punisher, The 17, 23, 24, 25, 26, 42, 96,
   112, 161, 169, 204

Q

Q 125
Q In Law 232
Quantum Beast 228
Quantum Leap 143, 215, 217
Quayle, Dan 42, 198, 230
Queen, Ellery 55
Quicksilver 161
QVC 127, 128, 129, 130, 131

R

Race Bannon 198
Raimi, Sam 135, 136
Ramada Hotel 171
Rambo 90
Randall, Tony 121, 139
Raub, Lori 116
Ray, Margaret 91
Reagan, Ronald 30, 119
Real Genius 92
Red Sonja 18, 19
Red Target 57
Reeves, George 53, 143
Reiser, Paul 140
Rembrandt 110
Remington Steele 200
Ren and Stimpy 141
Return of the Blasters, The 49
Return of the Jedi 168
Return to Oz 133, 135, 138
Rhino 132
Richard Lionheart 54
Riker 124, 126
Ripley 140

Robin 16, 35, 50, 161
Robin and Marian 54
Robin Hood 41, 54
RoboCop 135, 136, 137
Robojox 180
Rock and a Hard Place, A 147, 232
Rocketeer 180
Roddenberry, Gene 94, 108, 125, 126,
   127
Rogue 40
Romania 61, 174, 181, 182, 183, 184
Rozanski, Chuck 62, 63, 64

S

Saffel, Steve 114
Salicrup, Jim 79
San Diego 100, 122, 171, 174, 236
San Diego Comic Convention 59, 82,
   111, 156, 158, 165, 177, 228, 244
Sandman 41, 50, 74, 161, 179, 226
Sarek 124
Saturday Night Live 54, 90, 123
Savage Dragon 106
Scarlet, Will 54
Schechter, Sandy 168
Schwartz, Julie 13, 109, 110, 111
Schwarzenegger, Arnold 139
Schwarzkopf, Gen. Norman 90
Sci-Fi Channel 117, 165
Scissorhands, Edward 137, 138
Scotland 68
Scrooge 191, 192, 193, 194
Sebastian 190, 236
Seduction of the Innocent 34, 125, 164,
   165
Seidman, Dave 191
Sesame Street 33, 209
Seven Faces of Dr. Lao, The 121
Shade 39
Shadow, The 29, 114
Shakespeare 47, 65, 66, 181, 216
Shaw, Robert 54
She-Hulk 21, 57
Shooter, Jim 61, 63, 105, 106, 113, 162,
   163, 164, 168
Shrapnel 65
Shuster, Joe 51, 119, 120, 178
Siegel and Shuster 52, 66
Siegel, Jerry 51, 120, 121, 178
Silent Movie 71
Silver Surfer, The 106, 107
Sim, Dave 64, 70, 71, 72, 73, 145, 153,
   156, 159, 163, 164, 179, 228, 250
Simonson, Louise 106, 107, 246
Simonsons, The 78
Simpson, Bart 20, 151
Simpson, Don 142, 209
Sinbad 54
Sin-Eater 104, 105
Sistine Chapel 47, 62
Skrull 89, 116

Sleepwalker 50
Smith, William Kennedy 30, 204
Snow 187, 188, 189, 190, 191
Sondheim, Stephen 25
Son-of-Sam 29
Sotheby's 78
Soulsearchers and Company 187, 226
Soviet Union 89
Space: 1999 166
Space Ghost 198
Spawn 70, 71, 72, 73, 161, 162, 208, 250
Spectre, The 52, 203
Spider-Man 12, 16, 17, 23, 24, 32, 34,
   38, 42, 53, 54, 62, 66, 67, 77, 79, 80,
   81, 86, 87, 99, 101, 105, 106, 111,
   144, 160, 161, 195, 203, 228, 229
Spider-Man 2099 166, 172, 232
Spider-Woman 105
Spirit, The 228
Spock 108, 123, 124, 125
Sprite 155
Squadron Supreme, The 28
St. Cloud, Silver 42
Stallone, Sylvester 90
Star Trek 12, 19, 92, 94, 101, 111,120,
   121, 123, 124, 125, 126, 127, 128,
   146, 147, 174, 175, 176, 223, 227
Star Trek The Motion Picture 127
Star Trek The Next Generation 191, 192
Star Wars 128, 228
Star*Reach 158, 206
Starjammers 112
Starlin, Jim 162
Starr, Roxanne 179
Statler Hilton 171
Steranko 43
Stern, Howard 162
Stern, Roger 92, 99
Stewart, Jimmy 143
Stewart, Patrick 123, 124, 126, 191
Stewart, Terry 13, 114, 115, 168
Stolwitz, Benny 135
Stone, Oliver 63
Stone, Sharon 208
Stones, The 209, 227
Storm 40, 61, 111, 155
Stowe, Harriet Beecher 93
Streep, Meryl 22
Street Poet Ray 79
Streisand, Barbra 26
Stroman, Larry 168
Sub-Mariner 89, 103, 113
Superboy 56, 181
Superman 23, 32, 35, 39, 42, 47, 49, 50,
   52, 53, 54, 55, 56, 57, 58, 120, 136,
   160, 161, 162, 163, 169, 170, 195,
   203, 204
Supreme Court 29, 35, 230, 231
Surfer 17

Swamp Thing 15, 39, 50, 136, 161, 232
Swayze, Patrick 22

T

Takei, George 174
Talia 42
Tango & Cash 90
Tarzan 54, 55
Taxi 90
Teen Titans 73
Teenage Mutant Ninja Turtles 198
Terminator, The 139, 166, 199, 212
Terminator II 177
Thanos 16, 20
Theakston, Greg 111
Thing, The 57, 203
Third Chimpanzee, The 211
Thomas, Clarence 205
Thomas, Roy 162
Thomerson, Tim 180, 181, 182
Thompson, Don 172, 246
Thompson, Don and Maggie 11, 13, 69,
    93, 116, 132, 168, 171, 229
Thor 38, 42, 65, 66, 161
Thunderbird 111
Thunderbolt Ross 132
Tik Tok 133
Time Squared 124
Tiny Tim 192
Tiny Toon Adventures 198
Tiny Toons 97
Titans 51
Todd, Jason 50
Total Recall 134
Toys 'R' Us 69, 78, 201
Tracy, Dick 133
Trancers 1 80, 183
Trancers I 180
Trancers II 180
Trancers III 180
Trancers IV 182
Trancers V 182
Troi, Deanna 121, 126, 180
Trudeau, Garry 90
Tundra 160
Turner, Ted 164
Turtles 135, 199
Twilight Zone 212

Twin Peaks 19
Twins 139
Tyco 201, 202
Tyson, Mike 204, 205

U

Uncle Ben 92
Unforgiven 183
United States 123
Urkel, Steve 55

V

Valentino, Jim 67, 68, 69, 78, 108
Valiant 61, 62, 97, 160
Vanity Press 31, 32
Varney, Jim "Ernest" 180
Vendetta 176, 177
Venom 54, 104, 105, 107
Verona, N.J. 45, 207, 230
Vertigo line 60
Vietnam 94, 123, 125
Village Voice 86
Vincent 216, 217, 218, 220, 228
Vincent, Fay 51
Vinton, Will 133
Voice 88
Von Doom, Victor 20

W

WACKO theory 106, 107
Waldo 42
Wally West 73
Wal-Mart 35, 69
Ward, Burt 228
Warlock 161
Warner Bros. 199
Warner, David 175
Warners 35, 81, 164, 234
Warp Graphics 32
Warriors of Plasm 61
wartist 44, 210
Watchmen 50, 65, 72
Wayne, Bruce 18, 136, 137, 144
Wayne, David 55
Weaver, Sigourney 140
Wein, Len 112, 162
Weirdworld 64
West, Adam 228
Wheeler, Dan 129, 130

Wheelers 133
Whitman, Walt 95
Who Framed Roger Rabbit 223
Wicked Witch 134
Wide World of Sports 67
Wild Weasel 194, 195, 197
Wildcats 67
Williamson, Al 128
Williamson, Nicol 54
Willingham, Bill 177, 178
Willis, Bruce 16, 22, 89
Winkler, Henry 120
Winters, Ralph 126
Witterstaetter, Renee 103, 162
Wizard 85, 100, 101, 104, 132
Wizard of Oz 132, 133, 134, 135, 182,
    229
Wolfman, Marv 162, 168
Wolverine 15, 22, 24, 25, 41, 56, 81, 87,
    99, 111, 139, 153, 155, 156, 161,
    200, 204
Wonder Woman 21, 40, 50, 53, 161
WonderCon 61, 165, 174, 206, 211,
    213, 250
Woods, James 25
Worf 126
World's Finest 23
Wright, Steven 23

X

Xavier, Charles 111, 113
X-Cutioner's Song 83
Xenogenesis 149
X-Factor 37, 60, 76, 83, 84, 92, 112,
    114, 168, 232
X-Force 65, 67, 77
X-Men 15, 21, 23, 24, 38, 65, 67, 77, 79,
    81, 111, 112, 113, 157, 160, 161,
    163, 178, 200, 228, 244

Y

Yankovic, Weird Al 100
Yomtov, Nel 102
Youngblood 33, 67, 163, 208, 209, 211
Yronwode, Cat 64, 163

Z

Zeck, Mike 105